LIVES IN THE BALANCE

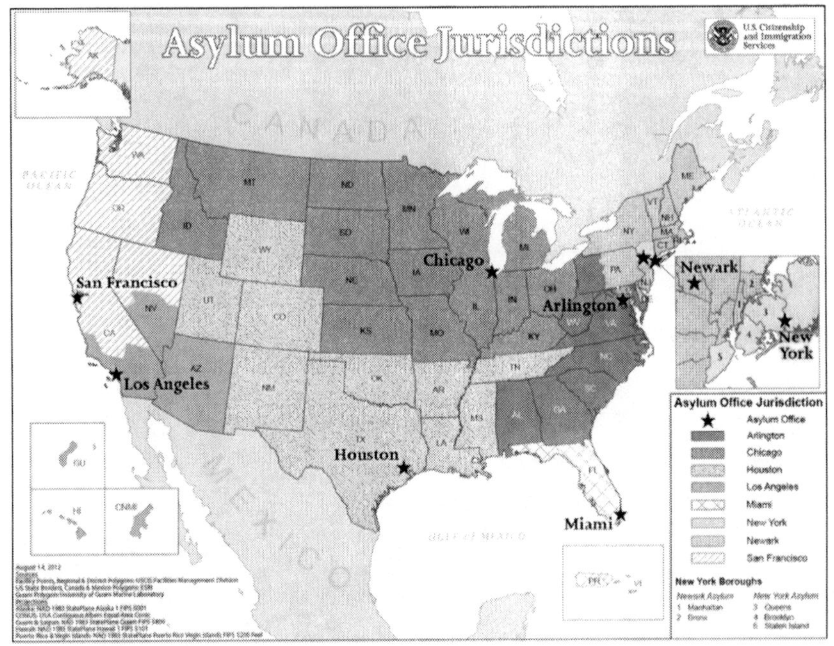
Asylum Office Jurisdictions
U.S. Citizenship and Immigration Services
CANADA
PACIFIC OCEAN
ATLANTIC OCEAN
MEXICO
San Francisco
Los Angeles
Chicago
Arlington
Houston
Miami
Newark
New York
Asylum Office Jurisdiction
Asylum Office
Arlington
Chicago
Houston
Los Angeles
Miami
New York
Newark
San Francisco
New York Boroughs
Newark Asylum
1 Manhattan
2 Bronx
New York Asylum
3 Queens
4 Brooklyn
5 Staten Island

Lives in the Balance

Asylum Adjudication by the Department of Homeland Security

Andrew I. Schoenholtz, Philip G. Schrag,
and Jaya Ramji-Nogales

NEW YORK UNIVERSITY PRESS
New York and London

NEW YORK UNIVERSITY PRESS
New York and London
www.nyupress.org

LIBRARY OF CONGRESS CATALOGING-IN-PUBLICATION DATA

Schoenholtz, Andrew Ian, 1951-
Lives in the balance : asylum adjudication by the Department of Homeland Security / Andrew I. Schoenholtz, Philip G. Schrag, Jaya Ramji-Nogales.
pages cm Includes bibliographical references and index.
ISBN 978-0-8147-0876-7 (hardback)
1. Asylum, Right of—United States. 2. Political refugees—Legal status, laws, etc.—United States. 3. Political refugees—Government policy—United States. 4. United States. Department of Homeland Security. 5. Administrative procedure—United States. 6. Emigration and immigration law—United States. I. Schrag, Philip G., 1943- II. Ramji-Nogales, Jaya. III. Title.
KF4836.S35 2014
342.7308'3—dc23
2013028448

New York University Press books are printed on acid-free paper, and their binding materials are chosen for strength and durability. We strive to use environmentally responsible suppliers and materials to the greatest extent possible in publishing our books.

Manufactured in the United States of America
10 9 8 7 6 5 4 3 2 1

Also available as an ebook

This book is dedicated to the officers of the Asylum Corps of the United States Department of Homeland Security, who work tirelessly, year after year, to protect those who seek freedom in America.

CONTENTS

FIGURES AND TABLES

Figures

Tables

ACKNOWLEDGMENTS

The authors appreciate the cooperation of the United States Department of Homeland Security, and particularly the Asylum Office of U.S. Citizenship and Immigration Services, which made public the raw data on which this analysis is based. The department made this data available because it is genuinely interested in understanding the effects of the laws that it administers and welcomes the contributions that scholars make to that understanding. We want to particularly acknowledge, as well, the assistance given to us by numerous asylum officers and supervising asylum officers, each of whom provided us with more than an hour of their time for interviews about their interpretations of our data. We are grateful to Professors Kathryn Zeiler, Joshua Teitelbaum, David Hoffman, David Law, and Shoba Sivaprasad Wadhia; Dr. B. Lindsey Lowell; Luis Carlos Ramji-Nogales; and the members of the Georgetown Summer Research Workshop for their comments and advice on statistical methodology. We appreciate the generous research support provided to us by our deans, T. Alexander Aleinikoff, William Treanor, and JoAnne Epps. We also appreciate the assistance of Mabel Shaw and the Georgetown University Law Library, and the encouragement of Deborah Gershenowitz, formerly of New York University Press. This work could not have been accomplished without the extraordinary help of our research assistants, Alexa Sendukas and James Dombach. As always, thanks to Janice, Lisa, Luis, Kala, and Javier, without whose support and patience we could not have completed this project.

An earlier version of our study of the one-year deadline appeared in the *William and Mary Law Review*.[1] We appreciate the editorial assistance of the editors of that review and their permission to reprint our findings in this book.

INTRODUCTION

The Department of Homeland Security (DHS), established by Congress in the wake of the September 11, 2001, terrorist attacks, is the third-largest federal agency, with more than 180,000 employees.[1] Most of its many functions are well known to the public and associated with national security or law and order. The department seeks to protect the nation against future terrorist attacks by disaffected citizens or foreign nationals. It houses the Federal Emergency Management Agency, which responds to natural disasters and, if necessary, major terrorist incidents. Through its Transportation Security Administration and its air marshals, it keeps air traffic safe, at times in controversial ways, by screening passengers and tracking potential hijackers. Its Customs and Border Protection (CBP) inspectors screen individuals arriving at airports, seaports, and land points of entry, seeking to exclude those who do not have a right to enter the United States, and CBP border patrol agents guard the southern and northern land borders to prevent entry by those who try to circumvent the established entry points. A cybersecurity unit works to safeguard the country from people who would attack its electronic infrastructure.

Within this sprawling national security bureaucracy lies a relatively tiny unit with a distinctly humanitarian mission: the nation's Asylum Office.[2] The office is one of three very important bodies that offer the protection of the United States to people who fear persecution in their home countries. Along with the Justice Department's immigration courts and Board of Immigration Appeals, the Asylum Office carries out the duties assigned to the executive branch by the Refugee Act of 1980. These responsibilities reflect the value that Americans place on providing safe haven to people across the globe who are threatened with imprisonment, torture, and death because of their political beliefs or activities, their religion, their race or ethnicity, or their membership in disfavored groups. The Asylum Office also helps to fulfill the United States' international obligations under the United Nations Refugee Protocol, a treaty to which the United States has been a party since the presidency of Lyndon Johnson.[3]

It is something of an historical accident that this humanitarian agency is nestled in a department whose principal duties are counterterrorism and law enforcement. When the Asylum Office was created, it was lodged, along with virtually all other offices concerned with immigration, in the Immigration and Naturalization Service (INS) of the Department of Justice. The INS was one of the casualties of 9/11. Part of the motivation of Congress when it created DHS in 2002 was to tighten border security, so it moved most of INS into the new department.[4] The Asylum Office was swept along, together with immigration officials primarily concerned with law enforcement: the border patrol and Immigration and Customs Enforcement (ICE) officers, who detain foreign nationals during removal proceedings and physically remove those who have been ordered to leave.

The Asylum Office has now been in operation, either in INS or in DHS, since 1990.[5] From October 1995 until June, 2009, 1,238 of its officers (usually fewer than 250 officers serving at any particular time) interviewed an average of more than 28,000 asylum applicants annually, deciding in each case whether or not to grant asylum. This enormous caseload makes the Asylum Office one of the largest adjudication systems in the United States.[6] Until now, however, there has been little systematic analysis of the office's decisions, and until we conducted the study reported in this book, there was only anecdotal evidence, and no statistical analysis, of the impact of the one-year filing deadline. This strict procedural bar, enacted by Congress in 1996, requires the Asylum Office to reject most asylum applications filed more than a year after the applicant entered the United States.

Each asylum decision potentially involves serious human suffering. The decisions of the Asylum Office therefore warrant careful investigation. All asylum applicants claim that they reasonably fear persecution if sent back to the country from which they fled. If the agency makes a mistake by wrongly excluding an applicant, that person could face detention, torture, and even death upon return to the home country. The refuge we offer to individuals fleeing such mistreatment because of their political activities, their religious beliefs, or the color of their skin is grounded in core American values. Moreover, our nation has bound itself under international law to protect to individuals within our borders who face persecution in their home countries.

On the other hand, an erroneous grant of asylum can allow fraudulent applicants to remain in the United States, using the asylum process to obtain immigration benefits for which they might not otherwise be eligible for many years, if at all. Mistakes in favor of people who should not be granted asylum also harm genuine asylum applicants. The press occasionally discovers a case in which someone won asylum by concocting a false claim or exaggerating a genuine claim.[7] False but successful claims threaten the accuracy of the asylum adjudication process, and reports of fraud can spur political attacks that weaken America's legal commitment to protecting refugees.

We undertook several related projects to understand the aggregate outcome of Asylum Office adjudication. We performed a range of statistical analyses on a database of over 380,000 asylum cases decided by INS and DHS between October 1, 1996, and June 8, 2009. First, we used the full database to ascertain the effect of the one-year deadline on asylum applications that Congress required the Asylum Office to enforce after April 15, 1998. We separately analyzed the approximately 303,000 of those cases in which the applicant met the deadline or was found to qualify for an exception thereto. We examined biographical data on the 221 asylum officers who decided 31,635 of the cases, and correlated these personal characteristics with case outcomes.

We supplemented our quantitative research with qualitative research. We analyzed the results of a questionnaire that the Asylum Office administered to its asylum officers and supervising asylum officers in 2011, which asked these officers about various aspects of adjudication that could not be understood by statistical analysis of the outcomes of cases. In order to further ground our hypotheses about our findings in experience rather than speculation, we reviewed the results of our quantitative work with experienced asylum officers from the eight different regional offices. Our interviewees had worked both as frontline officers who interviewed asylum seekers on a daily basis and as supervisors who reviewed the decisions of several asylum officers. We also presented the results to senior officials at the national headquarters of the Asylum Office. The interviews with the asylum officers and the headquarters staff were conducted with the understanding that we would not identify interviewees by name. We particularly asked all of these officials for their interpretations of some of the most surprising results of our data analysis. Many of the explanations they offered are reported in this book, particularly in chapters 6 through 10.

The results of all of these investigations are reported in the text and graphs that follow. In addition, we have posted on a website the original databases on which our studies are based, for those who might wish to replicate our analysis or perform their own investigations on this data.[8]

Chapter 1 describes the asylum adjudication system and the central role played by the Asylum Office. The first part of chapter 2 provides a statistical portrait of the refugees in terms of their nationalities, genders, ages, methods of entering the United States, and other personal characteristics recorded by the Asylum Office. In the second part of chapter 2, we turn to the asylum officers and provide two statistical snapshots of the officials who decide the fates of applicants for asylum.

Chapters 3, 4, and 5 discuss the one-year time limit on filing asylum applications that Congress imposed in 1996, which became effective on April 16, 1998. This limit precludes asylum for people who apply more than one year after entering the United States, with two exceptions. Chapter 3 describes the deadline and the exceptions that Congress allowed. It also considers why some asylum applicants are unable to file within a year, which explains why Congress saw fit to create exceptions to the deadline. Chapter 3 also explores how DHS interprets the exceptions to the deadline. Chapter 4 examines the characteristics of the applicants who were able to meet the deadline, and of those who sought asylum after the deadline had passed. In chapter 5 we investigate the characteristics of those who qualified for the deadline and those who did not, and we project how many applicants who otherwise would have been granted asylum by DHS were in fact turned down because of the deadline.

In chapters 6 through 10 we look at the adjudication of the "merits" of asylum cases; that is, whether an asylum officer found that the applicant had a well-founded fear of persecution on the basis of one of the five protected grounds. These chapters look only at cases that were not rejected because of the one-year filing deadline. In the asylum cases explored in these chapters, the applicant either sought asylum before the deadline went into effect, filed on time, or qualified for an exception to the deadline. In all of the cases discussed in these chapters, therefore, the Asylum Office considered whether the claim was credible and the applicant was eligible for asylum as a matter of law.

Chapter 6 looks at how grant rates changed over the fourteen-year period covered by the database. It examines the extent to which fluctuations in grant rates may have corresponded to major changes in asylum law and policy: particularly the recognition of gender-related claims at the outset of that period, the change in law creating the one-year deadline, the terrorist attacks of September 2001, and the congressional action in 2005 that tightened the credibility and corroboration standards that applicants had to meet.

Chapter 7 analyzes four characteristics of asylum cases—some related to the merits of the cases and some that seem unrelated—and their relationship to grant rates. In particular, it examines two sociological characteristics of applicants: whether they had dependents with them in the United States and their gender. This chapter also explores two factors relating to the asylum process: whether applicants entered the country with or without valid immigration documents and whether applicants were assisted by a representative in preparing their applications.

Chapter 8 looks at a subject that we first examined, with a smaller database, in our prior book, *Refugee Roulette*. We consider disparities in grant rates among the eight asylum offices, looking not only at the overall differences in rates but also at how the offices compared when adjudicating particular categories of applicants, such as those with dependents, those with representation, and those who applied in the aftermath of the 9/11 attacks.

In chapter 9, we focus our attention on differences in outcomes that depend on individual asylum officers. The chapter considers disparities within each regional office. Cases are assigned randomly to officers within each regional office, so in principle the grant rates of officers within an office should be approximately equal. The chapter looks at the degree to which disparities from this ideal occurred, both for cases as a whole and for high-volume nationalities within the office.

In chapter 10, we examine correlations between grant rates and the asylum officers' personal histories, such as the number of cases they previously decided, and, for those cases decided by officers on whom DHS had collected biographical data, the officers' personal characteristics such as educational attainments, ethnicity, and gender. We also explore several ways in which the officers' and the applicants' biographical characteristics interact.

We summarize our conclusions in chapter 11. We found that asylum officers granted more often to those fleeing the most abusive human rights situations, which reflects the kind of merits-based adjudications that policy makers and refugee advocates should hope to see. We also found that certain officer characteristics, such as gender, did not seem to matter in terms of outcome. But certain officer characteristics did correlate with higher or lower grant rates. This chapter discusses those findings and makes recommendations for policy makers and adjudicators to address the influence of external, non-merits-based factors on asylum outcomes.

Our statistical methodology, including further description of the databases we analyzed, the statistical analyses we conducted, and the variables we created for those analyses, appear on the website associated with this book along with additional relevant data.[9] The website also provides a link to the database made public by DHS, coding conventions used by DHS, and the outputs of the regressions that we conducted for this book.

We greatly admire the work done by asylum officers, who make difficult, stressful, decisions every day, decisions that are life changing for every person whom they interview. We hope that this book contributes to better public understanding of the work that these important public servants perform and to reforms that will ensure that, to the greatest extent possible, asylum claims are adjudicated based only on their merits.

1

Seeking Refuge

The United States was settled in part by waves of refugees, including the Pilgrims and Puritans, seeking freedom from religious and political persecution. Nevertheless, laws, regulations, and government programs to protect refugees systematically and apolitically are of surprisingly recent vintage, dating only from 1980.

In 1968, the United States ratified the United Nations Protocol Relating to the Status of Refugees. Parties to this treaty agreed that they would not deport refugees to other lands where their lives or freedom would be in danger.[1] Thirteen years later, Congress passed the Refugee Act of 1980 to implement its obligations under the Protocol.[2]

The Refugee Act formalized a system of resettlement through which the United States now protects tens of thousands of refugees from persecution each year.[3] Many of these individuals, displaced by ethnic violence, were living in United Nations refugee camps or in African or Asian cities. After careful screening by the departments of State and Homeland Security, the refugees are brought to the United States at government expense. With the help of local faith-based and community organizations, they are resettled in American communities.[4]

The 1980 Act also created a system of asylum for people who come to the United States to seek refuge on their own. The criteria for asylum eligibility are the same as those for eligibility for refugee resettlement: to be granted asylum, a person must be unwilling or unable to return to her own country because she has a well-founded fear of being persecuted there on account of her race, religion, nationality, political opinion, or membership in a particular social group.[5]

The Application Process

A foreign national who is physically in the United States may apply "affirmatively" for asylum by completing Form I-589 of the Department of Homeland Security (DHS) and mailing or delivering it to a DHS service center.[6] Nearly 80 percent of all asylum applications are initiated in this manner.[7] DHS adjudicates these affirmative applications in the first instance. If DHS does not grant an application, it may be renewed during a removal (deportation) hearing in a Department of Justice (DOJ) immigration court.[8]

The other fifth of asylum applications, termed "defensive" applications, are filed by individuals who are apprehended by federal officials before they apply for asylum. With the recent exception of unaccompanied-minor claims, these applications are adjudicated only in the immigration courts of the Department of Justice.[9] This book is concerned only with DHS adjudication and therefore is a study of only the affirmative asylum cases.

The asylum application, which much be completed in English, is neither short nor simple.[10] The current form is twelve pages long, with fourteen pages of instructions. It requires applicants to provide exhaustive information about their identity, family relationships, education, employment, travel, and reasons for fearing persecution or torture in her home country.[11] In particular, it requires applicants to describe their prior political, religious, and ethnic affiliations and activities, any past mistreatment or threats (including arrests, detentions, and torture), and the reasons they fear returning. Applicants must respond in detail and provide corroboration. The form directs claimants to

> provide a detailed and specific account of the basis of your claim to asylum or other protection. To the best of your ability, provide specific dates, places, and descriptions about each event or action described. You must attach documents evidencing the general conditions in the country from which you are seeking asylum or other protection and the specific facts on which you are relying to support your claim. If this documentation is unavailable or you are not providing this documentation with your application, explain why.[12]

An asylum applicant may receive assistance in filling out the form, either from a friend or relative or from a professional, such as a nongovernmental organization (NGO) or an attorney; a person who assists the applicant must also sign the form.[13] Although an affirmative asylum seeker may complete an application by writing brief answers on the form itself, many accept Form I-589's invitation to attach narrative statements describing past persecution or reasons to fear persecution in the future and to annex additional documents to prove identity and to support their claims.[14] These additional documents may include, among other things, statements or affidavits from fact and expert witnesses, copies of arrest warrants, medical records showing treatment for injuries received during demonstrations or imprisonment, and published reports about human rights violations in the applicant's country.[15]

Particularly when prepared by professionals, asylum applications can include hundreds of pages of supporting documents.

After receiving an application, service center personnel undertake two tasks. First, they enter much of the information from the I-589 form into a computer system known as RAPS (the Refugee, Asylum, and Parole System).[16] Data in RAPS are visible to all DHS personnel who subsequently participate in the adjudication of the case.[17] Second, they forward the application to the DHS asylum office with jurisdiction over the region in which the asylum seeker was living at the time she applied for asylum.[18] Upon receiving an application, the regional asylum office sets a date for the applicant to appear for a personal interview with an asylum officer.

Each of the eight regional asylum offices houses some dozens of asylum officers, several supervising asylum officers, at least one quality assurance officer, and a director and deputy director. The asylum officers are a part of a special corps of civil servants, within the DHS bureau known as Citizenship and Immigration Services (USCIS). They are recruited in two ways. Some of them are hired through internal vacancy announcements circulated within the federal government. Only current or former federal employees are eligible for appointment to positions advertised in this way. Because experience with immigration is a desired job qualification, asylum office managers often choose to limit the announcement to employees of DHS. As a result, officers hired in this manner may come from other parts of USCIS or from the agencies concerned with immigration law enforcement, such as the Border Patrol or Immigration and Customs Enforcement (ICE), the DHS bureaus responsible for preventing the entry of and deporting certain foreign nationals. Others are hired through public announcements on government's website, usajobs.gov. (When public announcements are used, applicants who are veterans have a strong advantage because the law requires the federal government to give them a "veterans' preference.")[19] Through public announcements, the Asylum Office has historically been able to attract and hire advocates, NGO attorneys, private bar attorneys, and returning Peace Corps volunteers—and continues to do so today. During the latter years of our study, many officers were hired through the now-defunct Federal Career Internship Program. Hence, the composition of the asylum officer corps has included a diverse mix of professionals from backgrounds that span multiple sectors and work experiences. Although national headquarters must approve the hiring of each new asylum officer, the person with the greatest influence over hiring policies and decisions in each of the eight regional offices is the director of that office. As a result, the particular mix of prior backgrounds among the officers in a region at any particular time strongly reflects personnel choices made by the individuals who were the office directors during the several previous years.

All of the officers undergo an extensive initial training course, which is currently a twelve-week residential program. They also receive weekly training on asylum law, human rights conditions around the globe, and interviewing techniques.[20] At any given time, nearly three hundred asylum officers are on duty among the eight offices.[21]

After the interview, the asylum officer makes a recommended decision on the case.[22] These recommended decisions are always reviewed by a supervising asylum officer.[23] Supervisors frequently give general guidance to officers about what to look for, how to analyze cases, how to assess credibility, and what they expect by way of a written report on a case. They cannot, however, spend the amount of time with each file that the interviewing officer spends, and they usually approve an interviewing officer's conclusions and recommendations. As a result, supervising asylum officers have told us that on a daily basis, the frontline officer who interviews the applicant has the most influence on whether asylum is granted.

In each region, asylum officers work under the pressure of high caseloads.[24] With a few minor exceptions, cases are assigned randomly to a particular officer.[25] In some of the regional offices, the random assignment is made several days before an interview is scheduled; in others, it takes place on the morning of the interview. Even when officers are assigned cases in advance, applicants often bring their supporting evidence with them to the interview, so whether or not an office assigns cases to officers before the interview date, an officer must study much or all of the documentary evidence while an applicant is in the waiting room. Officers usually have an hour or less to read an application or otherwise prepare for the interview.[26] On average, an asylum officer is expected to spend only four hours on each case, including reading the application, performing any necessary background research on conditions in the applicant's country, interviewing the applicant, checking the applicant's immigration history and fingerprints, and writing a recommendation and report to the supervisory asylum officer.[27]

The applicant has the burden of proving eligibility for asylum.[28] The task of the asylum officer is to separate the cases in which the applicant proves eligibility through testimony and documents from those in which the applicant fails to prove eligibility. When evaluating a claim, an asylum officer considers the applicant's written responses to the questions on the I-589 form, the corroborating evidence that the applicant filed, and the applicant's oral responses to questions posed during the officer's personal interview of the candidate, which usually occurs within forty-five days after the form is filed.[29]

An applicant who does not speak English must bring an interpreter to the interview; the government does not supply one.[30] The applicant may also bring a lawyer or a lay representative, but the government does not provide representation, even for indigent applicants.[31]

The interview by the asylum officer is not an adversarial proceeding, but it is nevertheless intended to be searching.[32] The asylum officer is charged with determining whether the applicant is eligible for asylum under the applicable statute[33] and regulations.[34] This task consists of four components: determining whether the applicant met the required time limit or an exception thereto; deciding whether the facts related, if true, would qualify the applicant for asylum under the well-founded fear standard; assessing whether she is telling the truth; and ascertaining whether any other law, such as the law prohibiting asylum for people who have committed certain nonpolitical crimes, bars the applicant from receiving protection.

Since April 16, 1998, when the one-year deadline on asylum applications became effective, part of the interview process involves an inquiry into whether the applicant sought asylum within one year of entering the United States.[35] If the applicant was admitted to the United States after being "inspected"—that is, after presenting a passport to an immigration officer at a port of entry (for example, at an airport, seaport, or land border crossing)—the determination of whether the deadline was met is generally simple; the asylum officer compares the date of entry stamped on the passport with the date the asylum application was received by DHS. If this comparison shows that entry was more than a year before application, the asylum officer must inquire into whether the applicant qualifies for one of the exceptions to the one-year deadline (described in chapter 3) and, if so, whether the applicant filed within a reasonable period of time after the exception no longer excused the late filing. Persons who entered without inspection (such as by crossing the Mexican or Canadian border at a place other than a designated border crossing) may apply for asylum, but because they do not have passport stamps to prove their date of entry, they must try to establish this date through other evidence.[36]

The asylum officer must also determine whether the applicant's history, if true, warrants a grant of asylum under current legal standards. In some cases, the law is relatively straightforward. For example, if the applicant was imprisoned and tortured because she was a human rights activist, a leader of a dissident party, a member of a minority tribe, or an adherent to a particular faith, she is clearly eligible under the law. But if she fled her country only to avoid a raging civil war and was not targeted because of one of the statutory grounds such as her political views or ethnicity, she is ineligible. Many cases fall in a middle ground in which the officer may have to do research on asylum law before coming to a decision. For example, the law does not define "persecution," and there are conflicting court opinions on whether political imprisonments of particular durations, without physical violence, constitute persecution. Asylum can be granted to someone who is at risk of persecution by a group that the government is unwilling or unable to control, but the law is in flux with regard to whether a person who is targeted by a violent gang because of his refusal to join the gang is a member of a "social group" and therefore eligible for protection. Sometimes, asylum officers are called upon to decide truly novel legal issues.[37]

The most difficult task for an asylum officer in most cases is determining whether the applicant is telling the truth. Some people come to the United States to seek a better life and are neither victims of past persecution nor threatened with persecution in the future. Some of these individuals apply for asylum after memorizing the facts of other people's lives or formulating claims based on stories of persecution that they heard on the radio. Sometimes smugglers coach their clients on how to tell a persuasive but fictitious story of persecution.[38] An asylum officer must distinguish the genuine refugees from the frauds. She has very few tools for making this judgment. Nevertheless, inconsistencies between the written application and the oral testimony, even those tangential to the applicant's asserted fear of persecution, may doom the claim.[39] The lack of documentary corroboration that, in the view of the asylum officer, should have been available, is also a basis for declining to grant asylum.[40] This is true even though genuine asylum applicants often do not have persuasive supporting documents such as arrest warrants; foreign dictators do not generally provide victims with clear evidence of persecution.

The asylum officer's work of separating genuine from false claims is made all the more difficult by language barriers and imperfect translation; cultural differences that make credibility judgments based on nonverbal behavior inaccurate; and the effects of torture and trauma itself. The latter often make it difficult for applicants to recall or relate the incidents of abuse that they suffered, particularly if they were raped or subjected to other humiliating treatment. An asylum officer generally tries to determine whether the applicant's narrative is sufficiently detailed, internally consistent, consistent with the written application and any other documents that were supplied, and consistent with published reports about the country in question, including, importantly, the State Department's annual report on each country's human rights record.[41]

In the oral interview, the applicant is sworn to tell the truth under penalty of perjury, and the asylum officer typically elicits details of the applicant's personal history. The applicant's representative is not permitted to question the applicant but may make a closing statement at the end of the interview.[42] If the interview discloses a significant error in the data that has been entered into the RAPS system (for example, if RAPS indicates that the applicant has Ethiopian citizenship, but the applicant demonstrates that although she lived for some time in Ethiopia, her nationality is Eritrean), the asylum officer corrects the RAPS entry.[43] However, asylum officers report that they rarely change data in RAPS except to correct the spelling of the applicant's name,[44] or sometimes to change the date on which the applicant entered the United States.[45]

At the end of the interview, the applicant is usually directed to return to the regional asylum office in two weeks for a written decision.[46] Interviewers and applicants generally have no contact with each other after the interview while the decision is pending.

After the interview, the asylum officer makes a written recommendation of a disposition, justifying the proposed decision to a supervising asylum officer by reference to the application and the officer's interview notes. Asylum officers have no quota of cases that they must approve, reject because of the deadline, or refer to immigration court because they do not think that the applicant has proved eligibility for asylum.

In cases in which the one-year filing deadline applies, the asylum officer is directed to conduct a thorough inquiry into both the merits of the claim and the applicability of the deadline.[47] But if the deadline was not met and no exception applies, the officer refers the case to an immigration judge based on the deadline regardless of the strength of the applicant's case on the merits.[48] For cases barred because of the deadline, the officer's write-up of the case need not include "a full account of the material facts of the applicant's claim, nor must they discuss whether an applicant has established past persecution or has a well-founded fear."[49] This written assessment must, however, include a great deal of detail establishing that the deadline was not met and that no exception applied.[50]

The supervising asylum officer may approve or disapprove the proposed disposition. The supervisor may also ask another asylum officer to review the case.

For the majority of applicants who have no other lawful immigration status, the asylum office makes one of three decisions. First, if it concludes that an applicant filed on time and met the statutory requirements for asylum, the office grants the application. Second, if the applicant cannot prove that she filed within a year of entering and has not proved a changed or extraordinary circumstance to justify a later filing (or if the applicant proves such a circumstance but did not apply within a reasonable time after the circumstance justifying the delay no longer applied), the asylum office "rejects" the application and "refers" the case to immigration court for a removal (deportation) hearing. Finally, if an applicant filed on time or proved a changed or exceptional circumstance but has not proved eligibility for asylum (or is barred by some other law, such as the ban on granting asylum to those who have committed certain crimes), the department also "refers" the applicant to immigration court, in the Department of Justice, for a removal hearing.[51]

An applicant who returns to the regional asylum office as directed is given the decision in writing. If the decision is a grant of asylum, the case is over. If asylum is not granted and the applicant has no other lawful immigration status at the time of the decision, the decision of the asylum office includes the summons (euphemistically called a "notice to appear") to immigration court. If the applicant does not attend the court hearing, she will be ordered "in absentia" to be removed to her home country.[52] If she participates in the hearing, her asylum application will be adjudicated de novo. However, unlike the asylum office interview, the immigration court hearing is adversarial in nature; an ICE lawyer will cross-examine the applicant vigorously and will usually argue against asylum and in favor of removal.[53]

Furthermore, even meritorious applicants may remember or state facts somewhat differently in court, compared to their applications or asylum officer interviews. The passage of time between interviews and hearings, the impact of trauma on memory, and different levels of preparation by representatives could all lead to such differences in accounts. "De novo" hearings are, in principle, proceedings in which the parties start over again, and the result of the DHS adjudication supposedly has no bearing on what the immigration judge decides. But during cross-examination, ICE lawyers often use any variations between statements that applicants made previously and those made in court to discredit the applicants by suggesting to the judge that they are lying.[54] If the judge does not grant the applicant some relief from removal such as asylum, the judge will order the applicant removed—deported—from the United States.

Even if the applicant ultimately prevails in immigration court, however, she is almost always much worse off than if she had succeeded during the asylum office interview. Immigration courts are badly backlogged, and it can take two years or longer to have a hearing on the merits of the case, during which many applicants have to live in poverty or off the charity of relatives, some of whom use them as unpaid laborers.[55] Her husband and children back home (who could join her if she wins asylum) may meanwhile be at risk of persecution or death because of her own apparent flight from the country, or because the persecuting regime identifies them with her.

In the small percentage of cases in which the applicant does not meet her burden of proof but has another lawful U.S. immigration status (such as a still-valid student visa) at the time of an asylum officer's decision, she is given a "notice of intent to deny" the application instead of a referral, because she is not subject to removal at that time. The notice explains the reasons for the proposed denial in more detail than the summary explanation that is given to applicants who are referred. She is given sixteen days in which to submit a written rebuttal to the notice.[56] If the asylum officer and supervisor are not persuaded by the rebuttal, her application is formally denied, but she may remain in the United States until her lawful status expires.

Tens of thousands of individuals submit themselves to this process every year, knowing that they are risking their chance of remaining in the United States on the hope that an asylum officer will rule in their favor. A refugee who does not apply may succeed in remaining in the United States without lawful status for years, working in an underground economy. But without proper documents, it will be very difficult if not impossible to get a driver's license, open a bank account, or obtain more than marginal employment. If the refugee is apprehended for even a minor offense, such as a traffic violation, he may be identified by name or fingerprints and jailed until deported.[57] On the other hand, if she applies for asylum and does not ultimately prevail, she will have identified herself and provided her address and other information to the United States government, making it much more difficult to remain unknown and in hiding, and more likely that she will be deported and barred from reentering the United States for many years.[58] It is likely, therefore, that many people who fear persecution but have scant evidence to support their claims, or who have strong claims and evidence but learn that they have missed the application deadline, do not apply for asylum, taking their chances on living underground.

Who are the affirmative asylum seekers who ask the Department of Homeland Security to judge their eligibility for protection in the United States? Where do they come from, how do they enter the United States, to what extent do they have legal assistance when they file for asylum, and what else do we know about them? And who are the asylum officers who decide whether to grant refuge to these applicants? Chapter 2 includes a statistical profile of the affirmative applicants over a fourteen-year period, from the fall of 1995 through the spring of 2009. Chapter 2 also includes a statistical profile of the asylum officers who decide whether to grant refuge to the applicants.

2

The Applicants and the Adjudicators

This study analyzes a database drawn from the Department of Homeland Security's RAPS system, providing information about 552,760 asylum applications filed between the beginning of FY 1996 and June 8, 2009.[1] We studied only the cases in which the applicants were really seeking asylum (as opposed to another form of relief) and were actually interviewed by asylum officers.[2] The Methodological Appendix, which is available on a website associated with this book, describes in detail why we excluded certain cases from our study.[3]

The resulting data on which this book is primarily based consisted of 383,480 cases. For most of our analyses of the one-year filing deadline, we used a smaller database of the 303,601 cases filed after April 16, 1998, when the deadline came into effect. For our analyses of cases decided on the merits, beginning in chapter 6, we explored the database of 329,361 cases (including those filed after April 16, 1998) that were not rejected because of the deadline. These cases were either filed before the deadline came into effect, filed timely, or filed late but subject to one of the exceptions to the deadline. And for our analysis of asylum officer characteristics in chapter 10, we analyzed a much smaller database of 31,635 decisions made by the 221 asylum officers who provided personal information as part of their Asylum Officer Basic Training Course (AOBTC).

For each case, the DHS data included the following information:

- A serial number assigned to the case[4]
- The applicant's age at the time of filing
- The applicant's date of entry into the United States[5]
- Whether the applicant was also seeking asylum for dependents (a spouse and any unmarried children under the age of 21) who were in the United States
- The applicant's gender
- The applicant's nationality
- The applicant's religion if she chose to list a religion
- Whether the applicant was represented when she filed her application
- The applicant's immigration status at the time of entry (whether the applicant entered the United States with a visa, and if so, which type of visa)
- The date of the asylum application

- A code number for the asylum officer who adjudicated the asylum claim[6]
- The regional asylum office in which the case was adjudicated[7]
- The date of the asylum office decision
- The outcome of the adjudication

Characteristics of the Asylum Applicants

The characteristics of the cases in the large applicant database of 383,340 cases are summarized below. We divide these summaries into four multiyear periods, which we discuss further in chapter 6.[8]

As might be expected, the composition of the applicant pool changed during the period of our study. Most of the changes reflected shifts in human rights conditions in the countries from which the applicants fled (for example, the signing of a peace agreement in Guatemala). In the case of the Chinese, they may have resulted from a change in U.S. asylum policy regarding flight to avoid sterilization and abortion.

As figure 2-1 shows, before 1998 the largest percentage of applicants (nearly 40 percent) came from Latin America and the Caribbean, with fewer than 10 percent coming from East Asia. However, the 1990s saw a large influx of immigrants from China, many of them asylum applicants,[9] and the proportion of East Asian

Fig. 2-1. Applicants' Regions of Origin, Percentages

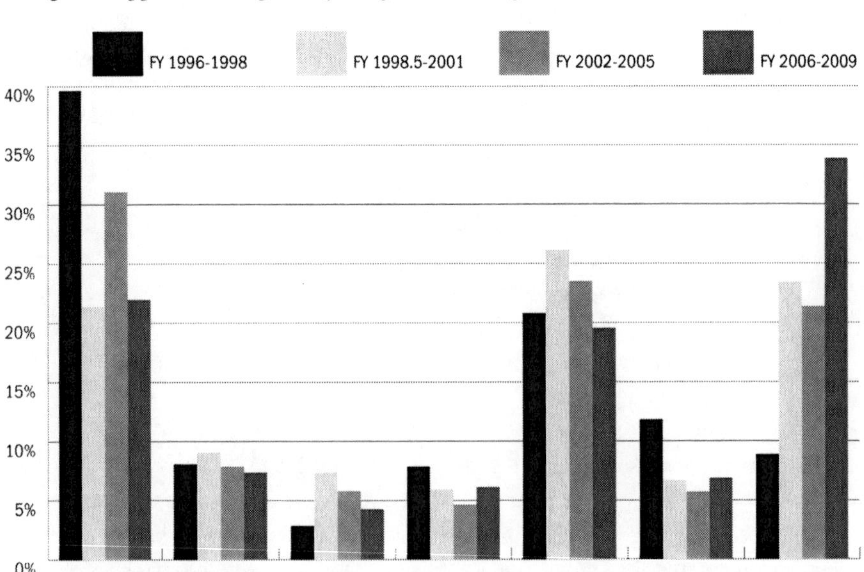

applicants increased dramatically, while the percentage of Latin Americans fell to about a quarter of the applicant pool. In the late 1990s, approximately equal percentages of applicants came from Latin America, Africa, and East Asia, but by the late 2000s, by far the largest proportion were applicants from East Asia.

Percentages tell only part of the story, however. As figure 2-2 shows, the percentage increase among East Asian applicants was really a result of the smaller number of Latin American and African applicants in the later years, as East Asian applications held rather steady after 1998.

Figures 2-3 through 2-6 show which countries were the principal nations of origin of the asylum applicants. Between 1995 and 1998, because of civil wars and related persecution in Central America, Guatemala and El Salvador produced the largest numbers of asylum applicants. Together, nationals of these countries constituted 27 percent of the applicant pool. Some of these applicants had fled to the United States much earlier, but as there was no deadline on applications in those years, they could apply until April 16, 1998, without regard to the length of time they had spent in the United States.

A few years later (mid-1998 through 2001), when persecution associated with the wars in their countries had diminished significantly, Guatemalans and Salvadorans constituted only 3.5 percent of the applicant pool. By then, the largest group of applicants by far consisted of Chinese people, with

Fig. 2-2. Applicants' Regions of Origin, Numbers

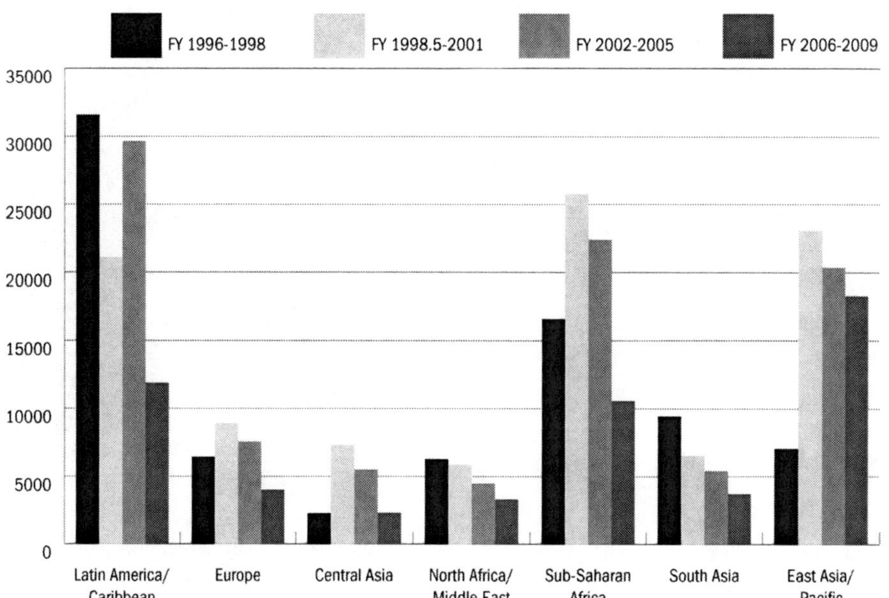

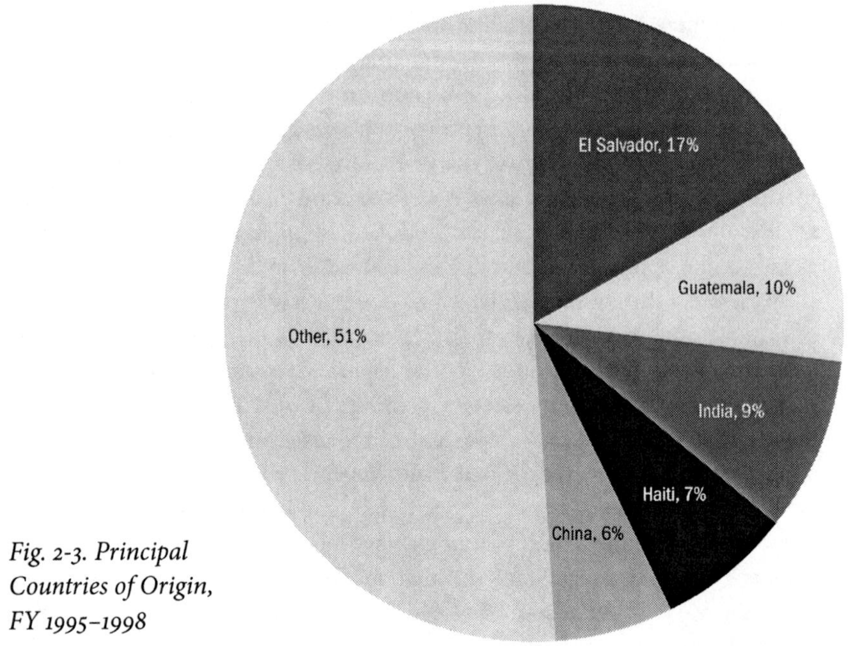

Fig. 2-3. Principal Countries of Origin, FY 1995–1998

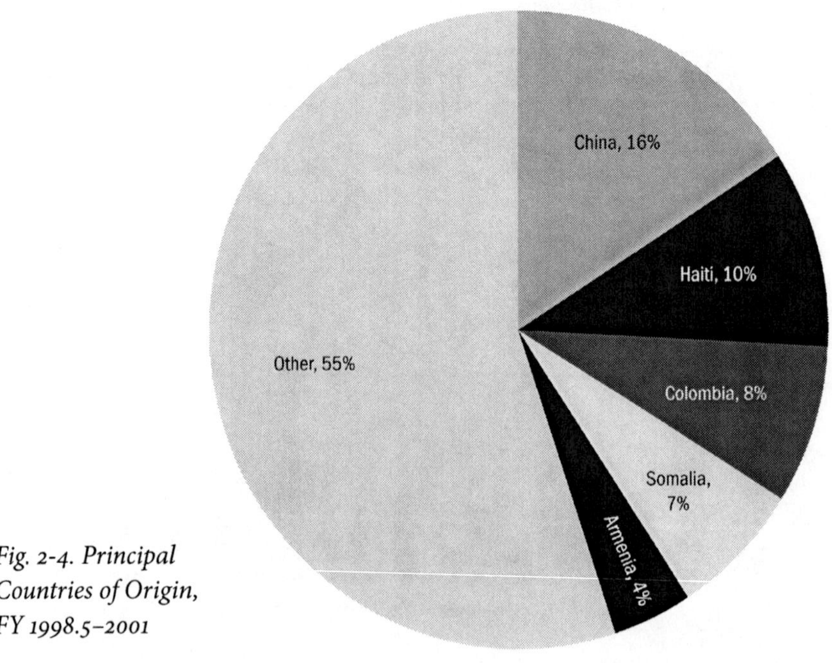

Fig. 2-4. Principal Countries of Origin, FY 1998.5–2001

Haitians, Colombians, and Somalis second, third, and fourth, reflecting the turmoil in those nations (figure 2-4).[10] The fact that so many Colombians applied for asylum reflected their flight from the threat of terrorist organizations, (particularly the Revolutionary Armed Forces of Colombia (FARC), which the Colombian government could not control. Armenians also made the top-five list in those years, with Indonesians close behind.

During the period after the September 11 terrorist attacks, Somalis no longer applied in large numbers. Perhaps it had become considerably more difficult to reach the United States, and perhaps many who had the means to flee the chaos in that country for the United States had already done so (figure 2-5). Chinese nationals remained the largest group of asylum seekers.

In the last period we studied, FY 2006–09, Chinese applicants were strongly predominant, but Haitians had again emerged as the second largest group of applicants,[11] with Ethiopians claiming the third spot after that country's 2005 elections, when "authorities arbitrarily detained, beat, and killed opposition members, ethnic minorities, NGO workers, and members of the press"[12] (figure 2-6).

Figure 2-7 reveals that in all periods, most applicants were male, although the percentage of applicants who were female increased in every period. In the period up to mid-April, 1998, only 32 percent of the applicants were female, but by the most recent period of our study, 43 percent were female.

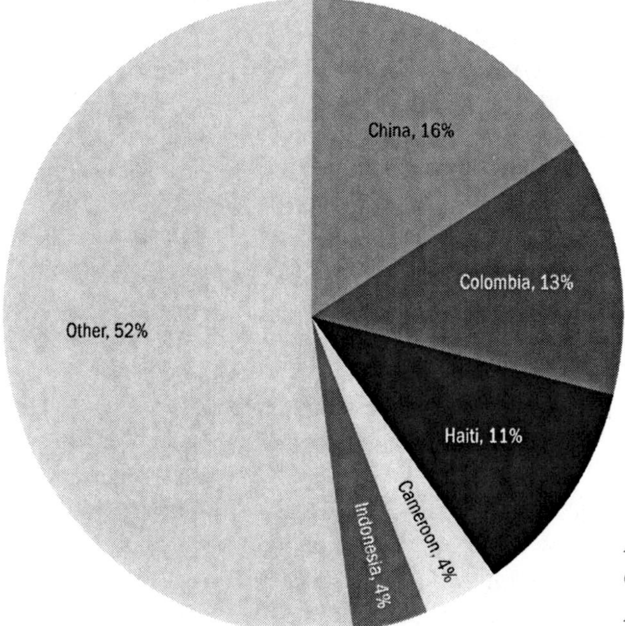

Fig.2-5. Principal Countries of Origin, FY 2002–2005

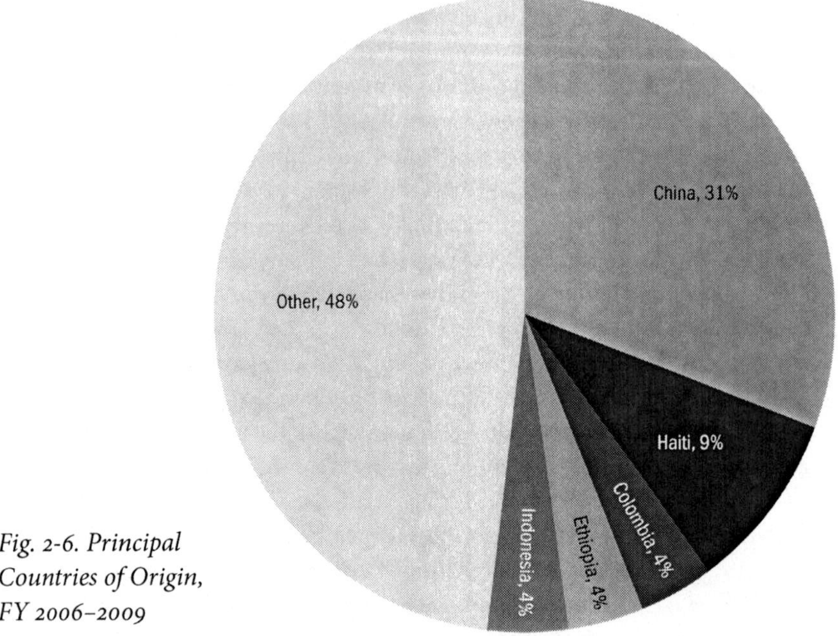

Fig. 2-6. Principal Countries of Origin, FY 2006–2009

Only 76 percent of the applicants in the database stated a religion. But as noted in figure 2-8, among applicants who stated a religion, by far the largest group in every period was Christian. Muslims were the second largest group. Before 1998, the next largest group consisted of Sikhs, perhaps reflecting the fear in that community in the wake of anti-Sikh violence after India's Prime Minister Indira Gandhi was assassinated by her Sikh bodyguards.[13] But in later years, the number of Sikhs and Jews, always relatively small, diminished, as flight from India, Russia, and other former Soviet Republics slowed.

In all periods, people in their twenties were the largest group of asylum applicants, accounting for 40 percent of all applicants between FY 1996 and FY 2009 (figure 2-9). Nearly all the rest of the applicants were more than thirty years old when they applied, as very few children and teenagers were among the applicant group.

As Figure 2-10 indicates, more than one-sixth of the applicants had a spouse or minor child with them in the United States and were also seeking asylum for that dependent. The percentage of applicants with dependents reached its highest level in the early years of the twenty-first century.

Representation increased significantly over the years (figure 2-11). This may reflect a greater perceived need for representation, as anti-immigrant sentiment hardened (particularly in the wake of the 9/11 terrorist attacks) and

Fig. 2-7. Percentage of Applicants Who Were Female

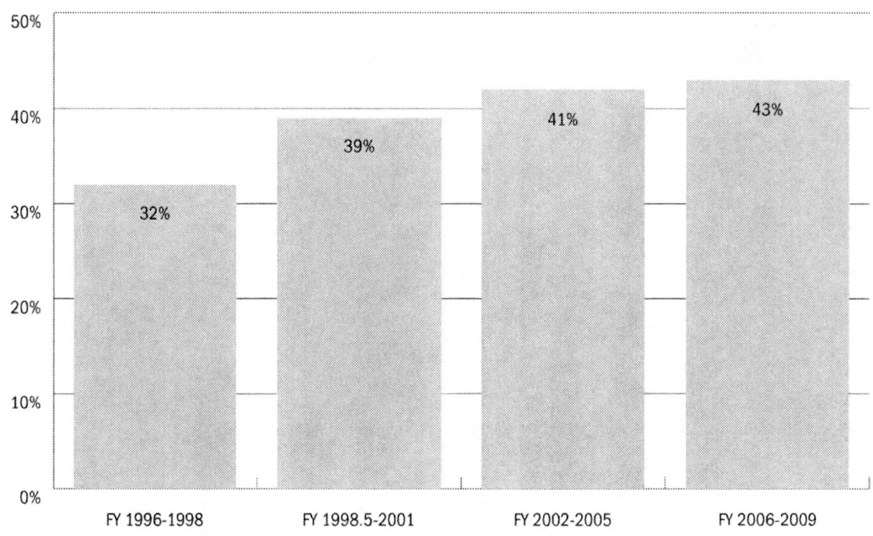

Fig. 2-8. Major Religions (>1%) of Applicants Who Stated a Religion

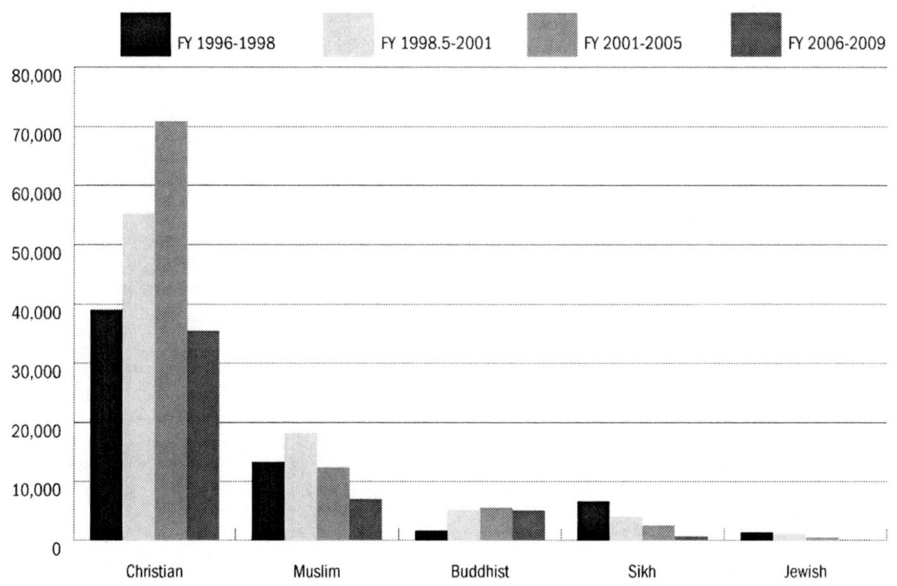

Fig. 2-9. Age at Filing

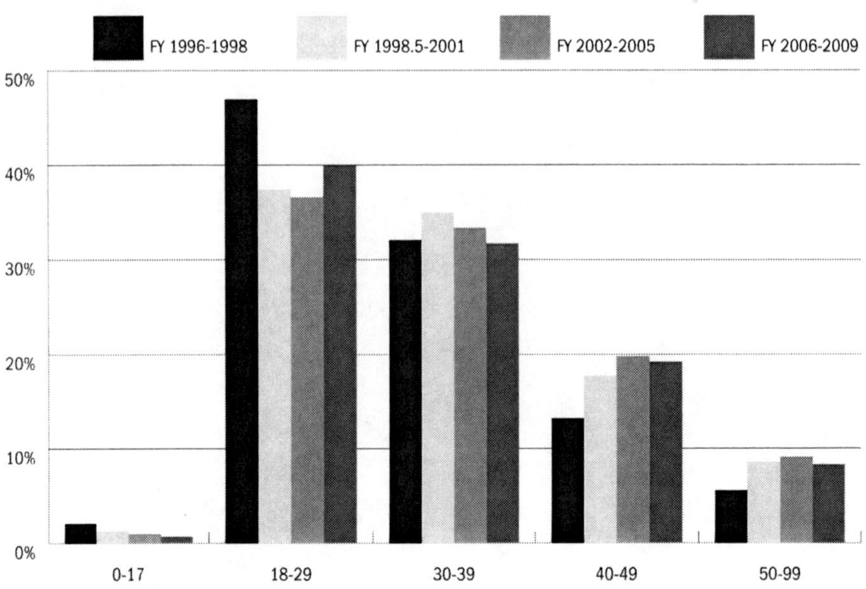

Fig. 2-10. Percentage of Applicants with Dependents in U.S.

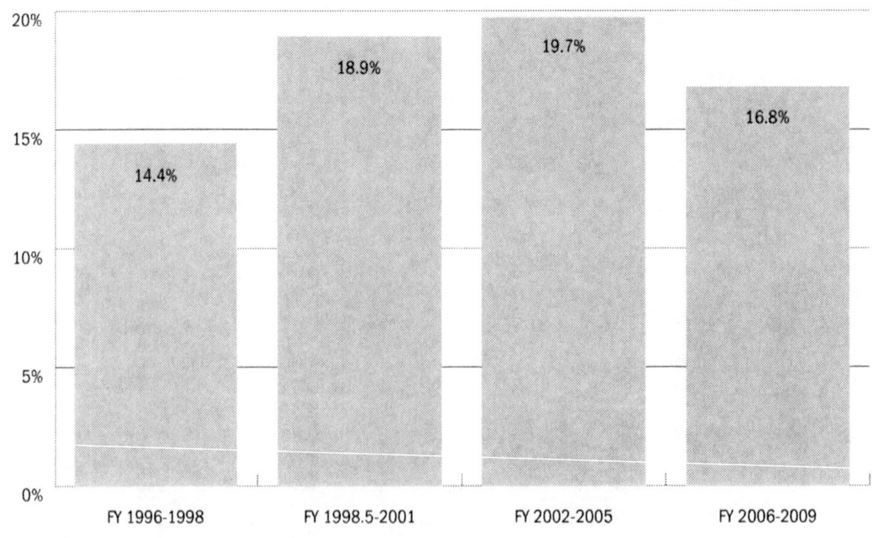

Fig. 2-11. Percentage of Applicants Who Were Represented

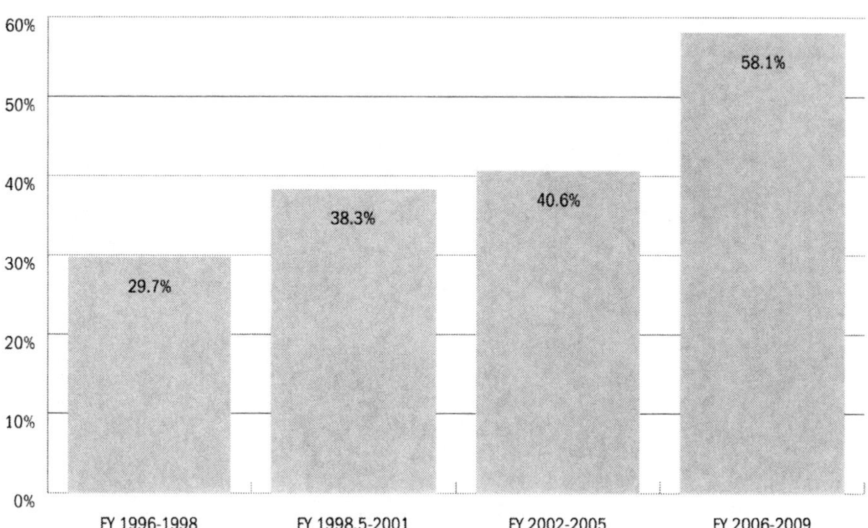

the asylum laws became more complex.[14] It may also reflect the greater availability of representatives as immigration and human rights became more prominent public issues. Another possibility is that notarios and predatory attorneys took advantage of a market for their services. Before 1998, only 30 percent of asylum seekers were represented at this stage of the process. By 2000, this figure increased to nearly 40 percent, and by FY 2008 it had risen to an all-time high of 61 percent.

The group of asylum seekers who applied before the spring of 1998 consisted primarily of individuals who had entered without being inspected (that is, crossed the border without presenting themselves to DHS for examination of their passports and visas). By contrast, two-thirds of those who applied thereafter were people who had entered with passports and visas but had overstayed their period of permitted presence in the United States either before applying for asylum or while awaiting a determination by DHS (figure 2-12).[15] By 2008, 70 percent of applicants were individuals who had entered lawfully. This shift may reflect the increasing difficulty of entering the United States after the mid-1990s, when the U.S. government began systematically increasing the number of border guards, sensors, and other border-crossing detection and prevention mechanisms, particularly along the Mexican border. It may also reflect, to some degree, the vastly reduced number of Guatemalans and Salvadorans who sought to flee to the United States by coming

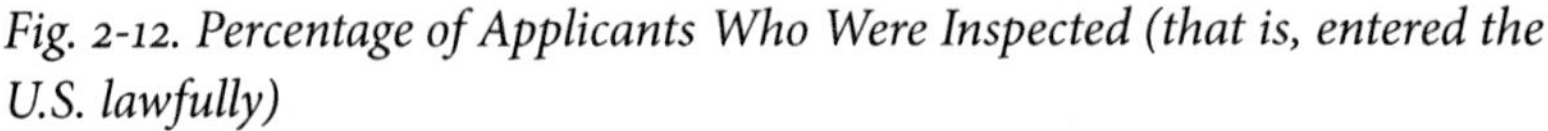

Fig. 2-12. Percentage of Applicants Who Were Inspected (that is, entered the U.S. lawfully)

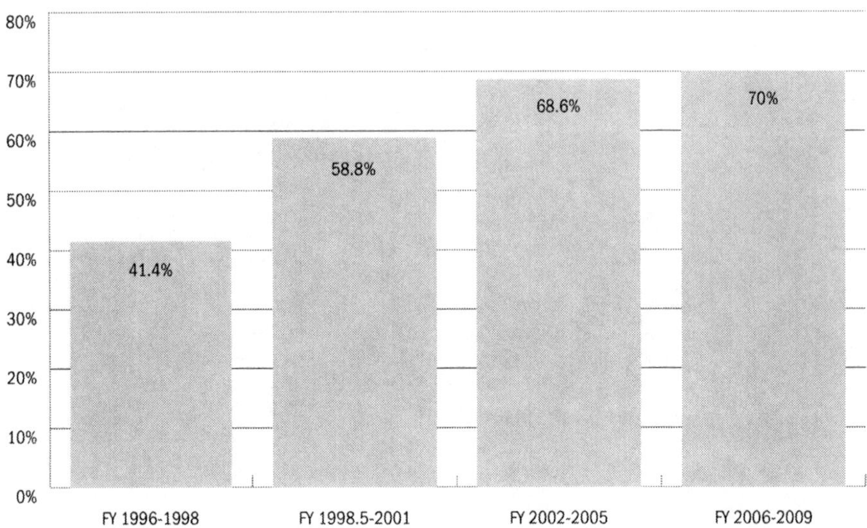

across the southern border after the end of the civil wars and major instability in Central America.

While the data suggest that the more recent asylum seekers are to some extent quite different from their earlier counterparts, these graphs reveal some striking constants. Asylum seekers continued to arrive from all over the world, but in all periods, only five nationalities made up nearly half—or in some periods more than half—of the applicants. Likewise, the percentage of applicants with dependents remained fairly similar over time. Among applicants who stated a religion, the percentage of applicants who self-identified as Christian increased somewhat as time went by, while the percentage of applicants who self-identified as Muslim declined.[16] The applicant population aged moderately over time. The percentage of female applicants and represented applicants increased steadily over the period of our study, as did the percentage of inspected applicants.

Characteristics of the Adjudicators

Our understanding of the characteristics of the adjudicators comes from two sources. First, from July 2003 through August 2008, 221 asylum officers attended a five-week training course at the Federal Law Enforcement Training Center (FLETC).[17] At the outset of the FLETC training, they completed a questionnaire about themselves, which was given to the trainers so that they knew the backgrounds of those in the class.[18] To fill in gaps in the FLETC questionnaire,[19] DHS also collected supplemental biographical information on most of these officers. In the database made available to the public, DHS removed all information that could have been used to individually identify asylum officers, including substituting names with a confidential code number.

Biographical Profile of the Officers Trained at FLETC

The officers who were trained at FLETC collectively decided 31,635 of the cases amassed in the data made public by DHS.

The biographical data reveal a diverse work force. Fifty-seven percent of the officers were female. Nearly half were nonwhite; figure 2-13 shows the ethnic composition of this corps.

The asylum officers were, on the whole, fairly young at the time they completed the questionnaire; two-thirds of them were under the age of forty. Figure 2-14 reflects their ages.

At the time of the training, approximately half of the asylum officers were single. Forty-three percent were married, and 5.5 percent were divorced or separated.

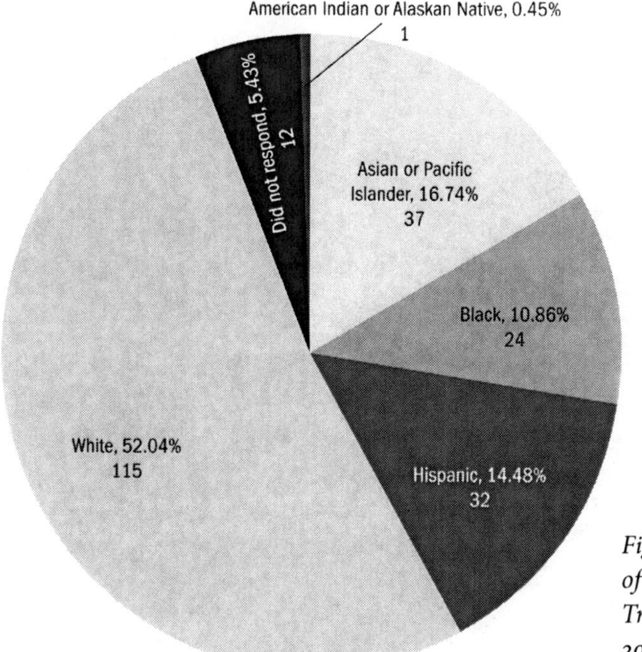

Fig. 2-13. Ethnicity of Asylum Officers Trained at FLETC, 2003–2008

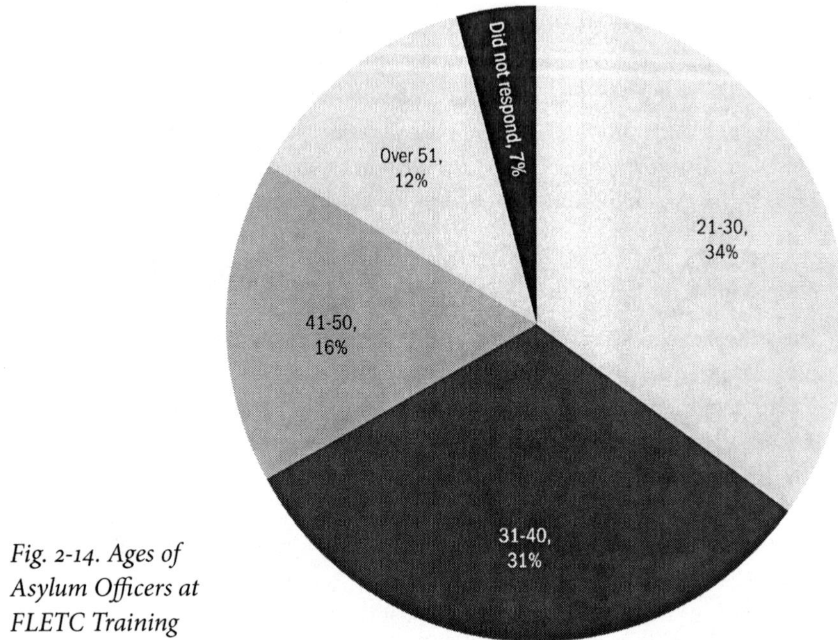

Fig. 2-14. Ages of Asylum Officers at FLETC Training

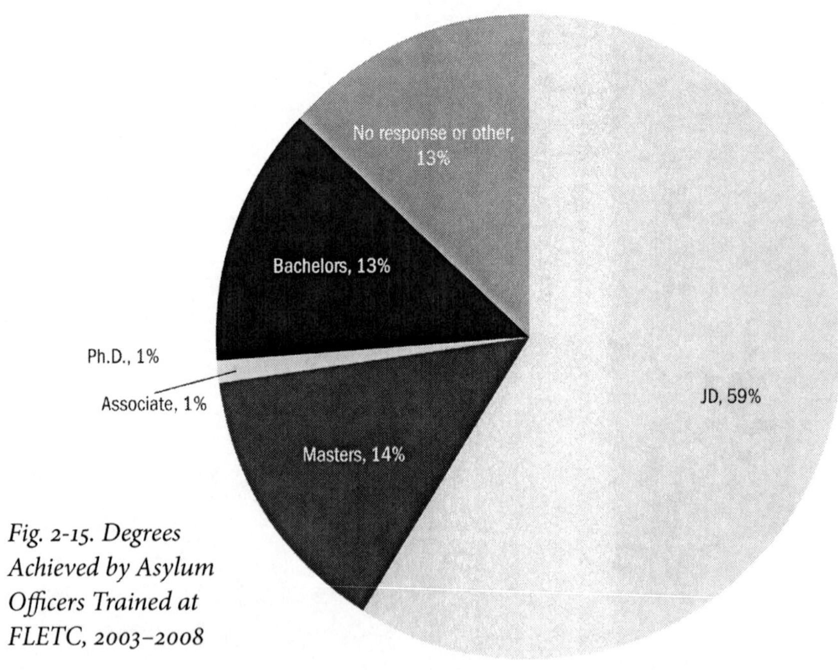

Fig. 2-15. Degrees Achieved by Asylum Officers Trained at FLETC, 2003–2008

More than two-thirds (68 percent) had no dependents. Thirteen percent had one dependent, and 19 percent had two or more dependents. Of course, their marital and dependent status may have changed during the time frame of the study.

The asylum officers were born in 34 states, the District of Columbia, Guam, Puerto Rico, and abroad; in fact, although all were U.S. citizens, 22 percent of them were born in another country, more than the percentage born in California (12 percent) or New York (8 percent).

The asylum officers were highly educated. Forty-five percent of them had completed four years of college education and three years of postgraduate education, and another 22 percent had completed more than three years of postgraduate education. Fifty-nine percent had law degrees. Figure 2-15 displays their educational attainments.

Ten percent of the asylum officers had taught before joining DHS, and an amazing 68 percent of them had lived overseas.[20] Perhaps individuals who had lived abroad were particularly drawn to adjudicating human rights cases. Ninety percent of the officers responded to a question asking whether, before joining DHS, they had worked with people who had received asylum. Of these, 53 percent had done so. Of the 91 percent whose foreign language experience can be determined from the questionnaire, only 15 percent did not speak a foreign language. The number of languages spoken by the asylum officers is displayed in figure 2-16.[21]

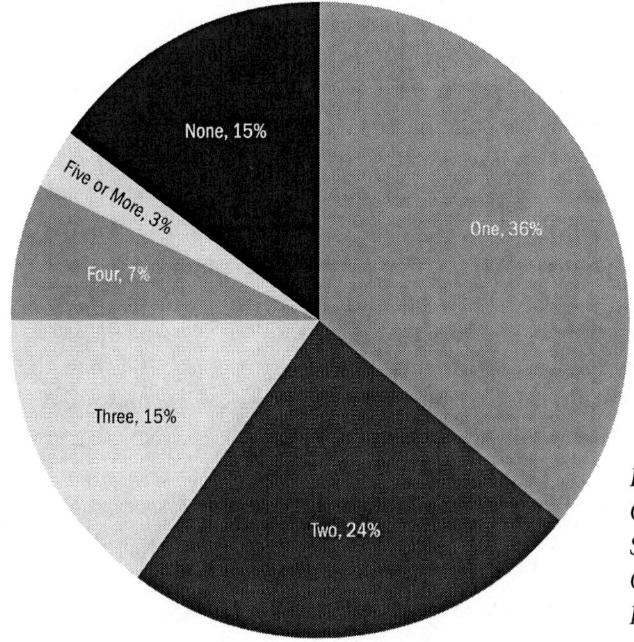

Fig. 2-16. Languages Other Than English Spoken by Asylum Officers Trained at FLETC, 2003–2008

Fifteen percent of the 221 officers had served for at least three years in the U.S. military. Of those who had been in military service, 17 had been in the Army, 10 in the Air Force, and 3 each in the Navy and Marines. Thirty-nine percent of the officers had prior civilian experience in a government agency. Most of those had worked in some other office within DHS or the Immigration and Naturalization Service (before its abolition in 2003), but some had worked in Defense, Labor, State, Justice, the FBI, the Social Security Administration, Health and Human Services, the Federal Reserve Board, and other agencies.

DHS's 2011 Survey of Asylum Officers

Our second source of data on asylum officer characteristics was a questionnaire that the Asylum Office distributed to all current asylum officers and supervising asylum officers in May 2011.[22] The opinions and other information provided by these asylum officers are helpful in clarifying various issues discussed in this book, and representative responses are included in the chapters that follow.

The questionnaire asked a few basic biographical questions. Unlike the data provided by the officers during several years of initial training classes, these data provide a snapshot of the characteristics of asylum officers at only one point in time. Furthermore, participation in the survey was voluntary.[23] The participation rate was 70 percent,[24] so it is possible that the respondents were not fully representative of the entire pool of asylum officers and supervisors during the month of the survey. While not ideal, the 70 percent participation rate is comparable to the 74 percent participation rate obtained when the Government Accountability Office surveyed asylum officers in 2008, on the basis of which it wrote its report on steps to improve the quality of asylum office determinations.[25]

Among the officers who responded, a majority (62 percent of the 194 officers who revealed their gender) were women, a proportion fairly similar to the proportion (57 percent) derived from the larger database. Of the responding officers, 175 answered a question asking about their ethnicity, and 39 did not answer this question. Figure 2-17 shows the responses, revealing a workforce in 2011 in which white and nonwhite officers served in roughly the same proportions as those who attended training in the period from 2003 to 2008 (figure 2-13).[26]

Fourteen percent of the respondents were serving as supervisors at the time of the survey. The median number of years of service of the asylum officers and supervisors was four, although there was a good deal of scatter. Figure 2-18 is a histogram showing the respondents' number of years of service.

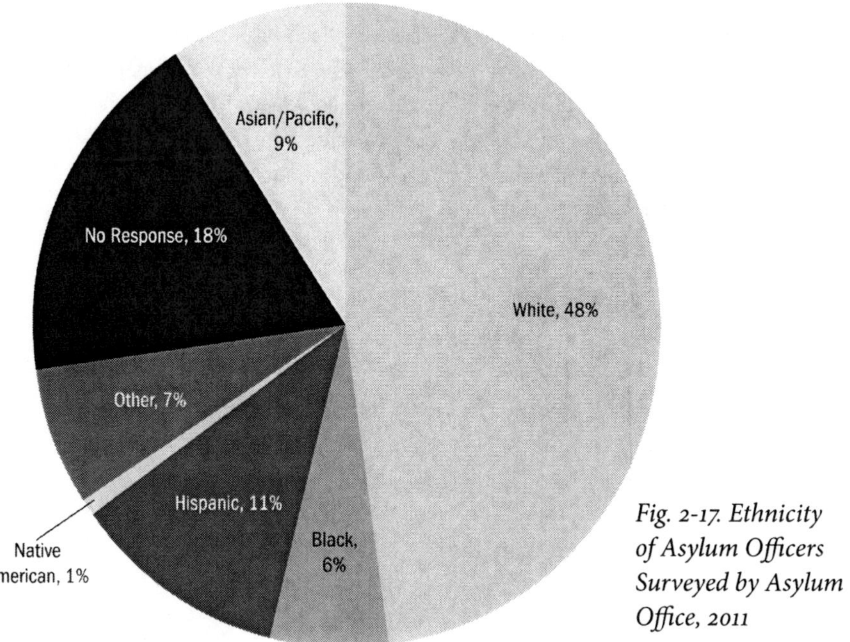

Fig. 2-17. Ethnicity of Asylum Officers Surveyed by Asylum Office, 2011

Fig. 2-18. Years of Service of the Asylum Officers Surveyed by Asylum Office, 2011

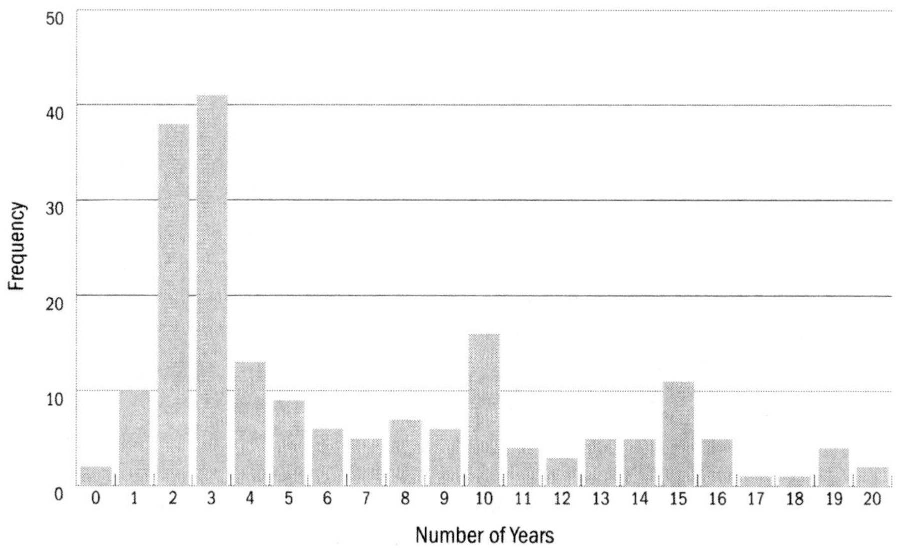

The survey does not fully reflect the actual distribution of asylum officers among the regions, because the response rate in New York was 95 percent while the response rate in the Houston office was particularly low (30 percent). Table 2-1 compares the regional distribution of eligible respondents with the distribution of those who responded and shows the different response rates to the questionnaire:

Table 2-1. Regional Distribution of Asylum Officers and Survey Respondents, 2011

Region	Number of officers	Percentage of all officers serving in this region	Percentage in region responding to survey*	Number responding to survey
Arlington	28	10%	75%	21
Chicago	18	6%	72%	13
Miami	44	16%	75%	33
Houston	33	12%	30%	10
Los Angeles	61	22%	70%	43
New York	42	15%	95%	40
Newark	23	8%	48%	11
San Francisco	29	10%	79%	23
No region identified				20
Total	278		77%	214
Total who responded to all questions				194

*Based on the region in which they had served for the longest period

The survey also asked officers to identify the degrees they had received. Figure 2-19 displays their responses. The percentages add up to more than 100 because some officers had more than one degree. The percentage with law degrees in 2011 was very similar to the percentage from the database from the years 2003 through 2008, while the percentage of those who had college and masters degrees appeared to have increased appreciably.

While the RAPS system contains a good amount of information about the asylum process, it has several shortfalls, which we discuss further in chapter 11. In particular, with respect to merits decisions, RAPS does not contain information about the type of evidence upon which officers relied in making their decisions, certain grounds for asylum, and the main reasons officers rejected asylum claims. The survey, however, contained questions about each of these parts of the adjudication process.

Fig. 2-19. Postsecondary Education of Respondents Surveyed by Asylum Office, 2011

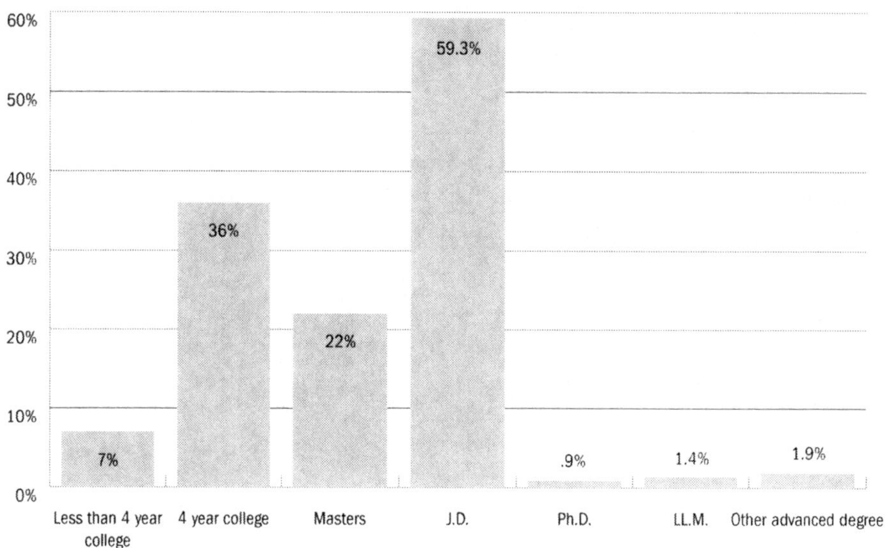

The responses we present below are the officers' recollections of how they made decisions. These data are not drawn from a database of case decisions or from a representative sample of case files, so they should be viewed only as estimates and perceptions rather than hard data. Because DHS does not systematically collect data on these questions, however, these responses may be helpful in rounding out a composite portrait of the asylum adjudication process in the United States.

Types of Claims

GROUNDS FOR ASYLUM

Asylum grants must identify at least one of five grounds upon which the applicant's claim is based: race, religion, nationality, political opinion, or membership in a particular social group. The latter basis for asylum was designed to expand over time and has been defined to include unions, families targeted for death, homosexuals, and social classes (like the educated elite). In 1996, Congress deemed flight to avoid coercive population control, such as was then being practiced in China, to qualify as a particular social group. In addition, as concern about gender-based persecution of women became widespread during the 1990s, case law established that certain kinds of gender-based persecution qualified for asylum under the social group rubric: forced genital mutilation and perhaps also domestic violence that a government was unwilling or unable to control.

The DHS survey asked, "In your experience as an asylum officer, please estimate the percentage of cases in which you have granted asylum that have involved persecution primarily based on [each of these grounds]." The question was worded to reflect the nature of successful cases, not of cases in which asylum was sought but not granted.

Table 2-2. Officers' Estimates of Types of Successful Claims

Estimated Percentage of Cases Granted Involving Persecution Primarily Based On . . .	0–10%	11–20%	21–30%	31–50%	> 50%
Political opinion	11%	18%	23%	22%	**26%**
Religion	17%	**30%**	23%	19%	11%
Gender (including sexual orientation and female genital mutilation)	**36%**	28%	17%	8%	11%
Membership in a particular social group not including gender	**49%**	30%	11%	7%	3%
Nationality or race	**57%**	25%	11%	4%	3%
Coercive population control (including forced abortion or sterilization)	**45%**	27%	13%	10%	5%

Note: The response that commanded the largest percentage of officers for each basis for persecution is **bolded**.

Table 2-2 displays the results of the survey of asylum officers with respect to this issue. The most important columns in this table are the last two columns, showing the grounds for persecution on which asylum officers believed they granted asylum most often. The officers perceived classical political asylum cases—those involving persecution because of the political beliefs or activities of the applicants—to be the largest group of cases in which they granted asylum. Religion was estimated to be the second most frequent ground for granting asylum. In the officers' recollection, gender-based cases made up a significant portion of asylum grants. But cases based on other "social group" grounds, while an important issue for appellate bodies because the law regarding what constitutes a valid social group remains in flux, represent a much smaller percentage of asylum grants. Half of the asylum officers reported that these cases account for 10 percent or less of their asylum grants.

Fig. 2-20. Officers' Estimated Percentages of Asylum Cases Involving Persecution by a Government

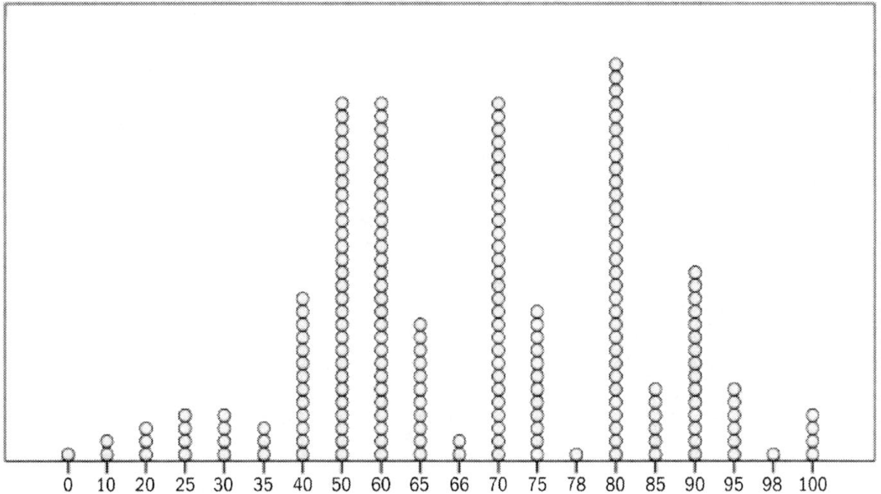

Note: Each circle represents the response of a particular survey respondent.

IDENTITY OF PERSECUTORS

Asylum can be granted when the applicant has a well-founded fear of persecution by his own government or, alternatively, by a group (such as a private militia) that the government is unwilling or unable to control.[27] To what extent do valid asylum claims involve fear of persecution by non–state actors, as opposed to governments?

The DHS survey asked, "Please estimate the percentage of the cases in which you have granted asylum that have involved persecution by the government [as opposed] to private militias, guerillas, gangs and individual abusers." This question, too, related only to cases in which asylum was granted, not to the larger group of all cases in which asylum was sought.

Figure 2-20 shows the asylum officers' responses. Each circle is the response of one survey respondent. The figure shows that most officers estimate that between 50 percent and 80 percent of applicants claim to fear persecution by their governments, as opposed to non–state actors.

PAST PERSECUTION AND THE FEAR OF FUTURE PERSECUTION

Under the Refugee Act, an applicant need not have been jailed or tortured in the past to win asylum; it is sufficient that the applicant have a well-founded fear of persecution in the future. So, for example, if the government is

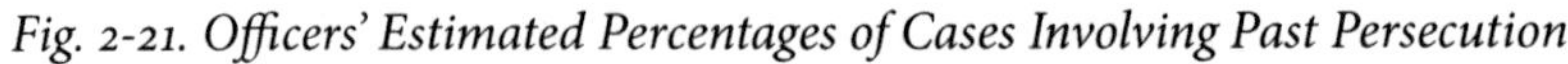

Fig. 2-21. Officers' Estimated Percentages of Cases Involving Past Persecution

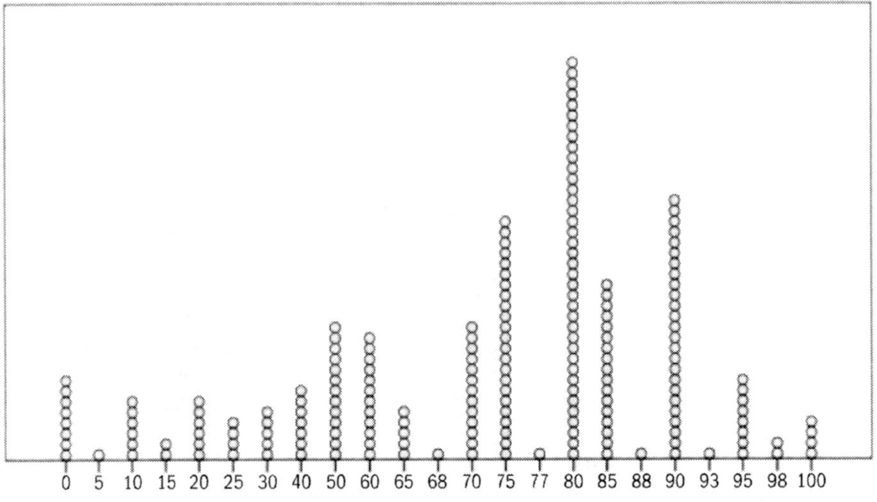

Note: Each circle represents the response of a particular survey respondent.

following a policy of ethnic cleansing of all members of a particular minority, a member of that minority need not personally have experienced harm in order to win asylum. Nevertheless, many asylum applicants are individuals who fled only after they personally suffered jailing, beatings, or other forms of abuse.

The DHS survey asked officers to "estimate the percentage of applicants whose cases you have granted within the last year who suffered past persecution, as opposed to having only a well-founded fear of future persecution."

Figure 2-21 displays these results.

Two-thirds of the officers surveyed believed that at least 60 percent of their asylum grants went to people who had already suffered persecution, and 43 percent believed that at least 80 percent of their grants went to past persecution victims. At the same time, 15 percent of officers recollected that 20 percent or fewer of the cases they had granted involved past persecution. Given the fact that applications (and therefore cases of victims of past persecution) are randomly distributed to officers, the survey results suggest that some officers may be much less willing than others to grant asylum to people who had not yet personally suffered persecution. However, because the data DHS provided did not indicate whether cases were decided based on past persecution, fear of future persecution, or both, we were unable to investigate this possibility more systematically.[28]

Reasons for Refusal to Grant Asylum

Except in cases in which the asylum seeker did not meet the one-year filing deadline, a subject treated in chapters 3 through 5, RAPS also does not record with specificity why an asylum officer declined to grant asylum. In any particular case, the reason could be that the asylum officer did not believe the applicant's story, or that the applicant did not provide sufficient evidence to corroborate that story, or that the asylum officer believed the applicant and found sufficient corroboration but the applicant did not qualify under the law (for example, if the applicant was fleeing from the ravages of a civil war rather than from threatened persecution on account of one of the five accepted grounds, or the applicant was ineligible because she had committed a serious crime).

The DHS survey asked officers to estimate how frequently, in cases where the deadline was met, they turned down applicants primarily for each of these reasons.

According to these asylum officers, lack of credibility is the most important reason why asylum is not granted, with 84 percent of the asylum officers stating that this is "very often" or "often" the reason for not granting asylum.[29] Twenty-seven percent listed legal ineligibility as being very often or often the reason, and only 14 percent reported lack of corroboration being very often or often the reason. (The percentages add up to more than 100 percent because officers could list more than one reason as being very often or often the explanation).[30]

RELIABILITY OF EVIDENCE

Asylum applicants use various types of evidence to prove their past persecution, threats made against them or against similarly situated individuals, and human rights conditions in their countries that are consistent with their claims. These include the applicants' testimony in their oral interviews; their own written statements, which they are encouraged to file with their application forms; letters or statements from witnesses (such as family members who know that they were imprisoned or tortured); statements from experts such as anthropologists familiar with the country or doctors who had examined the applicant for scars; documents such as political party cards or medical records; reports from human rights organizations such as Amnesty International; and the annual human rights reports from the U.S. State Department.

The DHS survey asked officers how reliable they considered each of these types of sources. For each source, they could indicate that the source was "usually quite reliable," "sometimes useful but I am sometimes skeptical," "somewhat useful but I am often skeptical" or "usually unreliable." Table 2-3 displays the views of the respondents:

Table 2-3. Officers' Perceived Reliability of Evidence

	Percentage of officers who regarded that type of evidence as:			
Type of Evidence	Usually quite reliable	Somewhat useful, but I am sometimes skeptical	Somewhat useful, but I am often skeptical	Usually unreliable
Applicant's oral testimony	27%	**47%**	23%	3%
Applicant's written statements	12%	**49%**	34%	6%
Letters or statements from fact witnesses	4%	24%	**49%**	23%
Documents from home country	4%	29%	**47%**	20%
Experts' statements	30%	**47%**	18%	5%
Reports from nongovernmental organizations	**79%**	17%	3%	2%
Official (e.g., State Deptart-ment) reports	**83%**	13%	3%	1%

The table includes several notable observations. First, among types of evidence offered, officers are most skeptical of the letters and statements of fact witnesses and of documents that originated in the applicants' home countries, with 72 percent and 67 percent of officers regarding these types of evidence with a great deal of skepticism. At the other end of the spectrum, both official reports, such as those from the State Department, and the unofficial reports of nongovernmental organizations were regarded about equally in terms of reliability. However, there is a big difference between government and NGO reports, on the one hand, and letters and other documents from home countries, on the other: the former address only general country conditions, while the latter are usually much more important in asylum adjudication because they tend to pertain to the situation of the individual applicant, who must prove that she personally had a well-founded fear of persecution.

It appears from the survey results that in terms of proving an individual's well-founded fear, the individual's own testimony and written statements, and those of experts, are considered much more reliable than evidence from other parties, such as relatives, and other documents, such as arrest warrants and foreign newspapers, which are sometimes forged or counterfeited, without the applicant's knowledge, by well-meaning relatives who think that they are helping the applicant to obtain safe harbor in the United States. Only 24 percent of officers reported being often skeptical of applicants' oral testimony (or find it usually unreliable), perhaps because they are able to probe that testimony through questioning in the interview—something that they cannot do with letters or documents from abroad. Applicants' written statements occupy something of a middle ground; they are seen as less reliable than applicants' oral testimony (perhaps because they can be prepared with the help of friends, relatives, or professional advocates), but more reliable than letters and documents from abroad.

In this chapter, we have introduced the characteristics of the asylum seekers and asylum officers in the databases on which we rely in the rest of the book, following an overview of the asylum system generally. In the next chapter, we describe the one-year filing deadline in greater detail, after which we move into the data analysis that constitutes the bulk of this book.

3

The One-Year Filing Deadline

The first step, for an asylum officer who is analyzing a new asylum application, is the determination of whether the claim was filed on time. This new twist to the asylum standard took effect on April 16, 1998, as part of the Illegal Immigration Reform and Immigrant Responsibility Act of 1996 (IIRIRA). Although the Refugee Act provides that any person from another nation who arrives in the United States may apply for asylum, the 1996 law states that this right to seek asylum "shall not apply" unless the would-be asylum seeker "demonstrates by clear and convincing evidence that the application has been filed within 1 year after the date of the alien's arrival in the United States."[1] The law, however, created two exceptions. A late-filing applicant may apply if he proves the existence of "changed circumstances which materially affect the applicant's eligibility for asylum or extraordinary circumstances relating to the delay in filing an application" within a year after entry.[2] Such a person must also have applied within a "reasonable period" of time after the changed circumstances occurred,[3] or within a "reasonable period given [the extraordinary] circumstances."[4]

The wording of the 1996 law did not simply make late filing a factor in the asylum officer's decision, or even a basis on which the asylum officer had to deny the application. Because it provided that an asylum seeker who filed late was not entitled by the Refugee Act even to apply for asylum, the law created a threshold requirement, a first line to be crossed even before the merits of an asylum application could be evaluated. At least, that is how DHS interpreted the law, for DHS required its asylum officers to analyze separately, in each case, apart from the officers' determinations of the merits, whether the applicant had met the deadline. If the deadline was not met, DHS codes the case in its record as one that was "rejected" rather than one in which asylum simply was not granted. Other legal bars to asylum, such as the prohibition of asylum for persons who had committed certain crimes, continue to be folded into the analysis of whether asylum should be granted, and these bars are not recorded by DHS as "rejected" cases.

The deadline does not bar applicants from being granted a different humanitarian status, called "withholding of removal."[5] Like asylum, this status allows an applicant to remain in the United States and, at least temporarily, avoid deportation to a country in which she fears persecution. A person who obtains withholding is allowed to work in the United States. But in an important way, withholding is harder to win than asylum. Although the deadline does not apply, a person seeking withholding must prove that persecution is more probable than not, a much higher standard than the "well-founded fear" of persecution used in asylum cases.[6] Despite having a higher burden of proof, an applicant who wins withholding receives many fewer benefits than an asylee (a person to whom asylum is granted). Unlike an asylee, she is not eligible to change her immigration status to that of a lawful permanent resident (and eventually, a citizen). She can not have her spouse or minor children join her in the United States, or pass along her lawful status to a "derivative" spouse or child in the United States, even though they may be at risk of persecution because of her past activities or her flight. She can be deported to a country other than the country from which she fled, and during her entire lifetime, her status can be revoked if human rights conditions in her country improve. Although the one-year bar does not prevent withholding from being granted, a DHS asylum officer may not grant withholding of removal to an affirmative asylum applicant who has missed the deadline and does not qualify for an exception. The officer must reject the application and require the applicant to appear for a removal hearing in immigration court, where she may seek a new determination of her eligibility for asylum and may seek withholding as an alternative form of relief from removal.[7]

It is not entirely clear why Congress imposed a deadline. The sponsors of a deadline, Representatives Bill McCollum, Chuck Schumer, and Romano Mazzoli and Senator Alan Simpson, originally proposed a deadline of only thirty days, with virtually no exceptions.[8] In their view, any person fleeing from persecution would know at once that she wanted asylum and would be able to apply for it immediately; anyone who did not apply for asylum immediately after entering the United States was probably not a genuine refugee.[9] McCollum and Simpson introduced this proposal in 1995, the first year in which Republicans had a majority in both houses of Congress since the early 1950s.

Other members of Congress apparently thought that the asylum adjudication system was broken because foreign nationals could remain in the United States indefinitely as a result of long delays in the adjudication of their cases. They claimed to be unaware that the problem of long delays had just been solved by recently adopted regulations eliminating temporary work permits for asylum applicants,[10] and they did not pause to consider the fact that a thirty-day deadline was a blunt instrument with which to solve a problem (if it had still existed) of ill-advised applications.[11] In the wake of several terrorist attacks in the United States (especially the 1995 Oklahoma City bombing, which had nothing to do with immigrants or asylum applicants) and growing anti-immigrant sentiment fueled by certain politicians, they wanted to demonstrate that they were doing something to make American borders more secure.[12] They supported the thirty-day deadline, among other proposals, to show their determination to do something about closing a border that many Americans, including President Clinton, thought too porous.[13] This restrictive measure was adopted by the House Immigration Subcommittee, the House Judiciary Committee, and the Senate Immigration Subcommittee.[14]

Critics of the thirty-day proposal argued that there were many reasons why some asylum applicants did not apply until they had been in the United States for a long time. Among other things, many asylum applicants had to flee with little more than the clothes on their back. They arrived in the United States traumatized and disoriented, unable to speak English, and their first priorities were to get housed and fed. Many suffered from posttraumatic stress disorder and other symptoms of torture. They distrusted governmental authorities, who had oppressed them in their home countries. They could not afford counsel and often did not know how to locate pro bono attorneys. Often they did not even know that the U.S. had a formal asylum application procedure.[15]

The critics were not able to defeat completely the idea of imposing a deadline on asylum applications, but in later stages of the legislative process, they were able to win significant modifications of the thirty-day proposal. The limit was changed to one year, and Congress adopted the two important exceptions to the limit—for "changed circumstances" and for "extraordinary circumstances"—that remain in the law.[16]

The Immigration and Naturalization Service, which was later dissolved and succeeded by DHS, wrote regulations[17] and a training manual[18] for asylum officers to flesh out the meaning of the exceptions. The regulations provide that the "changed circumstances" exception applies not only to the changed conditions in the applicant's home country but also to activities in which the applicant had become involved, outside of her own country, that placed her at greater risk. The regulations define "extraordinary circumstances" to include serious physical or mental illness, legal disability (as in the case of an unaccompanied minor), improper conduct by the applicant's counsel, the applicant's having other lawful status in the United States (and therefore no need to seek asylum), and the death or serious illness of a family member or legal representative.[19] The regulations do not list unawareness of the right to seek asylum, or of the existence of the deadline, as an extraordinary circumstance, but they do state that extraordinary circumstances "may include but are not limited to" the types of events listed in the regulations.

The training manual provides additional guidance for asylum officers who must apply the deadline. For example, it elaborates the "clear and convincing" standard for proof of the date of entry by stating that the proof need not be "conclusive" but somewhere between the "preponderance of evidence" standard and the "beyond a reasonable doubt" standard used in criminal trials.[20] It elaborates on most of the exceptions that are listed in the regulations. For example, it states that if the applicant has been tortured, "the asylum officer should elicit information about any continuing effects . . . which may be related to a delay in filing. Torture may result in serious illness or mental or physical disability."[21]

Some of the guidance is provided by way of example, such as this illustration of the changed circumstances exception:

> A Russian citizen of West African ancestry has lived in the United States since 1989. She filed an I-589 in June 2000. . . . [If government-tolerated abuse of West Africans had existed for a long time and remained constant, her application would be late, but] if there had been a [recent] escalation of violence between ethnic Russians and West Africans . . . the applicant would be eligible for an exception, provided the delay in filing is a reasonable period of time.[22]

The regulations state that "extraordinary circumstances" are "not limited to" the types of circumstances listed therein. Going a step further, the asylum officer training manual explicitly recognizes that an extraordinary circumstance may be based on patterns of facts that do not fall within the specified regulatory list of exceptions. It points out that other valid reasons may prevent an applicant from applying within a year, including "severe family or spousal opposition, extreme isolation within a refugee community, profound language barriers, or profound difficulties in cultural acclimatization."[23] The need to apply the regulations to specific facts, and particularly the fact that the regulatory list of extraordinary circumstances is not exclusive, gives asylum officers a degree of judgment or discretion in adjudicating cases in which an applicant appears to have a good reason for having missed the deadline. As in all cases in which officials exercise judgment, different officers may have different views about when it is appropriate to be lenient toward those who do not file on time.

The training manual also provides partial guidance to asylum officers on how to determine whether a late applicant who qualifies for an exception filed his application within a reasonable time, given the changed or extraordinary circumstances.[24] Rather than set inflexible rules, the manual encourages the use of good judgment:

> Asylum officers are encouraged to give applicants the benefit of the doubt in evaluating what constitutes a reasonable time in which to file. An applicant's education and level of sophistication, the amount of time it takes to obtain legal assistance, any effects of persecution and/or illness, when the applicant became aware of the changed circumstance, and any other relevant factors should be considered.[25]

The manual goes on to state that in cases in which the reason for lateness was that the applicant previously had a lawful immigration status, waiting more than six months would ordinarily be considered unreasonable.[26] In 2010, the Board of Immigration Appeals (the body that hears appeals from decisions of immigration judges) opined that one year was not per se a reasonable period of time in which to file, but that this "reasonableness" determination must be made on the facts of the particular case. The Board seemed to suggest that any delay of over six months will face a higher evidentiary hurdle to proving that the delay is reasonable.[27]

Notwithstanding the fact that the statute, regulations, and manual provide some exceptions, the deadline has been criticized over the years as harsh and unfair.[28] Professors Karen Musalo and Marcelle Rice examined 286 cases involving the one-year filing deadline in which the clients had been assisted by lawyers or psychologists associated with the Center for Gender and Refugee Studies, the East Bay Sanctuary Covenant, the International Gay and Lesbian Human Rights Commission, or Survivors International.[29] Musalo and Rice did not seek to reach conclusions through quantitative methods; they attempted only to illustrate types of problems in the implementation of the deadline through qualitative research. They concluded from cases that they examined that "the one-year bar . . . cause[s] the refoulement of legitimate refugees, . . . leads to arbitrary and disparate outcomes, deters bona fide claims, and squanders precious administrative resources."[30] They charged that some asylum officers and immigration judges apply the exceptions to the deadline formalistically and without regard to the manual's injunction that "asylum officers must be flexible and inclusive in examining changed or extraordinary circumstances, if credible testimony or documentary evidence relating to an exception exists."[31]

Similarly, Human Rights first examined case files of asylum claims that were handled by lawyers to whom it had referred potential clients. Based on this study, it found that the deadline "is barring legitimate refugees with well-founded fears of persecution from receiving asylum in the United States and is leading to the unnecessary expenditure of government resources."[32]

Musalo and Rice gave this example, among others, to support their view that asylum officers (and immigration judges) often apply the deadline with excessive rigidity:

> A Kenyan woman fled to the United States to avoid genital mutilation. She applied after the deadline. A psychologist diagnosed her with posttraumatic stress disorder that seriously impaired her ability to function. But the asylum officer "concluded that the applicant's disorders could not have directly related to her delay in filing because the applicant attended church during her first year in the United States."[33]

Reported cases offer examples, such as the following, of individuals who met the refugee definition, but were denied asylum because of this procedural bar:

> A Senegalese woman was ordered by her parents to undergo Female Genital Mutilation (FGM). She fled to the United States. For four years, she attempted without success to change her parents' minds so she could safely return to Senegal. She finally applied for asylum when her younger sister was forced to undergo FGM. DHS rejected her claim because she had not met the deadline, and the immigration judge concurred. The judge found the woman credible and observed there was "a reasonable possibility" that she would undergo FGM in Senegal. But she was ordered removed because of her late application and because she could not meet the higher burden of proof to qualify for withholding of removal.[34]

And in an even stronger claim handled by the clinic that two of the authors of this book direct, the applicant ultimately met the higher burden for withholding and proved that he would be persecuted if returned to his home country, but did not receive asylum because of the deadline:

> The applicant was a gay man from Peru, where the military and the police harass, abuse, assault and sometimes rape gay men. During his childhood and adolescence, he did not think of himself as gay, but he was twice suspended from school for effeminate conduct. A few years later, he was attacked by a gang of men as he was leaving a gay bar. They called him a faggot, punched him, put out their cigarettes in his arm, and knocked him unconscious. He was hospitalized as a result. He knew that the police would not protect him, and he fled to the U.S. on a tourist visa. He then obtained a student visa so that he could remain in the U.S. for postsecondary education. But he was struggling with PTSD

(as diagnosed by a psychiatrist) and depression and began taking prescribed antidepressants. He stopped attending school on a full time basis two years after entering the U.S. For the following year, with his school's permission, he took a reduced course load. At the end of that third year (in other words, a year after he stopped maintaining full time student status), he applied for asylum. His representatives argued that his PTSD and depression were an extraordinary circumstance; that his coming to terms with his sexuality and accepting it, after he had lived in the U.S. for a long time and had a relationship with a man in this country, was a changed circumstance; and that he filed his application for asylum as soon as he was able to do so.

The Asylum Office referred his case. It found that his change of status when he obtained his student visa was an extraordinary circumstance, but that the one year delay in filing his application after he ceased to be a full time student was more than a reasonable amount of time.[35]

Finally, Human Rights First reports similar cases, such as the following ones, in which immigration judges believed the applicants' testimony and corroborating evidence but agreed with asylum officers that the applicants were not eligible for asylum because they had not sufficiently proved that they met the one-year deadline or qualified for any exception:

A young Eritrean woman was tortured for her Christian beliefs after the Eritrean government forcibly conscripted her into military service. She applied for asylum four months after arriving in the United States, but her request was rejected by the Asylum Office because she did not have a passport showing her date of entry. In Immigration Court, the young woman provided three affidavits and documentary evidence to establish her date of entry. The Immigration Judge told her that she fit the definition of a refugee, but offered her only withholding of removal. Even though the court determined that she would probably be persecuted in Eritrea, the judge denied her asylum claim for failure to prove that she filed within a year of arrival.[36]

A Burmese student fled to the United States after being jailed for several years for his pro-democracy activities. The student did not know anyone in the United States, did not speak English, and did not learn about asylum until several years later when he met other Burmese refugees who told him how to apply. The Immigration Court ruled that the student's extreme isolation did not constitute an exception to the filing deadline. The student was denied asylum even though he was found to be credible and to face a clear probability of persecution, requiring the withholding of removal. The Board of Immigration Appeals and the Sixth Circuit upheld the decision.[37]

Because of the unavailability, until now, of the full statistical record of adjudication of cases involving the deadline, the published regulations and manuals and the critics' commentaries can tell only part of the story of the deadline's effects. The next two chapters seek to place these anecdotes in a broader perspective, at least with respect to adjudication by DHS.[38] Unfortunately, we are not able to analyze the application of the deadline by immigration judges, because unlike DHS, the Department of Justice does not keep records of which cases involve challenges to asylum applications based on the deadline, nor of which denials of asylum are based on the deadline. But at least we can examine, in depth, the effect of the deadline during the initial stage of asylum application adjudication.

4

Timeliness

The Department of Homeland Security's data reveal interesting and at times surprising patterns in asylum officer determinations of whether asylum seekers filed within the permitted one-year period.[1] This chapter describes basic but crucial information about the deadline—what percentage of asylum claims were determined to have been filed late and how late these claims were filed. It also examines whether determinations of lateness differed depending on certain personal characteristics of the asylum seekers—where they came from in terms of geographic region and nationality, their age, how they entered, whether they were represented, their gender, and in which of the eight regional asylum offices they filed their affirmative claims. Chapter 5 will examine, in depth, how asylum officers administered the two statutory exceptions to the deadline for those applicants who filed late.

A grant of asylum brings with it tremendous benefits, including the chance to become a lawful permanent resident and eventually an American citizen. Yet more than 30 percent of asylum applications submitted from April 16, 1998, through June 8, 2009—about 93,000 of the approximately 304,000 claims in our database—were determined to have been filed late. That is a very high number, in both percentage and absolute terms, given the nature of the U.S. government's protection responsibilities and the potentially deadly consequences of being denied asylum if one is a bona fide refugee.

To confirm the statistical significance of the data analysis presented below, we ran a binary logistic regression on the database of all cases, exploring the dependent variable of timely filing.[2] Unless otherwise noted, these variables were statistically significant[3] and confirmed the findings of the cross-tabulation analysis.[4] In other words, even with all other variables held constant, the relationship between timely filing and each of the independent variables described below was statistically significant.

Just how late were these 93,000 asylum seekers? The largest identifiable late group (about 28,000 people) filed within one year after the deadline had passed, as figure 4-1 demonstrates. They constituted 30 percent of all late filers. For 27 percent of untimely applicants, or about 25,000 asylum seekers, we do not know how late they filed because their date of entry was recorded

Fig. 4-1. DHS Determinations of Lapse between Entry and Filing

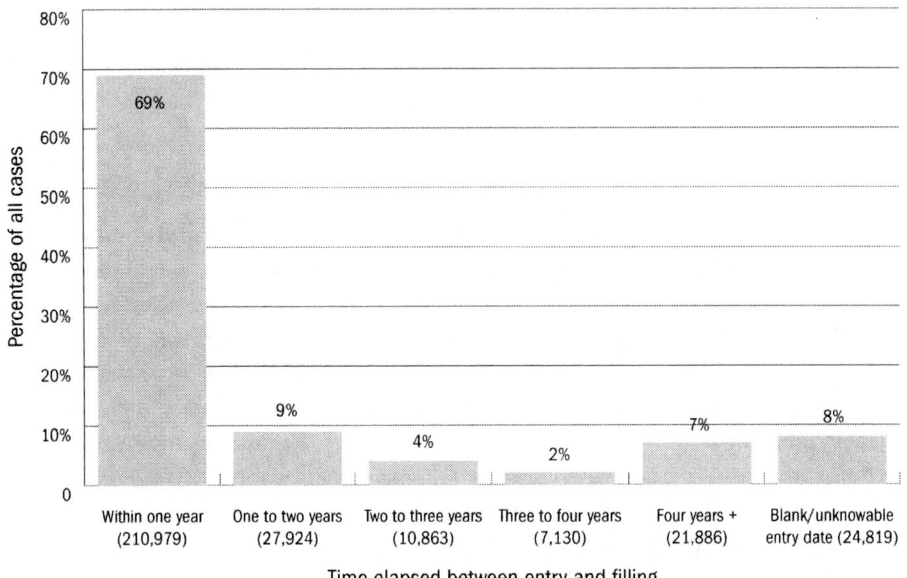

Fig. 4-2. Late Cases, by Fiscal Year of Filing

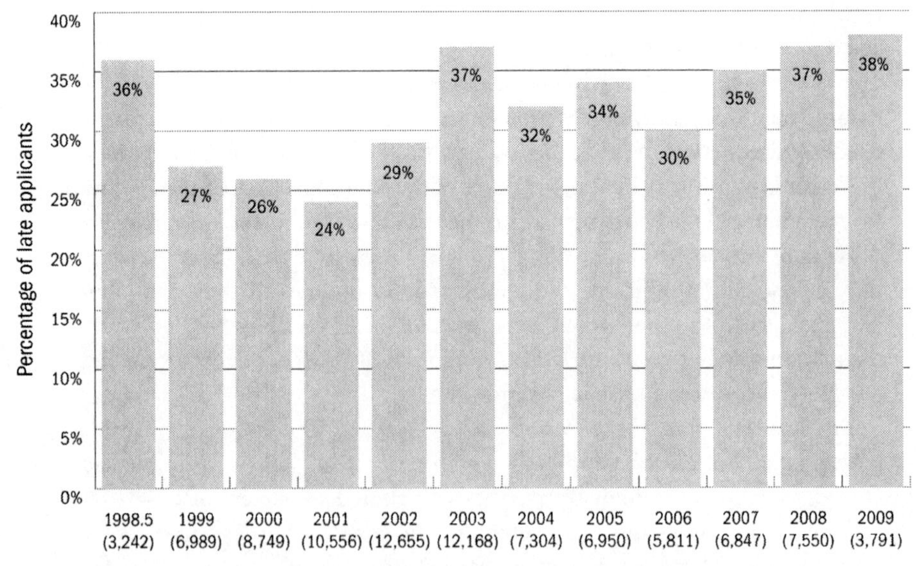

as blank or unknowable.[5] We do know that a significant percentage of applicants filed many years after entering the United States. Some 22,000 individuals (nearly 24 percent of all late filers) filed claims four years or more after entering the U.S.; 6,184 of these applicants (nearly 7 percent of all late filers) filed for asylum more than ten years after entry.

As figure 4-2 illustrates, in recent years, asylum officers deemed a higher percentage of cases late than in earlier years. From FY 2000 through 2002, about 26 percent of asylum seekers filed late. From FY 2007 through 2009, some 36 percent filed late. That represents a 38 percent increase in the percentage of cases that asylum officers determined were untimely filed.

As figure 4-3 shows, the greatest increase in filers regarded as late occurred within the group of asylum seekers determined to have filed three or more years late, from 6 percent in 1999 to just under 12 percent in 2009.[6] During the most recent five-year period (FY 2005–2009), the number determined to have filed more than four years after arrival jumped by 26 percent over the previous five-year period (FY 2000–2004).

Our finding that the percentage of late filers increased over time and that this was particularly true of very late filers is counterintuitive; one would expect that the deadline would minimize late filers over time. These increases could reflect a change in the behavior of the applicants. For example, in the years immediately following the enactment of the deadline, more would-be applicants might have heard the publicity surrounding the passage of the law that imposed it and filed on time as a result, but fewer knew about the deadline in later years. Perhaps in recent years there have been more applicants who lack ethnic or national communities that inform them about asylum or the deadline. Another possibility is that more news about raids and arrests of undocumented immigrants during the second administration of George W. Bush caused more refugees who had been living in the United States for a long time to apply for asylum rather than remain undocumented, given the perceived higher risk that they would be identified and detained. Alternatively, the increase in the number of applicants who were determined to be late could reflect a change in how strictly the asylum officers scrutinized each case; in other words, perhaps applicants were late at a constant rate, but asylum officers were less accepting of their evidence of the date of arrival as time went by.[7]

Figure 4-3 also shows a large increase in the number of applicants whose date of entry is blank. The proportion of applicants with blank or unknowable entry dates grew dramatically over time, constituting less than 2 percent of all applicants in the second half of FY 1998 and 15 percent of all applicants in FY 2009—more than a 600 percent increase in just over a decade.[8] At the same

Fig. 4-3. Lapse between Entry Date and Date of Filing, by Fiscal Year

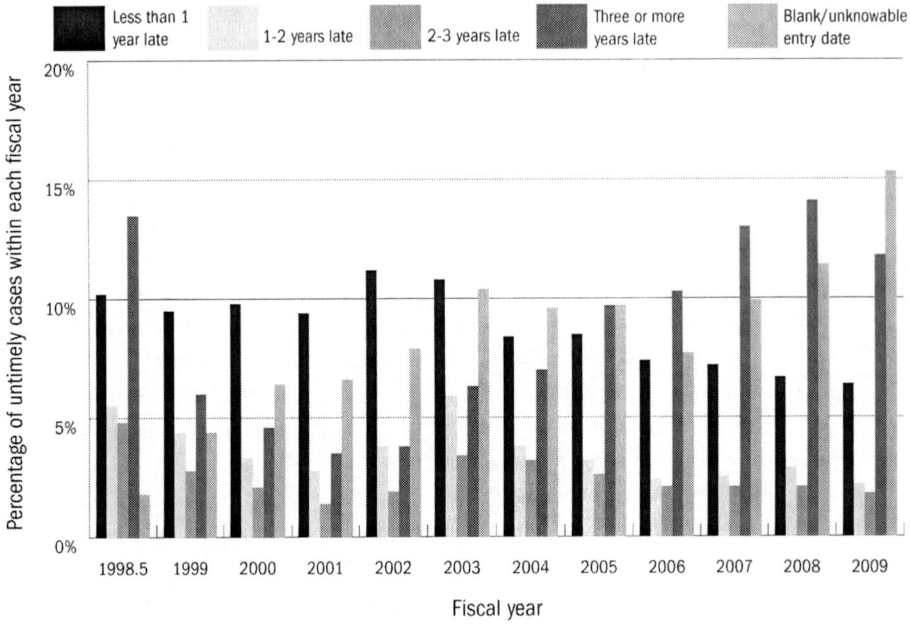

Fig. 4-4. All Applicants, Uninspected Entry, by Year

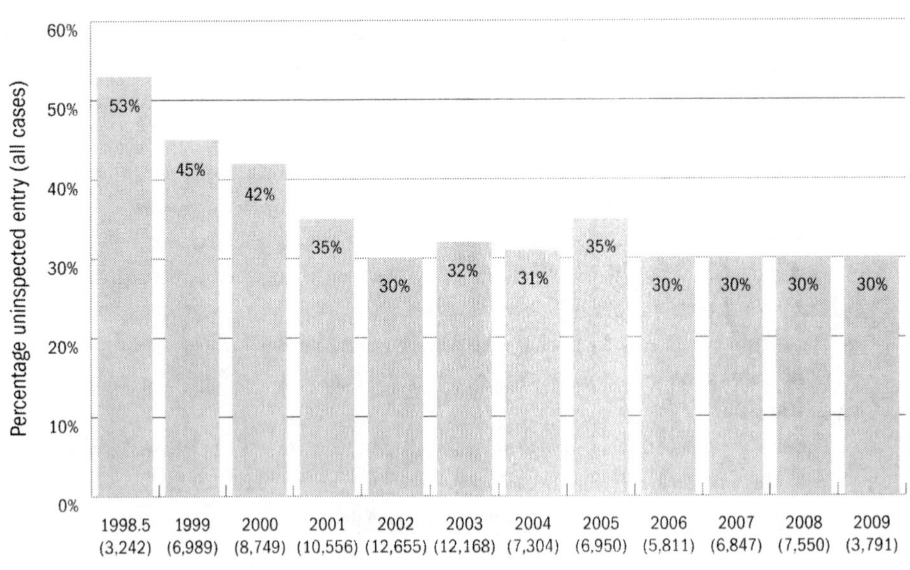

time, as figure 4-4 demonstrates, the number of applicants who entered without inspection dropped by 83 percent, from nearly 55 percent in the second half of FY 1998 to a fairly consistent 30 percent from FY 2002 through FY 2009.[9] These trends suggest that the growth in blank or unknowable entry dates may have resulted especially from stricter application of evidentiary standards by adjudicators—that is, more applicants missed the deadline because asylum officers were less accepting of proof of entry other than official documentation.

Representation

The data reveal interesting patterns in the characteristics of asylum applicants who were determined to have filed late.[10] To begin with, late filers generally were represented at higher rates than timely filers. Almost 50 percent of late filers were represented, in contrast to only 41 percent of timely filers.

One might expect that applicants with sufficient understanding of the asylum adjudication process that they apply on time would also more likely be aware of the value of being represented. So why were untimely filers more often represented than timely filers?

Asylum seekers who want to be represented may not be able to file their applications within a year of entry because of the information, the time, and the financial resources needed to secure representation, not to mention the psychological obstacles to discussing their claim for asylum with people they do not know.[11] Asylum applicants often arrive in the United States with virtually no money, and they may have to work for more than a year before they can afford to pay a lawyer. A few applicants are fortunate enough to obtain free assistance from a nongovernmental organization, law school clinic, or pro bono lawyer,[12] but for most, representation is very expensive. Private attorneys typically charge several thousand dollars to prepare an asylum application, amass the necessary supporting evidentiary documents, and accompany the applicant to the interview.[13] Some asylum applicants, realizing that they will need a lawyer but cannot afford one, may postpone filing until they can work (in most cases, without authorization) for long enough to be able to hire an attorney, meanwhile missing the filing deadline.[14] Other asylum seekers may be aware of the one-year filing deadline but not of the exceptions to the deadline or their eligibility for the exceptions. Once the deadline has passed, these asylum seekers might decide that applying for asylum is hopeless and might apply for asylum only after they are informed by friends or lawyers that they may still be eligible for asylum. Similarly, some asylum seekers might not understand that the mistreatment they suffered in their home countries could make them eligible for asylum and might apply only after they meet with lawyers who can explain the potential grounds for their claims.[15] It may also

Fig. 4-5. Applicants Represented, by Lapse between Entry Date and Filing Date

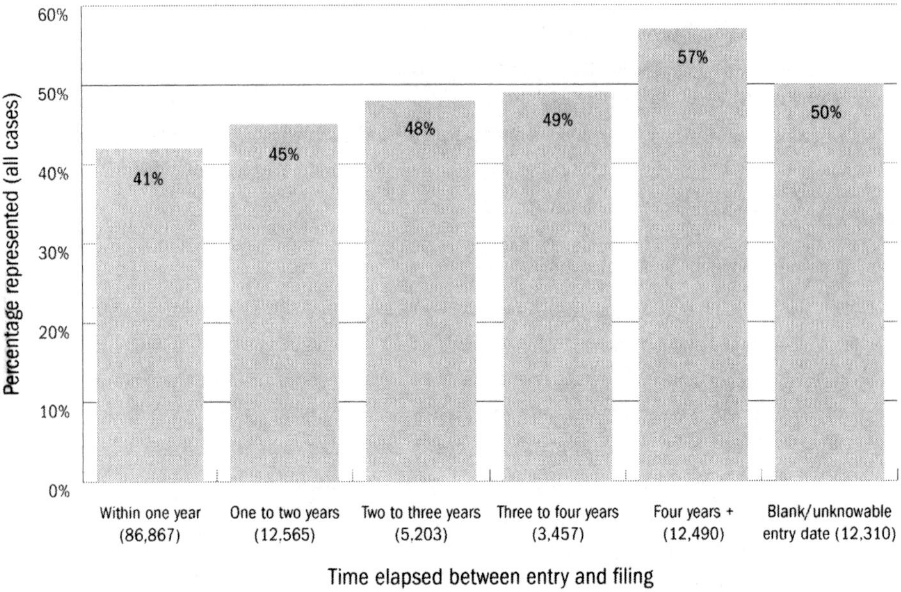

60%
50%
40%
30%
20%
10%
0%
Percentage represented (all cases)
41%
45%
48%
49%
57%
50%
Within one year (86,867)
One to two years (12,565)
Two to three years (5,203)
Three to four years (3,457)
Four years + (12,490)
Blank/unknowable entry date (12,310)
Time elapsed between entry and filing

be the case that those who missed the deadline perceived a greater need to obtain counsel to overcome this bar to asylum.

Figure 4-5 shows an increasing degree of representation for every year of lateness. Interestingly, for each cohort, the majority of asylum seekers were unrepresented—except for the group of asylum seekers who filed four years or more after entry.

Nationality

What are the demographic characteristics of those determined to have filed late? Figure 4-6 looks at applicants from the six most frequent nationalities of affirmative asylum seekers: Armenia, China, Colombia, Ethiopia, Haiti, and Indonesia. Considerably fewer Armenians, Ethiopians, and Haitians filed late compared to Chinese, Colombians, and especially Indonesians.[16]

Why did only 15 percent of the Armenians file late, while 45 percent of the Indonesians failed to meet the deadline? We cannot answer this question definitively, but we explored four hypotheses.

Our first hypothesis was that the time it often takes for applicants to find representatives caused applications to be filed late. As with the study's

Fig. 4-6. Late Filing by Applicants of the Six Most Common Nationalities

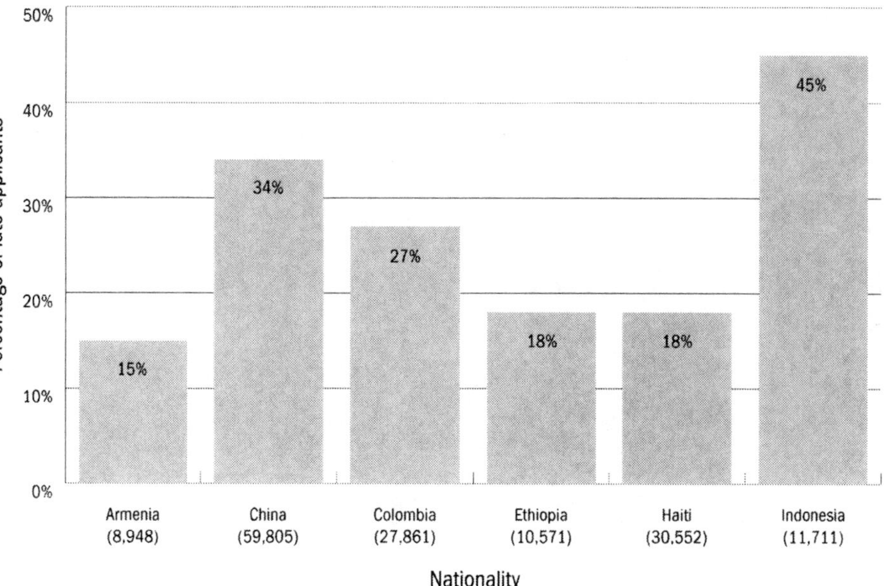

population more generally, there was an inverse relationship between these two variables: late filers were more often represented than timely filers. As figure 4-7 shows, the two major nationalities that filed late most frequently, the Chinese (34 percent) and Indonesians (45 percent), were the nationalities that were most often represented—the Chinese at a rate of 74 percent and the Indonesians at a rate of 55 percent. At the other extreme, Armenians and Haitians had low rates of late filing (15 percent and 18 percent respectively) and very low rates of representation (15 percent and 11 percent respectively). Ethiopians bucked the pattern, though, with a low rate of late filing of 18 percent and a relatively high rate of representation of 46 percent.[17] Therefore, the need to wait to file until an applicant has a representative does not fully explain the relationship between nationality and late filing. In fact, it may be the case that many applicants obtained counsel after they had already missed the deadline and realized that they needed representatives to help them persuade asylum officers that they could qualify for an exception.

Our second hypothesis was that timely filing correlated with inspected entry. Perhaps individuals who entered the United States with visas were more attuned to legal requirements and would be more likely to file on time. Or perhaps those who had entered without inspection would be more

Fig. 4-7. Representation for the Six Most Common Applicant Nationalities

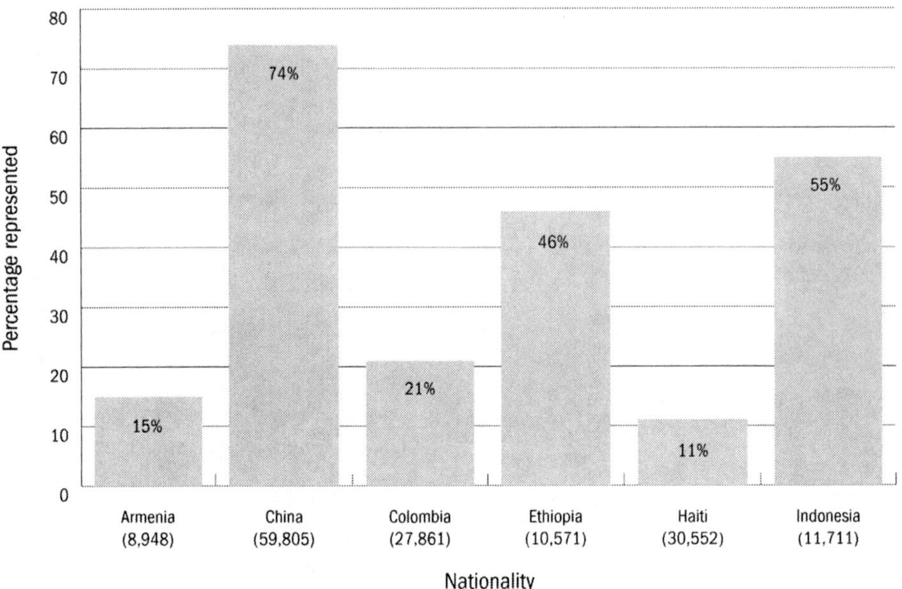

Fig. 4-8. Inspected Entry for the Six Most Common Applicant Nationalities

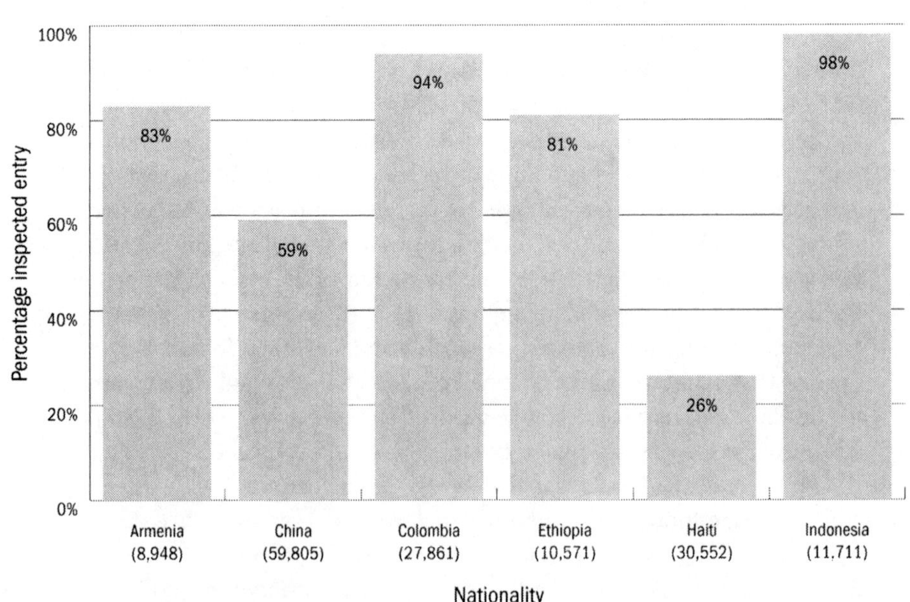

reluctant to identify themselves to immigration officials by filing a prompt asylum application.

For four of the six most common applicant nationalities, the cross-tabulation analysis did show a relationship between lawful entry and timely filing (figures 4-6 and 4-8), and the regression analysis tells us that, with all other variables in the model held constant, lawful entry correlated with timely filing.

Armenians, Colombians, and Ethiopians, who all had relatively low rates of late filing, overwhelmingly entered through official channels, with rates of inspected entry ranging from 81 percent to 94 percent.[18] Although more Chinese applicants entered with inspection than without inspection, the proportion of inspected entries was significantly lower, at nearly 60 percent, so it is perhaps unsurprising that over one-third of Chinese applicants were found to have filed late. But we see an inverse relationship when it comes to the Indonesians, who had the highest rate of inspected entry, at 98 percent, but also the highest rate of late filing. In the opposite direction, Haitians had the highest rate of entry without inspection (74 percent), but also one of the lowest rates of late filing.

So with Indonesians and Haitians in mind, we turned to a third hypothesis, that communities of immigrants from those nationalities already in the United States, among whom the new refugees may settle, are differently organized, leading to differences in levels and effectiveness of information-sharing regarding the deadline requirement. For example, Haitians have a large and long-standing diaspora in the United States. Nearly one in every twenty Haitians resides in the United States.[19] In 2008, there were about 535,000 Haitian immigrants in the United States, nearly half of whom were naturalized U.S. citizens.[20] Nearly a fifth of these Haitians had lived in the United States since before 1980, with over one-third residing in the Miami area and nearly one-third residing in the greater New York City area.[21] We surmised that the relatively tight-knit and well-established Haitian community helps its nationals file for asylum within a year and has figured out a way to prove their date of entry without providing official documentation.

The Indonesian immigrant community in the United States, in contrast, is relatively small and perhaps not as well organized in supporting its newly arrived nationals. As of 2005, there were only 75,000 Indonesian immigrants in the United States, approximately one-third of whom arrived before 1980.[22] In 2000, less than 37 percent of the Indonesians in the United States had obtained U.S. citizenship.[23]

Some of the data appeared at first blush to undercut the hypothesis that timely filing is related to a large diaspora. For example, among the six largest groups of applicants in FY 2008, Haitians and Ethiopians had the highest rates of filing on time, 88 percent and 83 percent respectively. Although there were large numbers of Haitian individuals living in the United States—535,000 including 8,707 recent (2003–2007) successful asylum applicants—the number of Ethiopian-born individuals living in the United States was much smaller—69,530, including 2,722 recent Ethiopian asylees.[24] Similarly, Armenians applied on time at a rate of 85 percent, but only 65,280 Armenians lived in the United States.[25] And although Colombia had a strong presence in America (509,870 Colombian-born individuals),[26] Colombians filed on time at a rate of only 73 percent.

So we turned to a fourth theory, a more focused variant of the co-national hypothesis. Perhaps an important influence on timely filing is the number of

Table 4-1. Regions with the Largest Number of Applicants of the Most Common Nationalities, and Those with the Highest Rates of Timely Filing, by Nationality

	Percentage of applicants who filed timely	Region with most asylum seekers from that country	Highest percentage of timely applicants from that country	Percentages of timely applicants in the other regions	Highest percentage of timely applicants, lawful entrants only
Less timely					
China	66%	Los Angeles	Los Angeles, 80%	49%, 51%, 54%, 60%, 69%, 70%, 75%	Los Angeles, 86%
Colombia	73%	Miami	San Francisco, 77% Miami, 76%	59%, 61%, 62%, 65%, 73%, 75%	San Francisco, 77% Chicago, 76% Miami ,75%
Indonesia	55%	Los Angeles	Los Angeles, 61%	33%, 40%, 45%, 46%, 54%, 56%, 59%,	
More timely					
Armenia	85%	Los Angeles	San Francisco, 87% Los Angeles, 85%	66%, 75%, 75%, 76%, 77%, 77%	Los Angeles. 88%
Ethiopia	82%	Arlington	San Francisco, 85% Arlington - 83%	62%, 76%, 79%, 79%, 80%, 82%	Arlington, 89%
Haiti	82%	Miami	Miami, 84%	58%, 61%, 62%, 68%, 69%, 70%, 72%	Miami, 83%

Note: The raw numbers of timely Colombian applicants in San Francisco and Chicago were quite small (345 and 412, respectively), compared with 22,062 in Miami. All other regions had timely percentages between 61 percent and 69 percent.

co-nationals in the same region as the applicant who have had recent experience in applying to DHS for asylum. To explore this possibility, we compared the number of asylum applicants in our database in each of the eight regional asylum office regions with the rate at which applicants filed within the deadline in that region. And here we found remarkable consistency: with one minor exception, for each of the six most common nationalities, the region with the largest number of asylum applicants was also the region with the highest or second-highest percentage of on-time filings, often by a very substantial margin compared to the least timely regions. Furthermore, to test the possibility that the differences between lawful and unlawful entrants was affecting the results, we also explored the relationship between numbers of asylum seekers and rates of timely filing for the subset of applicants who had entered lawfully. The results were similar. These results are summarized in table 4-1.

While these results do not conclusively prove that asylum seekers are more apt to meet the one-year deadline if they live near other applicants of the same nationality who have already applied, they do suggest that social networking with others who have experienced the challenges of seeking asylum may be a significant factor in filing a timely application. This conclusion is consistent with the impressions of asylum officers we interviewed. One of them told us, for example, that Armenians usually settled in towns where they had family, so they were able to find out about the deadline through family connections and therefore file on time. Another told us that most Haitians settled in Miami where

> there are plenty of organizations including pro bono organizations that help people prepare their applicants and also get the news out. They have Haitian radio and television, and many of them are well established from previous influxes. . . so you have a more established community.

Many Chinese asylum applicants also have family and can link up with organizations that provide immigration information. In addition, some of those applicants are individuals who are trafficked by professional smugglers who file fraudulent applications for them, on time, because they want to keep them in the United States long enough to pay off their debts to the traffickers. But one asylum officer suggested to us that the low rate of on-time filing for Chinese applicants could be related to the fact that in many cases, they are under the thumbs of traffickers who want these immigrants to remain undocumented. These traffickers may threaten deportation, violence, or other retribution if the immigrants apply for asylum (thereby becoming less vulnerable to smugglers' threats to report them) before paying off their debt for passage to the United States. Only after they pay off these debts do these individuals apply for asylum, but by that time the one-year deadline has passed.

It appears, therefore, that the one-year deadline differentially disadvantages refugees from countries that do not have large co-national populations in the regions in which they settle. It may also disadvantage victims of traffickers. We doubt that the members of Congress who voted for the deadline ever considered its differential impact favoring some nationalities over others or its effect on victims of trafficking. This differential impact tends to suggest that the one-year filing deadline is an arbitrary, inappropriate tool for weeding out weak asylum claims.

Gender

Women filed about forty-one percent of the claims in this database. Women had a rate of untimely filing 13 percent higher than men (32.7 percent, in contrast with 29 percent).[27]

The degree of filing within two, three, and four years of entry was similar for both males and females, as Figure 4-9 shows. Strikingly, however, women filed very late claims at a rate more than 50 percent higher than men. Almost 10 percent of female asylum seekers filed at least four years after entry. We suspect that this difference may be due to the particular nature of persecution inflicted upon these women. Women are more likely to have suffered sexual violence than men and may therefore be more reluctant to reveal to government officials—or anyone else—what happened to them in their home countries.[28] It may take many years before they are psychologically prepared to present an asylum claim. Moreover, women claiming asylum on gender grounds, such as domestic violence and female genital mutilation, may not be aware that they are eligible for asylum when they first arrive in the United States, and as a result they might not file within a year of entry.

The theory that the higher rate of very late filing by women is related to their gender-based claims is supported by the finding that these applicants were represented at a higher rate than very late male asylum seekers.[29] Perhaps the women were very late in filing because they did not know that their experiences warranted asylum, and they filed only after finally being advised by an attorney that asylum eligibility was not restricted to political dissidents or persons persecuted for their religious faith.

Finally, women filed late more often than men despite the fact that they entered without inspection less often than men did—31.1 percent versus 37.2 percent.[30] This, too, suggests that other factors, such as the nature of persecution suffered by women, accounted to a large degree for higher levels of late filing.

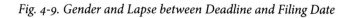

Fig. 4-9. Gender and Lapse between Deadline and Filing Date

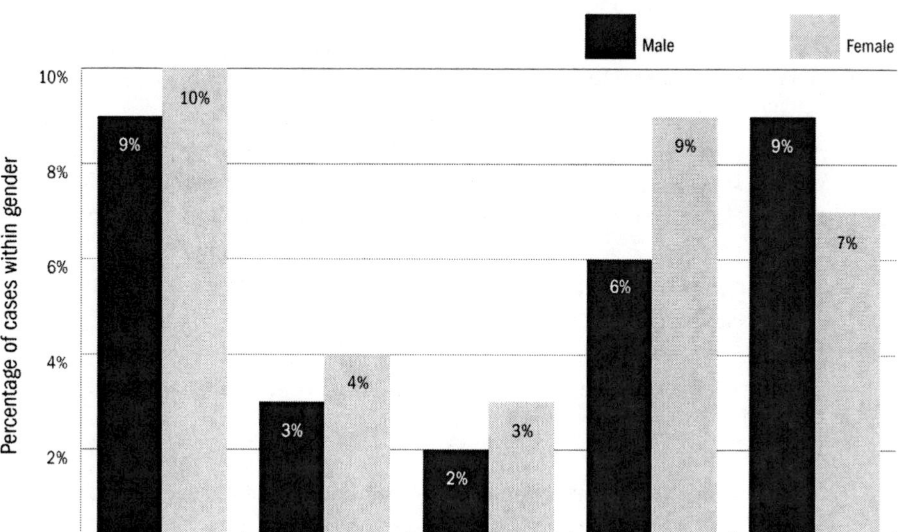

The DHS survey of current asylum officers asked their opinions on why more females than males filed four or more years after entry. The officers did not agree with the hypothesis that the nature of gender-based claims accounted for particularly late filing by women applicants. Only 14 percent of the 194 officers who responded to this question believed that many more women filed at such a late date because they were "more likely to have suffered sexual violence than men," and this answer revealed no significant difference of opinion among male and female respondents. But 46 percent of respondents thought that the difference could be explained by an information gap (as opposed to a psychological barrier). They thought that the primary difference between the rates of very late filing lay in the fact that "women more frequently file 'novel' claims (based on domestic violence or female genital mutilation) and might therefore have been unaware that they were eligible for asylum until many years after entry." Male asylum officers gave this reason more often than female officers (50 percent to 43 percent). A third explanation—that women were less likely than men to be able to find or afford lawyers or others to help them file prompt claims—was favored by a much higher proportion of female than male officers (15 percent to 4 percent). And 30 percent of officers thought that some "other" reason would be more explanatory. Officers who answered "other" to this question were permitted to provide narrative comments to explain their thinking. Among the comments were these:

—I think this can be attributed to the fact that many women who are asylum seekers are significantly more isolated than men and therefore may not be able to access the same information regarding eligibility for asylum.

—Women serve a different social role in many countries that I think may affect their ability to ask a stranger for help.

Some of the officers believed that the women who filed very late were not genuine asylum seekers:

—They heard that U.S. law now recognized domestic violence, or FGM, for example. Women are not stupid—they just need a way to stay in the U.S. that

Fig. 4-10. Age of Applicants from the Six Most Common Nationalities

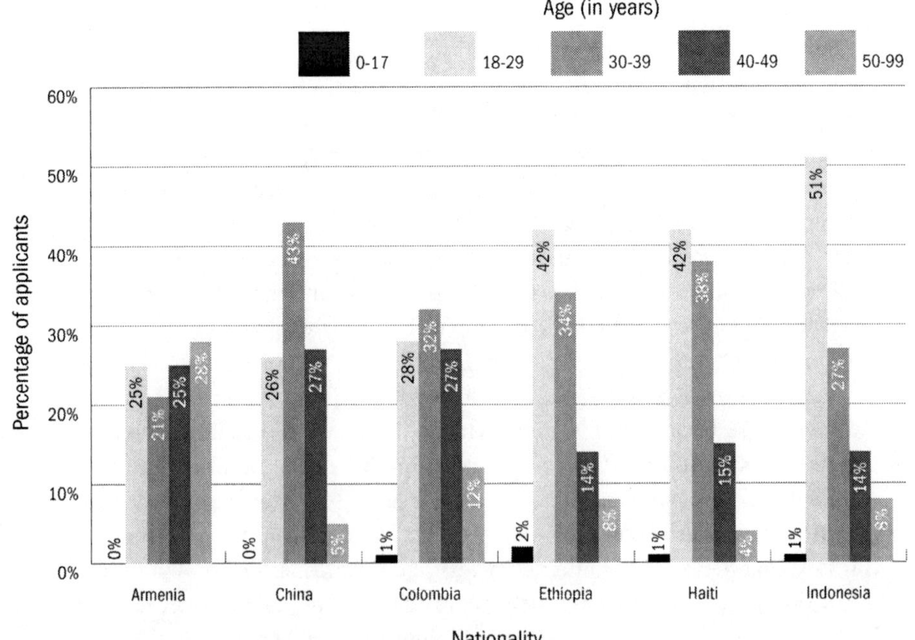

is tailored for them. I have seen many experts' opinions that are simply based upon the client's self-reported symptoms—the same symptoms are there on the Internet to emulate—but the underlying facts of the case turn out not to be true. Every ethnic group seems to be very well educated as to all of their immigration options— thank you, advocates, for doing such a thorough job.

Age

As noted in chapter 2, more than two-thirds of asylum applicants filed their claims when they were between the ages of eighteen and thirty-nine, although as figure 4-10 demonstrates, different nationalities produced very different populations of applicants in terms of age.

Figures 4-11 and 4-12 show that younger adult asylum seekers as a whole missed the deadline more frequently than older adult asylum seekers. Although about one in four claimants over fifty years old filed late, more than one in three between the ages of eighteen and twenty-nine did so. This relationship holds for those who filed in each fiscal year that we studied. For example, in FY 2003, more than 40 percent of asylum seekers between the ages of eighteen and twenty-nine filed late compared to less than 30 percent of

Fig. 4-11. Untimely Filing by Age

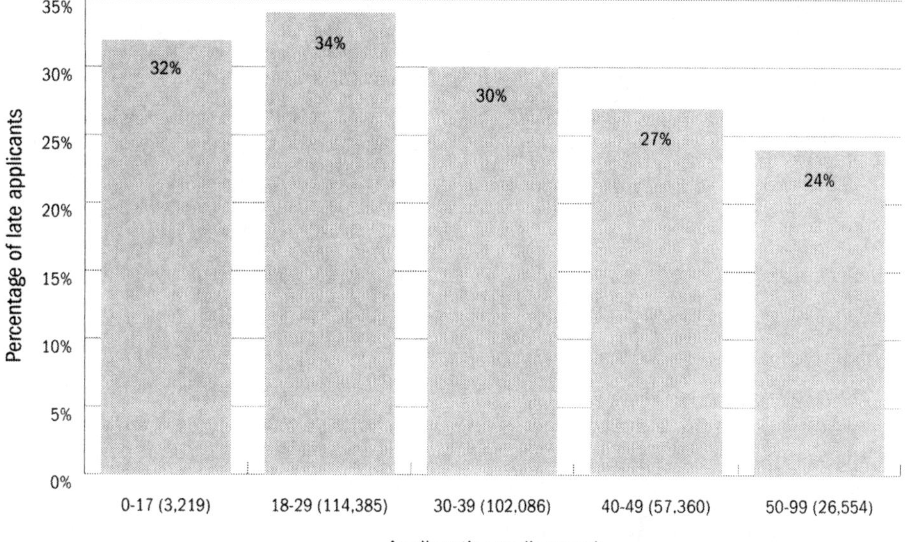

Fig. 4-12. Age and Lapse between Deadline and Filing Date

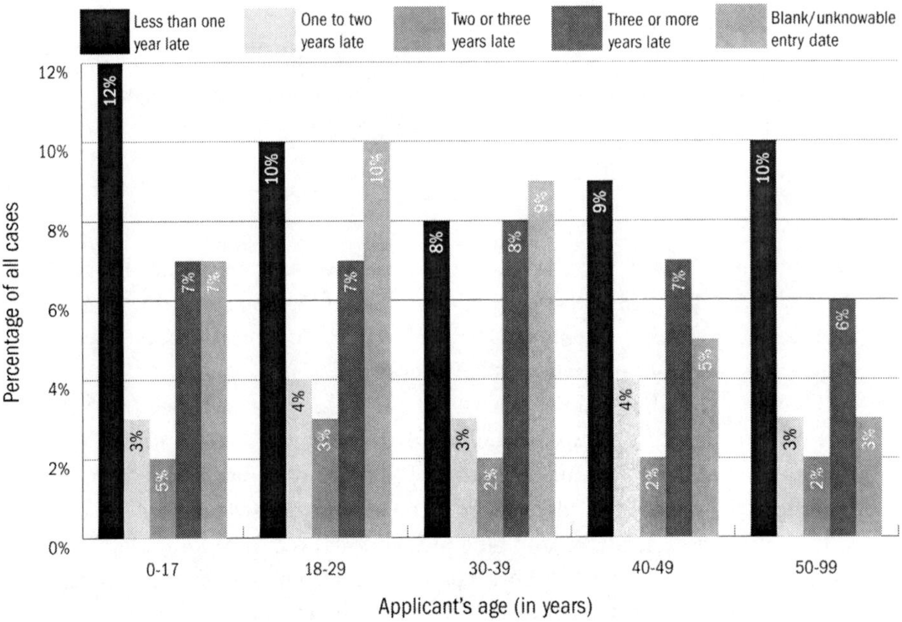

those age fifty and over. In other words, asylum seekers over fifty filed on time more than 20 percent more often than those age eighteen to twenty-nine.

We know that young adults entered more often without inspection (nearly 9 percent of that group had a blank or unknowable entry date as compared to just under 3 percent of the older group) and therefore did not have official documentation of entry. Yet even with all other variables in the model, including status at entry, held constant, the regression analysis confirms that greater age of the asylum seeker correlated with timely filing.[31]

Status at Entry

As noted in chapter 2, almost two-thirds of asylum seekers in our database gained admission to the United States lawfully. Late entry was determined for nearly 45 percent more of the applicants who entered the United States without inspection than for applicants who were inspected upon entry—38 percent of uninspected entrants, but only 26 percent of inspected entrants, filed late.[32]

This degree of difference in late filing has changed significantly over time. As figure 4-13 shows, those entering lawfully were deemed late filers at a

Fig. 4-13. Late Filing by Year and Status at Entry

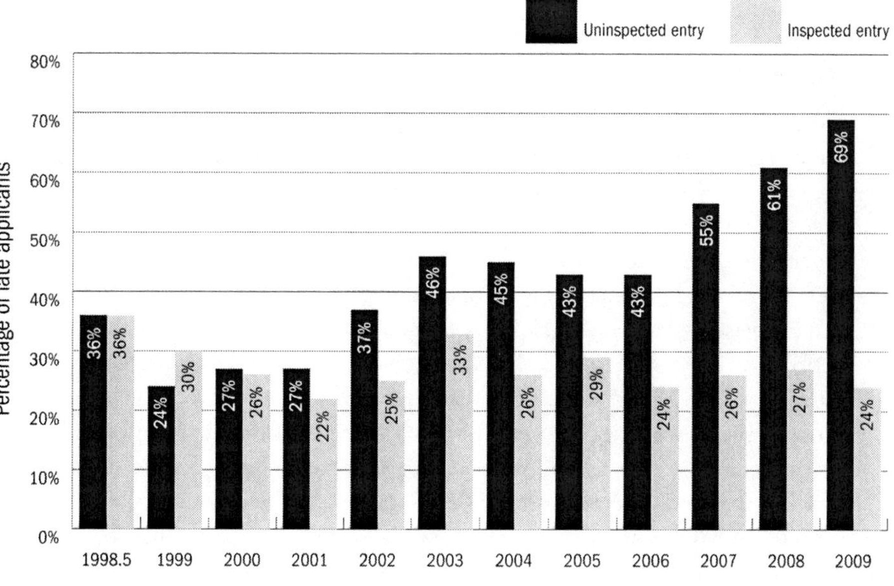

fairly consistent rate. Those entering without inspection, however, were over time increasingly deemed late filers.

The most recent years, 2007–2009, show an enormous increase in determinations of late filings by uninspected entrants, to the point that almost 70 percent of those who entered without inspection were determined to have filed late claims in 2009, compared to only 24 percent in 1999—a nearly 200 percent increase in a decade. The steady increase occurred despite the fact that the percentage of applicants who entered without inspection has remained almost constant since 2002 (figure 4-4).

What might account for the fact that the percentage of applicants deemed late increased substantially in the years after 2001, while the percentage who entered without inspection remained about the same? It is possible that since the September 11 attacks, asylum officers have required a higher degree of proof of the date of entry (for those who entered without inspection) than they had required previously. Those who are inspected most often have an immigration officer's "Arrival and Departure" record card stapled to their passports, including a date stamp indicating when they arrived in the United States. But those who enter without being inspected don't have such official evidence to corroborate their date of entry. Asylum officers must rely on other evidence, including testimony, to determine that date. Perhaps since 2001, their standards for evaluating that evidence became more exacting.

Asylum Offices

The DHS asylum adjudicators work at eight regional offices, whose catchment areas are shown in the map at the front of this book and described in an appendix. What about lateness of filings at these different asylum offices? The regional asylum offices determined asylum seekers to have filed late at very different rates. In the Newark regional asylum office, for example, applicants were found to have filed late nearly twice as often compared to those in Miami, San Francisco, and Los Angeles (figure 4-14). As shown in figure 4-15, those applying in the Chicago and Houston regions were found to have filed late, but by less than a year, about twice as frequently as those in Los Angeles, and those in the Newark region were found to have filed very late (four or more years after arrival) more than twice as often as those in the Miami region.[33]

We wondered whether these differences between asylum office regions reflected the status at entry of the relevant asylum applicant populations. As discussed, those who entered without inspection and therefore without the best proof of their dates of entry were more often unable to prove timely

Fig. 4-14. Untimely Filing by Regional Asylum Office

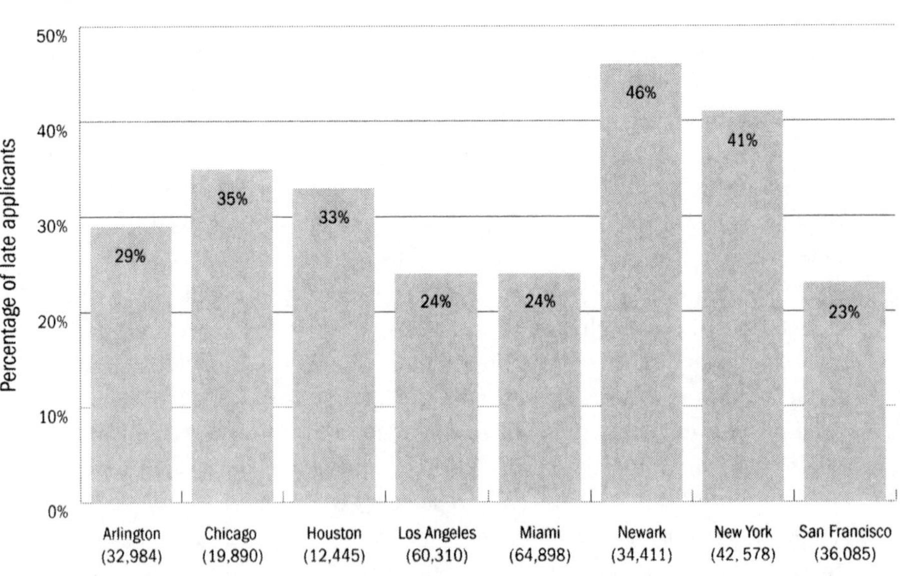

Fig. 4-15. Lapse between Deadline and Filing Date by Regional Asylum Office

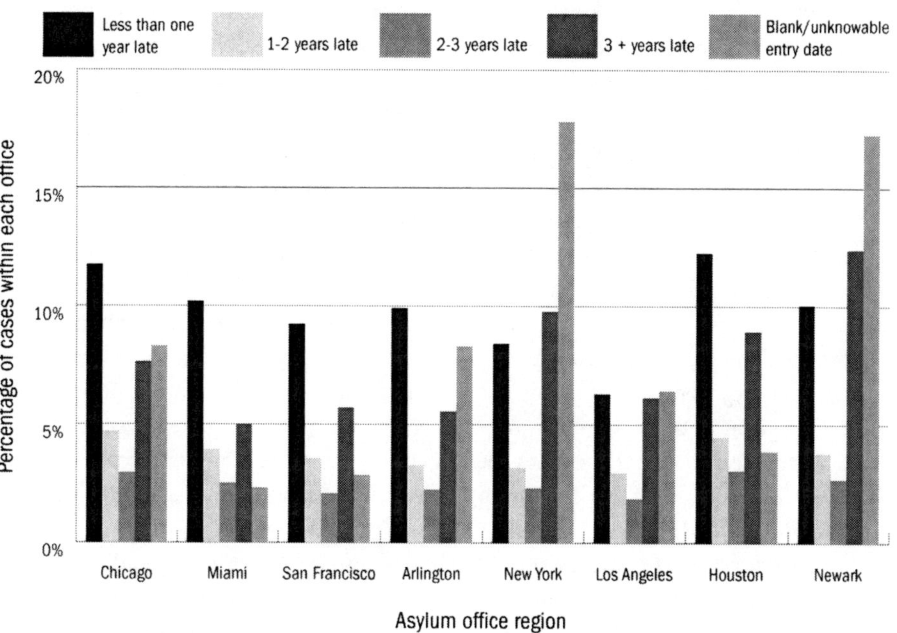

Fig. 4-16. Status at Entry and Regional Asylum Office

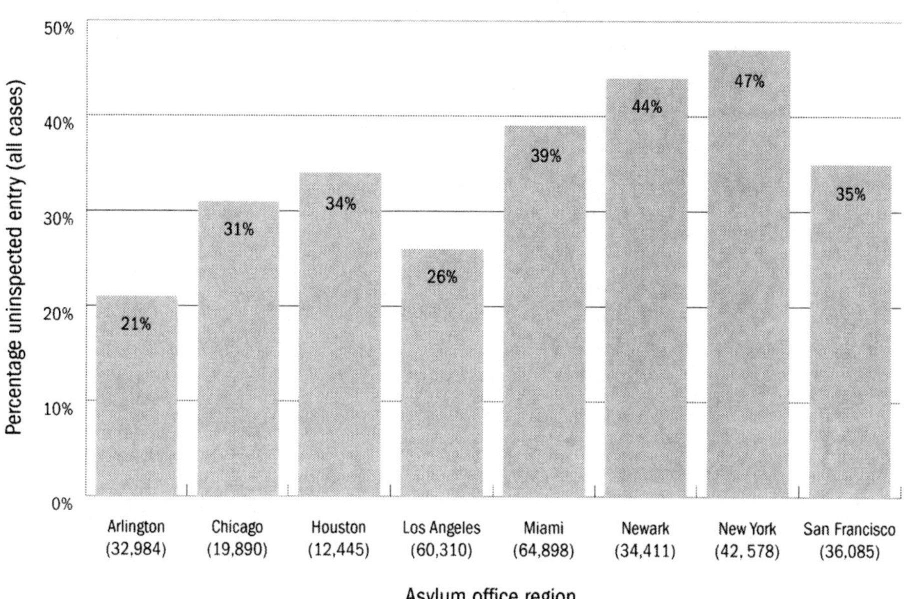

filing compared to those inspected upon entry. This relationship holds true for the New York and Newark offices, which had the highest levels of both late and uninspected filers. But as with nationality, a high rate of uninspected applicants did not necessarily correlate with a low rate of timely filing. Miami had the third-highest rate of uninspected (39 percent) but one of the lowest proportions of late filers (24 percent). Chicago had the third-lowest rate of uninspected (31 percent) and the third-highest proportion of late filers (35 percent). These data suggest the possibility that these differences in timely filing rates between asylum offices may reflect different operating assumptions or procedures in the different regional offices.

The data reveal that a very large percentage and absolute number of asylum seekers have been deemed to have filed late. This failure to meet a procedural requirement has major consequences for those who fear or suffered persecution and for the U.S. government. A number of characteristics of asylum seekers correlated with lateness and sometimes the degree of lateness. These include representation, gender, age, nationality, regional office in which they filed, and status at entry. We think it is very troubling that a procedural bar to asylum should affect refugees differently depending on these factors, which do not have anything to do with the severity of the persecution that the asylum seekers faced, the reasons why they were persecuted, or the credibility of their testimony. Unfortunately, the arbitrariness that is injected into asylum adjudication by these factors is compounded by how these same factors correlate with asylum officers' evaluation of how the changed and extraordinary circumstances exceptions apply to the applicants. How those officers applied the exceptions is the subject of the next chapter.

5

The Rejections

In chapter 4, we reviewed the numbers and demographic characteristics of applicants who did not establish to the satisfaction of asylum officers that they filed their asylum applications within one year of entering the United States. We saw that 92,622 individuals, 30.5 percent of all affirmative asylum applicants, fell into this "untimely" category during the period of our study. This figure understates the proportion of asylum seekers affected by the deadline because it does not take into account those who failed to apply because they knew that they had missed the deadline and therefore judged that the risk of applying late, and revealing themselves to immigration authorities, was greater than the risk of remaining in the United States without authorization.

In this chapter, we examine the relationships between the larger pool of all untimely applicants and the smaller pool of those who were ultimately rejected by DHS because they did not qualify for exceptions to the deadline. We ask what proportion of untimely applicants were actually rejected, and to what extent the rejection rate changed over time and was different for certain demographic subgroups within the population of untimely applicants. We also examine the extent to which asylum officers, to whom cases are randomly assigned within each of the eight regional offices, vary in the degree to which they found that applicants qualified for an exception. And we offer an informed estimate of the extent to which the rejected applicants would have won asylum if Congress had not imposed a one-year deadline.

Introductory Note

We begin this chapter with a note on terminology, discretion, and the limitations of the data provided to us. Following the practice of DHS officials, in this section we use the term "rejectable" to refer to a case in which the applicant could not prove, by "clear and convincing evidence," that he filed an application for asylum within one year after entering the United States.[1] "Rejectable" cases, in other words, are those to which the one-year deadline could apply. The law imposes a high burden of proof on applicants, many of whom lack documentation of their date of entry, and invests asylum officers with authority to determine whether an applicant has met that burden or is rejectable.[2]

The term "rejected" refers to a case that was referred to immigration court because of the applicant's failure to prove timely filing or an acceptable exception—that is, a case to which the one year deadline was actually applied as a bar. If an asylum officer rejects a case based on failure to meet the deadline, that applicant cannot be granted asylum by the officer based on the merits of the case. But an asylum officer can determine that a rejectable applicant's reason for filing late constitutes a "changed circumstance" or an "extraordinary circumstance," the two exceptions that Congress provided to the deadline. The statute provides an illustrative but not exhaustive list of exceptions to the one-year deadline, enabling asylum officers to approve exceptions not enumerated therein.[3]

If the applicant qualifies for an exception, the asylum officer then has the authority to determine whether the applicant filed within a reasonable period of time after the circumstance that prevented timely filing was no longer applicable.[4] Asylum officers, therefore, may make as many as three separate determinations pertaining to the deadline in a particular case: whether the applicant filed on time or was rejectable; whether a rejectable applicant qualified for an exception; and whether an applicant who qualified for an exception filed within a reasonable period after the exception was no longer applicable.

DHS statistics reveal which untimely applicants were deemed to qualify for an exception,[5] so we can analyze quantitatively who these people are, as well as who did not qualify, in relationship to the larger body of untimely filers. Unfortunately, DHS does not separately code (1) untimely filers for whom no exception was even arguably applicable, (2) untimely filers for whom an exception might be applicable but who did not establish that exception "to the satisfaction of the Attorney General,"[6] and (3) untimely filers whose exception was accepted but who were deemed not to have filed within a reasonable period of time after the exception was no longer operative. We were therefore not able to evaluate the rate at which exceptions were applied in relation to exceptions that were asserted or might have been applicable, nor were we able to determine whether cases were rejected because the asylum officer found that the asylum seeker had not established the existence of the potentially applicable exception or because the asylum officer found an exception but decided that the applicant did not file in a timely manner after the exception occurred.

Similarly, DHS does not record the nature of any potentially applicable exception, so we were unable to analyze statistically the types of exceptions that were offered by the asylum seeker or examined by the asylum officer and the proportions in which they were accepted. Moreover, DHS does not record the end date of accepted exceptions or the length of time after those end dates that applicants filed asylum claims, so we were also unable to analyze the range of postexception filing time periods and which of those were deemed to be "reasonable." And DHS does not keep records on how frequently exceptions were asserted by applicants compared to how frequently facts justifying these exceptions were elicited by asylum officers' astute questions. Nevertheless, the responses to the questionnaire that DHS administered in the spring of 2011 and data that DHS does record enable us to make some interesting observations about the exercise of discretion by DHS officials.

First, consider the questionnaire responses. As we have noted, these are of limited reliability because they offer only a snapshot at one point in time, and survey participation was 70 percent. Nevertheless, the questionnaire did address two areas of interest not captured by DHS' coding of its case information.

The first of these is how information relating to the exceptions is first raised. DHS asked its officers:

> In assessing exceptions to the one year filing deadline, how often do you develop a possible exception that the asylum applicant has not offered on her own?"

Many officers—41 percent of the 199 officers who answered the question—sought information and developed exceptions based on that information in fewer than 25 percent of the cases they heard. If accurate, this reflects a failure to properly implement the training that officers receive. The Asylum Officer Basic Training Course states:

> While the burden of proof is on the applicant to show that there are changed circumstances that now materially affect his or her eligibility for asylum, many applicants affected by changed circumstances may not be able to articulate this. The unique nature of assessing an applicant's need of protection places the officer in a "cooperative" role with the applicant. It is an asylum officer's affirmative duty "to elicit all relevant and useful information bearing on the applicant's eligibility for asylum."[7]

Fewer than 14 percent of officers stated that they developed exceptions in 75 percent or more of the cases they heard. The remaining 45 percent did so sometimes or frequently (25 percent to 74 percent of cases).

A second area in which the questionnaire produced some new information pertains to the type of exceptions that were adduced. The questionnaire asked,

> Consider only those cases in which applicants file for asylum more than a year after entry and in which you find that an exception to the deadline applies. Among such cases, please estimate how often these reasons justify an exception to the one year filing deadline: Physical disability, mental disability (including trauma or PTSD), legal disability, ineffective assistance of counsel, unsuccessful attempts to file, and changed circumstances.

Figure 5-1 displays the percentage of respondents who responded "very often" or "often" with respect to each type of exception.

According to the asylum officers surveyed in 2011, changed circumstances, including deteriorating human rights conditions in the countries of origin and changes in the situation of the applicant such as religious conversions, were the largest single justification for exceptions, followed by legal disability, which in most cases probably referred to children who because of their age could not have been expected to prepare legal documents.

Comments volunteered by respondents suggested that the single largest subcategory within the changed circumstances exception consisted of applicants who had entered legally, with visas, but feared returning and applied for asylum just before or just after their legal status expired.[8] The shortest bar in the graph is that of ineffective assistance of counsel, and indeed 73

Fig. 5-1. Types of Exceptions Encountered by Questionnaire Respondents

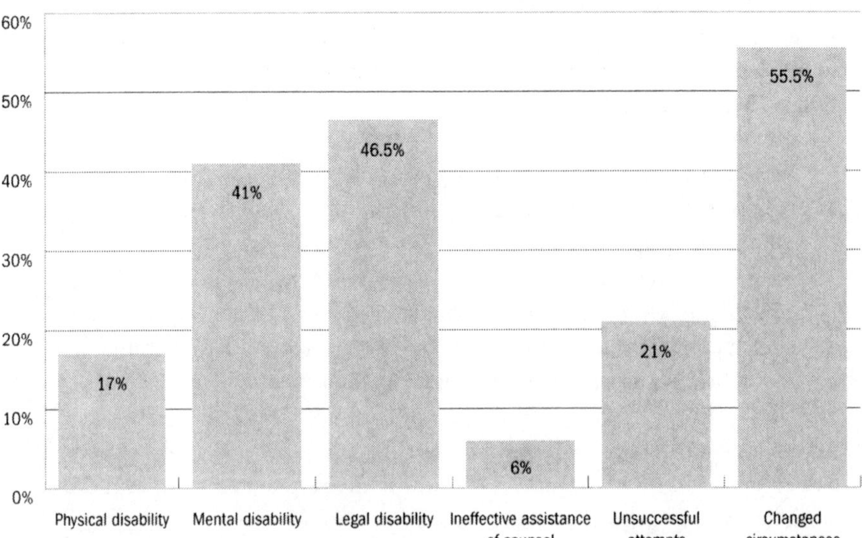

Note: The percentages exceed 100 percent, because many officers encountered several types of exceptions often or very often.

percent of the surveyed officers stated that they rarely encountered that type of claim. Interestingly, 52 percent of female respondents stated that they very often or often saw claims of mental disability, compared to 41 percent of the male respondents. It may be that applicants with mental disabilities feel more able to discuss their emotional difficulties with female officers, or that female officers are better able to discern or draw out such information.

We turn now to the data from the cases from April 16, 1998, through June 8, 2009. To confirm the statistical significance of the data analysis presented below, we ran a binary logistic regression on the database of all cases, exploring the dependent variable of rejection.[9] Unless otherwise noted, these variables were statistically significant and confirmed the findings of the cross-tabulation analysis.[10] In other words, even with all other variables in the model held constant, the relationship between rejection rates and each of the independent variables described was statistically significant.

The Rejection Rate

From April 16, 1998, when the one-year deadline went into effect, through June 8, 2009, DHS rejected 54,141 applicants for one of three reasons: they could not prove that they filed on time; if they conceded that they did not file on time, in the view of DHS officials they failed to prove the existence of a changed or extraordinary circumstance justifying a late application; having proved their eligibility for an exception, they failed to file within a reasonable period of time in light of the exception. These rejected cases constituted 17.8 percent of all of the asylum cases that DHS adjudicated and 59 percent of all cases that were filed more than a year after entry.

Figure 5-2 shows the outcomes by fiscal year of all of the cases in the database, including those filed in the two and a half years before the filing deadline was imposed as well as those filed timely.

The figure shows that rejections based on the deadline can be grouped into three periods. In cases filed before April 16, 1998, there were no rejections based on the deadline, because the deadline had not yet taken effect. From the onset of the deadline through FY 2002, between 10 percent and 17 percent of cases were rejected because of the deadline. Then, in FY 2003, there was a sudden increase, to 25 percent, in the percentage of rejected cases. And in every year but one since the end of FY 2002, the rejection rate has topped 20 percent, with the rate near 25 percent once again in the last year and a half covered by our study.

The figure also shows that from FY 1999 through FY 2009, the rate at which cases were denied or referred on the merits generally held steady, at roughly 43 percent. Of course if the rate of merits denials held steady, and the

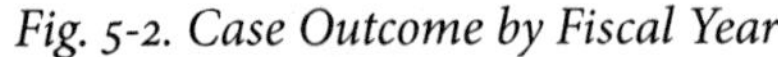

Fig. 5-2. Case Outcome by Fiscal Year

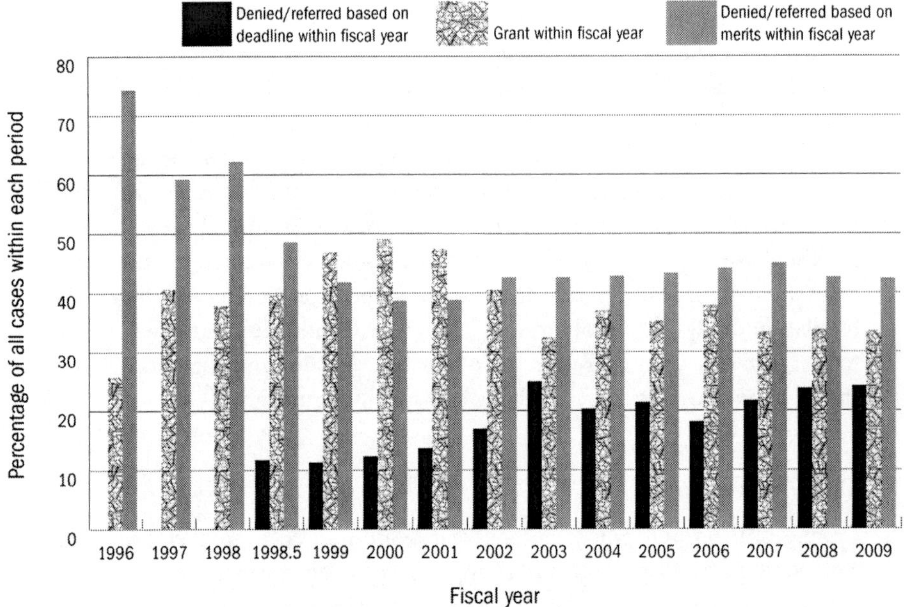

rejection rate went up, DHS's grant rate had to fall during the years in question, which it did. In every year from the second half of FY 1998, when the deadline first took effect, through FY 2002, that rate equaled or exceeded 40 percent. But in FY 2003 the grant rate dropped to about 33 percent and never reached 40 percent again. In the last two and a half years covered by this study, the grant rate remained at about 33 percent.[11]

What are the reasons for the increase in the rejection rate? We suspect that stricter enforcement of the deadline statute, as applied in the wake of the terrorist attacks, was the main reason for the increase in the rejection rate.[12] As we shall see in chapter 6, stricter enforcement of the one-year bar was part of a broader shift that also resulted in declines in the grant rate for timely filers. Some former DHS asylum officers anecdotally told us that they were informally advised by their superiors, around FY 2002, to apply the deadline more stringently, and the statistical evidence suggests that the advice was followed.

To test the hypothesis that officers may have been told to apply the deadline more strictly after 2001, DHS asked its officers in its anonymous questionnaire, "At any time, did a supervisor or director suggest, whether formally or informally, that you become more or less strict with respect to how you were applying the one year deadline?" Of the 197 officers who answered this question, 109 reported no such directions. Of the 88 other officers, 12 had been told to apply it more strictly, 28 had been told to apply it less strictly, and 48 had been given different directions at different times.[13] This would tend to suggest that supervisors' attitudes played some role in changing the rate at which officers would determine that applicants qualified for exceptions.

We cannot know from the data whether this decline in timely filing resulted from more applicants actually filing later or from some asylum officers becoming stricter in crediting applicants' testimony about their entry, or from both of these factors. The percentage of applications determined to be timely was 64 percent in the six months after the deadline went into effect and then climbed, running around 73 percent to 76 percent between FY 1999 and FY 2001, but as we noted in chapter 4, it dropped to about 65 percent in the subsequent years.

A major aspect of the adjudication of untimely asylum applications is the adjudication of exceptions to the deadline. As noted above, 59 percent of all rejectable cases were rejected over the entire period studied. But the rate of rejection was not uniform among years, nor was it uniform among subpopulations of asylum seekers.

Figure 5-3 shows the rate, by fiscal year, at which these rejectable cases were rejected. Here, too, we see the steady climb in the rejection rate after the first few years in which the deadline was in force.[14] In the first three years, DHS rejected an increasing number of rejectable cases, ranging from 33

Fig. 5-3. Rejectable Cases Rejected by Fiscal Year

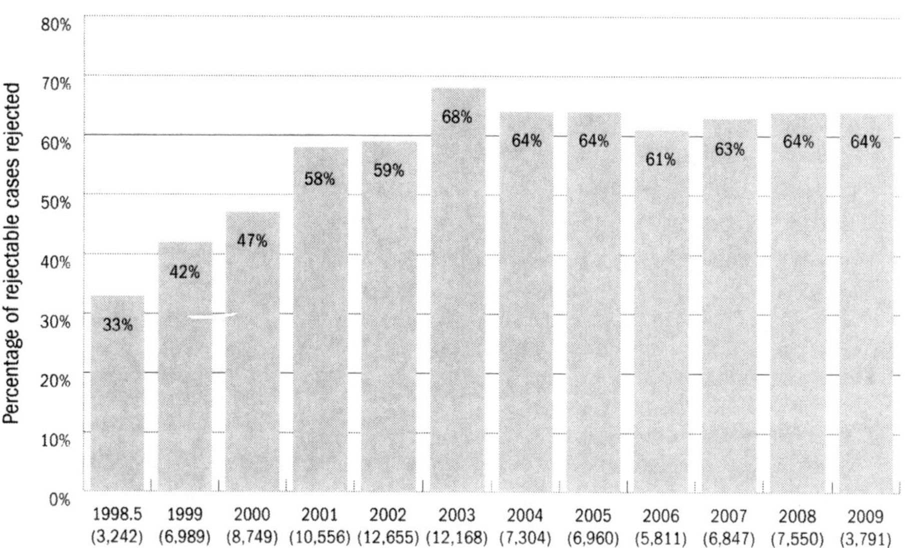

percent in the second half of FY 1998 to 47 percent in FY 2000. But in FY 2001, the rate jumped to 58 percent, in FY 2003 it reached a high of 68 percent, and in subsequent years it was never less than 61 percent.[15]

Magnitude of Lateness

The rate of rejection varied by how much later than one year the applicant filed. Those who filed late, but less than two years after entry, were rejected at a rate of 32 percent, while those who filed more than two years after entry were in every case rejected by a rate of at least 57 percent. Our regression analysis confirmed that longer lapses correlated with higher rejection rates. Moreover, having a missing entry date was like losing your ticket in a parking garage; applicants with no date of entry were penalized even more severely than those who filed four or more years after entry. Asylum applicants who could not establish any date of entry faced an 84 percent rejection rate—35 percent higher than the 62 percent rejection rate faced by those who filed four or more years after entry, and 65 percent higher than the 51 percent rejection rate faced by the entire cohort of those who could establish an entry date.

If we look more closely at the rejection rate for applicants who filed shortly after the deadline expired, we can see that those who were only a few days late often qualified for an exception. Figure 5-4 shows the rejection rate for those who were late but who missed the deadline by thirty-one or fewer days.

Figure 5-4 shows that the rejection rate remained at 15 percent or less for those who filed between the 365th and the 384th day after entry (20 days late), but that it began to climb after that, reaching 21 percent by 30 days after the deadline. Figure 5-5 reveals that the rejection rate climbed steeply after 20 days.

These two figures are not surprising, except that the statute reads as if it created an on-off switch at the one-year mark, whereas the two graphs show that in practice, asylum officers have in the aggregate created a sliding scale. Tardier filings resulted in higher rates of rejection based on the deadline.[16]

Rejections and Applicant Characteristics

Gender and Age

We were also interested in whether there were differences in rejection rates for different populations who filed more than a year after entry. Not all differences among the characteristics of the applicant pool correlated with disparate rejection rates. Women who were late filers were rejected at about the same rate as men; the rate for women was 56 percent and for men, 60

Fig. 5-4. Rejection Rates for Applicants Late 31 or Fewer Days

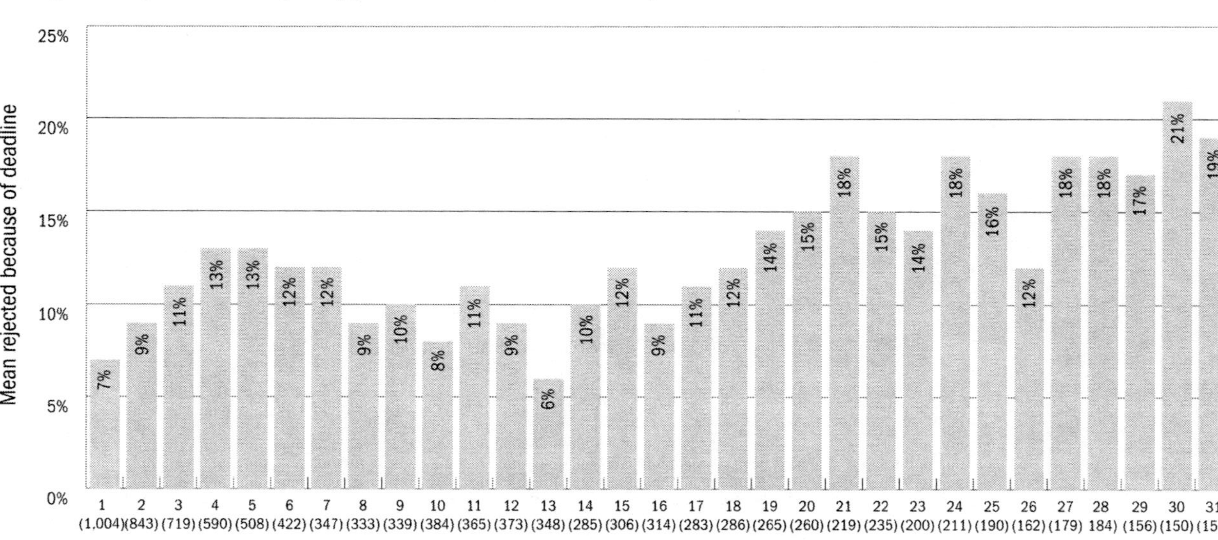

Fig. 5-5. Rejection Rates by Number of Days after Deadline

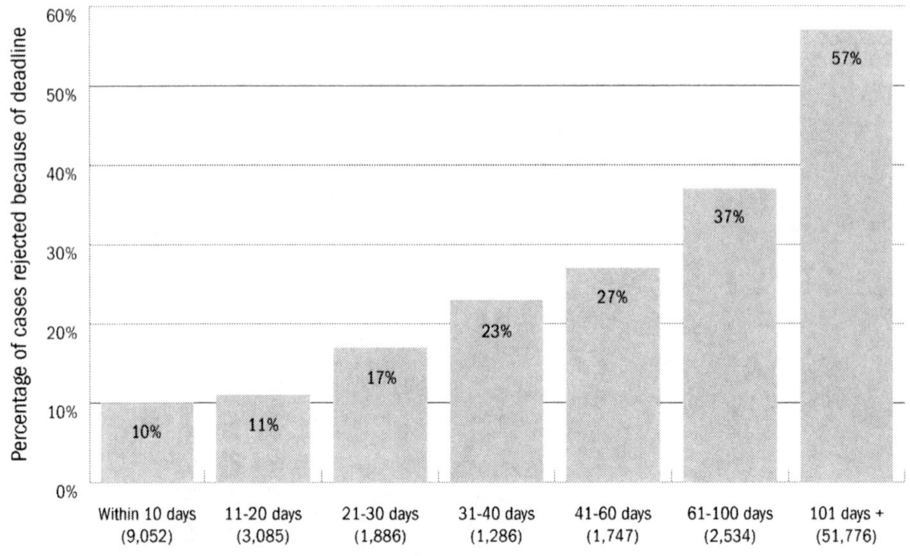

percent.[17] Except for applicants who were younger than eighteen (for whom the regulations provide a particular exception to the deadline), the rate of rejection was not much affected by the applicant's age.

Dependents

Late applicants with dependents were rejected at a rate of 52 percent, while those without dependents were turned down at a rate of 60 percent, perhaps reflecting some sympathy on the part of asylum officers for those with dependents.[18] Just as applicants with dependents were rejected less often than those without dependents, applicants with dependents whose cases were adjudicated on the merits were more successful than applicants without dependents whose cases were adjudicated on the merits. We report on this phenomenon at length in chapter 7.[19]

Representation

One particularly important attribute was whether the applicant was or was not represented when interviewed by an asylum officer.[20] Forty-four percent of all applicants were represented. As we have seen in chapter 4, applicants who filed late were more often represented (73 percent compared with 65 percent) than applicants who filed timely. Among those who filed late (and were therefore rejectable), those who were represented were rejected less often (55 percent compared with 62 percent).[21]

As we have noted, late filers may more often have had legal representation because lawyers may have helped them understand that they were actually eligible for asylum. Asylum seekers from a different legal and political culture might not expect that, for example, sexual orientation and domestic violence can be the basis for a successful asylum claim. It may also be that legal representatives helped late-filing asylum seekers to understand the exceptions to the deadline and their eligibility for these exceptions. In any case, our finding that represented rejectable asylum seekers were less often rejected based on the deadline confirms many studies showing the effect of representation on asylum outcomes.[22]

In its questionnaire to asylum officers serving in 2011, DHS asked why they believed that represented late asylum seekers were found to qualify for exceptions at a higher rate than unrepresented applicants. A majority (60 percent of the 200 officers who responded) believed that represented and unrepresented applicants qualified for an exception in equal proportions, but that representatives provided corroborating evidence, such as a psychologist's report showing posttraumatic stress syndrome, more often than unrepresented applicants did. Thirteen percent believed that represented applicants had valid justification (not merely proof of that justification) more often than unrepresented applicants did, and 11 percent believed that the represented applicants presented more credible testimony than the unrepresented applicants. Sixteen percent suggested a diverse set of "other" reasons. Some of them suggested that lawyers and other representatives are better able to help applicants articulate their valid reasons for late filing:

> Representatives are able to question applicants more completely and explain to applicants more fully how reasons they didn't file may be relevant. . . . For example, I have had cases in which it took a very long time and many questions to uncover that the person was involved in a controlling and abusive relationship during the time they had to timely file. People are not always willing to offer up this personal fact about which they were not prepared to testify unless they understand why it is important. Representatives have much more time to develop a rapport and uncover details that an officer may not be able to elicit even if they are really trying.

> Represented applicants are often prepared by counsel to provide exceptions to the one-year rule as reasons why they did not file.

> Unrepresented applicants are more likely to not to mention exceptions, even if they have them, because they do not know what the exceptions are.

> Unrepresented applicants are less likely to know the law and are more likely to be completely candid regarding their failure to file, and their candid answers typically do not qualify as exceptions.

Other respondents suggested that represented applicants were more successful because some representatives help applicants fabricate excuses:

> Represented applicant were told what to say to beat the one year deadline [*sic*]

> Represented applicants are counseled by their attorneys to create changed circumstances, such as beginning to practice Christianity or Falun Gong (for Chinese applicants).

One suggested that some asylum officers were simply intimidated by the presence of representatives:

Fig. 5-6. Rejectable Cases Rejected, by Asylum Applicant's Region of Origin, Inspected Entry Only

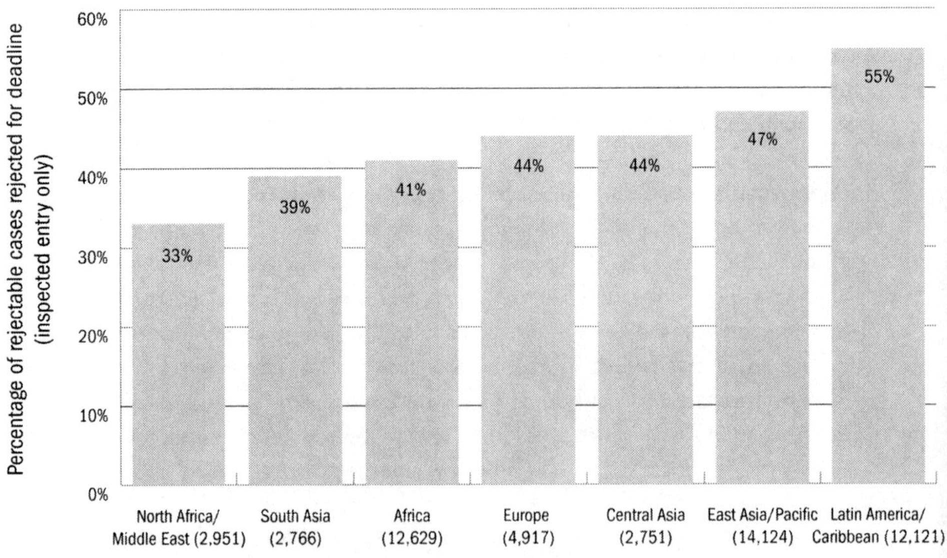

AOs and SAOs probably feel pressured when an applicant is represented and qualify the applicant on that basis alone rather than on any real merits to do so.

Region of Origin

Figure 5-6 shows the rate at which cases were rejected, broken down by the geographic region from which the asylum applicants fled, for only those rejectable applicants who were inspected at entry.[23]

Figure 5-6 shows that there were important differences in the ultimate rejection rates among inspected untimely filers, depending on their region of origin, and that those from North Africa and the Middle East fared best—only 33 percent of late applicants from that part of the world did not qualify for an exception—while those from East Asia and from Latin America and the Caribbean experienced significantly higher rejection rates of 47 percent and 55 percent respectively.[24] Inspected Central Asian and European applicants were more often rejected than inspected African and South Asian applicants.[25] Why were late inspected Latin American applicants rejected 66 percent more often than late inspected North African and Middle Eastern applicants?

Fig. 5-7. Inspected Entry, by Asylum Applicant's Region of Origin, Rejectable Cases Only

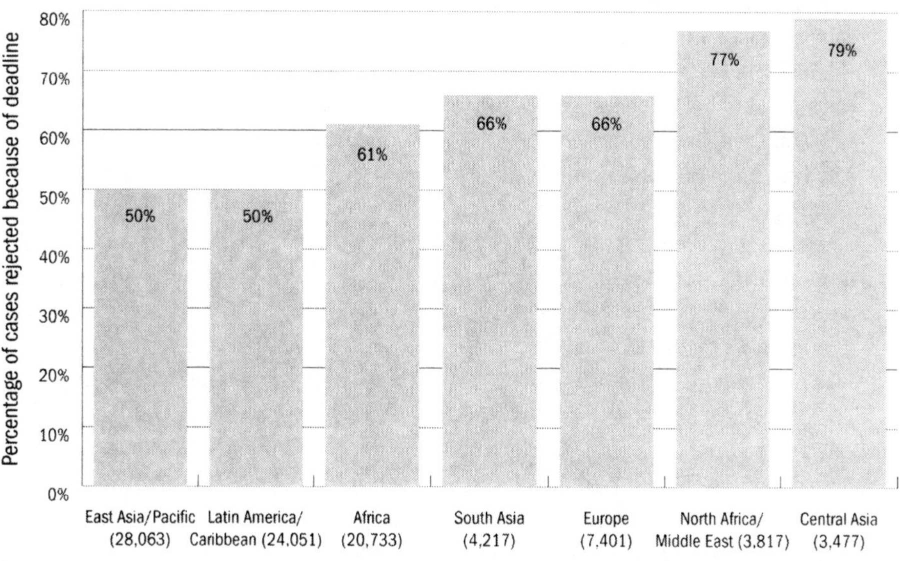

Perhaps part of the answer lies in the raw numbers of applicants shown on the x-axis in figure 5-7. There were much larger numbers of late-filing applicants from Latin America and the Caribbean and from East Asia than there were from North Africa and the Middle East. Moreover, the percentage of applicants who were uninspected was also much higher for the applicants from Latin America, the Caribbean, and East Asia. It could be that the large numbers of undocumented applicants from Latin America and East Asia contributed to negative perceptions even of inspected applicants from those regions. But this is not the whole explanation, because we see low numbers of uninspected rejectable applicants from Central Asia but relatively high rejection rates for inspected applicants from that region.

Nationality

Figure 5-8 shows the differences in the rejection rate of late filers from various countries.[26] It shows that while those who filed late from certain countries, including Iraq, Liberia, Togo, Nepal, and several others, were found eligible for an exception at very high rates, those from certain other countries, such as Mauritania, the Gambia, and Côte d'Ivoire, had much lower rates at which exceptions were found.

Even if we consider only those untimely applicants who were inspected at entry from these countries (figure 5-9), we see a similar pattern. Applicants from Iraq, Liberia, Togo, and Nepal benefited from findings of an exception at high rates, while applicants from Mauritania, the Gambia, and Côte d'Ivoire faced much higher rejection rates.

In chapter 4, we saw that different nationalities had different rates of late filing (or at least of being unable to prove on-time filing to the satisfaction of asylum officers). In figure 5-8, we saw that rejectable applicants of different nationalities also had different rates of rejection. For some nationalities these two variables reinforced each other, while for others, one reduced the impact of the other. To determine the ultimate effect of the deadline on different nationalities, we graphed the percentage of *all* applicants from these countries (rather than those who filed more than a year after entry) who were rejected by asylum officers.

Figure 5-10 presents these data, with the countries of origin listed in the same order as in figure 5-8. In this figure, we see very different overall rates of rejection for nationals of different countries. For example, only 13 percent of Haitians were rejected because of the deadline, compared with 58 percent of Gambians. Comparing figures 5-8 and 5-10, it is evident that although Haitians and Gambians who were late were rejected at about the same rate—72 percent and 77 percent, respectively—the deadline had a much smaller effect on Haitians because a much higher percentage of them applied on time.[27] Similarly, although late Indians and

Fig. 5-8. Rejectable Cases Rejected, by Nationality

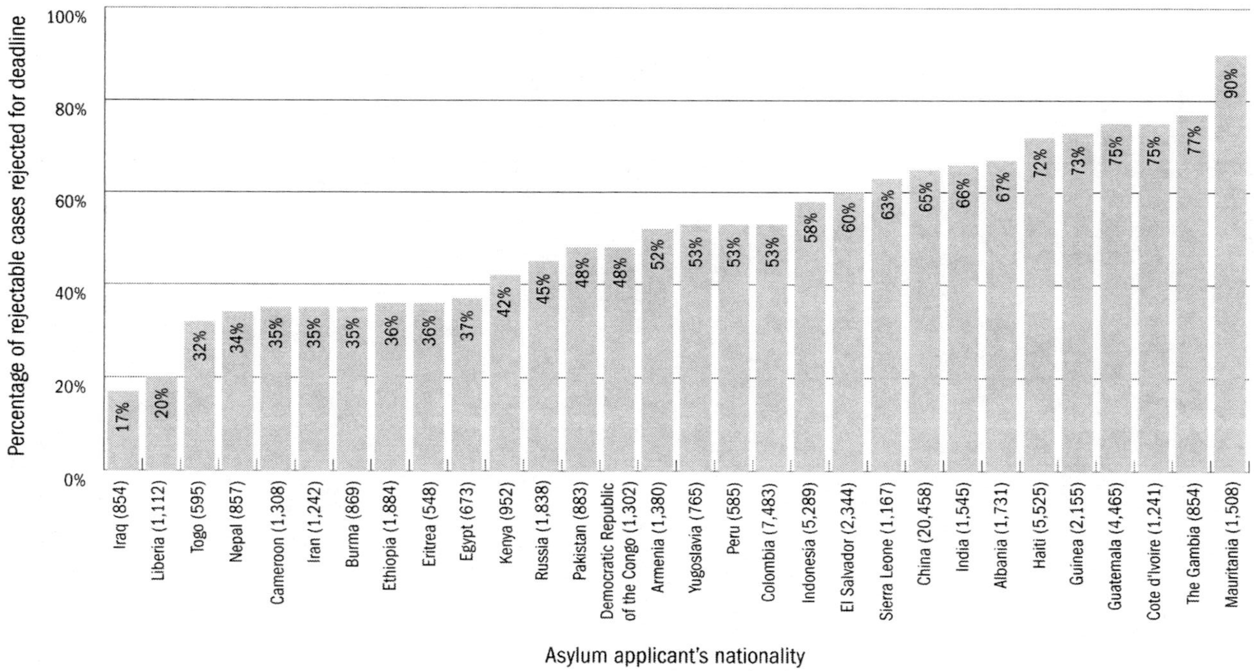

Fig. 5-9. Rejectable Cases Rejected, by Nationality, Inspected Entry Only

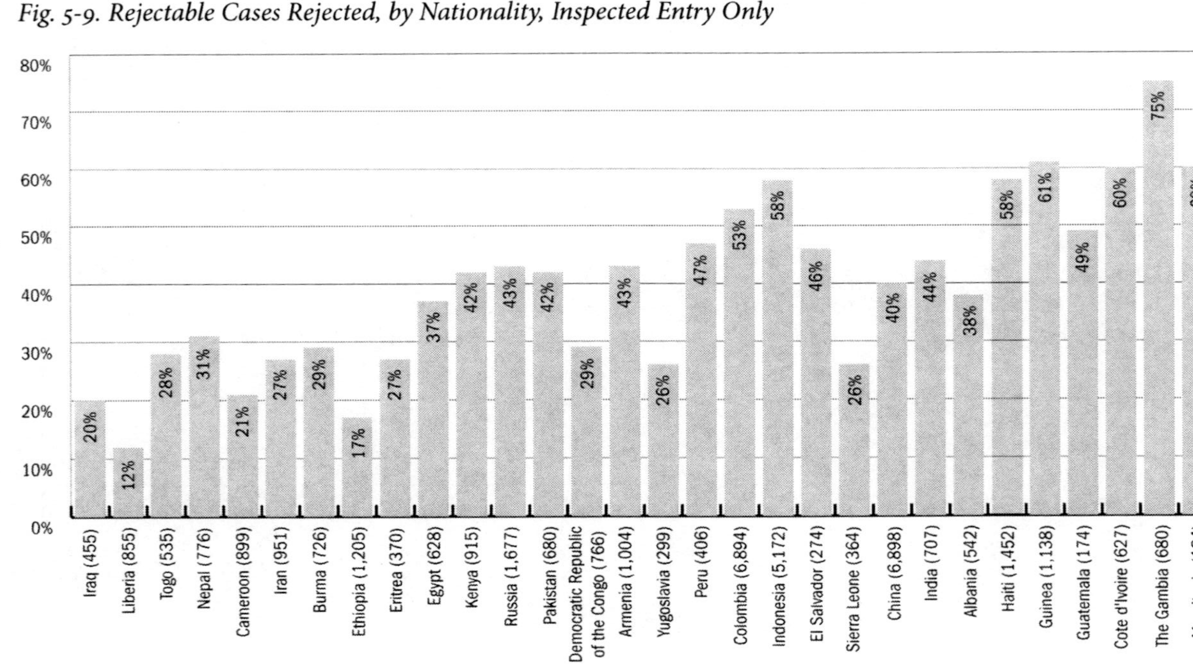

Fig. 5-10. Deadline Rejections by Nationality, All Applicants

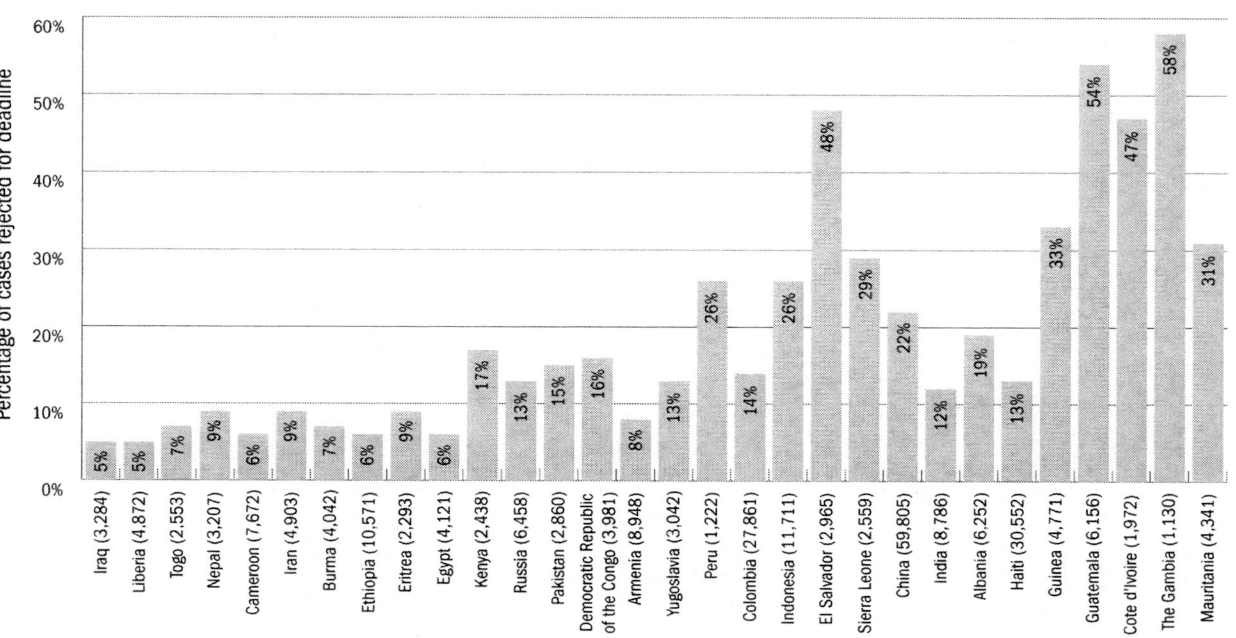

Sierra Leoneans were rejected at similar rates—66 percent and 63 percent respectively—more than double the percentage of Sierra Leoneans were rejected on the basis of the deadline because a significantly higher percentage of Indians filed timely.[28] These results probably reflect the much better developed social network of Indians and Haitians in certain regions of the United States where many of them have settled, compared to Gambians and Sierra Leoneans, and the support that those who are already here are able to give to newly arrived refugees.[29]

They may also reflect suspicions that some asylum officers hold about the testimony or documentation filed by nationals of certain countries. For example, asked to explain the high rejection rate for Gambians and the very low rejection rate for Liberians, one asylum officer told us that

> Gambians are a population perceived as having a lot of fraudulent cases. Sometimes purported Gambians are actually Senegalese or Mauritanians. [Also] Gambia has never been seen as being in as much trouble as Liberia. People would be more inclined to give Liberians the benefit of the doubt because of the horror and severity of what went on there.

The first two sentences of this statement do not necessarily suggest stereotyping, as it could be factually true that a disproportionate number of Gambian applicants committed identity fraud. The remaining sentences are even more clearly suggestions that perceptions of the merits of cases—in this case, the degree of abuse in the applicants' countries—actually influence determinations of whether or not the applicants have met the deadline.

To the extent that rejections are a function of either the fortuity of an extant local community of co-nationals and support organizations or of asylum officers' assumptions about applicants from certain countries, these determinations are arbitrary; they are not simply based on individualized determinations related to the risk that particular applicants face in their home countries or the likelihood that they are telling the truth to asylum officers. These outcomes demonstrate that the one-year deadline can have differential impact on various groups of refugees in ways that were probably not contemplated by Congress and that are unrelated to the persecution these individuals feared or experienced in their home countries.

Religion

Figure 5-11 breaks the data down by religion, for those who stated a major religion.[30] We start the discussion of the religion data by noting that of 92,622 rejectable asylum applicants, 13,315 were classified as "other" religions and

Fig. 5-11. Rejectable Cases Rejected, by Religion

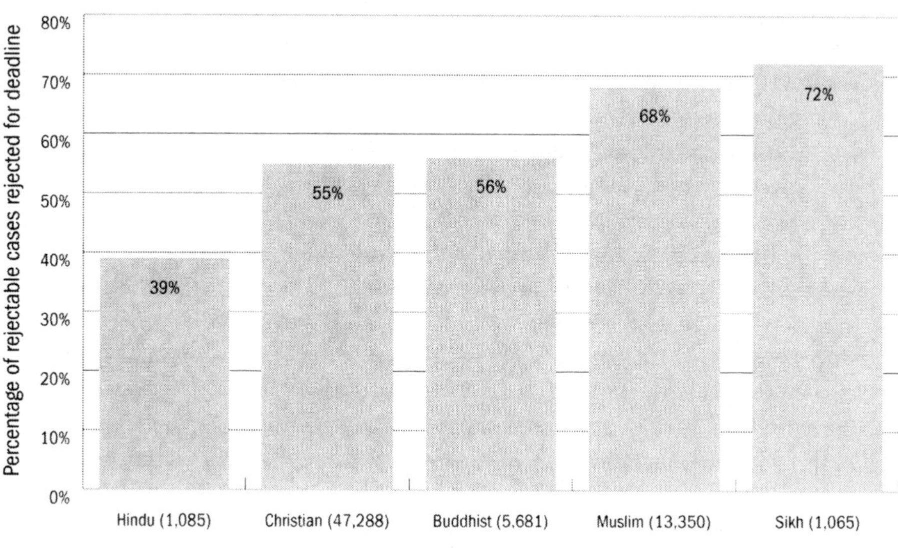

10,230 were classified as being of an "unknown" religion. As a result, the discussion below is descriptive only of the data we obtained, and should be treated as tentative. Despite these limitations, we find that the data offer interesting patterns worth cautious consideration.

This figure shows that among untimely filers who identified themselves by stating a religion, Hindus were rejected at the lowest rate (39 percent), while Muslims and Sikhs were rejected at a rate more than 70 percent higher than the rate at which Hindus were turned down (68 percent and 72 percent). This is similar to but slightly different from the regression, which found the strongest relationship between rejection and adherents of the Sikh religion followed by Muslims, Christians, Hindus, and Buddhists. Again, we wondered whether another variable might be driving the differences in rejection rates by religion. We decided to explore religion and nationality.

Unsurprisingly, the vast majority, or 1,049 of 1,065 of rejectable Sikhs came from India. Over half, 3,394 of 5,681 of rejectable Buddhists came from China, a country with a long-standing and well-documented pattern of persecution of Buddhists. Similarly, nearly half, 497 of 1,085, of rejectable Hindus came from Nepal, a country that is majority Hindu but whose residents suffered persecution at the hands of secularist Maoist rebels during the period we studied. Given the large number of Christian applicants, it was not surprising that they did not fit much of a pattern. Of the 47,288 rejectable Christians, over 1,000 came from each of the following countries: Armenia, Cameroon, China, Colombia, the Democratic Republic of Congo, El Salvador, Ethiopia, Guatemala, Haiti, Indonesia, and Venezuela.

Digging deeper into the numbers, it turns out that two-thirds of the 13,350 late Muslim asylum applicants during the time period studied came from sub-Saharan Africa, and that of the 11,535 sub-Saharan African asylum applicants rejected because of the one-year deadline, nearly 60 percent were Muslim. To slice the numbers a different way, figure 5-12 shows that 75 percent of late sub-Saharan African Muslims were rejected for failure to meet the one-year deadline; in contrast, less than 40 percent of late sub-Saharan African Christians were rejected. In striking contrast, for applicants coming from outside sub-Saharan Africa, Christians and Muslims were rejected at almost the same rate. And even if we look at only inspected or uninspected applicants from sub-Saharan Africa, the differences are exceptional. In the former group, 61 percent of Muslims were rejected compared to only 31 percent of Christians; in the latter group, 86 percent of Muslims were rejected compared to only 64 percent of Christians. We are not sure what caused this disparity, but the particularly high rejection rates faced by sub-Saharan African

Fig. 5-12. Rejectable Cases Rejected, by Religion and Region of Origin

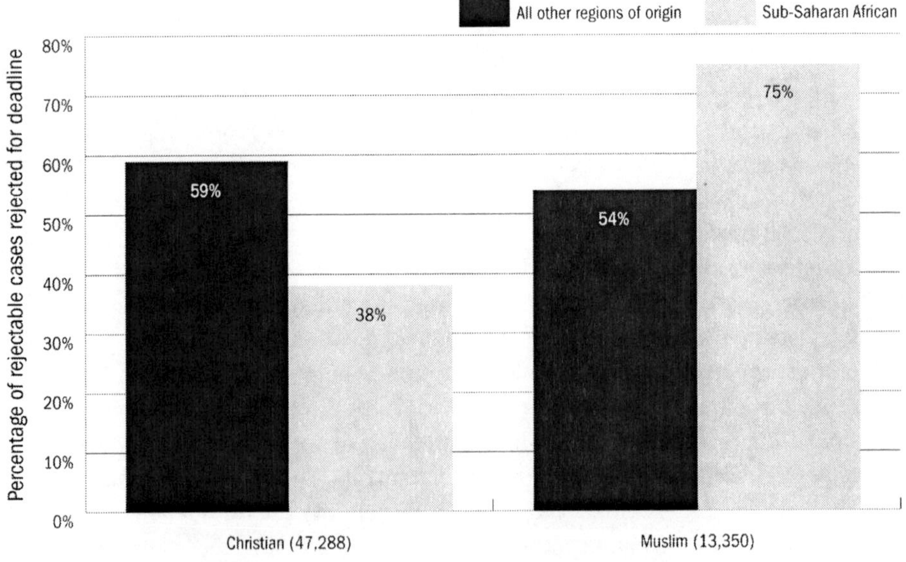

Muslims raise additional concerns about whether the one-year deadline and its exceptions have been and can be applied fairly.

Disparities across and within Asylum Offices

We next examined differences in rejection rates in different asylum offices, and differences in rejection rates of asylum officers in the same regional office (to whom cases were randomly assigned). In our earlier research, we found significant disparities across and within asylum offices in terms of the rate of granting asylum.[31] With the new data that DHS has supplied, we were able to look at disparities in the frequency of rejecting untimely applicants.

Disparities across Asylum Office Regions

Figure 5-13 shows that the rate at which rejectable cases are rejected varies significantly according to the region of the country in which the asylum officers (and perhaps more importantly, directors and other supervisory personnel) work.

As figure 5-13 shows, in two of the eight regions this rate is 43 percent or lower, while in three other regions the rate is 63 percent or higher. Were these

Fig. 5-13. Rejectable Cases Rejected, by Asylum Office Region

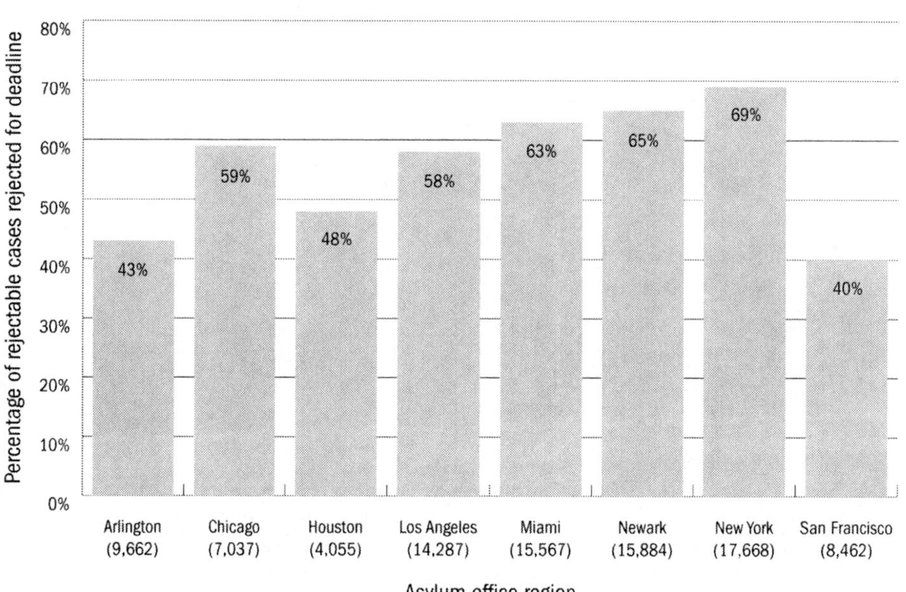

disparities due simply to easily explainable factors such as population differences in the different regions, or were there other factors at play? The regression analysis found statistically significant differences in outcomes between asylum office regions, even holding variables such as nationality of the asylum seeker constant. We were interested to learn, however, that the regression showed a different pattern in the asylum office regions' rejection rates than our cross-tabs did. According to the regression, the Miami regional office was most correlated with rejection and the Arlington, Virginia, office the least correlated with rejection. In the middle arrayed from most to least correlated with rejection, were New York, Chicago, Los Angeles, Newark, Houston, and San Francisco. This revealed that there are other variables driving the differences between asylum office regions. To investigate this puzzle further, we explored correlations between rejection rates and whether applicants had presented themselves for inspection when entering the country.

We started with a bird's-eye view, comparing how the eight regional asylum offices treated untimely applicants. The data points in figure 5-14 indicate, for each regional office, (a) the rate at which they found all late applicants to

Fig. 5-14. Qualification Rates for Exceptions, by Asylum Office Region

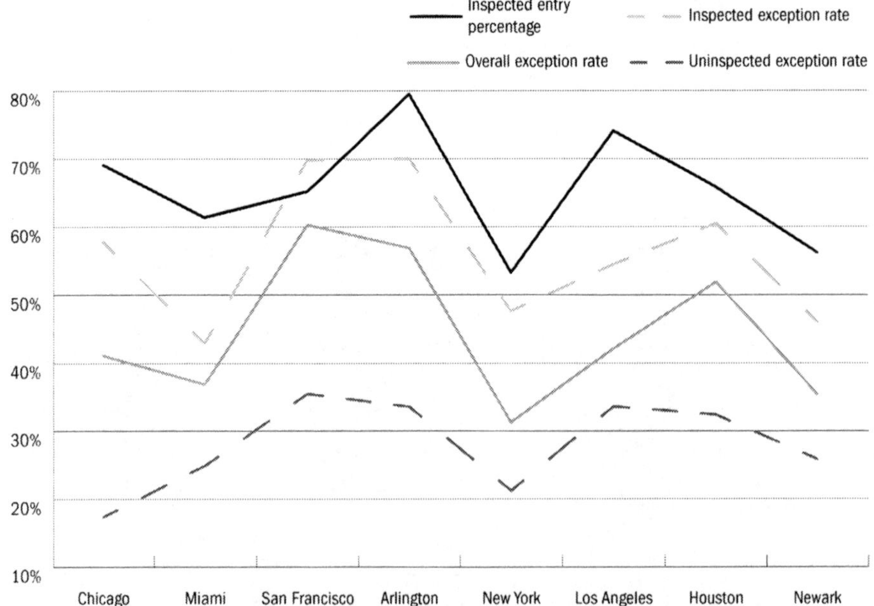

Note: The inspected entry percentage used for this figure is the percentage of all applicants on or after April 16, 1998 (when the deadline took effect), who were recorded in RAPS as having been inspected upon entry.

have qualified for an exception, (b) the uniformly higher rate at which they determined that exceptions existed for those applicants who had presented themselves for inspection when they entered the United States (that is, applicants who had entered the U.S. lawfully, even if they no longer had a lawful status when they applied for asylum), (c) the percentage of applicants in the region in question who had presented themselves for inspection; and (d) the uniformly lower rate at which the regional offices determined that exceptions existed for those applicants who had entered the U.S. without inspection.

This graph showcases two important and, to us, surprising findings. First, there was a wide disparity in the rate at which regions awarded exceptions to inspected applicants, with three regions awarding exceptions to about 40 percent of inspected applicants and two regions awarding exceptions to about 60 percent, a rate that is about 50 percent higher. In addition, there seems to be a strong correlation between the percentage of uninspected applicants in a region and the rate at which that region's officers granted exceptions to all late applicants, including those who were inspected at entry.

Disparities within Asylum Office Regions

For a more meaningful measure of consistency or disparity, we examined the rate at which the individual asylum officers within each region rejected rejectable applicants. To avoid any distortion that would come from examining the rejection rate of officers who decided only a few cases (for example, two cases, both of which or neither of which resulted in an exception), we limited this study to officers who had adjudicated the cases of at least one hundred late-filing applicants. By limiting our investigation to a particular region, we eliminate any effects caused by particular populations (for example, applicants from a particular country or region) having settled in certain regions of the United States. Within each region, furthermore, clerks randomly assign cases to the various asylum officers. Therefore, the rate at which each officer within the same office rejected late applicants should be approximately the same.

Figure 5-15 shows the percentage of rejectable cases that were rejected, by region. It reveals the disparities in individual asylum officer rejection rates within and between asylum offices. The boxplot provides several types of data for each region. First, it shows the median rejection rate for each regional office, which is the black line in the middle of each box.[32] Second, it reveals the degree of disparity in rejection rates for officers in the middle 50 percent of rejection rates for each office (that is, for the range of officers other than those whose rejection rates put them in the top 25 percent or the bottom 25 percent of their office). The range for the middle 50 percent is shown by the length of the shaded box. Third, it shows the full range of disparity in rejection rates, except for the few officers whose rates were extremely disparate. This range is shown by the lines protruding from the shaded box. Finally, the rejection rates of a few officers in three regions (Miami, Newark, and Los Angeles,) were extremely disparate from the mean, as measured by the distance of these rates from the end of the shaded box. The rejection rates of those officers are shown by circles and asterisks, known as "outlier flags." When a rate is 1.5 to 3 box lengths away from the *end* of the box, it is flagged by a circle. (The rate of one officer in Miami, more than 3 box lengths away, is flagged by an asterisk.)

As discussed, there were sizable differences in mean rejection rates across asylum office regions (from 39 percent in San Francisco to 69 percent in New York). The boxplot tells us that there were also large disparities among asylum officers within each region and that there were also serious disparities, from region to region, in the degree of disparities among officers within a regional office. For example, in Miami, the middle 50 percent of asylum officers

Fig. 5-15. Individual Asylum Officer Rejection Rates, by Asylum Office Region

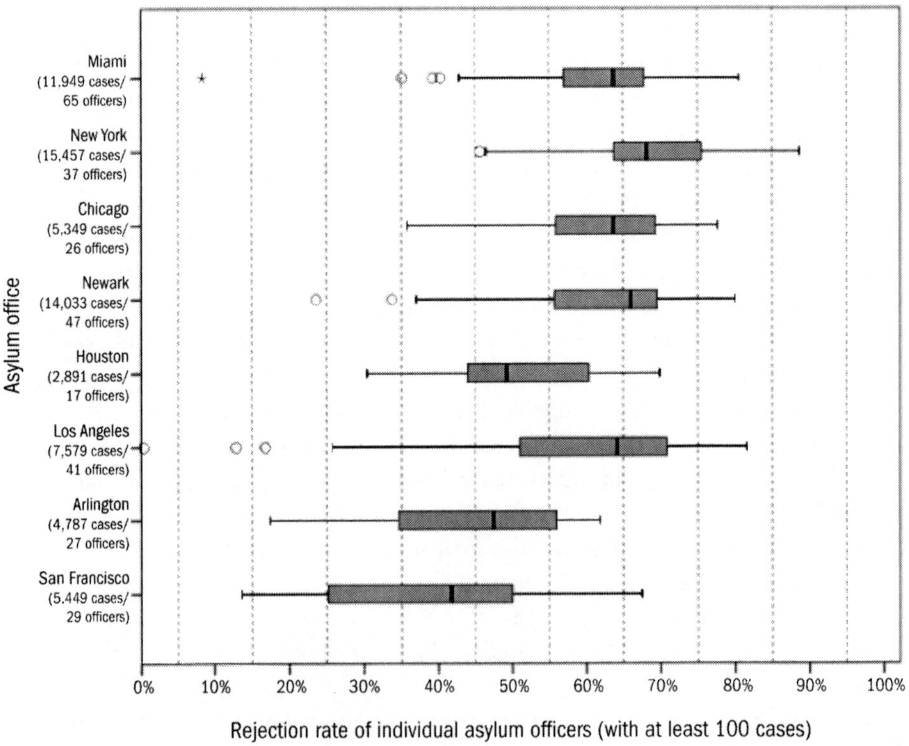

rejected cases at rates of between 57 percent and 68 percent, an 11 percentage point spread. But in Los Angeles, with a mean rejection rate nearly identical to that of Miami, the middle 50 percent of asylum officers rejected cases at rates of between 51 percent and 72 percent, a 21 percentage point spread.

Were Bona Fide Refugees Denied Asylum Because of the Deadline?

Our analysis shows that from 1998 through 2009, the deadline did not operate evenly across the population of asylum seekers. First, as chapter 4 demonstrates, subpopulations of asylum applicants (whether classified by region of origin, age, nationality, or other characteristics) varied in the degree to which they applied before the deadline, perhaps reflecting different degrees of support in co-ethnic communities in the United States or other factors. Second, among those who applied beyond the deadline, certain subpopulations were found to qualify for exceptions at different rates than others, though there is no reason to think that these differences reflected the merits of their cases. Among other factors, for example, those with representation fared better than those who lacked a representative, and those from some countries were much more affected by the deadline than those from other countries. Finally, even within particular regional asylum offices, where cases are assigned randomly to asylum officers so that they all decide approximately the same mix of cases, individual asylum officers granted exceptions at very different rates, in yet another example of "refugee roulette."

None of this would matter, however, if the late applicants who were rejected were undeserving of asylum; that is, if they would have been ineligible for asylum in any event because they did not have bona fide cases (or worse, had fraudulent claims). To explore this question, we first compared the grant rate for timely applicants with the grant rate for late applicants who qualified for an exception. If late applicants had generally weaker cases than timely applicants, we would expect the late-but-excepted applicants to have lower grant rates than the timely applicants.

In fact we find that the grant rate for both of these categories was exactly the same: 49 percent in each case.[33] Furthermore, this approximate equality persisted for virtually all subcategories of applicants. Men who filed on time won asylum 47 percent of the time; men who were late and qualified for an exception prevailed 48 percent of the time. For women, the corresponding percentages were 51 percent and 50 percent. Represented asylum seekers who filed within the deadline won asylum at a rate of 51 percent; those who qualified for an exception won at a rate of 52 percent. For unrepresented applicants, the corresponding figures were 47 percent

Fig. 5-16. Grant Rates for Timely Applicants and Rejectable Applicants Who Qualified for an Exception, by Region of Origin

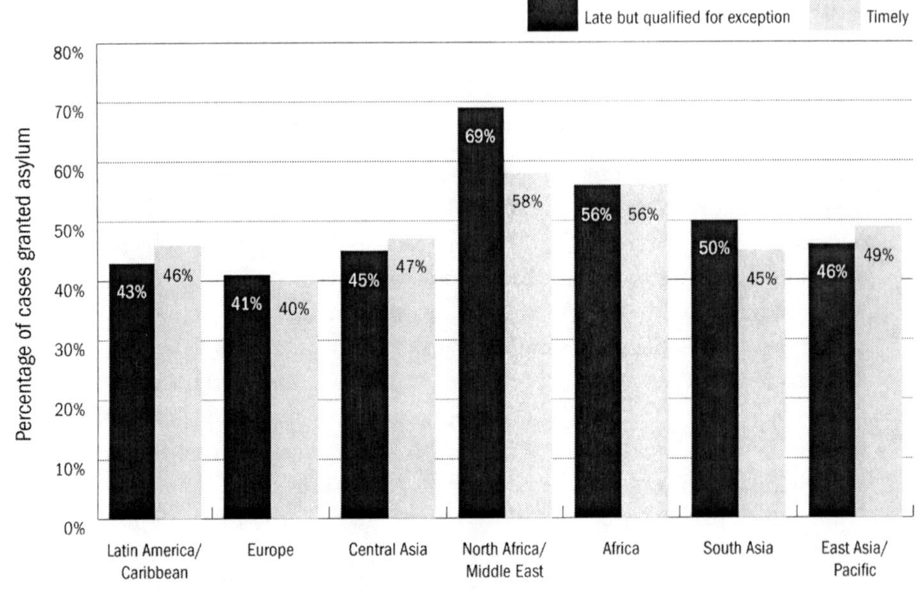

Fig. 5-17. Grant Rates for Timely Applicants and Rejectable Applicants Who Qualified for an Exception, by Age at Filing

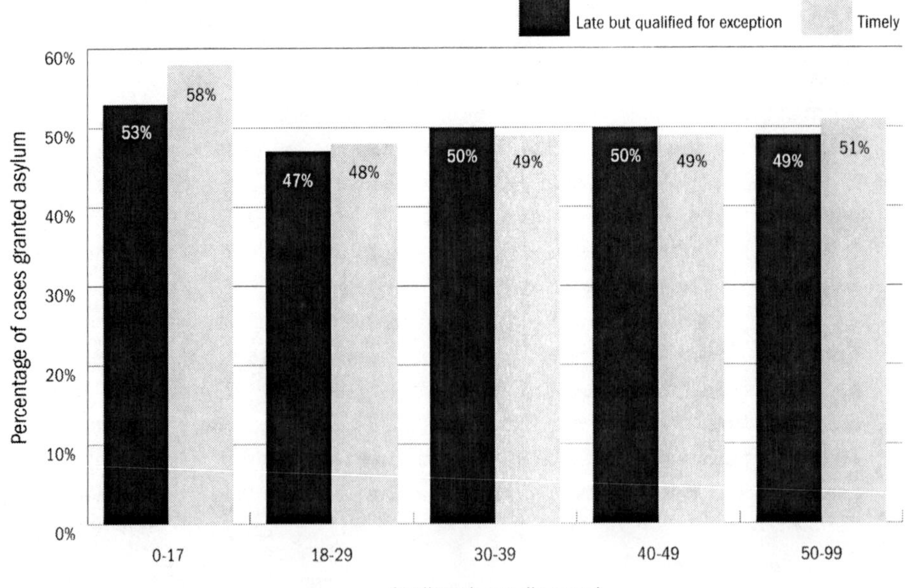

and 47 percent. As figure 5-16 shows, for every region of the world from which substantial numbers of applicants arrive, the excepted, late applicants had approximately the same grant rate, or, for North Africa and the Middle East, a higher grant rate, as timely applicants.

Similarly, these relationships generally held true for each age bracket among the applicants (figure 5-17).

They also hold true for applicants who self-identified as Christian, Muslim, and Buddhist.[34]

Fig. 5-18. Grant Rates for Timely Applicants and Rejectable Applicants Who Qualified for an Exception, by Stated Religion

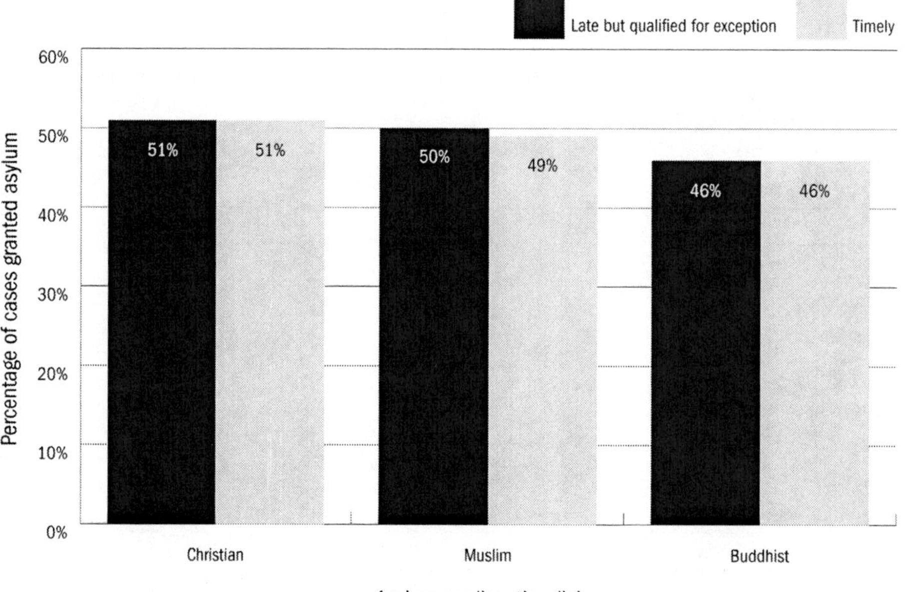

Among inspected applicants who filed within the deadline, the grant rate was 51 percent; among late applicants who qualified for an exception and had been inspected at the time of entry, the grant rate was a very similar 54 percent. There was, however, a significant difference in the grant rate of applicants who had entered without inspection in the two groups. For those who proved that they filed within one year, the grant rate was 43 percent, but it was only 33 percent for those who were late but qualified for an exception.

These numerous correspondences may suggest that the pools of applicants who filed on time and those who filed late but qualified for an exception were similar. But it is a further stretch to conclude that those who were actually rejected because of the deadline were also similar in their characteristics (except for having filed late) to those who filed on time, and that they too would have had a grant rate as high (49 percent) as the two other groups.

For a first pass at comparing these two groups, we simply listed the demographic characteristics of the individuals populating each of them. Table 5-1 shows this comparison:

Perusal of this table suggests that while the makeup of the two pools of applicants is not identical, they are remarkably similar. There was a somewhat higher percentage of Chinese and a somewhat lower percentage of Haitians and Colombians in the pool of rejected applicants, but the differences

Table 5-1. Who Is in the Database? A Comparison of Grant Rates for Timely and Rejected Applicants

	Timely applicants	Rejected applicants
Gender		
Male	60%	58%
Region		
Latin America	26%	28%
Europe	8%	7%
Central Asia	6%	3%
N. Africa & Middle East	5%	2%
Africa	24%	21%
South Asia	6%	4%
East Asia/ Pacific Islands	24%	32%
Most frequent nationalities		
China	19%	24%
Haiti	12%	7%
Colombia	10%	7%
Religion		
Christian	54%	48%
Muslim	12%	17%
Buddhist	5%	6%
Has dependents in U.S.	19%	17%
Unrepresented	59%	53%
Inspected	69%	44%

are generally not huge. The one exception concerns inspected applicants. Those who entered with inspection had an easier time proving their date of entry by clear and convincing evidence than did those who entered without inspection. Accordingly, a much lower percentage of inspected applicants appears in the pool of those who were ultimately rejected.

Table 5-2 compares the demographics among three groups of applicants, considering only those applicants who were inspected:

Tables 5-1 and 5-2 demonstrate that although there are a few demographic differences among the sub-populations considered in the columns of each table, they are remarkably similar virtually across the board. These tables hint at the possibility that because the populations of late, rejected applicants are similar in many respects to the population of timely applicants, the late applicants, particularly the 65 percent of them who were inspected upon entry, would have been granted asylum at a rate something like the 49 percent rate at which asylum was granted to timely and untimely but excepted applicants, if there had been no deadline.

To refine our estimate of the percentage and number of rejected applicants who would have been granted asylum by DHS if no deadline existed, we used an out-of-sample prediction. We performed a binary logistic regression on untimely but excepted cases.[35] This regression provided coefficients that described how certain variables in the database affected an applicant's chances of receiving asylum. The regression equation was then applied to those cases rejected because of the deadline. For each case, the values for the database variables were plugged into the regression equation, and the computation provided the percentage chance of that particular case being granted asylum. The mean of these values was then found to determine the percent of all rejected cases that would have received asylum had the one-year deadline not been in effect.[36]

The total percentage of rejected applicants who would have received asylum was predicted to be 43.6 percent.[37] Applying this percentage to the 36,220 applicants who did not have blank dates of entry in DHS's records,[38] we estimate that an additional 15,792 applicants would have won asylum during the 11 years from April 16, 1998, to June 8, 2009, if the deadline had not been in force.[39] This number is already unacceptably high, but it impacts an even greater number of individuals, as many asylum applicants have dependents. Including the dependents, we estimate that 21,635 genuine refugees were refused asylum by DHS during the time frame studied solely because of the deadline.[40]

As noted in chapter 3, some of these rejected asylum seekers may ultimately have been granted asylum by immigration judges who concluded

Table 5-2. Demographic Characteristics of Timely and Untimely Applicants (Inspected Entrants Only), April 16, 1998–June 8, 2009

Percentage of each category listed to the right who were:	Timely applicants	Late applicants who qualified for an exception	Late applicants who did not qualify for an exception
Male	58%	54%	54%
Inspected	100%	100%	100%
From:			
Latin America	22%	19%	28%
Europe	8%	10%	9%
Central Asia	7%	5%	5%
North Africa & Middle East	6%	7%	4%
Africa	23%	26%	22%
South Asia	6%	6%	4%
East Asia/Pacific	27%	26%	28%
From:			
China	20%	15%	12%
Haiti	4%	2%	4%
Colombia	13%	12%	15%
Indonesia	4%	8%	12%
Ethiopia	5%	4%	1%
Religion:			
Christian	60%	58%	58%
Muslim	9%	11%	15%
Buddhist	5%	6%	4%
Sikh	2%	1%	1%
Jewish	1%	1%	1%
Age:			
0-17	1%	1%	0%
18-29	32%	42%	31%
30-39	33%	30%	34%
40-49	23%	18%	24%
50-99	11%	9%	11%
Has dependents in U.S.	23%	25%	27%
Unrepresented	54%	46%	53%

either that they did prove entry within one year or that they did not but met an exception and filed within a reasonable period of time after the exception was no longer operative. Or they may have avoided removal from the United States by winning "withholding of removal" in immigration court. However, because the immigration courts do not keep statistics on how many cases involve deadline issues or how immigration judges rule on cases referred by DHS because of the deadline, we do not have sufficient information to report what happened to rejected cases after they were referred to immigration court. So we are left with the possibility that between 1998 and 2009, more than 15,000 asylum applications, involving more than 21,000 refugees, would have been granted but were instead rejected because of the one-year deadline.

6

Four Eras of Asylum Adjudication: Grant Rates Over Time

During the fourteen-year period we studied, DHS granted asylum to 45 percent of the 329,336 asylum seekers who applied on time or qualified for an exception to the one-year deadline.[1] Two factors should most strongly affect whether a particular applicant wins or loses. The first is whether the applicant's home country is a human rights abuser (very few British people win asylum, but many Ethiopians are successful). We explore in the next few pages the extent to which grant rates correlate with this factor. The second is whether the applicant testifies credibly and provides sufficient corroboration to show that she has a well-founded fear of persecution.[2] But our previous research showed that other factors may have also influenced the decisions of immigration judges deciding asylum cases.[3] Our ample database allowed us to explore the relationship between many of these factors and decisions by DHS asylum officers.

Because our database included hundreds of thousands of cases that were randomly assigned to asylum officers, we assumed that each officer received an approximately equal proportion of honest applicants and frauds, and applicants with solid corroboration and applicants who could not back up their stories. We would then expect significant variations in grant rates to be related to the prevalence of persecution in the applicants' countries, but in an adjudicatory system that evaluated only the applicant's eligibility for asylum, we would expect (or at least hope to find) no such correlation with other factors, such as whether the United States had recently been attacked by terrorists who had nothing to do with the applicant, or even her country of origin; whether the applicant had a visa when she entered the country; whether she had fled from her country alone or with a spouse or child; whether she applied while residing on the east or west coast of the United States; or whether the asylum officer had a law degree. Controlling, to the extent possible, for frequency of persecution in countries of origin, we explored whether these and other factors might also have influenced asylum officers' decisions.

This chapter and the four chapters that follow it examine in detail the relationship between those other factors and grant rates. This chapter focuses primarily on how the rate at which DHS granted asylum changed over time, with particular emphasis on the impact of four events: (1) the issuance of guidelines and the publicity associated with cases, in the late 1990s, that focused attention on violations in many countries of the human rights of women; (2) the imposition of the one-year filing deadline in April 1998; (3) the terrorist attacks on the United States in 2001; and (4) Congressional enactment, in 2005, of statutory provisions that tightened the evidentiary standards for grants of asylum. In chapter 7, we consider demographic and other characteristics of the applicants that have a statistically significant relationship with outcomes. In chapter 8, we look at how the region of the United States in which the applicant happened to have settled and from which he or she applied for asylum correlates with grant rates. In chapter 9, we report disparities in grant rates among individual asylum officers within the regional offices. Finally, in chapter 10, we examine the relationship between demographic characteristics of the asylum officers and their rates of granting asylum.

At first glance, it may appear that outcomes attributed to one variable (such as whether applicants entered with a visa or not) were actually caused by some other variable (such as whether the home countries of those applicants were or were not one of the worst abusers of human rights). Of course asylum applications may be approved for many reasons. We employed regression analysis to test whether or not the variables we discuss retain their explanatory power—their statistical significance—after controlling for the effects of other variables.

Fig. 6-1. Grant Rates by Fiscal Year

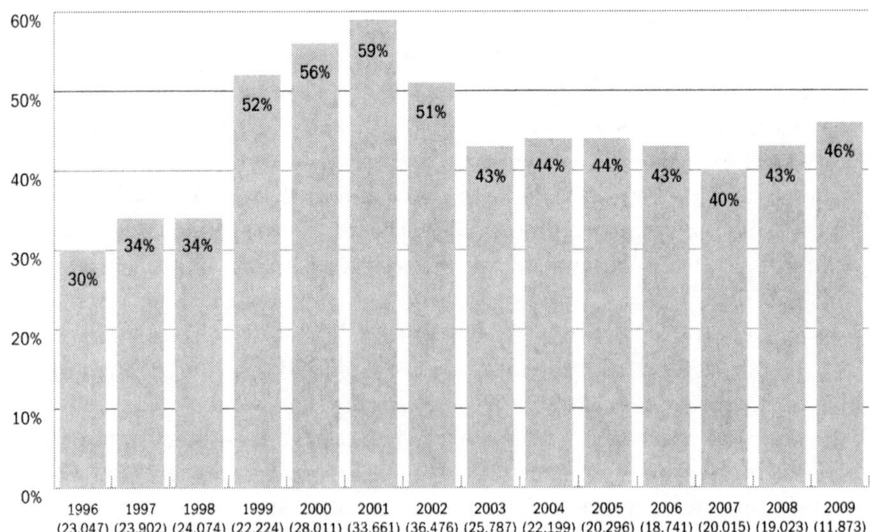

We describe the regression analyses we performed further in the Methodological Appendix.[4] In the text or in footnotes, we note the direction of each variable's effect holding other variables constant.[5] We also performed three-way (or more) cross-tabulations to evaluate the nature of variable relationships in the context of a detailed discussion of the socio-legal context. Chi-square tests were performed to test for the statistical significance of those bivariate relationships (which, in turn, were further subjected to multivariate regression).

The Four Asylum Eras

An initial examination of asylum grant rates over the time frame studied uncovers a few striking trends. Figure 6-1 lays out, for each fiscal year, the grant rates for cases decided in that year. [6] We see a steep increase (over 50 percent) between 1998 and 1999, then steady increases (5–10 percent) through 2001, followed by significant declines (15–20 percent) in 2002 and 2003, after which grant rates remain fairly even, between 40 and 45 percent.[7]

We categorized these trends into four periods of time, which we call "asylum eras," covered by our database.[8] These eras are identified in table 6-1:

Table 6-1. Eras of Asylum Adjudication, FY 1996–2009

Era	Explanation	Dates
1	From the beginning of our study until the one-year deadline became effective	October 1, 1995 - April 15, 1998
2	From the effective date of the one-year deadline until the terrorist attacks	April 16, 1998 - September 11, 2001
3	From the terrorist attacks until asylum officers had been trained to implement the credibility and corroboration requirements of the REAL ID Act	September 12, 2001 - June 30, 2006
4	From full implementation of the credibility and corroboration requirements of the REAL ID Act until the end of the study period	July 1, 2006–June 8, 2009

Note: The cutoff dates for each era refer to dates of adjudication, not dates on which an application was filed.

We selected the beginning and ending dates of these four periods for a reason. We wanted to determine whether changes in asylum grant rates were related to changes in laws, policies, or political events. We explored these three different types of events by creating time categories that reflect changes in federal statutes, DHS training and regulations, and the terrorist attacks of September 11, 2001.

Era 1

The asylum reforms promulgated by DHS in 1994, effective in January 1995, prevented applicants from obtaining U.S. work authorization until they won asylum, unless the government unduly delayed decisions on their applications. This reform aimed at curtailing fraud. If successful, the reform would result in lower proportions of nonmeritorious claims and therefore higher grant rates in the two or three years after 1995, as word spread through the immigrant community that fraudulent applications would no longer enable an applicant to obtain employment and send money to relatives back home.[9]

Era 2

New immigration legislation enacted in 1996 imposed the one-year filing deadline on asylum applicants who applied on or after April 16, 1998.[10] As we saw in chapter 3, some legislators believed that this law would deter fraudulent applications, although the deadline may in fact have operated primarily as a trap for unwary applicants who did not know of its existence or could not quickly obtain the evidence to prove their claims. In addition, the deadline excluded those applicants who could not prove their date of entry into the United States, and if DHS had adjudicated their cases on the merits, these applicants might also have had trouble providing proof that they had reason to fear persecution. Either way we should expect an increase in the grant rates of cases adjudicated on the merits (that is, those that met the deadline or qualified for an exception to the deadline) in the second era, compared to the first era.[11]

In the second era, we might also see the impact of the INS Asylum Gender Guidelines, which were issued in 1995. As asylum officers were trained on these guidelines, and as they assessed the impact of other developments in the late 1990s particularly affecting female applicants, asylum officers learned to better elucidate and assess gender-based asylum claims. We might see grant rates rise in general because of the deterrent effect of the new one-year deadline, and we might detect a more rapid rise in the grant rate for female applicants.

Also, the imposition of the deadline may have had the salutary effect of prompting some applicants to file cases sooner than they otherwise would have. As a result, during the second era asylum officers were hearing testimony from applicants whose memories of events were fresher, and who may have had better access to corroborating documentation, some of which tends to be destroyed or lost as years go by. These factors could contribute to higher grant rates as well.

Era 3

The September 11, 2001, terrorist attacks sent shock waves through the government and particularly the INS (the predecessor agency of DHS), because the federal government had permitted the terrorists to enter and remain in the United States. We would intuitively expect grant rates to fall between the second era and the third era as adjudicators became more leery of ruling in favor of applicants from countries in which anti-American terrorist groups operated, and perhaps from other countries as well. Moreover, it seems likely that the increased security check requirements in the wake of September 11 revealed additional information about applicants that was inconsistent with testimony offered in some cases, again leading to decreased grant rates.

Era 4

Four years later, the REAL ID Act codified adjudicators' authority to require corroborating evidence beyond the testimony of the asylum seeker and make credibility findings on the basis of immaterial inconsistencies. The act became effective in May 2005 and was fully implemented through asylum officer training by July 1, 2006. If the act significantly changed the behavior of asylum officers, we would expect grant rates to fall from the third era to the fourth era.

The data support all but one of these hypotheses. During the first era, grant rates rose, from 30 percent in FY 1996 to 34 percent in FY 1997 and FY 1998 (figure 6-1). When the second period began, grant rates rose again, from an average of 30 percent during the first era to 56 percent in the second era, as figure 6-2 demonstrates. In the wake of the September 11, 2001, terrorist attacks, grant rates dropped precipitously, from 56 percent to 46 percent. After full implementation of the REAL ID Act, grant rates fell slightly, but a breakdown of grant rates by fiscal year during the fourth era reveals that they recovered and were soon higher than the rate at which asylum was granted in the years immediately preceding the adoption of the REAL ID Act (figure 6-1).

The regression analyses confirmed that grant rates climbed from the first era to the second era, dropped after September 11, 2001, and remained fairly constant during the third and fourth eras. In contrast, however, to the grant rates reported in figure 6-2, when we controlled for the other variables in the model using regression analyses, there was little difference in grant rates among eras one, three, and four. In fact, two of the three regression analyses failed to confirm the statistical significance of grant rates among those three eras.[12] In other words, the grant rates in figure 6-2 show the rates at which officers granted asylum in the four eras, but other variables

Fig. 6-2. Grant Rates in the Four Asylum Eras

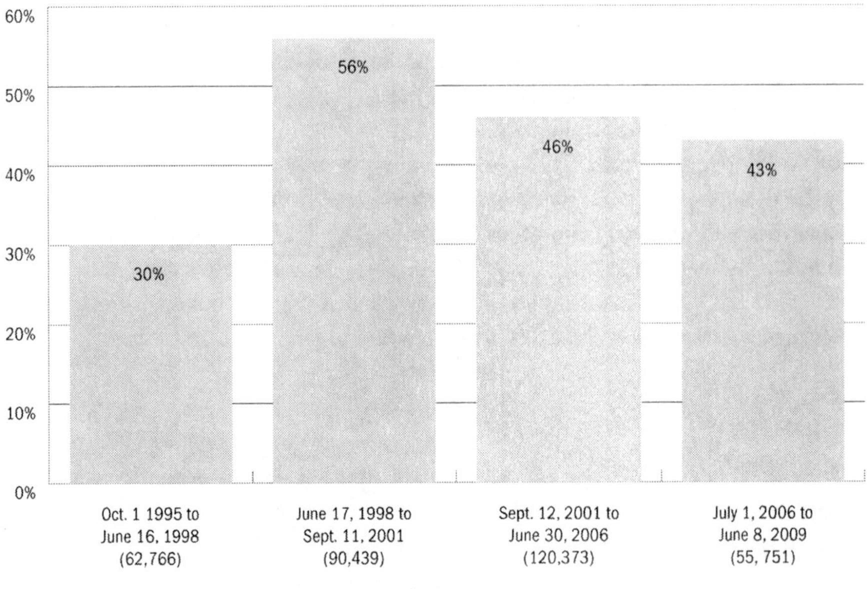

included in the regression models accounted for the lower grant rates in Era 1 compared to Eras 3 and 4.

Which variables, then, were responsible for the difference that we see in figure 6-2 among grant rates in the first, third, and fourth asylum eras? These changes in grant rates might be due to differences in the quality of asylum claims over time—for example, in some eras, there may have been more cases from countries with severe human rights abuses than in other eras. To explore this hypothesis, we used, as a measure of human rights abuse, the "Freedom in the World" scores assigned to countries by Freedom House.[13] This measure of repression enabled us to compare decisions involving applicants from severe human rights violators from one era to another, while also examining decisions in the cases of applicants whose countries were not as abusive.[14]

We first examined this variable in the aggregate to test its reliability. If DHS is adjudicating cases appropriately, we would observe higher grant rates for asylum seekers from countries deemed the most abusive by Freedom House. Indeed, that turned out to be the case: over the entire time frame studied, DHS granted asylum about one-third more often to claimants from the most abusive countries compared to claimants from countries with greater respect for human rights (53 percent compared with 40 percent).[15]

Fig. 6-3. Grant Rates by Asylum Era and Human Rights Assessment

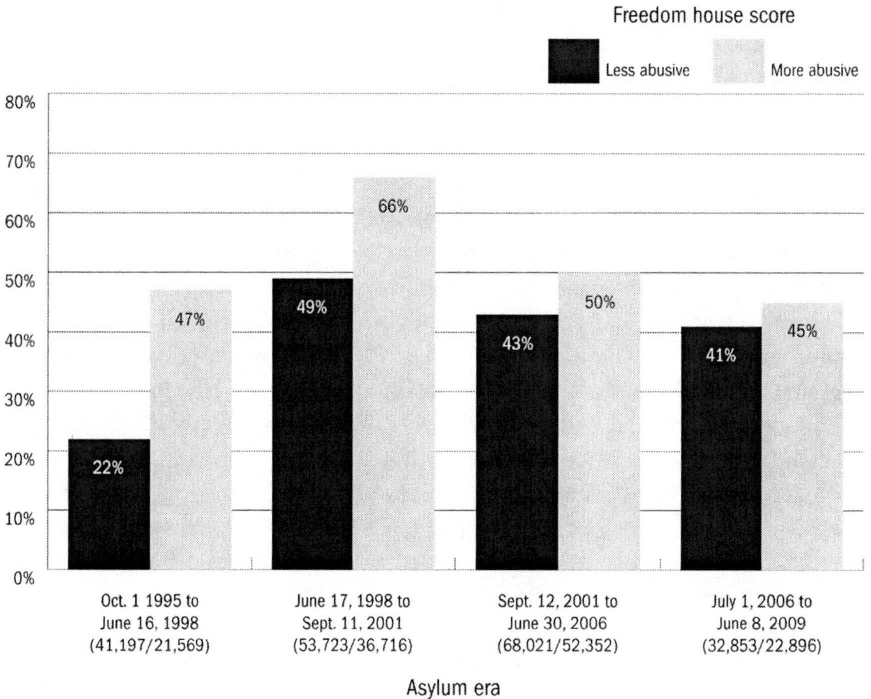

Note: In this figure, the mean Freedom House scores are the mean scores for each individual era, not for the entire period of the study.

Figure 6-3 reveals that, as we would expect, in every era, DHS granted asylum more often to applicants from countries with the worst human right abuses.[16] This tends to show that the asylum officers are doing their work conscientiously and accurately: on the whole, asylum adjudication is not random. But the figure also shows that external events, particularly the September 11 attacks, differentially affected applicants from countries with varying records of abuse. After the attacks, the grant rate fell more precipitously for applicants from countries with the worst human rights records. We were dismayed to discover that countries with a "more abusive" Freedom House score faced a 24 percent decrease in grant rates, as opposed to a 12 percent decrease for countries with a "less abusive" Freedom House score.

Some asylum officers suggested to us that the convergence in grant rates, after 2001, between those for applicants from more abusive and less abusive countries may have resulted from an influx of claims based on female genital mutilation and domestic violence. These grounds would not necessarily be captured by Freedom House scores, which focus on factors related to governmental and political persecution. However, because DHS does not code for female genital mutilation and domestic violence as a ground for asylum, we were not able to test this hypothesis.

The First Asylum Era: Employment Authorization Reforms

This first era immediately followed the major reforms that the Immigration and Naturalization Service initiated in 1995 to address large numbers of applications made by those seeking work authorization without valid asylum claims.[17] Prior to January 1, 1995, all applicants could obtain a work permit three months after filing an asylum claim.[18] Very large numbers of immigrants applied for asylum simply to obtain work permits. The incentives to do so were substantial, and the downsides minimal, particularly since unsuccessful affirmative asylum seekers were not automatically placed in removal proceedings in immigration court (as they are today). The large number of applicants resulted in a huge backlog of more than 425,000 claims by 1993.

The 1995 regulatory reforms decoupled work authorization from the asylum application, placed those without legal immigration status who did not receive asylum into removal proceedings, and committed to making most initial asylum decisions within sixty days. Importantly, INS increased the

Fig. 6-4. Asylum Claims Filed by Fiscal Year, 1991–1999

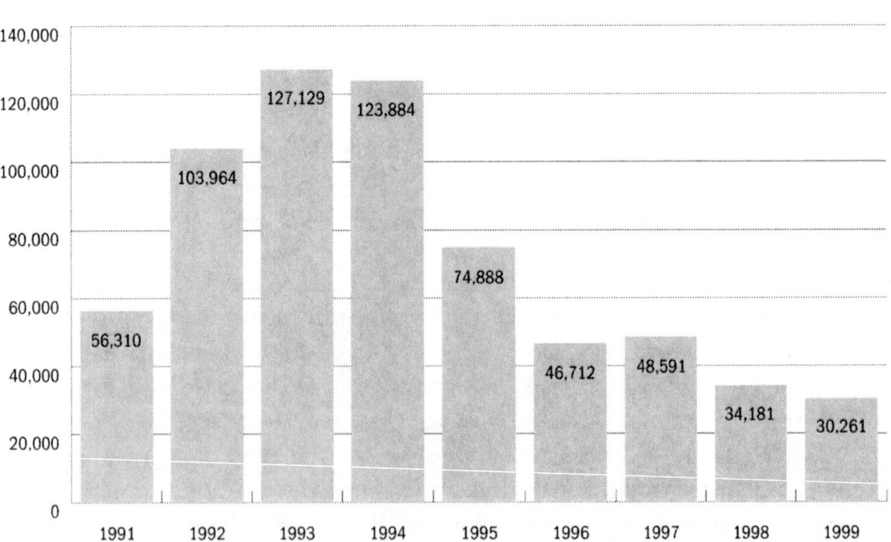

number of asylum officers and prioritized the new applications to be able to demonstrate to potential applicants that the government could handle all new claims in a timely fashion. Those without valid claims would not be able to hide in a backlog but would instead be referred to immigration court.

INS implemented these major reforms successfully. The number of asylum applications decreased significantly during the initial post-1995 reform years, from over 140,000 in each of FY 1993 and 1994 to about 30,000 in FY 1999. The decline did not all take place in the first year. As figure 6-4 shows, FY 1995 applications dropped to about 75,000 new claims, followed by 47,000 in FY 1996, 49,000 in FY 1997 and about 34,000 in FY 1998.[19] The number of claims declined during this period as asylum officers demonstrated the capacity to adjudicate most applications within sixty days of filing.

The numbers of asylum applicants declined beginning in FY 1995, and grant rates began to rise steadily in FY 1997. This suggests that applicants who in earlier years might have applied in order to receive work authorization learned, over a two-year period, that making an asylum claim would no longer provide this benefit.[20] As INS reported, this shift—declining absolute numbers of claims and, likely, nonmeritorious ones—resulted in grant rates that increased from approximately 15 percent of all cases filed in FY 1993 to 22 percent in FY 1996 and to 38 percent in FY 1999.[21] Our own data,

Fig. 6-5. Asylum Office Grant Rates, FY 1996–1999

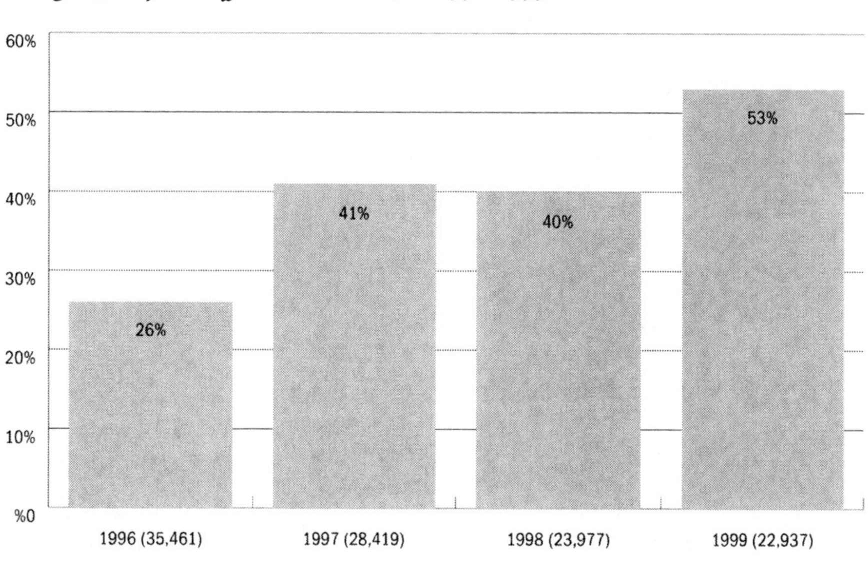

which begin only with cases filed in FY 1996, similarly show an increasing grant rate, although our percentages are higher than those reported by INS because the database on which figure 6-5 is based excludes cases of Mexican nationals, cases denied or referred because the applicant did not appear for an interview, and (after April 15, 1998) cases rejected because of the deadline.

The Second Asylum Era: The One-Year Filing Deadline and Increased Awareness of Gender-Related Human Rights Violations

The Effects of the Deadline

As discussed in extensive detail in chapters 3 through 5, the Illegal Immigration Reform and Immigrant Responsibility Act of 1996 created a one-year filing deadline for asylum seekers who applied on or after April 16, 1998. Figures 6-2 and 6-5 demonstrate the increase in grant rates beginning in FY 1999, after the implementation of the deadline.

What were the reasons for this increased grant rate? There are likely several. Remember that this database includes only asylum claims that were filed within one year of entry or met an exception to the one-year filing deadline. For the claims filed within a year, the evidence was fresher and therefore probably more compelling than claims filed later. Moreover, asylum officers may have perceived the applicants' claims to be more legitimate because they had voluntarily come forward to apply for asylum very soon after arriving in the United States. And if an asylum officer found that a claim met an exception to the deadline, she already believed the applicant to be credible with respect to the deadline, so was likely to also find the applicant credible with respect to the merits of the case.[22]

These hypotheses are supported by the particularly striking grant rate increases for asylum applicants who entered the United States without authorization. As figure 6-6 illustrates, from the first asylum era to the second, grant rates for unlawful entrants increased by 118 percent, in contrast to the grant rates for lawful entrants, which increased only by 42 percent.[23]

The Gender of the Applicant

In general, over the entire period of our study, DHS granted asylum about 11 percent more often to women than to men (48.1 percent compared with 43.2 percent grant rates for females and males, respectively).[24] But this aggregate difference hides an interesting trend over time. In the first asylum era, in FY 1996 and 1997, men and women won asylum at about the same rate. But in

Fig. 6-6. Grant Rates by Asylum Era and Status at Entry

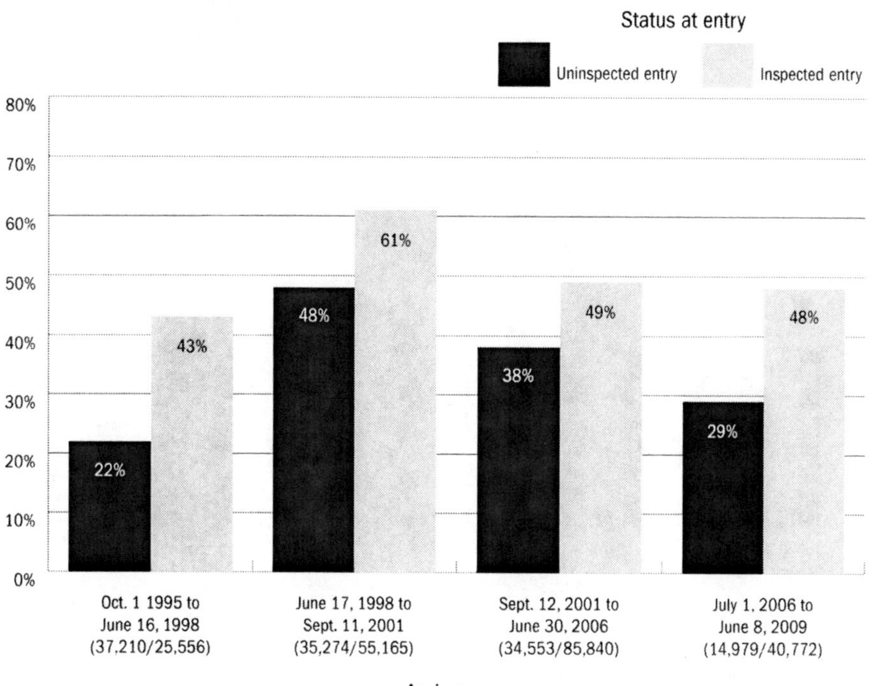

the second asylum era, in the late 1990s, women began to prevail at considerably higher rates than men.

When we break the shift in grant rates down into individual fiscal years, we see that in FY 1996 and 1997, women and men won asylum at the same or nearly the same rate.[25] Women first experienced higher grant rates in FY 1998, winning asylum at a rate 20 percent higher than men (38.1 percent compared to 31.8 percent). In FY 1999, women won asylum at a rate 14 percent higher than men, a trend that has persevered, as shown in figure 6-7.[26]

The most likely explanation for this shift in grant rates for women is that until the late 1990s, the Immigration and Naturalization Service (DHS's predecessor agency) did not give special training to asylum officers on the particular ways in which women are often persecuted, nor did officers receive training on how to address sensitive issues involving women, such as whether they had been raped. In May 1995, INS issued its Asylum Gender Guidelines,[27] on which officers were subsequently trained.[28]

Fig. 6-7. Grant Rate by Fiscal Year, by Gender of Applicant

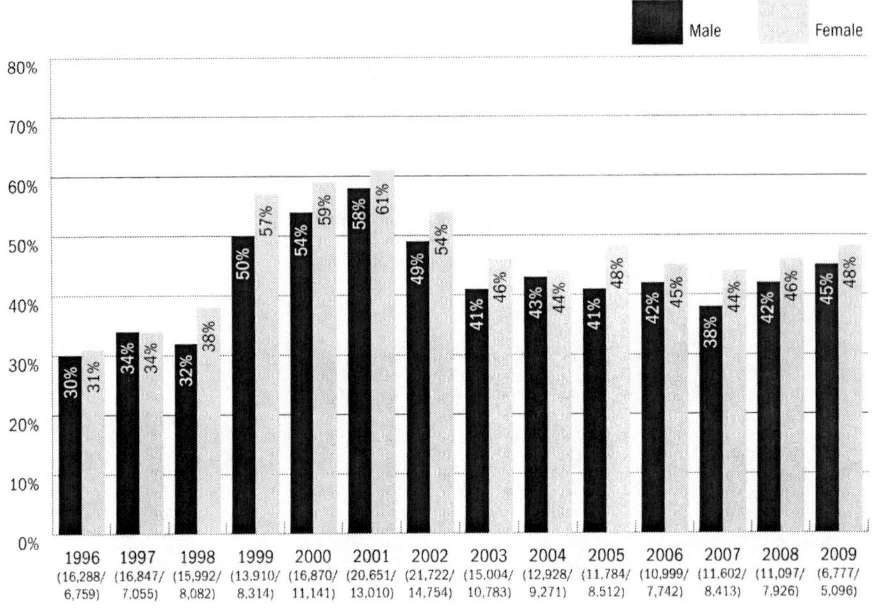

Moreover, three other events in the same time frame called attention to human rights violations directed at women, and in particular female asylum seekers. In the June 1996 *Kasinga* decision, the Board of Immigration Appeals extended asylum protection to specifically gender-based claims (in that case, female genital mutilation).[29] Later in 1996, Congress passed legislation deeming persons fleeing to avoid forced abortions and sterilizations to be refugees eligible for asylum.[30] And in 1999, a great deal of publicity was generated by the Board of Immigration Appeals' rejection of an asylum application by a woman who had fled from violence perpetrated by her abusive husband, after the Guatemalan police had refused to protect her.[31]

It is not possible to know with exactitude how each of these four developments affected the grant rate for women, because DHS's database does not include a code to distinguish gender-based asylum claims from other types of claims.[32] The combination of these developments, however, apparently called asylum officers' attention to human rights abuses of women and changed how they looked at gender-based claims. One officer told us, as an explanation of why women won at higher rates than men after 1997,

> In 1998, there was a tremendous focus on training on gender cases, at weekly caselaw training. Then there was *Kasinga* in 1996, the Karen Musalo paper on developing jurisprudence in gender-based claims (referenced in the lesson plan), which was incorporated into training, and constantly evolving . . . caselaw from that point on.

Another said,

> We worked out that [resistance to domestic violence was] a political opinion and decided that saying "don't treat me that way" was the expression of a political opinion, and even [just] leaving the relationship was a huge statement.

Yet another who had become a supervisor stated, perhaps more bluntly,

> When I was interviewing and I had a woman from Afghanistan, I was going to grant her even if her testimony completely fell apart, because you just know about what it's like to be female in those countries.

The fact that the grant rate for women was lower before FY 1998 than after that date suggests that female applicants had been persecuted at a greater rate than male applicants all along, but that the officers may not have fully recognized or elicited information about gender-related persecution until these four developments occurred. If this hypothesis is correct, it is a textbook example of how changes in the law (including, particularly, changes in informal agency guidelines) can result in changes in adjudication outcomes.

The Third Asylum Era: The Impact of the Terrorist Attacks of September 11, 2001

As figure 6-1 shows, in the aftermath of the September 11 terrorist attacks, asylum grant rates fell from 59 percent in FY 2001, which ended a few days after the attacks, to 43 percent just two years later.[33] The data reveal that this change in grant rates was not caused by a change in personnel. In FY 2003, asylum officers who decided cases before September 11, 2001, granted asylum at a rate of 42.9 percent; those who began work after the attacks granted at essentially the same rate (42.7 percent).[34]

Applicants from certain countries with very poor human rights records experienced substantial declines in their grant rates immediately after the September 11 attacks. Figure 6-8 sets out the grant rates for the period before

Fig. 6-8. Decrease in Grant Rates after Terrorist Attacks, for Nationals of Selected Countries with High Freedom House Scores

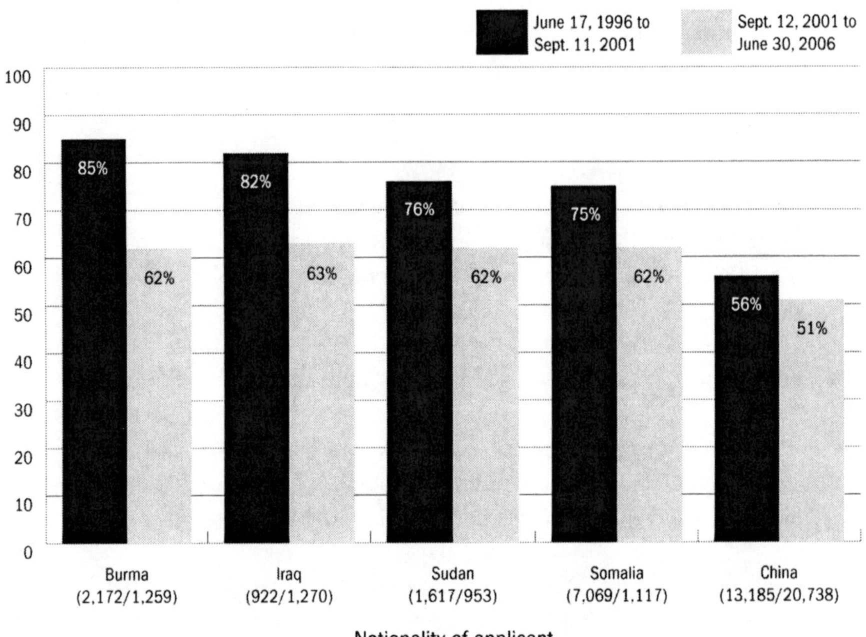

Note: The numbers of cases in parentheses indicate the numbers of cases decided in Era 2 and Era 3.

and after the attacks for five of the countries determined by Freedom House to have among the most abusive governments in the world during the entire time frame studied.[35] Chinese asylum seekers faced a drop of only 9 percent after the attacks. But during the era immediately following 9/11, DHS granted asylum 27 percent less often to Burmese, 23 percent less often to Iraqis, 18 percent less often to Sudanese, and 17 percent less often to Somalis. Though the degree to which these countries violated human rights did not change, the rate of asylum for applicants from these nations dropped precipitously.

To learn more about this striking decline, DHS asked asylum officers the following question in its 2011 survey: "In the first years after the September 11th terrorist attack, asylum grant rates came down significantly. Indicate the two most important reasons why you think this happened."[36]

The reason given most often for this drop in grant rates was that "security check requirements increased, delaying many approvals until later years and providing officers with negative information to which they did not previously have access."[37] While delays should not per se affect the grant rate (and we can see from figure 6-2 that the grant rate did not recover when the delayed cases were eventually decided), negative information certainly could. Several officers provided brief explanations about this and other reasons for the decline:

> The increase and effectiveness of security checks enabled the AOs to have access to adverse entry and other helpful information for proper adjudications, specifically related to the one-year deadline rule, fraud and other security related issues.

In particular, some of the asylum officers we interviewed pointed out that after the attacks, other government agencies began to cooperate more with DHS, providing data that could cause applications to be rejected. For example, asylum officers were able to obtain fingerprint data showing that certain applicants had made prior attempts to obtain a visa or to enter the United States, contrary to information that they supplied in their asylum applications. One officer told us that although applicants from Colombia were obviously unconnected with Al Qaeda terrorists, the data that became available to asylum officers revealed a considerable amount of fraud in cases filed by Colombian applicants.

Another factor probably influenced the post-9/11 drop in the grant rate more strongly than increased security checks. As one officer observed in response to the survey, "Asylum officers were afraid of granting potential terrorists." Another officer noted that "it became more acceptable to supervisors at all levels and asylum officers to refer cases because of excessive concerns of fraud and terrorism." A third said,

> I think people were looking for potential terrorists everywhere. I don't know if that means that humanity comes into play in a way that it shouldn't but you do have to be careful. It may be that some things were sent to court to let the IJ determineif there were questions about credibility at that time because people might have given extra scrutiny to identity.

Corroborating this account, a senior DHS official told us that "nobody wanted to approve someone who later turned out to commit a terrorist act." (These remarks are consistent with the observation of Wendy White, director of the Board of International Scientific Organizations, that, after 9/11, approving a visa for a prospective U.S. visitor who later turned out to be a terrorist would likely be a "career-ending" move for a State Department consular officer, a reality that caused consular officials to become much more cautious about granting visas in the years immediately after the attacks.)[38]

One asylum officer explained:

> Asylum officers became a little more observant about certain things, maybe less willing to accept certain discrepancies. At SAO [supervisory asylum officer] training, one of the general counsels heading one of the national security teams presented a new policy that seemed to run contrary to the basic asylum training. [This policy was essentially,] "Where there are inconsistencies and doubts, refer the case to the judge, and let the judge weed it out." The message changed when JTTF [the Joint Terrorism Task Force] came on board and FDNS [the Fraud Detection and National Security program] started.

Figure 6-1 shows that the decline in grant rates did not take place instantly in FY 2002, which began just days after the attacks; there was just as large a drop in the following year, which ran from October 2002 through September 2003. We wondered what happened in the months following the attacks that could have continued the impact on asylum officers of the increased concern about terrorism. One answer may be that, as a senior asylum office official told us, "it took a couple of years for the asylum officers to realize how much granting asylum to a terrorist could damage their careers." What focused their minds was what became known within the asylum office as the "massacre" of key employees. The director of the INS Office of International Affairs, who had responsibility for the asylum office among other duties, was transferred out of his position immediately after his office mailed, care of a flight school in Florida, a visa renewal to the late Mohamed Atta, one of the suicide pilots in the 9/11 attacks. Other senior government officials also lost their jobs amid congressional hearings into the agency's apparently insufficient attention to national security.[39]

Also, Commissioner Ziglar sent out what became known as the "zero tolerance" memo:

> Effective immediately, I am implementing a zero tolerance policy with regard to INS employees who fail to abide by Headquarters-issued policy and field instructions. I would like to make it clear that disregarding field guidance or other INS policy will not be tolerated. The days of looking the other way are over. . . . Individuals who fail to abide by issued field guidance or other INS policy will be disciplined appropriately.[40]

We understand that some officers interpreted this memo to mean that referrals were a lot less risky than grants.

Another reason for the decline, even for applicants with no possible connection with terrorism, was simply that it took time for asylum officers to evaluate the additional security data that became available to them, but they were not given additional time (beyond the average of four hours per case) to process each application.[41] One asylum officer told us that as a result, officers had less time to research human rights conditions in applicants' countries and had to devote less time to the personal interview with each applicant. Thus officers may have had somewhat less ability to adduce evidence supporting the applicant's claim and may have been more inclined to refer the case to immigration court, leaving it to someone else to take the time for a thorough exploration of the merits of a case.

Fifteen officers who responded to DHS's survey said that legal changes making asylum more difficult to obtain accounted for the most or second most important reason for the decline in grant rates. One major change brought about by the USA Patriot Act involved an expansion of the bar to asylum in connection with the provision of material support for terrorist activities.[42] But we doubt that this change had an immediate effect on DHS asylum adjudications. The bar did not immediately cause asylum officers to turn down applications. Instead, the agency placed potentially affected asylum applications on hold for a number of years, so cases affected by this bar were not referred to immigration court and did not affect the statistics during the years immediately after law was passed. On the other hand, another change in the law (at the beginning of 2003) abolished the Immigration and Naturalization Service and transferred its functions to DHS. It is possible that the change of departments itself conveyed to asylum officers the message that they should be more concerned with terrorism than before.

The Fourth Asylum Era: The Credibility and Corroboration Requirements of the REAL ID Act

In 2005, Congress passed the REAL ID Act, authorizing asylum officers to refer cases based on immaterial inconsistencies in testimony or the absence of corroborating documentation in cases filed after the Act was passed.[43] We wanted to examine whether these more arduous evidentiary requirements contributed to lower grant rates. We learned from DHS officials that officers were trained on how to implement this law during 2006, and they advised us to use July 1, 2006, as the date when this law was first applied by most of the asylum officers.

Figure 6-2 shows only a slight decline in grant rates in this fourth, post-REAL ID era, and figure 6-1 suggests that by FY 2009, grant rates may have exceeded those of the period immediately before the REAL ID Act was passed. In the aggregate, then, it appears that the REAL ID Act may not have contributed to lower grant rates. In most parts of the country, the legislation largely codified long-established case law regarding when asylum officers could require corroboration beyond the applicant's testimony and how they can make credibility determinations.[44]

But the REAL ID Act made serious changes to the law in two asylum office regions, Los Angeles and San Francisco, both of which fall under the jurisdiction of the Ninth Circuit Court of Appeals. The case law in the Ninth Circuit with respect to credibility and corroboration was considerably more generous to the asylum applicant than the jurisprudence in other parts of the country.[45] The REAL ID Act appears to have been intended to overturn that case law,[46] so we further explored asylum officer decisions in the Ninth Circuit only.

When we break out the third and fourth eras by fiscal year, we do not see a decline in grant rates in the Ninth Circuit in the wake of the REAL ID Act. Grant rates in the Los Angeles and San Francisco offices dropped steadily from FY 2001 through FY 2005. But in FY 2006, just after the passage of the REAL ID Act and during which asylum officers were trained on the implementation of the Act, grant rates began to rise again. Grant rates

Fig. 6-9. Grant Rates by Fiscal Year, Los Angeles and San Francisco Asylum Offices

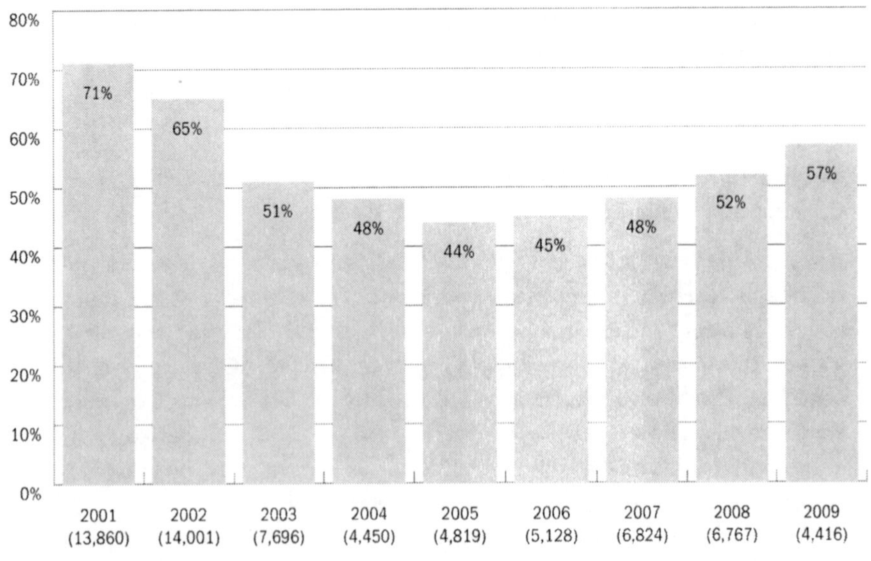

rose consistently, increasing by nearly 30 percent between FY 2006 and FY 2009 (figure 6-9).[47]

Grant rates declined, overall, only from 46 percent to 43 percent between the third and fourth eras (figure 6-2). For applicants who entered the United States with visas, grant rates remained fairly constant between these two eras (figure 6-6). However, for asylum applicants who entered without inspection, grant rates dropped by 24 percent in the era after the implementation of the REAL ID Act.[48] It may be that asylum seekers who entered without inspection had fewer resources than those who entered with inspection and may therefore have had a harder time obtaining the necessary corroboration. Asylum officers may also have perceived uninspected entrants to be less credible than applicants who presented documents to border officials.

However, when we break the grant rates out by fiscal year during the fourth era (figure 6-10), we see that the decline in grant rates in the wake of the REAL ID act's implementation did not last for long even for unlawful entrants.[49] Although grant rates to asylum applicants who entered without inspection dropped by nearly 30 percent from FY 2005 to FY 2007, grant

Fig. 6-10. Grant Rates by Fiscal Year and Status at Entry

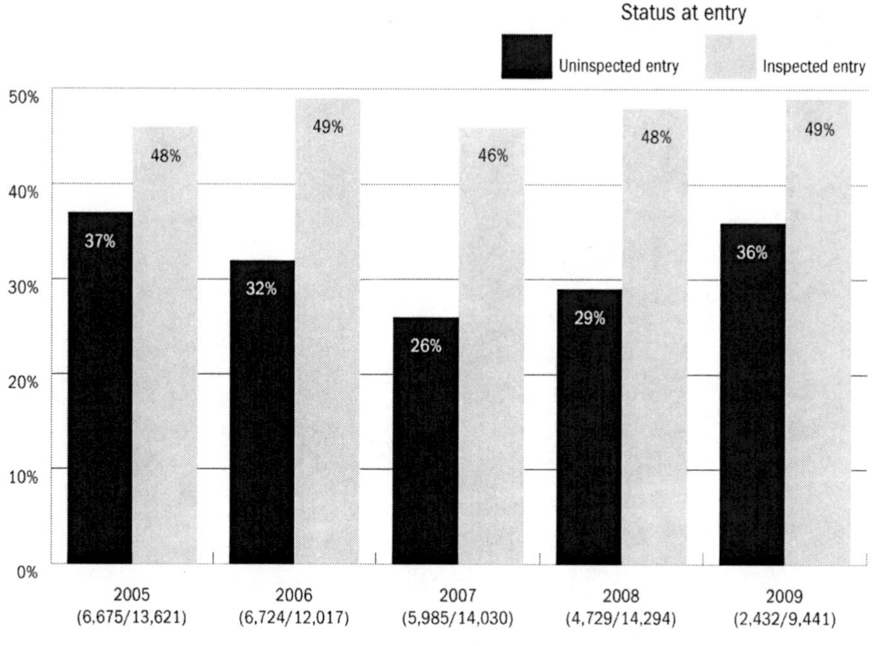

rates for those entrants then increased in FY 2008 and again in FY 2009, ultimately reaching a rate similar to that for FY 2006.

In this chapter, we have considered the relationship between grant rates and changes over time, accounting for different degrees of respect for human rights in various countries. We focused on changes over time in asylum officer training (particularly regarding gender-related persecution), the legal framework, and the nation's response to terrorist attacks. In the next chapter, we turn to the relationship between asylum officers' perceptions of particular categories of applicants and grant rates. It should not matter to the legal analysis of an asylum claim whether an applicant fled with or without dependents, entered with a visa or fled without one, or had a legal representative. But do these facts matter in practical effect?

7

Perceptions about the Asylum Seekers

In chapter 6, we explored asylum adjudication over time, investigating the relationship between grant rates and changes in laws, policies, and politics. In this chapter, we shift our focus to examine variables that may have shaped asylum officers' perceptions of the asylum seekers. We start by discussing the ways in which two sociological characteristics of the applicants—their dependents and their genders—correlated with grant rates. We then look at two factors relating to the asylum process—status at entry and representation—and their relationships with grant rates.

Dependents

DHS granted asylum 18 percent more often (52 percent compared to 44 percent) to asylum seekers who applied with at least one dependent present in the United States than to those who applied without any such dependents. The regression analyses confirm that, even with all other variables held constant, applicants' dependents correlated with higher grant rates.

Why did DHS grant asylum more often to applicants with dependents? In our book *Refugee Roulette*, we observed a similar phenomenon in immigration court and speculated that sympathy for spouses and parents might play a role:

> It could be that asylum seekers who bring children or a spouse appear more credible, or that immigration judges are more sympathetic to asylum seekers who have nuclear family members to protect.[1]

Sympathies may similarly have affected the judgments of asylum officers, who met the applicants (and sometimes any accompanying family members) and learned their family histories and structures. In addition, in some situations, accompanying family members suffered persecution or observed the persecution of the principal applicant. Family members' testimony and affidavits sometimes provided corroborating evidence of actual or feared persecution.

The asylum officers with whom we spoke corroborated our hypothesis that they had more sympathy for applicants with dependents than for those who did not have dependents. One of them told us, "You have to ID [personally see] dependents. Seeing family members, it can be very persuasive if they have a cute son or daughter. I don't know how much of the decision is informed by that." Another officer put it this way:

> To grant entire families is certainly more work [but] when you see a person with their family, their wife and their children, generally you would think that the person is more stable, perhaps more honest, I don't know why. [When you judge whether a person is genuinely a refugee] it should be the law, it should be the facts [that influence your decision] but if we use this idea that males from Muslim countries are more likely to be terrorists, I'm going to look at that claim more closely, and if there are things that are wrong with it I'll find them. . . . [It's a matter of] perceptions of the applicant before you. . . . A person who has their spouse and children, one thinks, well, this is a person who is responsible and, in discretion, worthy of an asylum grant.

Of course, it could be that applicants with dependents had more at stake, so spent more time and effort on their applications. As one officer said:

> The claims, maybe it's how they presented their claim. As [applicants with dependents] fled, they made sure they had their ducks in a row so they met their burden. They had children so they had more at stake maybe? They all have a lot at stake, but if you're protecting your dependents you'd want to have all your ducks in a row.

Another asylum officer suggested two additional reasons why those with dependents won more often. First, a spouse and children above a certain age can be questioned by the asylum officer, and testimony consistent with that of the principal applicant adds credibility to the claim of that applicant. Second, asylum officers might wonder why persons who were really at risk of persecution would leave their families behind. Families are in fact often left behind because they could not obtain exit visas from persecuting governments; because the U.S. consulate would not give them visas; or because the principal victim of persecution could not afford travel expenses for his or her entire family.

And of course, the constraints of the process may have had an impact. An asylum officer told us:

> Applicants with dependents take longer to process during the pre-interview review. If the kids are over fourteen and a husband or wife is involved, the asylum officer has to run the whole battery of background checks on those

> individuals and that takes time – time away from the interview. Whenever somebody on my team has a family pack of four, he's usually starting the interview late or if he's starting it on time he's likely to be less prepared.[2]

In other words, officers who had less time to interview may have been more likely to rely on their instincts and sympathies and may have spent less time rigorously assessing the facts of the case.[3]

With respect to claimants from Europe and Central Asia, DHS granted asylum to those without dependents at or at about the same rates as those with dependents.[4] The greatest grant rate differential concerned those from Latin America/Caribbean, where DHS granted asylum about 55 percent more often to claimants with dependents than to those filing alone.[5]

As figure 7-1 shows, applicants from certain Central American and Caribbean countries in this region may have contributed particularly to this difference.[6] DHS granted asylum 81 percent more often to Guatemalans, 76 percent more often to Salvadorans, and 47 percent more often to Haitians with

Fig. 7-1. Grant Rates for Applicants with and without Dependents from Selected Countries

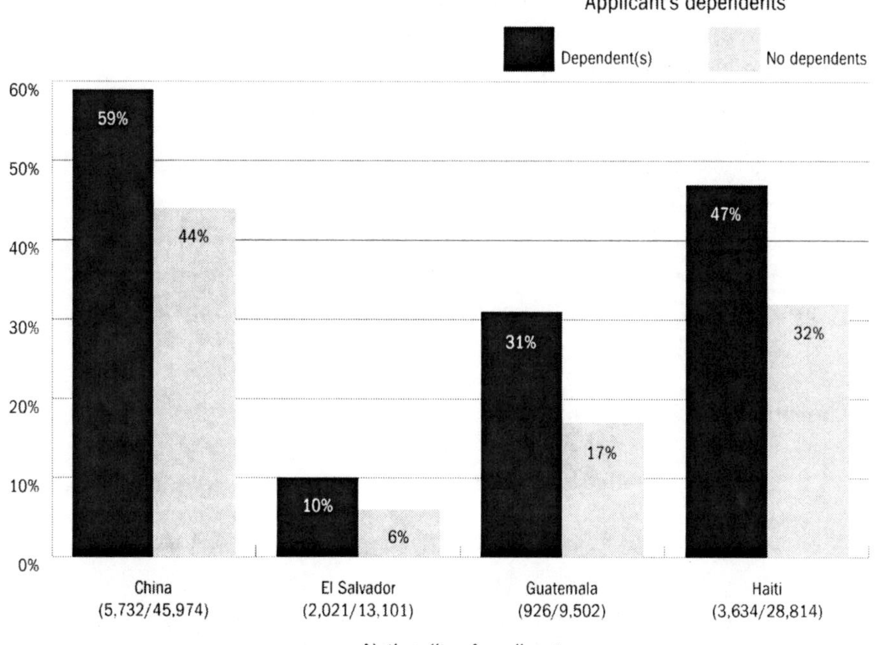

dependents than to those filing by themselves. Outside of Latin America/Caribbean, China also stood out as a nationality where DHS granted asylum considerably more often than the overall average to applicants with dependents. DHS granted asylum 33 percent more often to Chinese applicants with dependents as opposed to those filing alone.

Whatever factors led to higher grant rates in general for applicants who arrived with dependents may have been especially significant for applicants from these countries. For Chinese applicants in particular, coercive population control claims may have been better received where one spouse had not left the other spouse and children back in China. Both credibility and sympathy may have affected Haitian adjudications of applicants with dependents because of asylum officers' knowledge that during most of the study period, Haiti was the most impoverished and poorly governed country in the Western hemisphere.[7]

Gender

We have already seen in chapter 6 that the grant rate for women exceeded the grant rate for men, possibly because asylum officers were trained in recognizing gender-based persecution and in sensitively interviewing female applicants who may have experienced such persecution.[8] The gender differential may also have resulted from officers' perceptions that women were more credible, or at least more sympathetic.

One asylum officer told us:

> One of the things that we see day in and day out with female applicants is that they much more often cry in our offices. Women claim rape . . . and they burst into tears and I think that affects the emotions of adjudicators sometimes. I know this may not sound like a good basis but demeanor and behavior in the course of the interview have some influence on the person on the other side of the desk.

Similarly, a supervisory officer said:

> Because I do have officers that get so caught up in the emotion of the case . . . Sometimes you just have to separate yourself, because we've seen it all as supervisors, and as a supervisor I just want to see it in the record and if it's not in the record, I kick it back to the officer and I ask them—you know, this isn't really that developed, I don't see much detail about this person's role and this particular human rights organization. And what I get

back from the officer is, oh my goodness, if you could have just seen this person, she was so credible, she was crying about this.

Another asylum officer suggested that it was supervisors who favored women:

Almost all of my managers were women, showing deference to women.[9]

We broke apart the gender data, investigating whether these female applicants had dependents with them in the United States and whether their religion may have further impacted asylum officers' perceptions of them.

Gender and Dependents

The gender grant rate differential disappeared when we looked at applicants with dependents. Female and male asylum seekers with dependents had nearly identical grant rates: 51.6 percent for males and 51.7 percent for women.[10] That means that the gender grant rate differential was driven by asylum seekers without dependents. For applicants without dependents, the female grant rate (47.1 percent) was 13 percent higher than the male grant rate (41.7 percent).[11]

Perhaps men who arrived alone in the United States were more often perceived to be economic migrants than women who arrived alone. In fact, one asylum officer told us that "single men may be seen as possible dangers to society. Females generally don't belong to the military or join terroristic groups or be involved in violent activity." That officer also noted that men without dependents were more likely than women without dependents to be perceived as people seeking better economic opportunity rather than fleeing from persecution. "Men are the ones who are more likely to be here to earn money . . . whereas a woman who has left her family behind, maybe there is something there." Men with dependents were also somewhat older than men without dependents and may therefore have been thought less likely to be economic migrants.[12] Another officer pointed out that women who are victimized by domestic violence in Central America were often forced to leave their children behind when they escaped by the dangerous route across the Mexican border, so their arrival without their children was unlikely to raise suspicions.

Gender and Religion

As previously noted, our data concerning the religion of the applicants is not as robust as most of the information collected by DHS, since 23 percent of

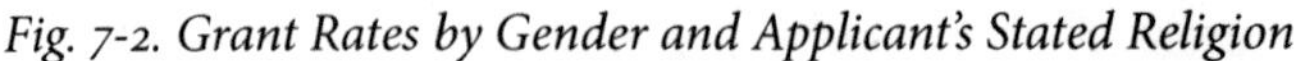

Fig. 7-2. Grant Rates by Gender and Applicant's Stated Religion

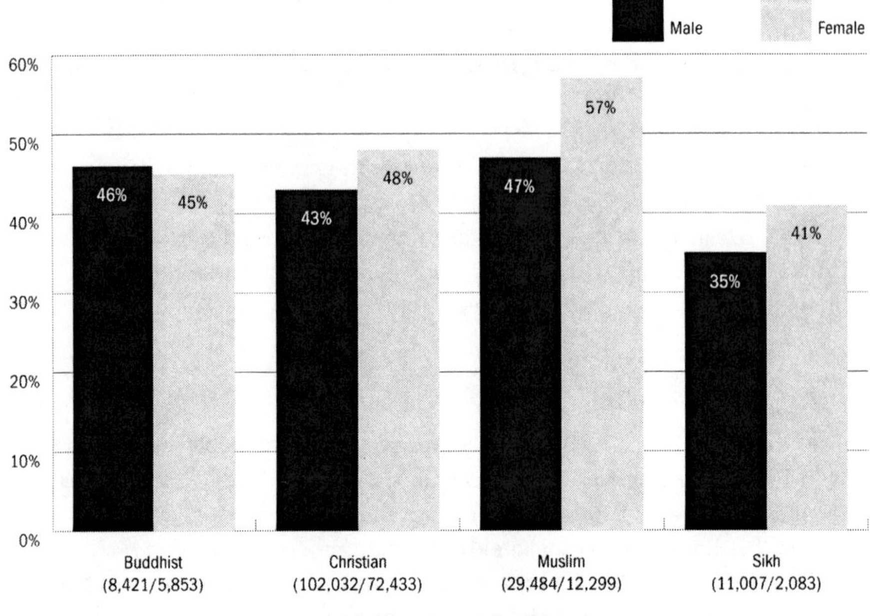

applicants did not indicate any relationship with a religion. We do not know whether that means they did not identify with a religion or they simply did not provide that information on their asylum applications.[13]

With that caveat in mind, we note that DHS granted asylum at nearly the same rate to male and female asylum seekers who identified themselves as Buddhists, and at somewhat similar rates to male and female Christians and Sikhs. But as figure 7-2 shows, DHS granted asylum 21 percent more often to females who self-identified as Muslim than to males who self-identified as Muslim (57 percent versus 47 percent).[14]

Some of the asylum officers with whom we spoke had no hesitation in explaining the higher grant rate for women who self-identified as Muslim, but they had two different theories. One said that "in these countries, military service is almost obligatory. And I hate to say this, but women may be seen as not as potentially dangerous." Other officers put it in terms of the perception that women in countries such as Pakistan and Bangladesh were highly likely to have been abused. One offered, "these results probably have to do with honor killings and more restrictive conditions for women being more prevalent in Muslim countries." Another suggested, "it may be a perception on the part of asylum officers. . . that women in Muslim families have much less independence and freedom to decide than in Christian countries."

We found that among the regions of the world, South Asia and Sub-Saharan Africa contributed the most to the greater gender gap among applicants who identified themselves as Muslim.[15] The grant rate for female applicants from South Asia who identified as Muslim was 60 percent, compared to 42 percent for males who identified as Muslim from the region.[16] Among sub-Saharan African applicants who identified as Muslim, females won asylum at a rate of 57 percent while males won at a rate of 43 percent.[17] In contrast, the grant rates for male and female applicants who self-identified as Muslim from North Africa and the Middle East were virtually identical: 74 percent to 76 percent.[18]

We can't be certain of the reason for the large gender gap among asylum seekers who identified as Muslims from South Asia and sub-Saharan Africa, but we suspect that these figures reflect a considerable degree of gender-based violence in the countries from which these refugees fled. Among such women are those who do not accept the mores (including forced marriages and genital cutting) of certain social, ethnic, and religious groups within these countries and have been persecuted or fear persecution in connection with their behavior challenging those mores.

But this does not explain the curious result that male and female applicants from North Africa and the Middle East who identified as Muslim had very similar grant rates. While gender-based persecution is prevalent in that region, nearly 50 percent of those applicants were from Iraq, which also suffered significant political persecution during the time frame studied. This might explain the higher grant rates for male applicants from that region. Further research into particular human rights violations in the countries within these regions could shed light on the reasons for greater differentials in some regions than in others.

Status at Entry

Over time, lawful entrants (those arriving with visas) have increasingly constituted a larger percentage of the total asylum applicant pool. In FY 1997, asylum seekers were evenly divided between lawful and unlawful entrants. By FY 2001, lawful entrants made up about two-thirds of the total number of claimants. As of FY 2009, lawful entrants were about 70 percent of all applicants and about 80 percent of the applicants who filed on time or were found eligible for an exception to the deadline.

The dramatic decrease over time in the number of asylum applicants who entered improperly is probably a testament to the significant border control measures put in place by the administrations of Presidents Bill Clinton and George W. Bush. During the period covered by our study, the U.S. government put major funding into a range of border control measures, from personnel to equipment and fences, and the cost of smuggling has increased significantly.[19] In addition, it is likely that fewer people were able to enter the United States with false documents, thanks to the embedding of electronic information in the passports of many countries and the training of airport and security personnel at transit points in Europe.[20]

Under the Refugee Act, eligibility for asylum does not depend on whether the applicant entered the United States lawfully or by evading a border crossing, or by using false travel documents. The United Nations Convention Relating to the Status of Refugees, which the Refugee Act aims to implement, specifically notes that refugees should not be penalized for entering without valid papers as long as they have good reasons for lacking papers and present themselves to immigration authorities promptly.[21] So in theory, the grant rates for inspected and uninspected applicants should be about the same, particularly given that the applicants in the database used in this chapter met the one-year filing deadline or an exception thereto. As one asylum officer put it to us, "If an asylum officer is affected in his or her decisions by whether or not the person entered legally, that person should not be an asylum officer."

Nevertheless, among applicants who were timely or who qualified for an exception to the deadline, DHS granted asylum about 45 percent more often to those asylum seekers who entered with inspection. Inspected entrants gained asylum 51 percent of the time compared to 35 percent for those who entered without inspection.[22]

Some of the difference is readily understandable. The law permits the State Department to grant tourist, business, and student visas only to people who persuade American consular officers that they do not intend to move permanently to the United States. As a practical matter, this means that the department grants those visas to persons who are established enough in their own countries, and who have sufficient funds for return tickets, to be likely to return home at the end of their visit to the United States. Applicants who arrive with visas are, by and large, wealthier and more educated than those who come without visas.

One reason, then, for the higher grant rate for persons who were wealthier and better educated (and therefore more likely to have received a visa) is that officers perceived that they were more likely to have been persecuted or to be at risk of persecution. As one officer put it to us, "The higher your education, the more likely you are to be involved in politics at least at a level that would make you susceptible to persecution. You are more likely to be a threat to the status quo."

In addition, better-educated applicants were more likely to be able to explain their stories articulately. An asylum officer told us

> It's not that they did or did not have a better claim, but they were better able to present it. . . . Many times [education] does make a difference because [those who lack education] don't know what they experienced [or] why they experienced it. An educated person will be able to go behind things . . . . An uneducated person will just say "I had problems," and [some officers] don't investigate as much because it's the applicant's burden of proof.

Moreover, asylum officers knew much more about inspected entrants because they had online access to their visa applications and to information that they told the consular officers. They could at least determine whether the identity information presented to them dovetailed with what the applicant told a consular officer, whereas there is no State Department "track record" on an uninspected applicant, whose very identity may be in question.

As one officer explained:

> If you have a B-2 visa, you can go to the Consular Consolidated Database,[23] you can see what the individual told the State Department, whereas somebody who [entered without inspection], you don't get anything from the State Department and you think, "How can I trust this person?"

Status at Entry and Region of Origin

Our data allowed us to further explore the source of the substantial discrepancy in grant rates between inspected and uninspected applicants. Much of it may be attributable to claims from nationals of countries near the United States, in the Caribbean and Latin America. Of the 8,716 Haitians who entered the United States with visas, 47 percent won asylum, but of the 23,732 Haitians who entered without presenting themselves at a border, only 29 percent were granted asylum. And among the 1,263 Salvadoran nationals who entered the United States with visas, 11 percent won asylum, but of the 13,859 Salvadorans who crossed into the United States without inspection, only 6 percent were granted asylum. Chinese claims also accounted for a large part of the difference. Fifty-five percent of the Chinese who entered with visas won asylum, compared to only 28 percent of the Chinese who entered without inspection (including many who were conveyed by smugglers and were likely economic migrants). If we remove from the database all applicants from the Caribbean, Latin America, and China, the rate at which DHS granted asylum to inspected and uninspected entrants is exactly the same: 50 percent for each group.[24]

The grant rate gap for natives of the Caribbean, Latin America, and China was huge: the rate was 24 percent for unlawful entrants and 52 percent for lawful entrants. How can this differential treatment be explained? In the case of China, many of the unlawful entrants were undoubtedly correctly identified by asylum officers as economic migrants who had been smuggled into the United States by professionals and armed with boilerplate asylum applications. The differential for Caribbean and Latin American applicants is more difficult to explain.

As we have suggested elsewhere, perhaps asylum officers attributed greater credibility to those who entered lawfully compared to those who enter without inspection. Some may have considered the very act of "sneaking in" as subterfuge rather than an act of someone who is desperate. This may have been particularly true when asylum officers had some doubt about an uninspected applicant's explanation of how he or she got to the United States (a part of the story that applicants may fabricate to protect the identity of smugglers who helped them or other people who entered with them). As one asylum officer said,

> Just because you don't find the manner of entry credible doesn't mean you can taint the claim with that, but in reality there are a lot of asylum officers who feel that "this person is not being on the level with me about how she came in, so how do I know that she handed out these flyers and did all this stuff?"

Another officer informed us that the difference in wealth and education was particularly great between inspected and uninspected applicants from Latin America and the Caribbean, and that the nature of the claims of wealthy and nonwealthy people of this region differed. In particular, according to this officer, the wealthy, educated applicants tended to have well-defined claims of political persecution, whereas the poorer applicants, who were much more likely to be uninspected, had claims that suffered from vagueness.

Some of the difference between inspected and uninspected Latin Americans may be due not to their status at entry but to their nationality (and the corresponding degree of human rights violations in their country). Of inspected applicants from Latin America and the Caribbean, 55 percent were Colombian, 21 percent Haitian, and 11 percent Venezuelan, while of uninspected applicants, 45 percent were Haitian, 27 percent Salvadoran, and 19 percent Guatemalan.

Status at Entry and Age of Applicant

To better understand the difference in grant rates for inspected and uninspected applicants from particular regions, we examined the age ranges of inspected and uninspected applicants from the entire world and also from various regions.

For most age groups, DHS granted asylum to lawful adult entrants more often than to unlawful entrants (figure 7-3).[25] But for those over 50, grant rates for both types of applicants were essentially identical, and unlawful entry did not present a particular obstacle. Asylum officers may have viewed members of this oldest cohort as particularly likely to be motivated to leave their home country for reasons of persecution as opposed to livelihood challenges. The fact that there was very little difference in grant rates for this older group of applicants tends to confirm the hypothesis that the taint of possible economic migration, rather than the moral taint of "sneaking in," is the more likely explanation of the differential in grant rates for lawful and unlawful entrants.

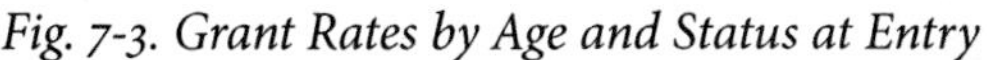

Fig. 7-3. Grant Rates by Age and Status at Entry

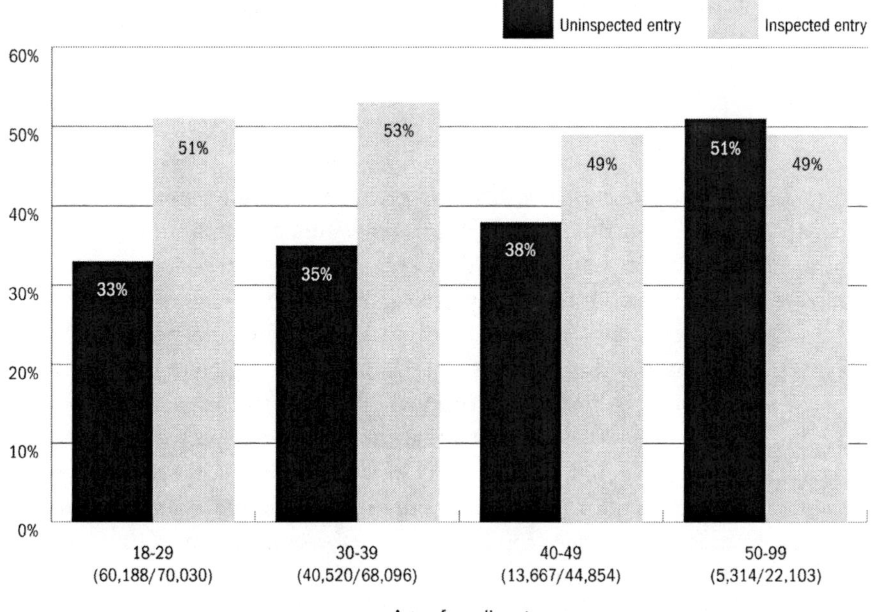

Fig 7-4. Grant Rates by Status at Entry and Age, Latin American and Other Applicants

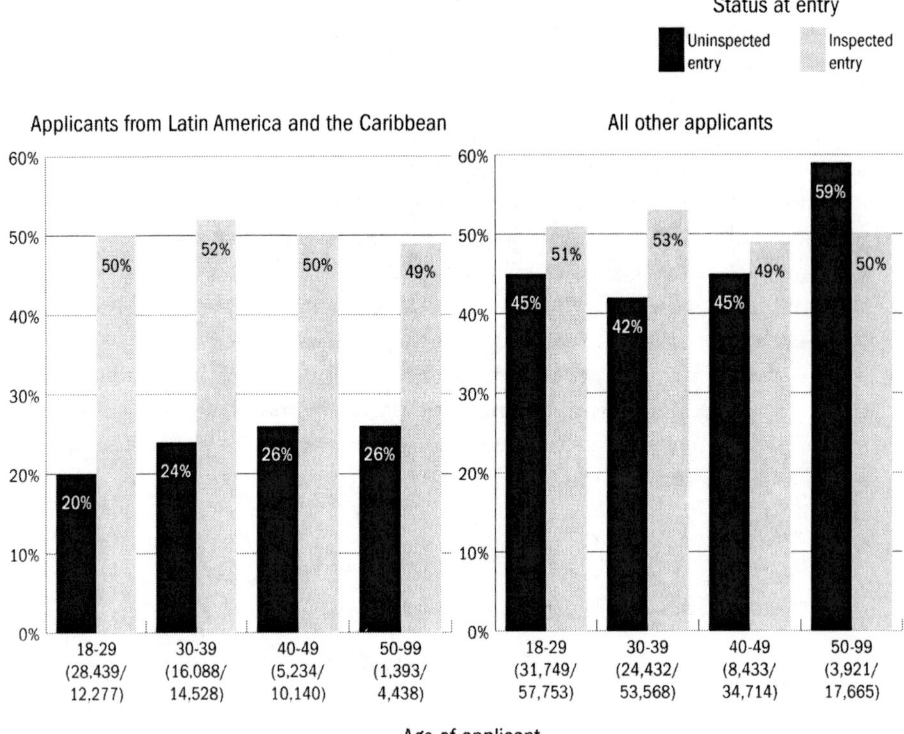

When we disaggregate these data by region, we see a quite interesting disparity. Although on a global basis the grant rate for older applicants seems to be about the same for those who were inspected and those who were not, that rate was in fact higher for the uninspected applicants from regions other than Latin America and the Caribbean, and much lower for uninspected applicants than for inspected applicants from that particular region (figure 7-4).[26]

We were initially baffled by this regional difference, but a senior official at asylum office headquarters surmised that the older, uninspected applicants from Latin America could well be people seeking reunification with undocumented relatives in the United States, rather than genuine asylum seekers, just as uninspected younger applicants from all regions might come under greater suspicion of having come to the United States for economic gain rather that because they feared persecution.

We are left with a question in our minds: is the difference between grant rates for inspected and uninspected applicants from Latin America and the Caribbean a reasonable one, based on a reality that many uninspected asylum seekers from that region (unlike their counterparts from Africa and Asia) are actually not eligible for asylum, or is this difference the result of a perception among asylum officers that uninspected applicants from this particular region are actually migrating for a reason other than a fear of persecution?[27]

Representation

DHS granted asylum 19 percent more often to represented asylum seekers compared to pro se applicants (50 percent compared with 42 percent).[28] The regression analyses confirmed that, with all other variables in the model held constant, representation correlated with higher grant rates.

Our findings about representation warrant two caveats. First, as we noted previously, DHS codes as "attorney" (and we therefore treat as a person with representation) anyone with a representative accepted by DHS, but some of the representatives were not attorneys; they may have been law students, accredited representatives, or other persons acceptable to the asylum officer. Second, the fact that DHS coded the applicant as having had an attorney does not necessarily mean that the representative actually helped the applicant fill out the application and showed up at the asylum office interview; the representative may only have helped with the forms or only appeared at the interview. In addition, some applicants may have been helped with the forms by an attorney or other representative who for whatever reason concealed his or her participation by not completing the form through which representatives register their appearance in a case.

The most obvious reason why representation matters is that representatives have the knowledge and skill to know what facts an asylum officer will deem relevant and to collect the necessary corroborating evidence to support a case. Sometimes this information will require scouring public or publicly available records; in other cases, the representative will have to collect the information from witnesses in the applicant's home country, obtain difficult-to-access records (such as records of medical treatments after torture), and retain experts in the United States on both human rights conditions in the applicant's country and on the physical and mental health of an applicant who has suffered torture and trauma.

To understand better how representation may have shaped asylum officers' perceptions of applicants, we studied how this variable changed over time, and its relationship with three characteristics of the asylum seeker: age, status at entry, and dependents.

Fig. 7-5. Grant Rates by Representation and Asylum Era

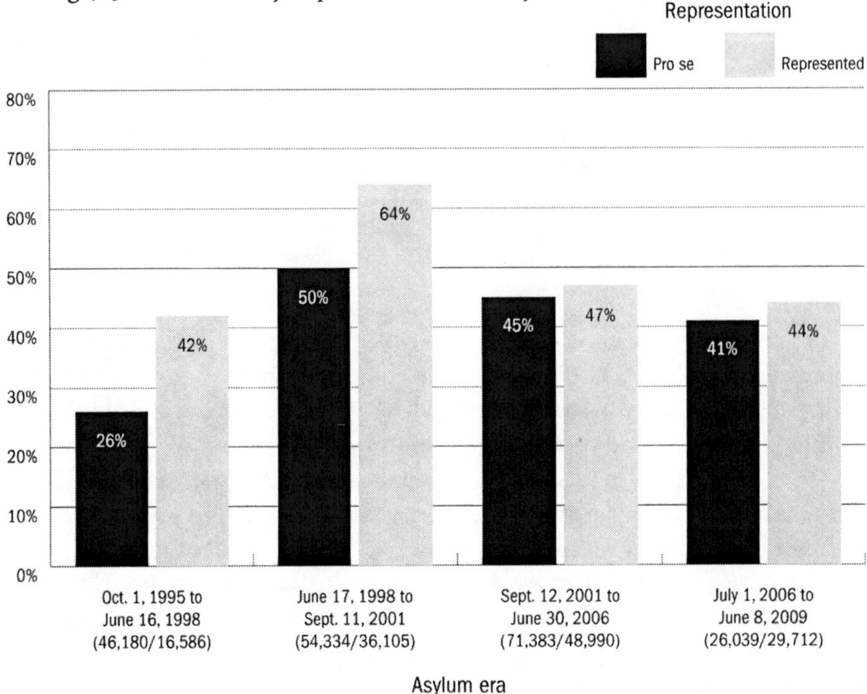

Fig. 7-6. Grant Rates for Adults by Age and Representation

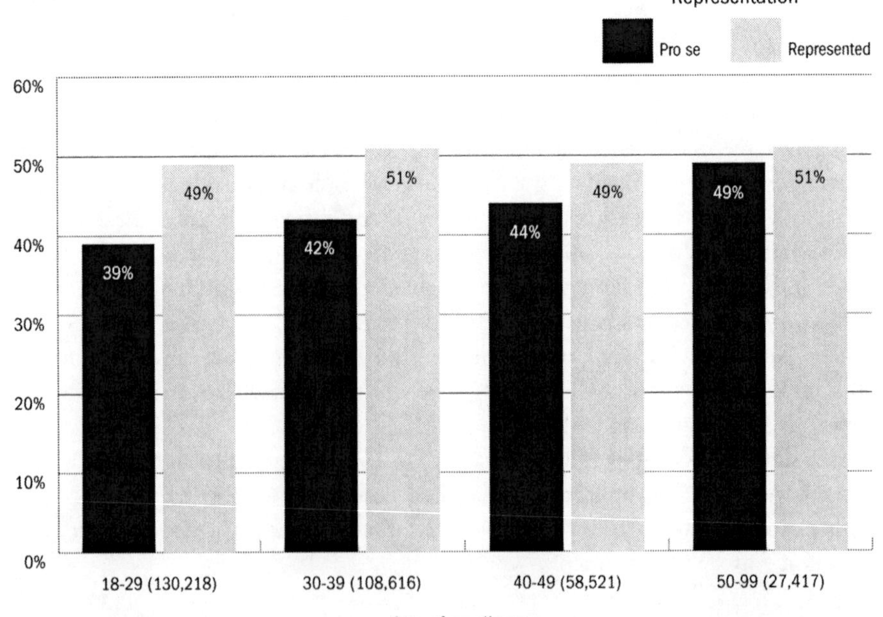

Representation over Time

We were surprised to learn that the positive relationship between representation and grant rates diminished over time. DHS granted asylum considerably more often to represented applicants in eras 1 and 2. As figure 7-5 shows, that difference diminished in Era 3, when DHS granted asylum only 4 percent more often to represented claimants. It grew slightly in Era 4, when we saw a 7 percent differential favoring represented asylum seekers.[29]

Why has representation apparently been of less advantage in recent years? One explanation might be that the asylum corps has become more professionalized over time. As a result of improved training, asylum officers have become more capable of adjudicating claims from applicants without representatives.

In addition, the Fraud Detection and National Security program (FDNS), which was established in 2004, may have made asylum officers more skeptical of certain representatives.[30] An asylum officer explained:

> We have fraud roundtables where the FDNS officers come out and talk to the asylum office about trends. The focus of the FDNS officers . . . is usually "Beware of applications from Attorney X, who is using the same boilerplate. Attorney Y is doing this that and the other thing." The focus is not on the applicant but on the attorneys who might be gaming the system, attorneys who are in cahoots with certain interpreters . . .

Some asylum officers suggested to us that representatives had a much less significant impact on outcomes in the twenty-first century because of the advent of widespread access to the Internet. They told us that cases are, in general, much better prepared in recent years than they previously were, and that most applicants now present a file of corroborating evidence that is "at least an inch thick." The World Wide Web has enabled more sophisticated pro se applicants to collect information not only on human rights conditions in their countries but also on the standards that DHS used to evaluate cases.[31] The Internet has also enabled asylum officers to better investigate some of the facts, both positive and negative, pertaining to applicants' cases.

Representation and Age

Among adult applicants, the older the asylum seeker, the smaller the difference in grant rates between represented and unrepresented claimants.[32] Figure 7-6 shows that the gap closed steadily as the age of applicants increased.[33] Perhaps this is because the younger applicants were more likely to be perceived as economic migrants and were thus in greater need of a lawyer, while older applicants were perceived as more credible simply because of their age. In addition, older applicants may have been more educated and more able to articulate their fear of persecution than younger applicants.

Representation and Dependents

We noted earlier that DHS granted asylum more often to applicants who had dependents in the United States. For applicants with dependents in the United States, having a representative appeared to make little difference. But for those who did not have dependents, it helped to have a representative. DHS granted asylum at about the same rate to represented and pro se applicants who had dependents, but claimants without dependents won 25 percent more often when they had representatives (figure 7-7).[34]

As discussed previously, applicants with dependents may have been viewed as more credible and more sympathetic than those without dependents and may therefore have had a greater chance of being deemed credible whether

Fig 7-7. Grant Rates by Representation for Applicants with and without Dependents

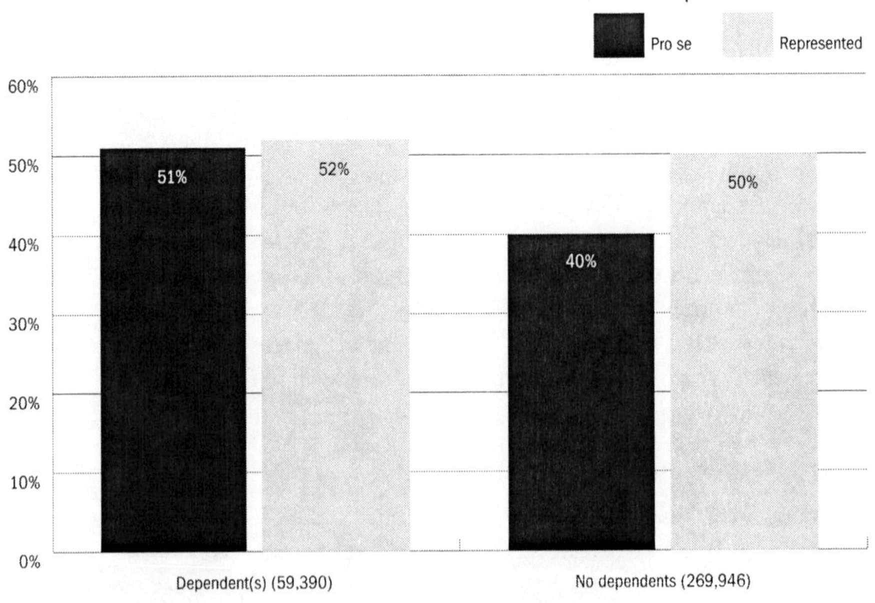

or not they had representatives. This might explain why representation made more of a difference for applicants who were not accompanied by dependents.

A senior asylum official at headquarters put it succinctly: "If you are EWI [you entered without inspection] and have no dependents, you are probably a single male. That is the least sympathetic category." The data bear out at least the first part of this theory. Of the 110,902 asylum seekers who entered without inspection and had no dependents, 76,659, or 69 percent, were male. Even more striking: of the 81,861 male asylum seekers in our study who entered without inspection, 76,659, or 94 percent did not have dependents.

Representation and Status at Entry

We also examined the relationship between representation and status at entry. Having a representative was much more important for applicants who had entered without inspection than those who had entered with visas. For uninspected entrants, DHS granted asylum to represented claimants 34

Fig. 7-8. Grant Rates by Status at Entry and Representation

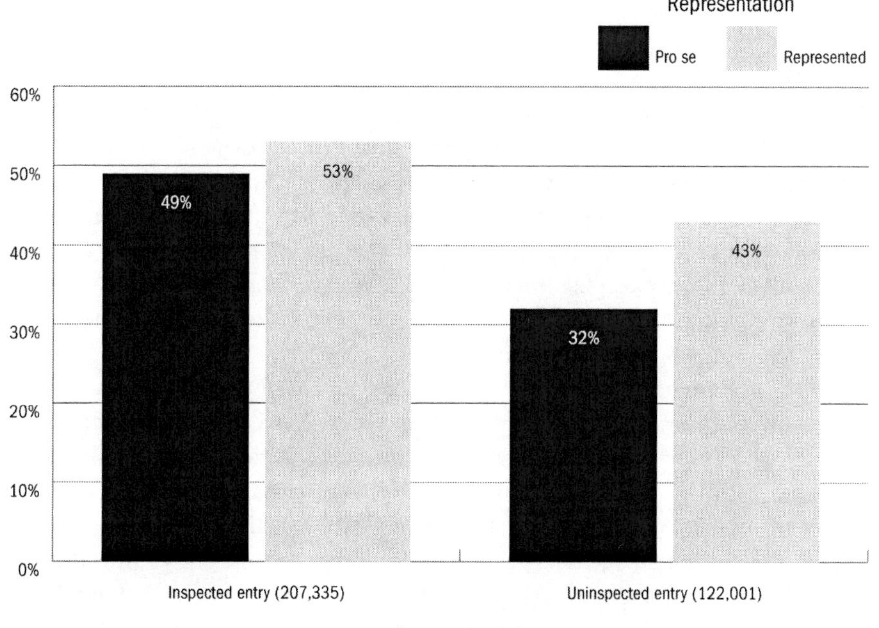

percent more often than to pro se applicants (43 percent compared with 32 percent). But for inspected entrants, DHS granted asylum to represented claimants only 8 percent more often than to pro se applicants (53 percent compared with 49 percent) (figure 7-8).[35]

As discussed earlier with respect to status at entry, this differential may suggest suspicions on the part of some asylum officers regarding the credibility of applicants who "sneak in" to the country. It may also show that representatives can help some applicants overcome such suspicion, particularly by substantiating claims through corroboration.

The difference in grant rates for uninspected entrants may also have involved the value of competent representation to applicants who may have been somewhat less educated than those who entered the United States with a visa. As an asylum officer told us:

> In any country, the more educated you are, the more likely you are to earn money and get a visa. If you are poor, they aren't going to grant you a visa, so if you come, you are going to come uninspected. If you are educated you should be able to put forth your claim without representation. An attorney isn't going to add much. It seems unfair, but the reality is that people coming [without inspection are more often uneducated and] when they present their claims by themselves, they can't make it out.

Another officer said that representatives prepare those who enter without inspection much better than that applicant could prepare herself. According to this officer, the representative explains in advance the questions that will be asked, such as, "When did you enter the country?" Applicants with representatives will have time to prepare an answer to that question. In contrast, those without representation may answer that question by saying "I don't remember, I wasn't keeping track." A DHS official further suggested that representatives can help uninspected applicants collect the documents necessary for a successful asylum claim.

One asylum officer with whom we spoke surmised that the group with the lowest grant rates would be unrepresented males without dependents who entered the United States without inspection; these would be viewed with the most suspicion as possible economic migrants, persecutors of others, or even terrorists. Lacking lawyers, they would be least able to allay the suspicion, or, to view it as this asylum officer did, they would be unassisted by a representative who would "somewhat mediate the threat." This officer suggested that we separate out, by gender and representation, those applicants who lacked dependents and entered without inspection.

We did so, and the result (figure 7-9) supports this officer's hypothesis.[36] Unrepresented males had the lowest grant rate among uninspected applicants without dependents (29 percent), while represented females had the highest grant rate among this population (45 percent). The rate for represented females was 54 percent higher than the rate for unrepresented males. By contrast, among applicants with dependents who entered after having been inspected, gender and representation made had little effect on the grant rate. Represented females won at a rate of 56 percent, while unrepresented males won at a rate of 55 percent. We note, also, that represented females who entered with inspection and had dependents won at a rate (56 percent) that was 93 percent higher than unrepresented males who entered without inspection and had no dependents in the United States (29 percent).

Fig. 7-9. Grant Rates by Status at Entry, Dependents, Gender, and Representation

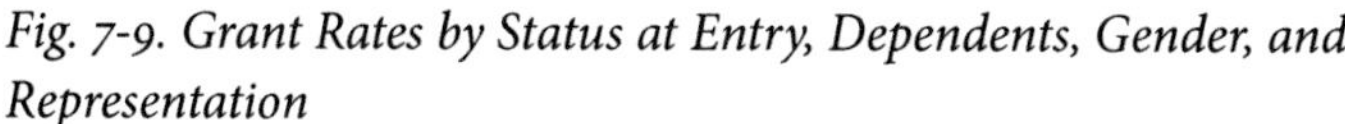

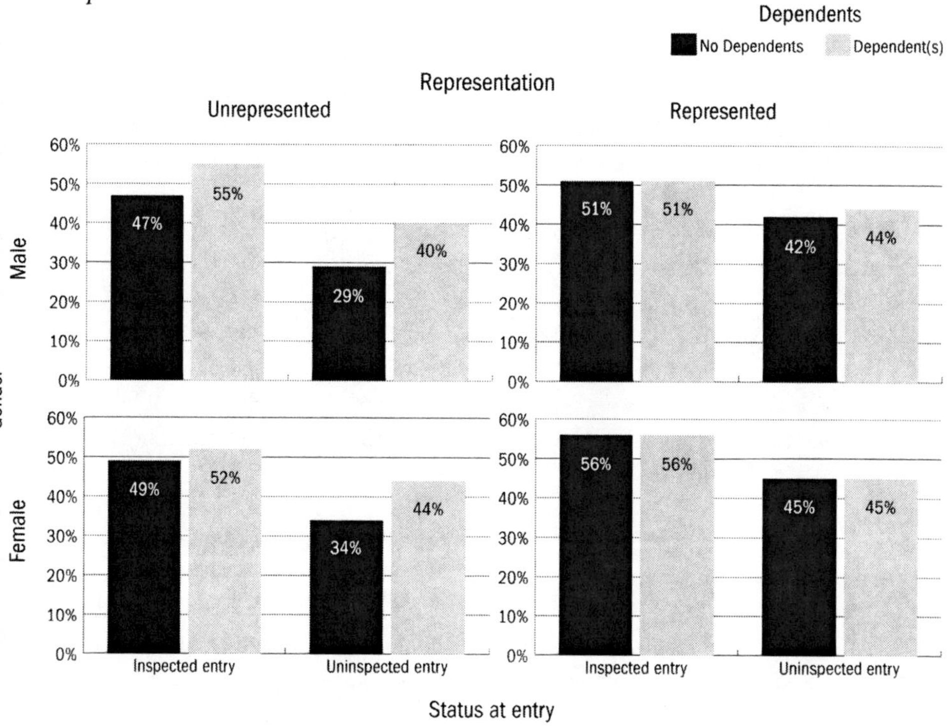

Why Representation Mattered

More than 60 percent of asylum officers surveyed by DHS in 2011 thought that the main reason represented asylum seekers won more often than unrepresented asylum seekers was that "representatives better prepare applicants to testify more clearly and consistently and to address weaknesses in their cases." In the words of one asylum officer:

> Competent attorneys better prepare both the applicant and any supporting documents submitted. As a result, the applicant testifies more clearly and materially, submits more relevant documents, and (not on your list above, but to me the most important) is [that able lawyers] PREVENTED [applicants] from submitting fraudulent or detrimental documents or making incredible statements, thereby reducing the likelihood an applicant will have problems with fraud or be seen as incredible. Also, attorneys seem to take the stronger, more meritorious claims only. I appreciate good representation, as it benefits all.

Another officer said:

> If the case is well-prepared, they have an advantage when they walk into the office; we have time constraints. When you can see that everything is in order, the nexus is very clear, when you ask the applicant and they can tell in detail the harm they suffered, no inconsistencies. . . . Preparation really helps.

Similarly, an officer described how competent representatives help to alleviate the time pressure that asylum adjudicators face:

> If the applicant is prepared, the officer has more time to focus on the merits of the claim. It takes more time for the officer to complete an interview with someone who is not represented, but the officer simply does not have that time, and so makes a judgment based on the amount of time he or she is given for all cases.

Competent representatives were also more likely to select cases that were meritorious. One officer explained:

> There are lawyers, law school clinics, and accredited representatives that screen their clients before they accept their cases, so that they are not filing applications for those who are not credible or who do not have viable

asylum claims. This is another reason why represented asylum seekers may have more success in the asylum office.

Moreover, the reputation of representatives mattered in credibility determinations. For representatives who are repeat players and have proved their integrity to particular asylum officers in past cases, the officers may feel more comfortable trusting the veracity of their clients' claims. This factor cut both ways, however: if an officer knew that a representative had previously presented false or weak cases, the officer may have been disinclined to believe other clients of that representative.

So representation was not always a benefit. In fact, the surveyed asylum officers conveyed a picture of three very different types of representatives: competent counsel; incompetent counsel; and lawyers who knowingly filed fraudulent applications. Poor representation was often worse than no representation, in that it prevented officers from uncovering any viable claims. Here's how one officer summarized this problem:

> Most applicants would have been better off without a representative as the latter gives them very bad counseling, oftentimes not having a clue concerning the claim at all, or not knowing the immigration law well enough to represent their clients. They charge hefty sums more often just to fill the application and do not bother to show up at the interview.

Similarly, another officer explained in detail:

> I agree that when applicants are represented by a good lawyer, they are better able to collect corroborating evidence related to medical/psychological conditions, they better prepare their applicants to testify clearly and consistently, and they are better able to show the relationship between the evidence and the law. *However, in my personal experience, I have rarely interacted with an attorney whose representation influenced the outcome of the case. Most attorneys that appear before me barely know or have never met their clients before the interview, are not familiar with the case, do not make closing statements or any comments at all, and submit no brief or supporting documentation that helps support the applicants' claims for asylum.* . . . In VERY rare cases, I have had an applicant who appeared ineligible and the attorney was able to provide evidence and an argument to support granting the claim where the applicant would otherwise have been referred. But this is generally uncommon, and the presence of a representative rarely has an impact on my grant rate. Based on rumors about other officers alone,

> I can imagine that the presence of attorneys is likely helpful to applicants who appear before officers who have very low grant rates and who are not always fair or kind to the applicants before them [emphasis added].

But even these officers are aware of different types of representatives:

> At [the Newark Asylum Office] I don't think represented cases are more meritorious on average than non-represented ones—there are a lot of bad lawyers here. I suspect that at other asylum offices they are seeing more reputable attorneys, who only accept the stronger cases. (This seems to be the case at our Boston suboffice.)

We asked several asylum officers why applicants of certain nationalities (Armenians and Haitians, for example) won asylum more often when they did *not* have representatives. They explained this phenomenon in terms of particular attorneys who specialized in claims by nationals of certain countries and who had bad reputations with asylum officers. One officer named a particular group of attorneys who represented Haitians and submitted

> the same boilerplate claims . . . again and again. [Perhaps they] take claims from anyone who files, just to get the money. They tell the applicants that they have valid claims just to get good money.

In the words of another officer:

> There are certain preparers who represent people from certain groups of countries and have poor reputations, for providing suspicious documents or information on applications that is later found not credible. That affects the stream of applicants from that group later on.

This chapter has explored factors that may impact the asylum officers' perception of asylum seekers, and the ways in which these characteristics of the applicants affect grant rates. But it has not taken into account another factor: what difference did it make whether an asylum-seeker applied while living in one region of the United States as opposed to another? We take up this subject in the next chapter.

8

Variations across the Regional Asylum Offices

Up to this point, we have examined changes in the grant rate over time and the impact of officer perceptions of the asylum applicants on grant rates. In this chapter, we shift our focus to the asylum offices as the locus of decision making, looking at variations across these offices. As the map at the front of this book shows, all of these offices have very large catchment areas; all but the New York office interview applicants from several states. In the next chapter, we explore variations in adjudication by officers within these offices.

In our book *Refugee Roulette*, we found large variations in grant rates across the eight regional asylum offices between 1999 and 2005. Of course, as we noted there, these differences could be due to the fact that different regional offices receive applications from different populations of applicants. For example, Haitians tend to settle in Miami and apply primarily to the Miami office, while Chinese tend to settle on the coasts and apply primarily in New York and Los Angeles. To make our comparison more reliable, we confined our analysis in that study to countries with a high volume of applicants *and* high grant rates.[1]

Our current database enabled us to repeat this study with three improvements. First, the database for the current study is larger, covering seven more years of adjudication. Second, we were able to eliminate a set of cases not decided on the merits of the claims; specifically, those rejected because of the one-year filing deadline.[2] Third, we used the Freedom House index[3] to assess whether this independent measure of country conditions would also show large variations in grant rates for countries that were serious human rights violators.

Variations by Nationality of the Applicant

Applicants from All Countries

When we look at asylum applicants from *all* countries over the entire time frame studied, officers at different regional offices granted asylum at very different rates. As figure 8-1 indicates, DHS officers in the San Francisco region granted asylum almost twice as often as did officers in the New York region

Fig. 8-1. Grant Rates by Regional Asylum Office

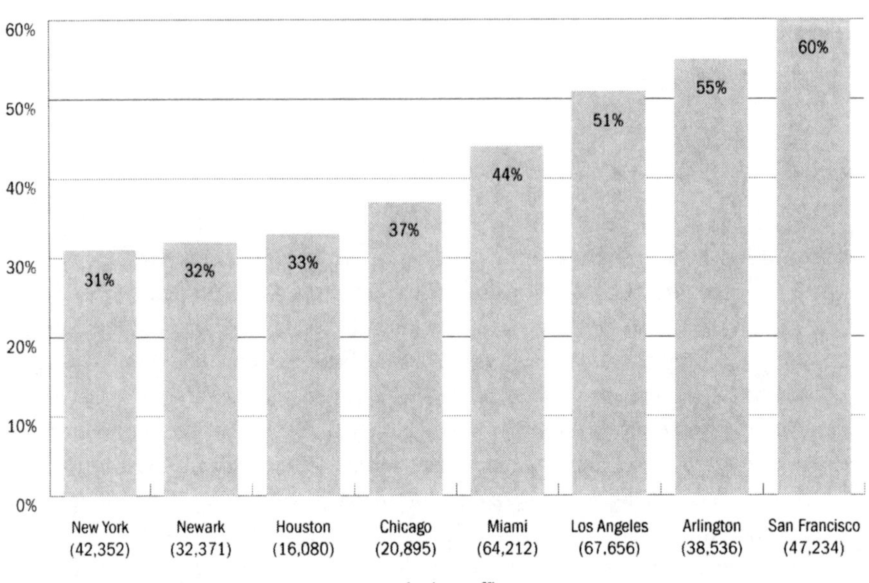

(60 percent versus 31 percent). In fact, three regional offices granted asylum to more than 50 percent of applicants (in addition to San Francisco, Arlington and Los Angeles granted at rates of 55 percent and 51 percent, respectively), while three regional offices granted asylum in the low 30 percent range (in addition to New York, Newark and Houston granted at rates of 32 percent and 33 percent, respectively).

Of course, this variation in grant rates might result from the different populations of asylum applicants residing in the eight regions.[4] For example, in New York, the regional office with the lowest grant rate, the largest population of asylum seekers—13,422 cases constituting 32 percent of the New York caseload—was from China. In San Francisco, the regional office with the highest grant rate, the largest population of asylum seekers—12,455 cases constituting 26 percent of the San Francisco caseload—was from India. Only 4,614 asylum cases, or 10 percent of the San Francisco caseload, were from China.

The regression analyses demonstrate that the variation in grant rates is real, as there are sizable differences in grant rates across asylum offices even with all other variables held constant.[5] We begin our analysis by exploring nationality and human rights conditions, to determine whether some of

Fig. 8-2. Grant Rates by Regional Office and Human Rights Assessment

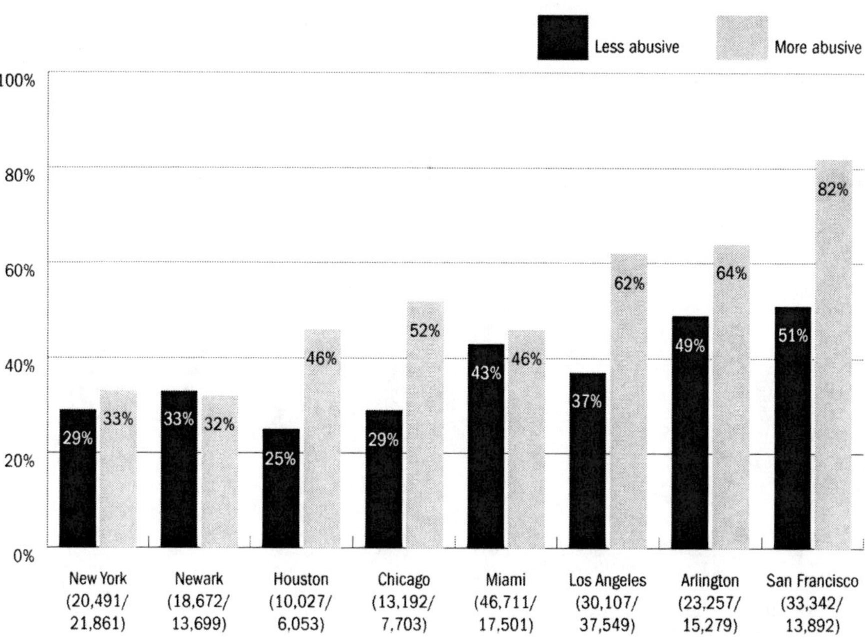

these differences in grant rates are due to the different mix of populations applying to the eight regional asylum offices.

Applicants from Countries with Poor Human Rights Records

We first analyzed cases only from countries with the most abusive human rights conditions, those with high (12–14) mean Freedom House scores. Surprisingly, the grant rates for applicants from these countries varied widely among the eight offices: officers in Newark granted asylum to such applicants 32 percent of the time, while the grant rate for countries with equally bad human right records was nearly three times as high (82 percent) in San Francisco. Figure 8-2 displays the range.[6]

As figure 8-2 shows, most of the offices (Houston, Chicago, Los Angeles, San Francisco, and Arlington) granted asylum, as one might expect, much more often to applicants from the most abusive countries.[7] But Miami, New York, and Newark did not in the aggregate differentiate much with respect to the reported severity of human rights violations.

Fig. 8-3. Grant Rates by Regional Office and Human Rights Assessment, Excluding Chinese Cases

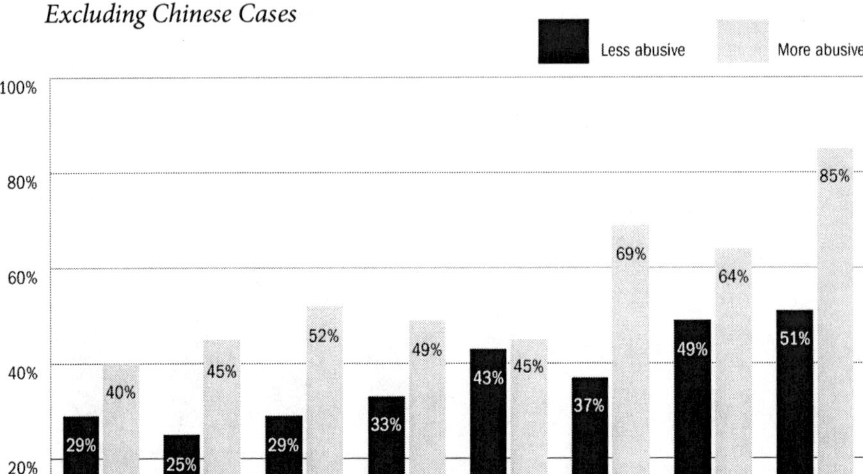

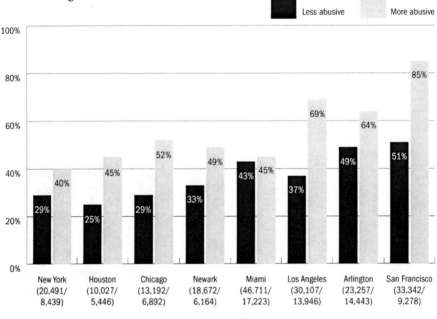

Newark actually granted asylum slightly more frequently to claimants from countries with greater respect for human rights (33 percent compared with 32 percent). But that anomaly was apparently caused by the Newark office's referrals of large numbers of possibly fraudulent cases from China, a country with a high Freedom House score. If we look at the array of the regional offices based on all cases other than those from China, as in figure 8-3,[8] we see that every office granted asylum more often to applicants from those other most abusive countries, but the grant rates for cases from those nations still varied considerably depending on the office. The range was still sizable, from 40 percent in the New York office to 85 percent in the San Francisco office.

Likewise, if we exclude Haitian cases from the mix, the anomaly in the Miami regional office disappears. Without Haitian cases, officers in Miami granted asylum to applicants from more abusive countries at a rate 29 percent higher than applicants from less abusive countries (67 percent versus 52 percent). At least some of this difference in grant rates among asylum offices is due to the different applicant pools in each region.

Particular Countries with High Volumes of Applications to Several Regional Offices

Of course, these differences in grant rates could be due to the different mixes of applicants from various countries who applied to different offices. In order to address this concern, we unpacked regional office grant rates by nationality of the applicant. That is, we looked at the success rates, in different DHS regional offices, of nationals of certain countries from which large numbers of people applied for asylum. Although China was the single largest source of applicants, we did not study Chinese applications, because we understand from talking to asylum officers that groups of Chinese applicants from different provinces, with very different degrees and types of persecution,[9] have tended to settle in different parts of the United States, which could account for differences in regional grant rates.

We identified fifteen other countries whose nationals had filed at least 5,000 applications during our study period: Albania, Armenia, Cameroon, El Salvador, Ethiopia, Guatemala, Haiti, India, Indonesia, Iran, Iraq, Liberia, Mauritania, Russia, and Somalia. We compared asylum office regions only when at least four of the regions had at least 500 applicants from a particular country.

That test excluded Albania (whose nationals' applications were adjudicated primarily in Chicago, Newark, and New York), Armenia (Los Angeles and San Francisco), Haiti (Miami, Newark, and New York), India (Los Angeles, New York, and San Francisco), Iran (Arlington, Los Angeles, and San Francisco), Iraq (Chicago, Los Angeles, and San Francisco), and Mauritania (Chicago, Houston, and New York). We do not present here results from El Salvador and Guatemala, both because the caseload from those countries is so heavily skewed to the early years of our study, and because the grant rates from those countries were so low as to render comparisons less meaningful.[10]

Accordingly, we compared regional office grant rates, one country at a time, for applicants from Cameroon, Colombia, Ethiopia, Indonesia, Russia, and Somalia. Figures 8-4 through 8-9 display the results of those studies, ordered from least to greatest disparity between the regional asylum offices with the lowest and highest grant rates for the country in question.[11] In each case, grant rates are displayed only for the regional offices with at least 500 adjudications from nationals of the country in question.

Collectively, these six graphs tell a disturbing story. Disparities exist, to varying degrees, across the regional offices. At one end, Cameroonians won asylum at rates of 40 percent and 56 percent rates in Houston and Chicago, the lowest- and highest-granting regions in which they filed in substantial numbers. This

Fig. 8-4. Grant Rates for Cameroonian Asylum Applicants

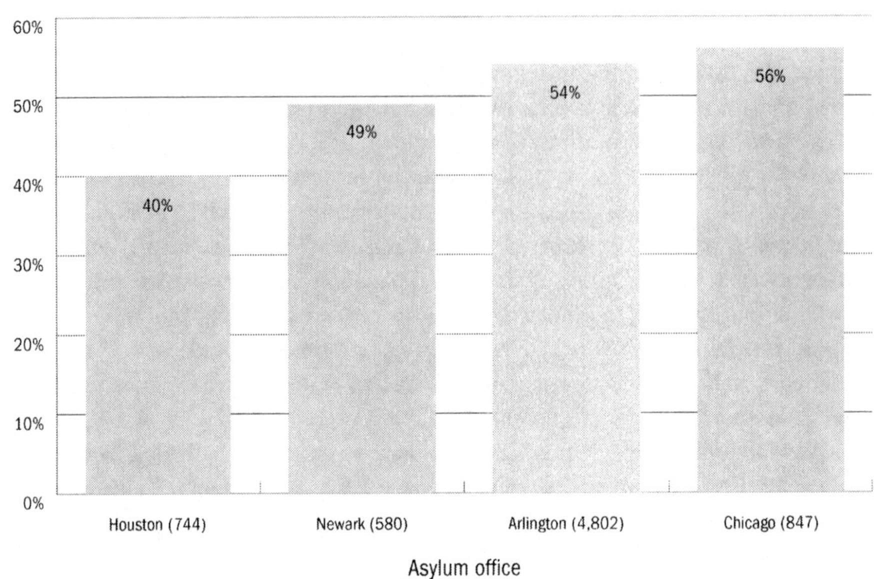

Fig. 8-5. Grant Rates for Ethiopian Asylum Applicants

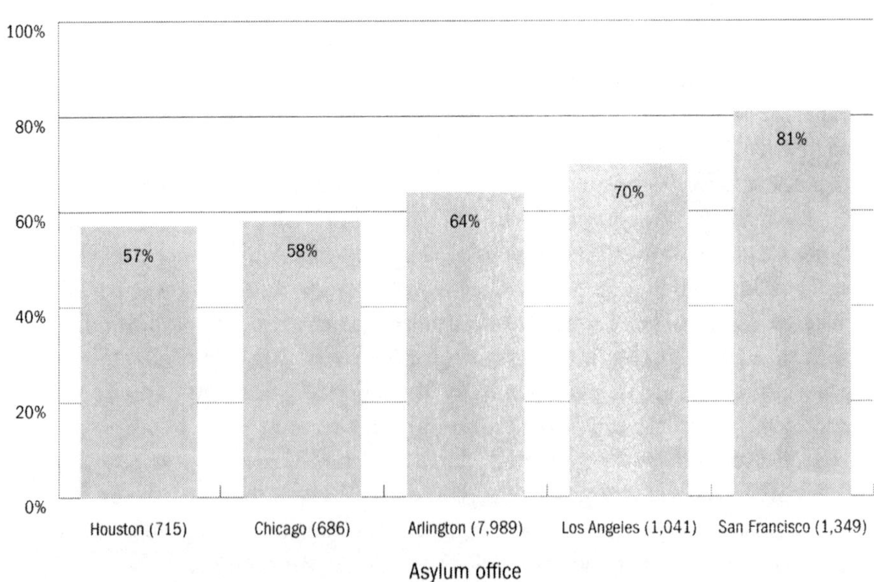

Fig. 8-6. Grant Rates for Colombian Asylum Applicants

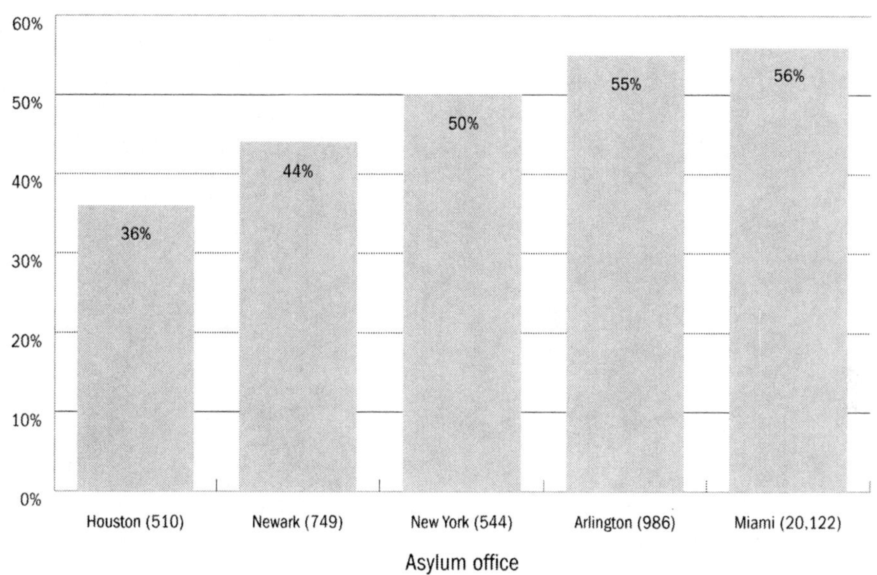

Fig. 8-7. Grant Rates for Somali Asylum Applicants

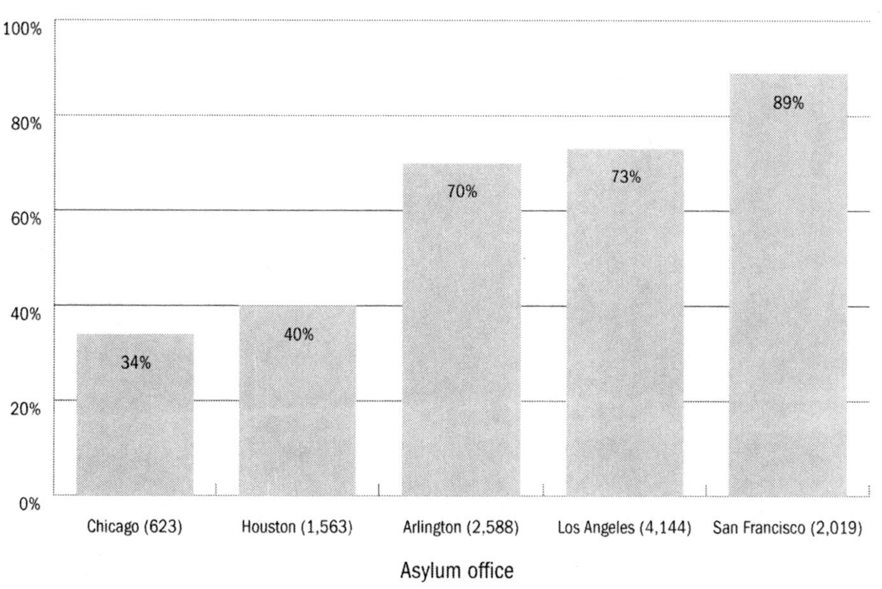

Fig. 8-8. Grant Rates for Indonesian Asylum Applicants

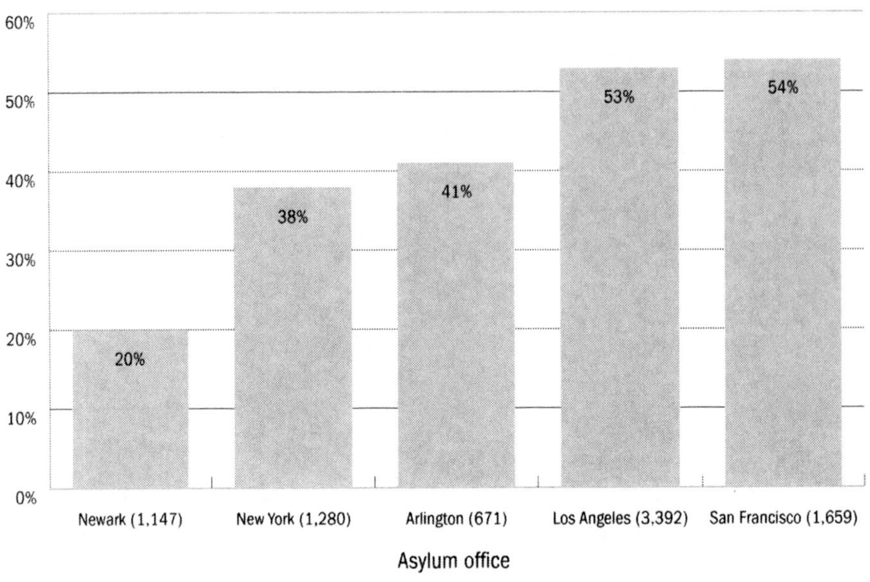

Fig. 8-9. Grant Rates for Russian Asylum Applicants

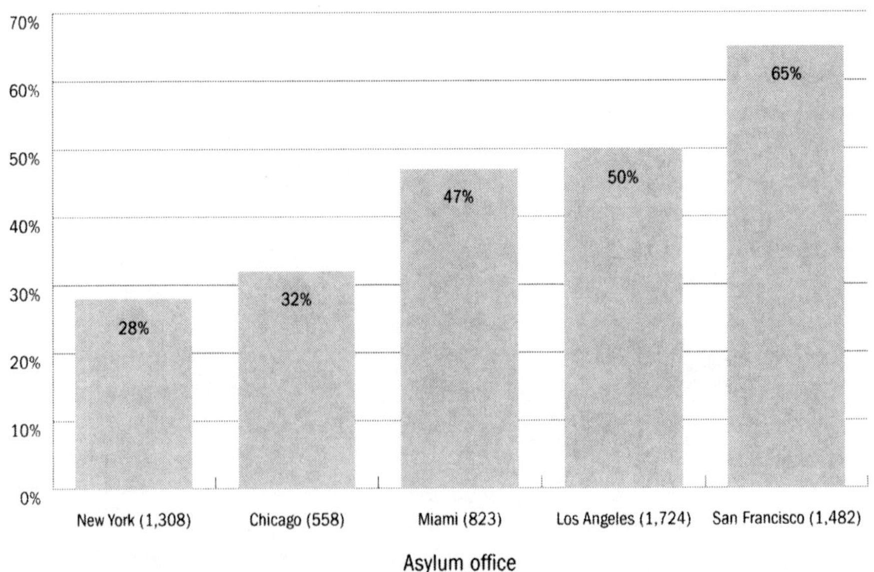

was the smallest difference among these six nationality analyses; nevertheless, the rate in Chicago was 40 percent higher than the rate in Houston. Ethiopian asylum seekers won asylum at high rates (over 50 percent) in all five offices in which they filed in substantial numbers, which is not surprising given the poor human rights conditions in that country during the time frame studied. Yet Ethiopians in the northwestern (San Francisco) catchment area experienced a grant rate 42 percent higher than their co-nationals in the southern states who were interviewed by Houston asylum officers. Colombian asylum seekers suffered an even greater disparity: the vast majority, who filed their claims in Miami, had a grant rate of 56 percent in that office, more than 50 percent higher than the 36 percent granted by the Houston office. But Somalis, who faced an undeniably dire human rights situation at home, had even more dramatically disparate grant rates. Their grant rate in San Francisco, 89 percent, was 162 percent higher than the 34 percent grant rate for that nationality in Chicago.

For Indonesians and Russians, there was a curious split between the east and west coasts. The San Francisco and Los Angeles offices granted asylum to Indonesians at rates of 54 percent and 53 percent, respectively, while the rates in New York and Newark were 38 percent and 20 percent. Russians succeeded at a rate of 65 percent in San Francisco, more than double the 28 percent grant rate at the New York office.[12]

The asylum officers with whom we spoke offered several explanations for the discrepancy in Indonesian grant rates. One rationale was simply that the office cultures varied from region to region. A second explanation was that supervisors in different offices sent different signals to asylum officers regarding the appropriate degree of skepticism that they should afford applicants' testimony. One officer suggested that the types of Indonesian claims might differ, as the West Coast offices heard many cases of Indonesians who belonged to a Chinese Christian minority, while the cases heard on the East Coast might have been those of people who, like the Mexican claimants whom we excluded from the study, may have been trying to get into the asylum system to obtain other forms of relief, such as cancellation of removal.

Several asylum officers suggested that the West Coast, which falls under the jurisdiction of the U.S. Court of Appeals for the Ninth Circuit, has case law that is more favorable to Indonesian nationals. In particular, they pointed to the case of *Sael v. Ashcroft*,[13] which held that even if members of a group are not persecuted systematically, the persecution of some group members may support a successful asylum claim for applicants similarly situated to the persecuted members.[14] The First, Third, and Seventh Circuits have rejected this "disfavored group" standard and require that asylum applicants establish a "pattern or practice" of persecution of other members of a similarly situated group.[15] Persecution of Chinese Christians in Indonesia, officers noted, may meet the *Sael* standard but not the stricter standards in other federal circuits.

An alternative proffered explanation was the effect of Operation Jakarta, an investigation of fraud perpetrated by Indonesian immigration application preparers based in Northern Virginia and Maryland.[16] In 2004, the U.S. Attorney's office charged 26 people for, among other acts, assisting with fraudulent Indonesian asylum claims in more than 27 states, including California.[17] These

> brokers tapped into the perceived sympathies of asylum officers and immigration judges, claiming that applicants had been raped, sexually assaulted, beaten or robbed by Muslims because of their ethnicity or their Christian beliefs . . . . Applicants were told to cry, plead and avoid positive references to Indonesia.[18]

Though it is possible that asylum offices on the East Coast were more sensitive to fraud in Indonesian cases because the prosecutions occurred in Virginia, it is likely that the West Coast offices also knew about the fraud ring.

For the Russian claims, an asylum officer noted that the Fraud Detection and National Security (FDNS) program focused in their trainings on fraud by J-1 visa holders. These are nonimmigrant visas for work and study exchanges, used by au pairs and other temporary visitors. This explanation does not appear to account for the disparities in Russian grant rates, as the percentage of Russian asylum applicants holding J-1 visas were similar in the New York (21 percent), Chicago (26 percent), Los Angeles (17 percent), and San Francisco (23 percent) asylum offices.

As to both of these populations, one asylum officer suggested that different subgroups of asylum seekers from these countries may have gravitated to the two coasts, with more educated and wealthier individuals heading for Silicon Valley, while working-class refugees settled in the East.[19]

Reasons for Variations

What could account for such large differences in grant rates from one regional asylum office to another with respect to applicants from the same country? Why is it that certain offices (San Francisco and Los Angeles) frequently had the highest grant rate, while other offices (Newark and Chicago) frequently had the lowest grant rate? Our hypothesis is that the cultures of the offices played an important role. Those cultures were likely influenced by the outlooks and experiences of office directors and other supervisors, by the office caseloads, by applicable legal standards, and by the patterns of nonmeritorious or fraudulent applications that certain of those offices had previously encountered.

The asylum officers we interviewed suggested that some offices have a culture of greater or lesser conservatism or skepticism about claims than other offices. One asylum officer told us that variations depend "on the background of the officer and the culture of the office . . . some offices have more conservative outlooks on adjudicating cases." Another, who was not from Chicago, said, "I have the perception that Chicago is a conservative office."

Supervisory Directives

The asylum officers surveyed by DHS in 2011 identified different management directives or management-influenced cultures at various regional offices as the most important factor contributing to regional disparities in grant rates (almost one-quarter identified this reason). In comments, a number of officers highlighted the influential role of supervisors, who may have set different norms regarding prevailing cases and put different amounts of pressure on officers to decide cases quickly. Some of the comments offered in response to an open-ended question on this subject are revealing.

> The biggest factor is office management and culture, as I have realized that my office is more 'enforcement minded' than other offices. I think differences in asylum law and different applicant pools also matter.
>
> Different asylum offices appear to have different quality of staff selection, case review, work standards and over all competency.
>
> Different offices get applicants from different countries, and rates will vary with country of origin due to variations in credibility, economic migration and country conditions. However, I do believe that office culture plays a strong role in setting the tone.

Several officers observed that office cultures and supervisory directives are intertwined. The culture of an office affects which officers are promoted to supervisory positions and how those officers exercise their authority once appointed. The supervisors, in turn, contribute significantly to creating a particular office culture, one that may be more or less skeptical of applicants' testimony. Of course, the regional director plays a central role in creating an office culture, not least because that director selects the supervisors (although the national director has a rarely exercised veto).

As an example of how such supervisory approaches may have contributed to disparities in grant rates across offices, one asylum officer explained that the San Francisco office has a more objective approach to negative credibility analyses than other offices. In San Francisco, any negative credibility finding must be based on specific factual findings. In contrast, other regional asylum offices allow denials based on gut reactions, putting the burden on the applicant to prove credibility to the officer's satisfaction.

Caseloads

Some of the surveyed officers suggested that caseload pressures in different offices may have contributed to grant rate differences. Officers are allowed, on average, only four hours in which to complete a case, including reading all of the background material submitted by the applicant or available from the State Department and from public sources; performing background security checks on the applicant by consulting FBI and other databases; interviewing the applicant; and writing a proposed decision to be reviewed by a supervisor.[20] If it takes more time to justify a grant than a referral, offices with the greatest workload pressure (that is, the greatest imbalance between the number of cases to be decided and the number of available officers) may have a greater tendency to refer cases.[21] The following comments were offered by asylum officers who responded to the survey:

> Different offices have both a heavier pressure to refer as well as to keep interviews short.
>
> Caseload dictates how much time an AO spends interviewing a case. A stressful environment, where being efficient may mean [having to identify] three credibility points in order to [grant asylum] creates a mindset that is pro-referral.

One officer suggested that even if the same amount of time per case was allocated in each regional office, supervisors in one office might emphasize spending most of the time reading the file and understanding the case, while those in another office might urge officers to spend more time interviewing the applicant. More interview time, he suggested, would expose officers to more information that could raise concerns about credibility, and therefore lower grant rates for the office as a whole.[22]

Legal Standards and Review

Asylum officers correctly noted in the survey and in interviews that the different federal circuits have different standards for asylum. Though asylum law is based on one federal code, the interpretations of that statute differ across the different federal circuits, with some circuits having a pro-immigrant reputation and others having a more conservative interpretation of the law. The Court of Appeals for the Ninth Circuit, which includes California, has probably written more precedential asylum opinions than its sister courts elsewhere, and over the years, most of them have tilted in a direction favoring applicants.[23]

The federal courts of appeals do not hear cases that come directly from the asylum office, but they do review decisions of the Board of Immigration Appeals, which often simply affirm denials of asylum by immigration judges. Federal courts of appeals decisions may therefore affect the outlooks of the immigration courts to which asylum officers refer cases, and the rulings of the immigration courts may affect the behavior of the asylum offices that refer those cases at the very first stage of adjudication.

Some asylum officers suggested that the culture of the immigration courts to which an asylum office refers cases might have an impact on that office's approach to asylum adjudication. An officer who had worked in a different region stated that, in a region with a more immigrant-friendly immigration court, the asylum officers might be more likely to simply grant cases because they know the applicant is likely to win in the immigration court anyway. Another officer thought, to the contrary, that an office in a region where the immigration courts had high grant rates might impose stricter standards to avoid an influx of applications, lowering the grant rate of the asylum office in that region.

Self-Selection by Applicants

Some academic colleagues have suggested to us that the West Coast offices may have reputations for high grant rates and that sophisticated asylum seekers with strong cases may deliberately move to the West, further increasing the grant rates in San Francisco and Los Angeles. In addition, one asylum officer we interviewed believed that asylum seekers may move to a certain region because they have heard that the immigration court there is more likely to grant their case.

While it would not be out of the question that a particularly well educated applicant would move to the Northwest because the San Francisco office has historically had a high grant rate, we are skeptical for two reasons of theories involving large numbers of applicants choosing where to live on the basis of where they might have the best chance of winning asylum. First, the Center for Applied Legal Studies at Georgetown University, at which all of us have worked, has represented approximately 200 asylum seekers. In almost all cases, their choice of residence was based on where they could obtain free or low-cost shelter and other support from relatives or acquaintances, rather than on where they would most likely win an asylum case. Second, even if applicants had the relevant statistical information and could afford to live in the "best" region for a favorable decision, it would be very difficult for a potential applicant to perform a calculation based on expectations of average rates of favorable decisions of three different fora: the asylum office, the immigration court, and the courts of appeals.[24]

Differences among Professional Preparers and Advocates

The differences among the regional offices may also be strongly influenced by differences among the professionals who help applicants file documents and prepare for interviews. Several asylum officers with whom we spoke believed that lawyers who represented applicants in the San Francisco office were very well prepared and devoted to their clients, nearly always appearing at the interviews, asking questions that the interviewer had not asked, and arguing for their clients. San Francisco may also be home to more nonlegal support groups—nonprofit organizations offering a spectrum of services from psychological evaluations to access to mental health services—than other cities, which strengthens the asylum claims presented there.

In contrast, asylum officers told us that attorneys in Newark and New York filed G-28 forms to register as the official representative of their asylum-seeking clients but didn't bother to show up for those clients' interviews. Officers told us that in Los Angeles, the preparers do all of the work on the cases. The attorneys show up to the interviews but get the case files from the preparers in the parking lot and collect their fees without doing anything in the interviews. As one officer said, given what a great job the San Francisco attorneys do compared to lawyers in other parts of the country, it's no wonder that San Francisco has the highest grant rates in the nation.

Another officer focused on unscrupulous "coaches" who helped applicants fabricate stories of persecution. He surmised that East Coast coaches advised their clients to make up stories of political activism followed by governmental persecution that were easily checked against human rights reports and found to be false, while West Coast coaches told applicants to make up simple stories of being farmers who were attacked by nameless paramilitary bands, which were not so easily shown to be false.

Patterns of Applications

Offices may also have approached credibility determinations differently for different nationalities, based on their past experiences with that nationality.

The survey that DHS administered to its asylum officers revealed that fraudulent applications affect officers' approaches to credibility determinations in subsequent cases involving the applicants of the same nationality. When asked to what degree, if at all, the submission of fraudulent applications affected officers' approaches to future credibility decisions regarding the same cohort, about one-third of the 195 officers surveyed said that this "substantially" affected attitudes and a little more than one-third said it did so "somewhat."

Many officers explained how this occurs with frankness and professionalism. Here are samples of their observations in response to the questionnaire:

> Officers become more aware of apparent patterns that are common in cases involving fraud or incredible testimony. When these factors are present, we (reasonably in my opinion) ask better, more probing questions. At the end of the day, you still have to decide each case on its record. So if an applicant has good explanations, or gives detailed testimony, that's the end of it. In short, such awareness from other cases is a starting place, not the ending place.
>
> Each case is adjudicated on its merits, but if there is a pattern of fraud in a certain community or preparer/attorney, it does affect your initial take on a case before actually interviewing the applicant.
>
> The existence of fraud does not make me believe that all applicants from a given country are fraudulent, but it makes me more alert to the level of detail applicants provide and more intent on asking focused questions that require the applicants to provide detail about their personal experience and veer away from third-person, general accounts. . . .I work hard to write referrals that appropriately address all of the evidence and the reasons it is not credible. I strive to follow the law, write legally-sufficient decisions, and treat applicants fairly. I believe in the asylum program and believe it should be available to those in need of protection.
>
> I think officers are more skeptical towards cases from known high-fraud areas like China. However, I personally do my best to enter each interview with an open mind, despite this knowledge.
>
> The claim itself must also be similar, not just the country of origin. For example, if there was a pattern of fraudulent cases concerning family planning in China, that would not affect credibility determinations for Chinese Christians.

It is clear, however, that suspicions of fraud related to a particular country's nationals can affect asylum officers in challenging and sometimes troubling ways where enough fraud is encountered. For some officers, these suspicions change their approach to the interview:

> When an AO starts to recognize fraud patterns, it definitely affects the line of questioning, which will inevitably affect the credibility determinations.

For others, experience with fraud impacts their perception of applicants represented by certain preparers/attorneys:

> We see many boilerplate applications submitted by several attorneys in our office so all of our officers have received fraudulent applications. I believe most still try to evaluate each case individually although I think that gets harder over time.
>
> When there are multiple applications from the same country, with the same story, same evidence, same preparer/attorney, the credibility of the applicant is in question.

And in some cases, officers begin to view all applicants from specific countries with skepticism:

> Over a long period of time and in consideration of a significant number of fraudulent applications from nationals of a particular country, it does affect the approach to the credibility determinations in the cases of nationals of the same country.
>
> Some AOs now think everyone from certain countries are lying as a result of this discovery.

Perhaps of greatest concern, these experiences of fraud can then bleed into all asylum determinations:

> In our office, we are so frustrated with our main demographic/nationality that I believe it affects our overall grant rate with respect to all nationalities. I cannot decide whether I think the grant rate would increase for other nationalities just because they are not from X country, or whether the grant rate for other countries would decrease because we tend to feel overwhelmed by the amount of fraud in the system.

The Asylum Eras

Responses to the Terrorist Attacks of September 11, 2001

As figure 8-10 shows, in all but one of the regional asylum offices, the grant rate dropped after the September 11 attacks.[25] But the drops were much more dramatic in some regions than in others. The grant rates in the Houston and

New York offices dropped by 36 percent in the third asylum era. In contrast, the grant rate in Miami increased slightly between the second and third eras. Even more curiously, the grant rates in Arlington and Newark, offices located very close to buildings hit by planes in the September 11 attacks, dropped only 18 and 13 percent, respectively, between the two eras. Why did the grant rate drop so much more sharply in Houston, which is much further from the locus of the attacks?

One officer suggested that the drop in Houston's grant rate was a result of the increased security checks after September 11. According to this officer, these new security processes provided officers with much more data about border crossers, and given Houston's proximity to the border, it may have received proportionally more negative information about its applicants than did other regional offices. Another officer suggested that the culture of the office came into play, and that Houston has a more conservative approach than other offices.

Two other officers provided explanations that we think particularly worthy of consideration. For officers in Houston, unlike in other regions, adjudication of affirmative asylum cases is only a small part of the workload (or, as one of these officers put it, a "side show"). Much of their work involves interviewing people who have crossed the Mexican border without inspection and were apprehended before applying for asylum. Such individuals are detained and are interviewed while in detention. They are deported without an immigration court hearing unless the interviewing asylum officer finds that they have a "credible fear" of persecution. An additional category of work for these officers requires them to determine whether certain persons who already have been ordered deported by an immigration judge have a "reasonable fear" of persecution. The Houston officers, therefore, deal to a much greater degree than others with officials of the Immigration and Customs Enforcement (ICE) branch of DHS, have much closer professional and in some cases social relationships with those officers, and are accordingly much more oriented to "law enforcement" than those in other regional offices. One officer attributed the substantial drop in Houston's grant rate after the terrorist attacks to the office's culture of enforcement. Another officer simply opined that "in Houston, it's all about documentation."

One explanation for the grant rate increase in Miami after September 11, notwithstanding the terrorist attack or reactions such as the Ziglar memo, is that a high proportion of the Miami caseload consists of applicants from Haiti and Venezuela.[26] In both of those countries, human rights conditions deteriorated markedly in Era 3, and grant rates for asylum seekers from those countries correspondingly increased.[27]

Considering only applicants who identified themselves as Muslims, the drop-off in the New York regional office was even greater. New York granted

Fig. 8-10. Grant Rates by Regional Asylum Offices, before and after September 11, 2001

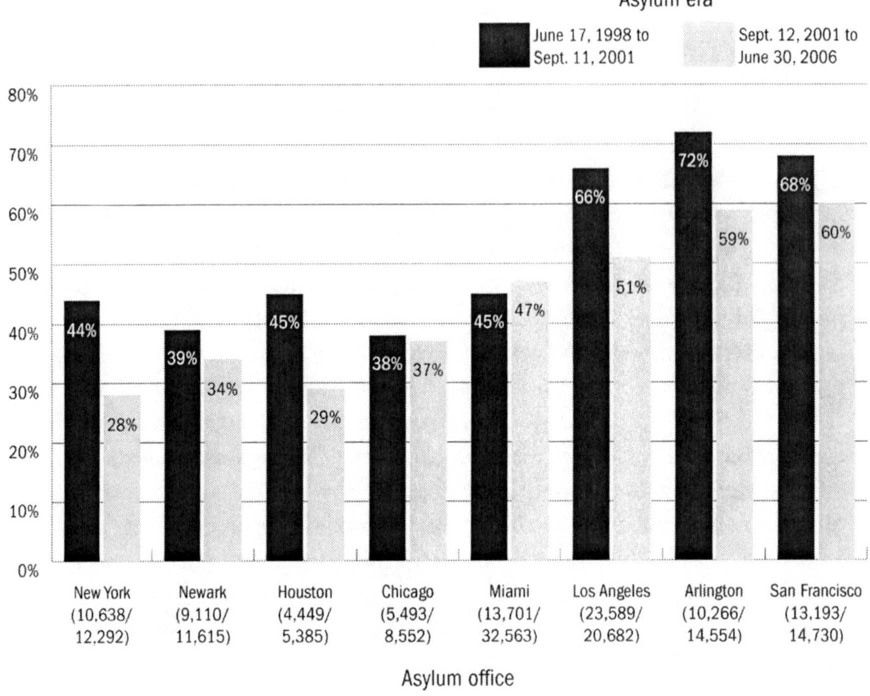

asylum to 47.5 percent of its 3146 Muslim applicants in the second era, but to only 21.5 percent of the 2229 Muslim applicants in the third era, a drop of 55 percent. In contrast, the decline in the Muslim grant rate in the San Francisco office was much smaller: from 85 percent of 1,830 applicants to 70 percent of 1,000 applicants, a drop of 18 percent. In Arlington, the rate fell only from 76 percent (2,532 applicants) to 62 percent (1,541 applicants), a drop of 18 percent.[28] But the dramatic drop-off in New York was not limited to Muslims. The New York office granted asylum to those who identified as Christian at a rate 43 percent lower in the third era than in the second era.[29]

Perceptions of Asylum Seekers

The Effects of Representation

There were interesting differences among the eight regional offices in the grant rates for represented and unrepresented asylum seekers. Nationally, DHS granted asylum 19 percent more often to represented claimants

Fig. 8-11. Grant Rates by Representation and Regional Office

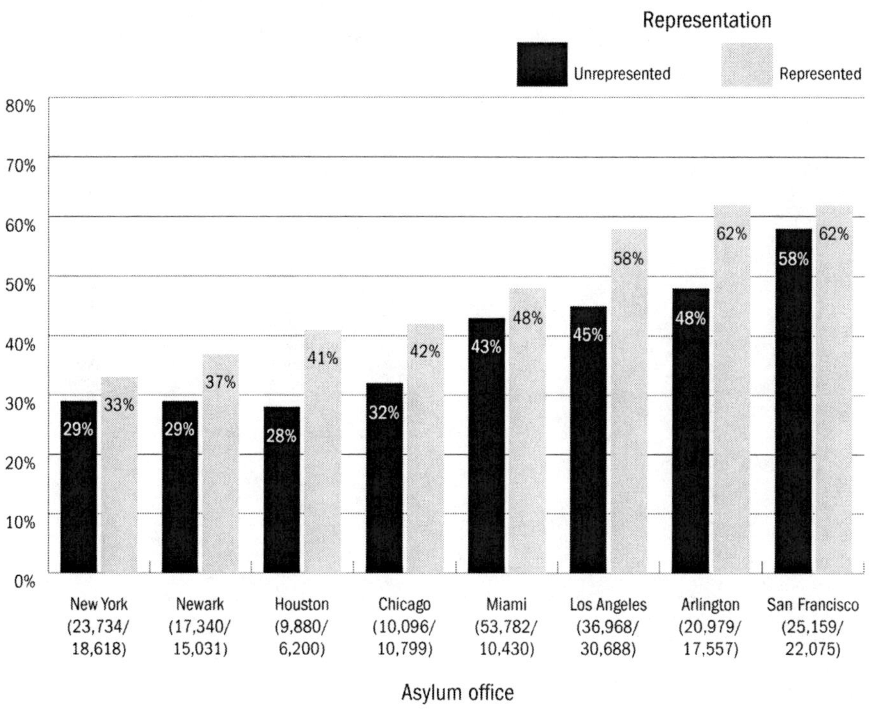

compared to those without representation (50 percent compared with 42 percent). As figure 8-11 shows, that difference narrowed considerably in San Francisco, where DHS granted asylum only 7 percent more often to represented applicants.[30] But that difference widened considerably in Houston and Chicago, where DHS granted asylum 46 percent and 31 percent more often to represented claimants, respectively. Why did regional offices differ to this degree with respect to representation and outcomes? Perhaps lawyers and other representatives are relatively more competent in some jurisdictions than others. Conversely, perhaps there are concentrations of lawyers who file boilerplate applications in certain offices.[31]

One of the asylum officers offered this explanation:

> Typically there is a general distrust of attorneys in certain asylum offices because of the fraudulent cases that they put forth. As a result, a pro se applicant is usually given more of the benefit of the doubt than one who is represented.

Fig. 8-12. Regional Office Grant Rates and Dependents

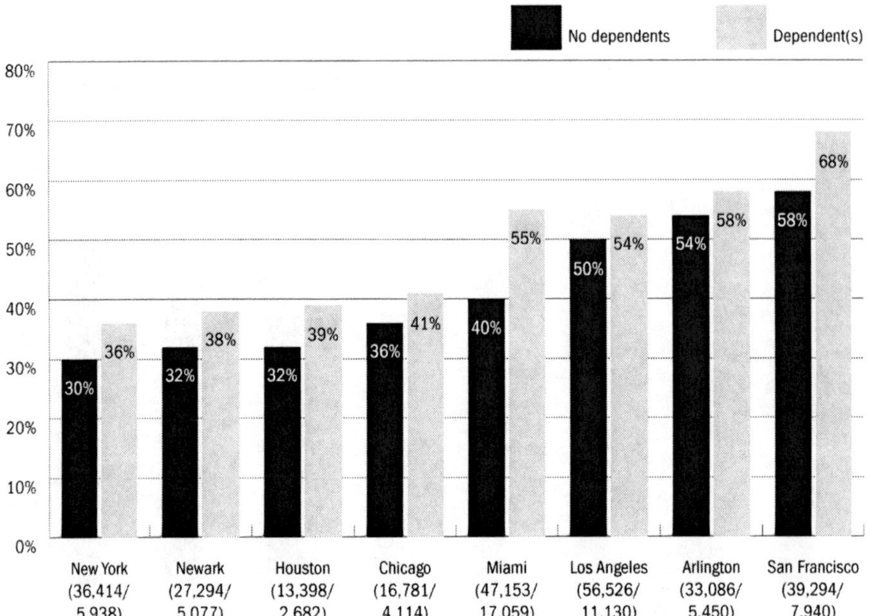

Applicants' Dependents

We also found a surprising pattern of disparities relating to dependents across the regional asylum offices. Nationally, DHS granted asylum 18 percent more often to claimants with dependents versus those without dependents (52 percent versus 44 percent). Arlington and Los Angeles granted at rates only 7 percent and 8 percent higher, respectively, to those applicants with at least one dependent. Miami, on the other hand, granted 38 percent more often to such asylum seekers (figure 8-12).[32] What might account for these differences? We return to this issue in chapter 10, in our discussion of asylum officer characteristics.

In this chapter, we have discussed disparities in grant rates across the regional asylum offices, which may be driven by different supervisory directives, variations in caseloads, diverse legal standards, and distinct patterns of applications. In the next chapter, we explore variations in grant rates within the different offices, and possible reasons for these disparities.

9

Disparities within Asylum Offices

In *Refugee Roulette,* we reported that asylum officers within some of the regional offices, to whom cases were randomly assigned, granted asylum at very different rates, even to nationals of the same country or group of countries. We now return to that issue, using the database from which the studies in the three previous chapters were drawn. This chapter reports on disparities in grant rates among officers within the eight regional asylum offices. We first examine all cases adjudicated by officers who decided at least one hundred cases, reporting these data for three asylum offices. We next hone in on a single nationality, presenting, for each regional office, grant rates of officers who decided at least one hundred cases of applicants from that office's most frequent country of origin. We then discuss reasons for these disparities offered by the asylum officers in the DHS survey and our interviews. In the chapter that follows, we explore some of the biographical characteristics of the adjudicating officers that correlate with higher or lower grant rates and that therefore might account for the disparities.

The data show that in every regional asylum office, individual officers granted asylum at very different rates, making it appear that the chance of winning asylum depended a great deal on which officer was randomly assigned a file.[1] In the graphs that follow, each bar represents the grant rate of an individual asylum officer.

With two exceptions, officers who adjudicated fewer than one hundred cases of the type identified in the graph were excluded, because an officer who adjudicated very few cases might have a grant rate that was 0 percent, 100 percent, or any other percentage just by chance. In other words, an officer who interviewed only five randomly assigned applicants might have happened by chance to have been assigned five interviewees with strong cases or five interviewees with weak cases. But it is reasonable to assume that the dockets of each officer with a large caseload was assigned approximately the same proportion of strong and weak cases as any other officer in the same regional office, so that any large disparities were caused by something other than the validity of the cases themselves. By "strong" and "weak" we refer to the sum of all characteristics of the cases that might warrant a grant or a

Fig. 9-1. Grant Rates by Asylum Officer, Chicago Office, All Nationalities

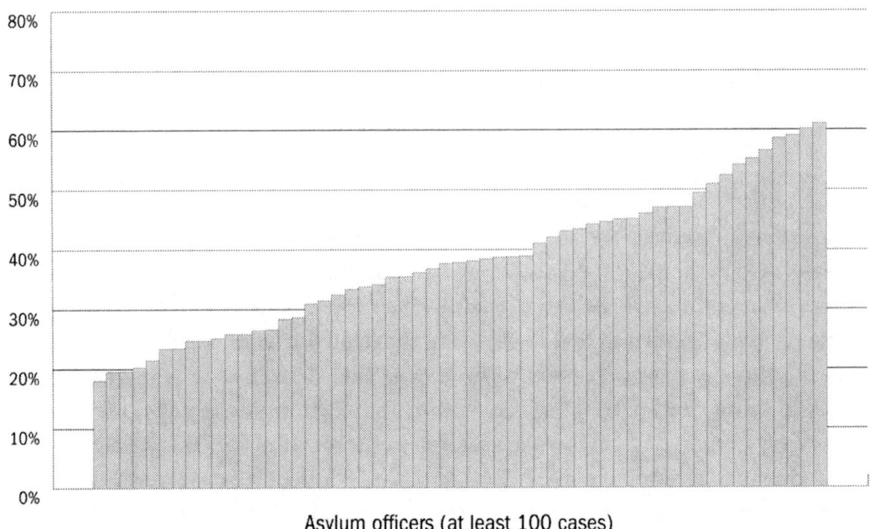

Fig. 9-2. Grant Rates by Asylum Officer, New York Office, All Nationalities

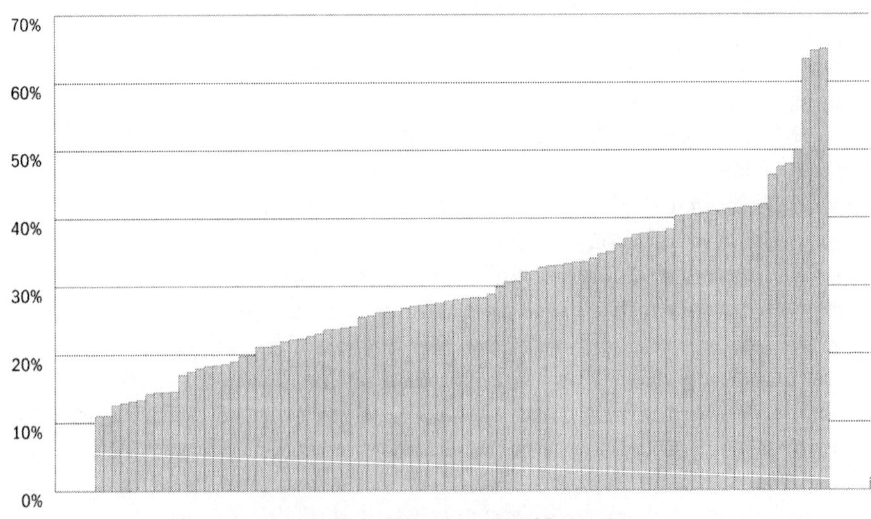

referral, including the human rights record of the country and the believability of the applicant's personal testimony and documentary evidence. If, in a particular regional office, 40 percent of the cases were strong candidates for asylum and 60 percent were too weak to justify a grant, we assume that each officer who decided a large number of these cases received about 40 percent in which the applicants were strong candidates.

Grant Rate Disparities, All Nationalities

We begin our study of grant rate disparities within particular asylum offices by exploring decisions for all nationalities by office. In the Chicago office, there were fifty-five officers who had decided at least one hundred cases. Their grant rates ranged from 18 percent to 62 percent. The mean grant rate in Chicago was 37 percent.

At the New York asylum office, which had a mean grant rate of 31 percent, grant rates ranged from 11 percent to 65 percent. There were eighty-six officers who had decided at least one hundred cases.

Newark's average grant rate was 32 percent, yet individual grant rates varied from 2.5 percent to over 90 percent (or to 80 percent, if we disregard the single officer with a 93 percent grant rate). Newark had eighty officers who decided at least one hundred cases.

Fig. 9-3. Grant Rates by Asylum Officer, Newark Office, All Nationalities

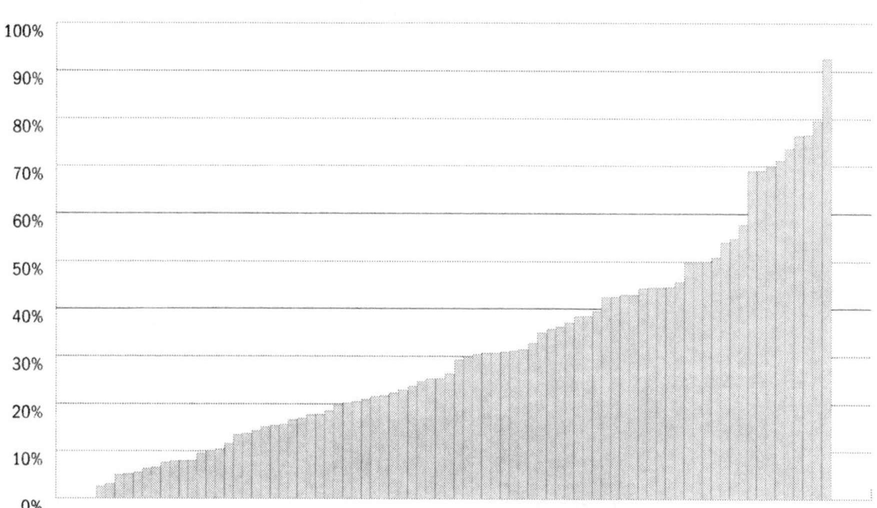

Fig. 9-4. Grant Rates by Asylum Officer, Newark Office, All Nationalities, Era 3 Only

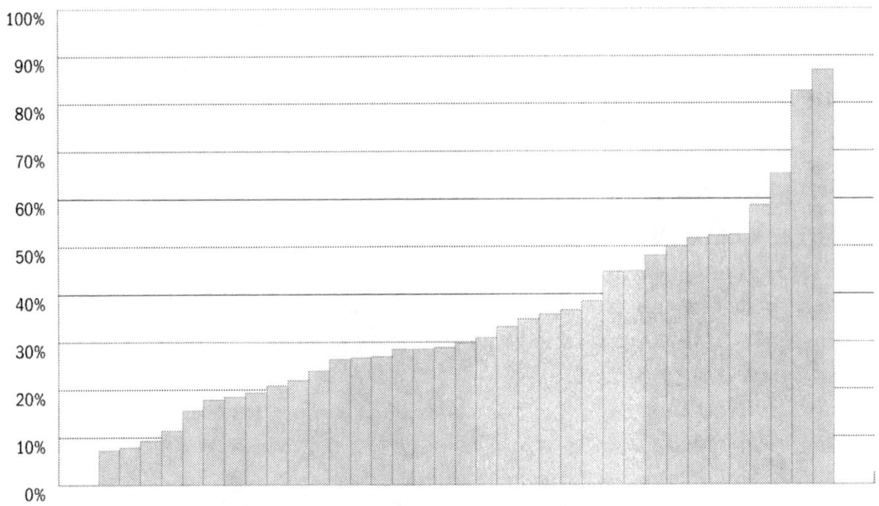

Fig. 9-5. Grant Rates by Asylum Officer, Newark Office, All Nationalities, Era 4 Only

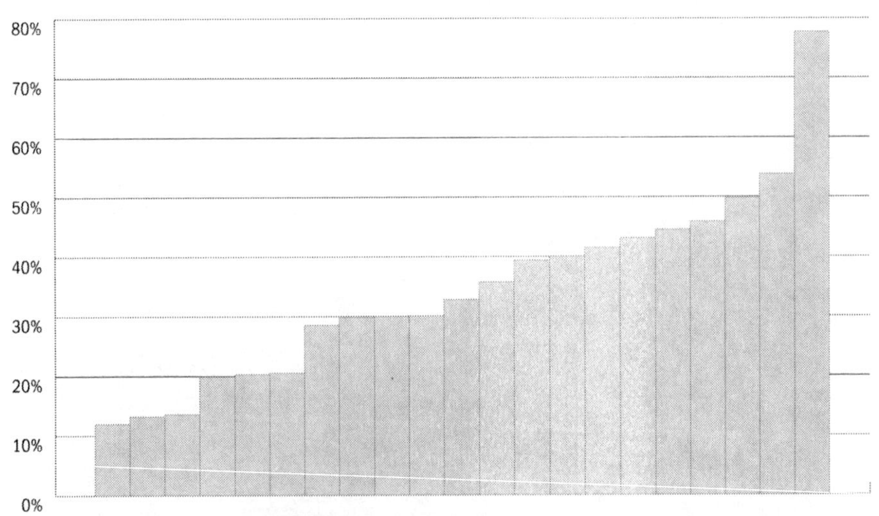

The disparities in Newark appear to have decreased in recent years. Figure 9-4 shows individual grant rates for asylum officers who had decided at least one hundred cases in Newark during Era 3, which ran from September 11, 2001, through June 30, 2006. Figure 9-5 shows the same for Era 4, from July 1, 2006, through June 8, 2009. In Era 3, the office's average grant rate was 34 percent, and thirty-three officers who had decided at least one hundred cases were adjudicating. Their grant rates ranged from 7 percent to 87 percent. In Era 4, the average grant rate was also 34 percent, but only twenty-five officers who had decided at least one hundred claims were making decisions. Grant rates ranged from 12 percent to 78 percent, and grant rates were generally more consistent. The high granter appears to be an outlier, as all of the other officers granted at rates below 55 percent. In addition, the relatively flatter slope of the graph in figure 9-5, compared to the steeper slope in figure 9-4, demonstrates the greater degree of consistency after the summer of 2006.

It may be that the national discussion of disparities in asylum adjudication helped to bring the issue of disparities to the attention of the Newark office, thereby increasing consistency in that office.[2] It is also possible that the reduction in disparity resulted instead from access to more information. Reports to asylum officers from other agencies of government, particularly reports from U.S. Customs and Border Patrol about prior entry attempts, gave asylum officers progressively more concrete information about applicants that they could check against applicants' testimony and thereby test credibility. As credibility determinations became less subjective, officers with high grant rates may have become a little more skeptical and those with low grant rates a little less skeptical, resulting in a somewhat greater consensus. In addition, in Era 4 there was a good deal of turnover of officers in the Newark office, with newly hired officers replacing officers who had worked their way up from being inspectors in the Immigration and Naturalization Service. Many of the new officers had law degrees, the significance of which we will explore in chapter 10. Therefore there may have been somewhat greater homogeneity of outlook among the officers as time passed.

Figure 9-6 is a boxplot comparing the degree of disparity in decisions on the merits within the eight regional offices. As we explained in chapter 5, the boxplot provides a variety of measurements of disparity. First, the black line in the middle of each shaded box shows the median grant rate for each regional office.[3] Second, the shaded box shows the grant rates for officers whose rates were in the middle 50 percent of grant rates in their own office. The more stretched out the box, the greater the degree of disparity for those in the middle. Third, it shows the full range of disparity in grant rates

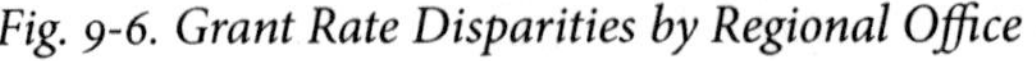

Fig. 9-6. Grant Rate Disparities by Regional Office

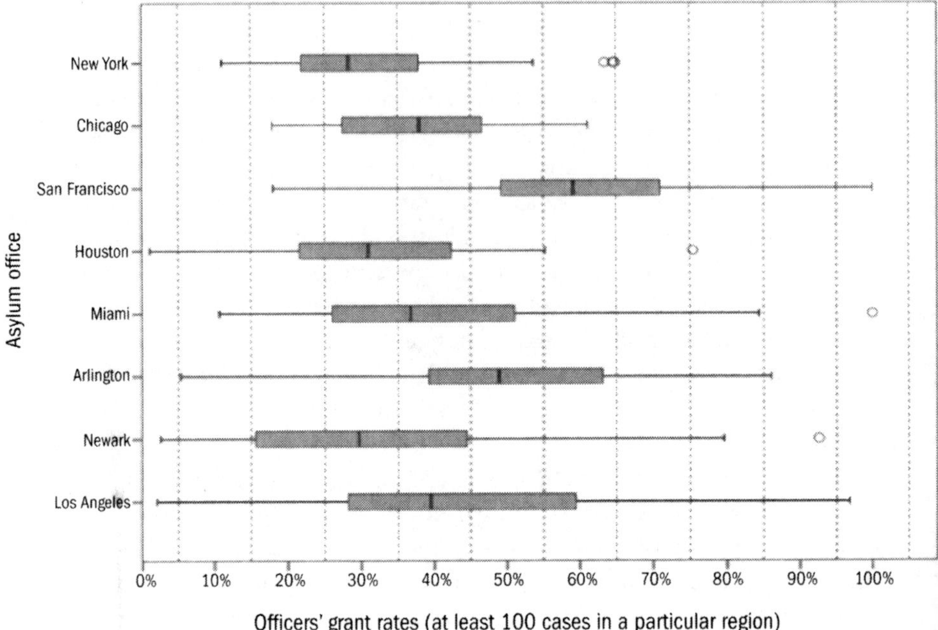

by the lines protruding from the shaded box. When a rate is 1.5 to 3 box lengths away from the end of the box, it is flagged by a circle, known as an "outlier flag." The figure reveals that judging by both the middle 50 percent and by all of their officers, New York and Chicago have the least degree of disparity. San Francisco has relatively little disparity among the middle 50 percent, but a very large spread in grant rates overall. Los Angeles and Newark have a great deal of disparity both among the middle 50 percent and among all officers.

To test whether most of the variation in this graph resulted from the fact that some officers served during the early years reported in the database while others served later, we also ran a graph showing disparities in grant rates for cases decided only during Era 4 (July 2006–June 2009). Only five officers in Houston had more than one hundred adjudications during this period, so the Houston bar in figure 9-7 is not reliable. The other bars show that large disparities persisted, though the regional offices with the most disparities changed, with Miami, Los Angeles, and Chicago having the greatest degree of disparity in the most recent years of our study.

Fig. 9-7. Grant Rate Disparities by Regional Office, Era 4

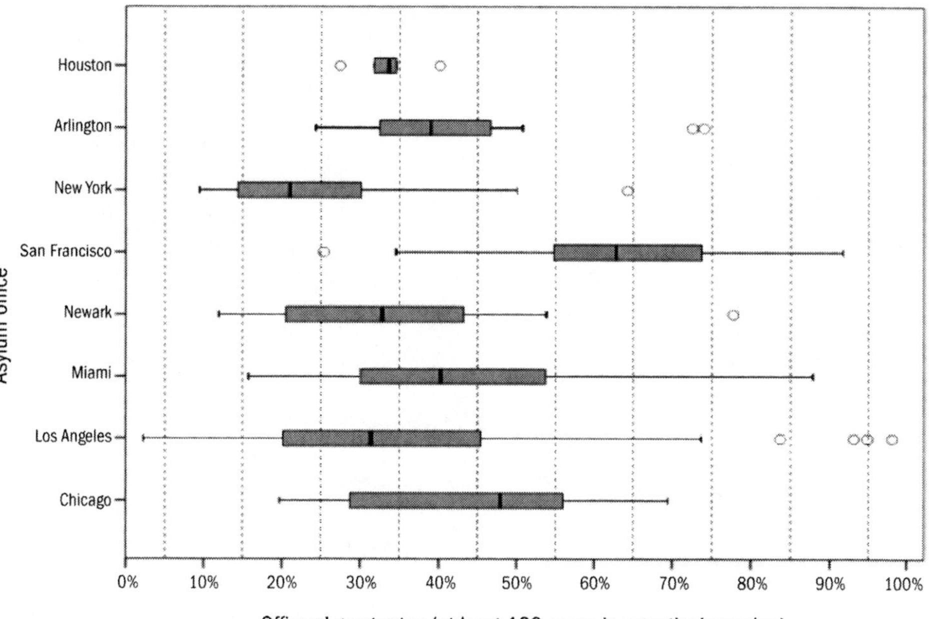

Grant Rate Disparities by Most Prevalent Nationality

We next explored individual officer variations in decision making by individual nationality. For each asylum office, we selected the nationality with the greatest number of applicants in that office, to ensure that we had a large enough pool of cases to make our data as reliable as possible. For six of the eight offices, we looked at asylum officers with at least one hundred decisions for that nationality. The two offices with the smallest number of cases overall, Chicago and Houston, did not have a sufficient number of officers with one hundred decisions for the relevant nationality, so they are not included in this discussion.

We first examine individual asylum officer decisions with respect to Ethiopian cases before the Arlington asylum office. Ethiopian applicants had a high national average grant rate, at 66 percent, and an average grant rate of 64 percent in Arlington; these numbers reflect Ethiopia's consistently poor human rights record over the time frame studied. The Arlington office decided by far the largest number of Ethiopian cases of any asylum office.[4]

Fig. 9-8. Grant Rates by Asylum Officer, Arlington Office, Ethiopian Applicants Only

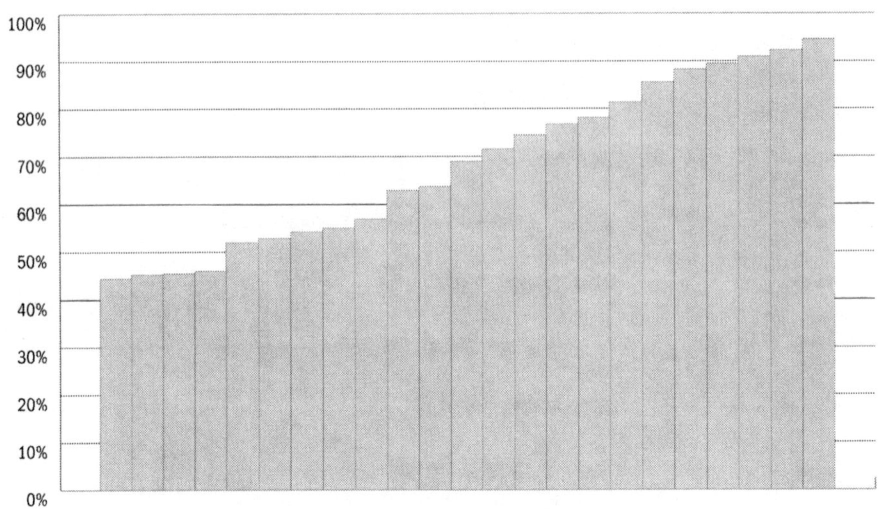

Fig. 9-9. Grant Rates by Asylum Officer, San Francisco Office, Indian Applicants Only, FY 1996–2004

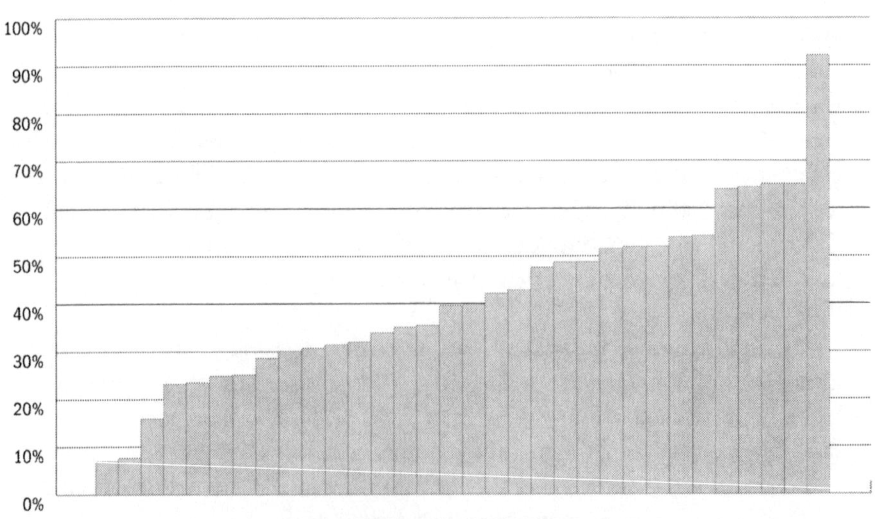

Twenty-three officers there decided at least one hundred Ethiopian cases. Their grant rates ranged from 45 percent to 95 percent.

The disparities become more marked when we turn to countries with lower national grant rates, perhaps because credibility plays an even greater role in these decisions. Indian asylum seekers represented the largest nationality group in the San Francisco office, which decided by far the most Indian cases of any asylum office.[5] Because a large-scale fraud indictment in 2004 against a law firm that represented Indian asylum seekers may have impacted grant rates, we look only at Indian cases decided before FY 2004. The average grant rate for Indian cases in San Francisco over this time frame was 41 percent; thirty-three officers decided at least one hundred Indian cases. One officer granted only 6 percent of the Indian cases before her, while another granted 91 percent.[6] For Haitian asylum seekers in Miami, individual officer grant rates were even more disparate. Miami decided the vast majority of Haitian cases, at an average grant rate of 34 percent.[7] Eighty-five officers decided at least one hundred Haitian cases. Their individual grant rates ranged from 5 percent to 85 percent, demonstrating little consistency in decision making.

China was the largest nationality for three asylum offices: Los Angeles, New York, and Newark. These were also the three offices that heard the

Fig. 9-10. Grant Rates by Asylum Officer, Miami Office, Haitian Applicants Only

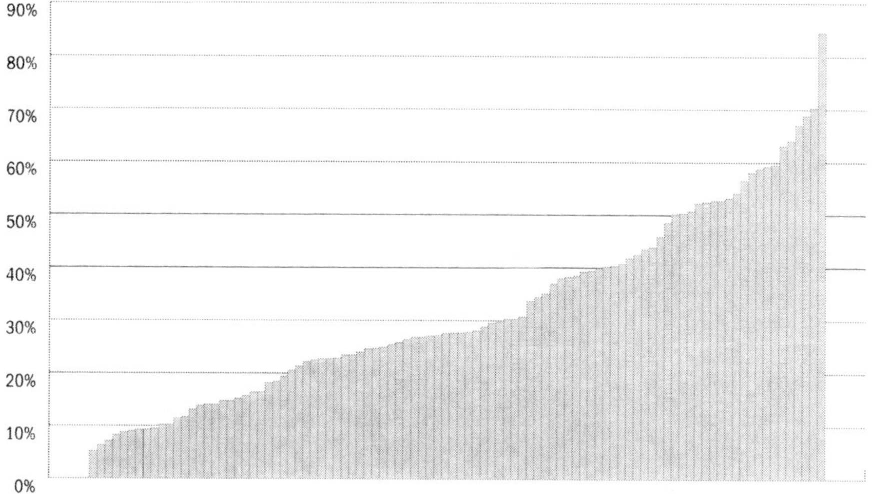

Fig. 9-11. Individual Asylum Officer Decisions, Chinese Cases Only

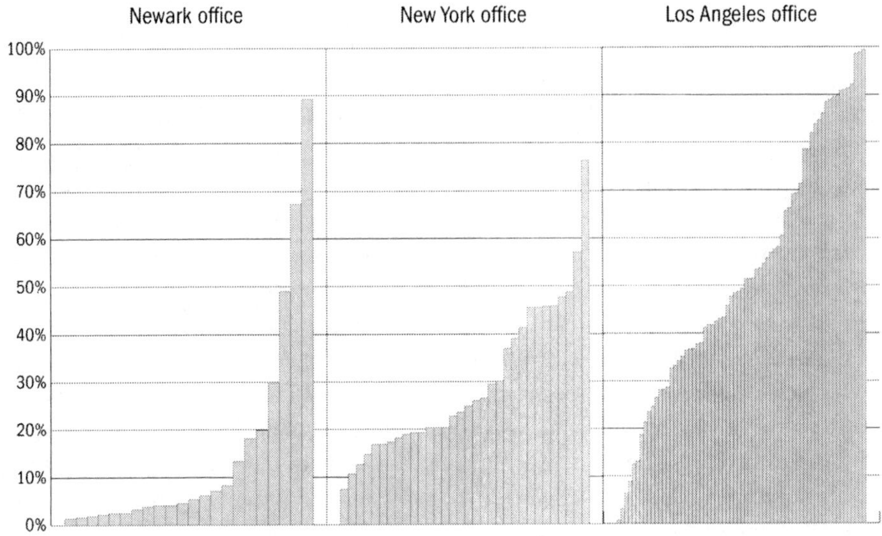

Fig. 9-12. Individual Los Angeles Asylum Officer Decisions, Chinese Cases Only, July 1, 2006–June 8, 2009

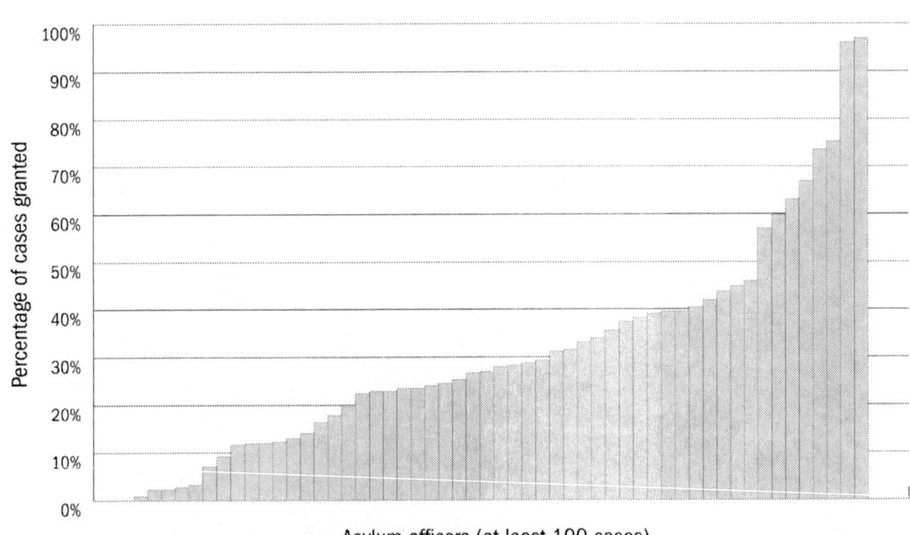

largest number of Chinese asylum claims: of the 51,706 total Chinese cases decided over the time frame studied, the Los Angeles office decided 21,882, the New York office decided 13,422, and the Newark office decided 7535. Though the nationwide grant rate for Chinese cases was 46 percent, the Los Angeles office mean was 59 percent, the New York mean was 28 percent, and the Newark mean was 18 percent. Figure 9-11 shows quite different levels of disparities in these three offices. In New York, 31 officers decided one hundred or more Chinese cases; their grant rates ranged from 7 percent to 77 percent. In Newark, 22 officers decided at least one hundred Chinese cases. One officer granted 2 percent of the Chinese cases he heard while another granted 89 percent. Fifteen Newark officers granted Chinese cases at rates under 9 percent. Sixty-seven officers in Los Angeles decided at least one hundred Chinese cases; their rates varied from less than 1 percent to 99 percent.

Because the grant rates for Chinese cases in the Los Angeles office appeared to be so disparate, we wondered whether the difference might be due principally to the fact that some officers served early in the period that we studied and others served much later. We therefore examined the rates of the 53 officers in Los Angeles who decided at least one hundred cases of Chinese applicants during Era 4 (July 1, 2006 through June 8, 2009). Figure 9-12 displays the results of this study. It shows that even with the time period so limited, the grant rates spanned a very large range, from 1 percent to 97 percent.

Explanations for Individual Officer Disparities

The Department of Homeland Security's survey of and our interviews with asylum officers provided at least two reasons exogenous to the asylum officers for these disparities: supervisory asylum officers and caseload pressures. In the next chapter we discuss certain factors, endogenous to the asylum officers, that may also have contributed to these disparities.

Several officers told us that supervisory asylum officers, who give general guidance to the asylum officers as well as approve or disapprove all their decisions, accounted for much of the disparity:

> [Some] supervisors are more or less strenuous, so the [asylum] officer's natural tendencies are either accentuated or not. If a [high-] granting officer by nature is paired with a supervisor who doesn't like to grant, you'll still get grants but not as many. If you have an ex-advocate paired with an ex-advocate, that's a deadly duo, whereas if you have an ex-CBP [Customs and Border Patrol] paired with another ex-CBP, you aren't going to get much out of them. It shouldn't be that way but it probably is.

Another officer emphasized the differences between new and more experienced supervisory asylum officers, suggesting that changes in supervisory approaches over time might be yet another cause of inconsistency:

> As new officers come on and have been around for a few years, they get promoted, they become supervisory asylum officers. Newer supervisory AOs have a tendency to be much more by the letter of the lesson plans than the older officers. And what happens when you get an old-timer, someone who's done thousands of asylum interviews, heard it all before and they get matched up with a brand-new supervisor. What are the chances that supervisor will say, "He's been here for a while, his work is not so great, but I'll just sign off on it." I would be much more inclined with ten years of experience to think that way; it's just the path of least resistance.

Furthermore, another officer, who had become a supervisor, suggested that it was difficult for supervisors to enforce any kind of policy that would lead to greater consistency:

> I had one person on my team [with an] Indonesian ethnic Chinese claim and they said, "It's a pattern and practice of persecution that has been going on since 1998, and [the Supreme Court's case law says that if a reasonable person in her shoes would fear persecution] I should grant the case." The very next file I pick up, it's asylum officer B, and it says, "There isn't a pattern and practice, [and] it's just discrimination [rather than persecution because they only burned down the store]." And I thought, "That makes sense, I'll sign off on it." So there I was, on the same day, the same fact pattern, signing off on two legally sufficient arguments that were vastly different. That is just the name of the game. [Suppose] one of my colleagues told her team, "If you have an ethnic Chinese Indonesian, you are not granting that case unless that person says I was raped or I was beaten up." I always told myself that I was never going to set these blanket kinds of things, but by doing that [that is, by not making blanket rules for grants and denials] the fallout is that it looks like you're really inconsistent.

One supervisory asylum officer told us that time constraints are the biggest obstacle to consistency. For asylum officers, the lack of time leads to underdeveloped records, which are difficult for supervisory officers to review accurately. According to this officer, even supervisors can't be as thorough in their reviews as they would like given time constraints and productivity requirements.

Some asylum officers offered rationales for disparities that we are not able to test with our data:

> It's based on some officers' personal agendas; some officers think that no one is deserving of an asylum grant.

> As long as human beings adjudicate claims and not computers there will be discrepancies in the grant rate. Some officers base their decisions on emotional arguments, not necessarily based in fact, and some may adjudicate in an intellectual vacuum of certain perceptions and another may adjudicate on the basis of determining the truth rather than "legal sufficiency," which is the standard, and legal sufficiency can mean different things to different officers.

In chapter 10, we take up the question of sociological characteristics that may relate to personal agendas, predilections, or biases, and explore their impact on grant rates.

10

The Asylum Officers

In chapter 9, we saw that there was great variability among the grant rates of asylum officers deciding similar cases within the same regional office. What might account for these striking disparities? One asylum officer with whom we spoke closed our interview by saying "there are so many factors that play into the data—the age of the asylum officer, whether they have an old or a new supervisor, whether they are close to retirement, their background, whether they had breakfast that morning."[1] To the extent possible, we used the data that DHS supplied to us to identify relationships between personal characteristics of the asylum officers and grant rates. DHS did not record which officers ate breakfast on which days, but the agency did keep records on many attributes of officers who were trained during a particular five-year period.

This chapter studies the 31,635 decisions made by the 221 asylum officers who attended Asylum Officer Basic Training (AOBTC) classes at the Federal Law Enforcement Training Center (FLETC) between July 2003 and July 2008.[2] Of those 221 officers, 196 were new hires trained shortly after beginning service, while the other 25 officers had joined DHS before July 2003. Most of the cases in that database (a subset of the larger database used for the analysis in chapters 6 through 9) were therefore decided by officers who joined the asylum officer corps between 2003 and 2008.

At FLETC, the officers completed a questionnaire that collected certain biographical characteristics, including their educational degrees, ethnicity, gender, and prior work experience.[3] We examined the relationship between these variables and the officers' asylum grant rates. To confirm the statistical significance of these relationships, we ran two logistic regressions, including one with standard errors clustered by asylum officer. We also ran a hierarchical logistic regression. The three regressions contained the same independent variables.[4] Unless otherwise noted, the relationships between these variables and the dependent variable of grant rate were statistically significant[5] and confirmed the direction of the relationships presented in the cross-tabulation analyses.[6]

We also constructed a variable from our primary database of 329,336 decisions on the merits made by 1,232 asylum officers between October 1995 and June 2009. This variable measured, for each case, the number of asylum

Table 10-1. Percentage of Officers by Regional Asylum Office in the Two Databases

Asylum office	Full database	Biographical database
Arlington	12%	19%
Chicago	6%	6%
Houston	5%	3%
Los Angeles	21%	15%
Miami	20%	28%
Newark	10%	12%
New York	13%	4%
San Francisco	14%	14%

decisions previously made by the officer who decided the case, enabling us to learn how prior experience correlated with the officer's grant rate.

It is important to note that the smaller database we describe below does not precisely reflect the composition of the larger database. As described in table 10-1, there were more officers from Arlington, Miami, and Newark and fewer officers from Houston, Los Angeles, and New York in the smaller database.

The overall grant rate for the subset of the 31,635 officers trained at FLETC was 46.6 percent. This overall rate was similar to the 45.1 percent grant rate of the officers in the much larger database discussed in chapters 6 through 9 (and used in this chapter to measure prior experience). The percentage of cases coming from countries with the highest (12-14) Freedom House scores (representing the greatest degree of human rights abuse) was also similar: 41 percent in the larger database, 43 percent in the smaller one.

Gender of the Asylum Officers

Much of the data show little by way of unexpected variations. In our previous research, we found surprisingly disparate grant rates for male and female immigration judges. From January 2000 through August 2004, female immigration judges granted asylum at a rate 44 percent higher than that of their male counterparts.[7] By contrast, there was little difference (only 1.7 percentage points) between the average grant rates of the 94 male (45.7 percent) and 127 female (47.4 percent) asylum officers during the time frame of this study.[8] As figure 10-1 demonstrates, the difference was slightly greater between the grant rates of female officers for male applicants (47 percent) and the grant

Fig. 10-1. Grant Rates by Gender of Officer and Applicant

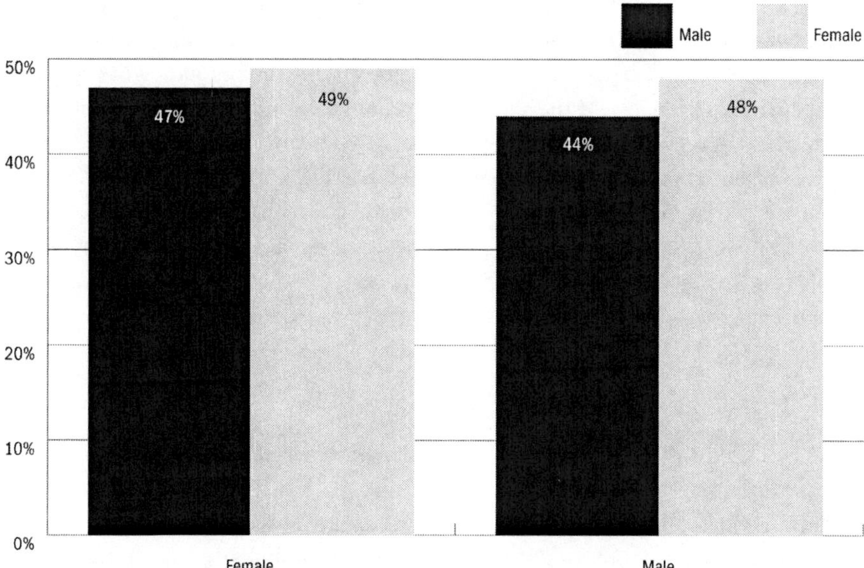

rates of male officers for male applicants (44 percent); in other words, female officers granted asylum to male applicants at a rate 7 percent greater than their male counterparts' rate.[9] These rather small differences put in perspective some of the much larger differences reported in this chapter and elsewhere in this book.

Prior Government Service

Some asylum officers we spoke with speculated that disparities between individual adjudicators within an office were caused by the prior work experiences of the officers. One officer observed that officers who have relatively lower grant rates are

> those who came into the system earlier, having been INS inspectors or border patrol agents. They never made the transition to asylum. . . . Some mind-sets are not capable of ever letting go. There is always a tangential document in the case that bothers them. Of course there are also people who don't pay attention, and grant everything. That's just as bad.

Our findings concerning prior government work experience did not necessarily support this theory, and they differed from our findings in *Refugee Roulette*. In immigration court, we found that immigration judges with prior government work experience had lower grant rates than adjudicators without such experience.[10] At the asylum office, however, adjudicators with prior government service had higher grant rates (49 percent) than officers with no government experience (46 percent).[11] One possible explanation for this difference is that, for immigration judges, prior government experience often involved work as a trial attorney prosecuting cases in immigration court. In contrast, the asylum office may have attracted adjudicators with prior government experience of a more varied nature.[12]

Ethnicity of the Asylum Officers

We analyzed self-reported ethnicity information for 208 of the asylum officers participating in the FLETC training.[13] At first blush, it seemed as though Black asylum officers had lower grant rates than Hispanic and White asylum officers.[14] As figure 10-2 shows, the grant rate of the Hispanic officers (50 percent) was 32 percent higher than that of the Black officers (38 percent).

Fig. 10-2. Grant Rates by Ethnicity of Asylum Officer

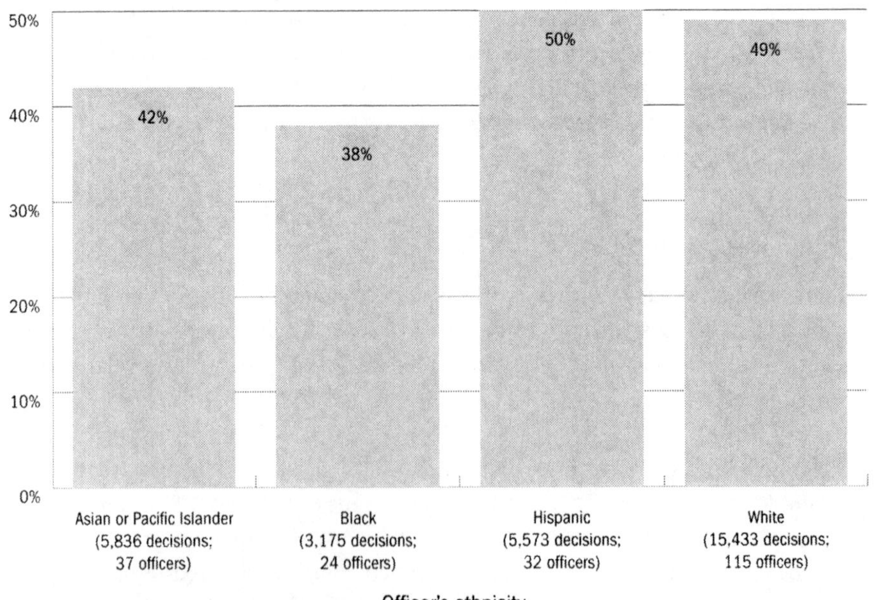

The grant rates of the Asian or Pacific Islander and White officers were in between these two figures.[15]

The regression analyses, however, showed that factors other than race contributed to these differences.[16] In fact, holding all other variables in the model constant, two of the regressions failed to confirm a statistically significant relationship with grant rates for either the Black or Hispanic categories.[17] This lack of significance probably resulted from the fact that the grant rates for these ethnicities (once all other variables are held constant) were indistinguishable from those of White officers (the control category). But in all three regressions, with all other variables in the model held constant, Asian or Pacific Islander ethnicity of the officer correlated with grant rates lower than those of the other three self-reported ethnic groups.

Officer's Ethnicity and Applicant's Status at Entry

The ethnicity variable played out in interesting ways when combined with other variables.[18] Black and Asian or Pacific Islander asylum officers granted

Fig. 10-3. Grant Rates for Inspected and Uninspected Applicants, by Ethnicity of Asylum Officer

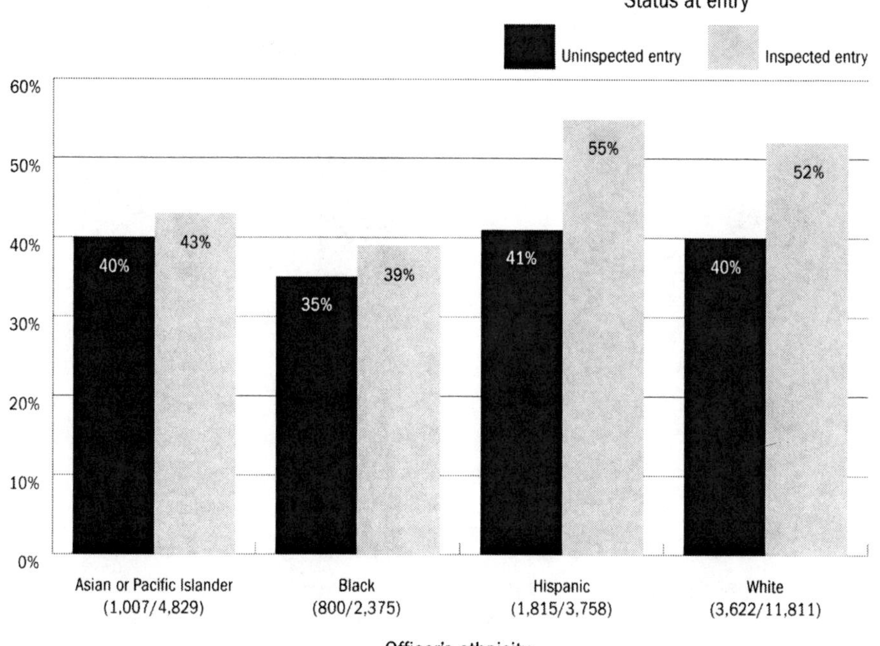

asylum at approximately equal rates to inspected and uninspected applicants. But Hispanic and White asylum officers had grant rates for inspected applicants that were 34 and 30 percent greater, respectively, than their grant rates for uninspected applicants (figure 10-3).[19]

Officer's Ethnicity and Representation of Applicant

When we look at the asylum officer's ethnicity and whether the applicant was represented, we see that having a representative improved the prospects of prevailing, on the whole, only for applicants who were assigned to White officers. We first note that in this smaller database on which this chapter is based, unrepresented applicants won asylum more often than represented applicants. This contrasts with the finding reported in chapter 7 that, over the time frame of the entire study, represented applicants won asylum more often than unrepresented applicants. It does, however, comport with the finding also reported in chapter 7 that the difference between represented and unrepresented applicants diminished over the course of the study, given

Fig. 10-4. Grant Rates by Ethnicity of Officer and Representation of Applicants

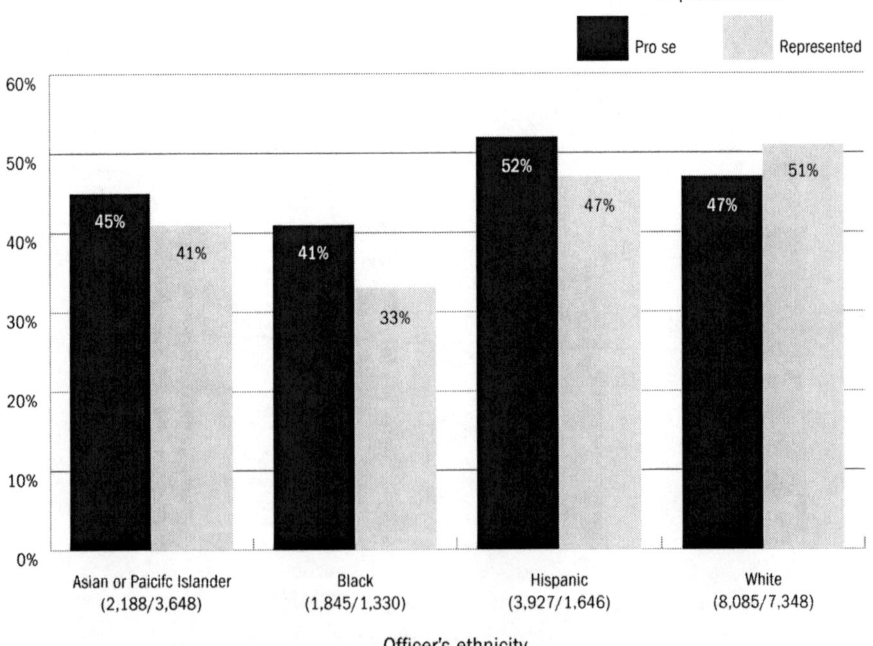

that this smaller database focuses on decisions made toward the end of the time frame of the study.

Asian or Pacific Islander, Black, and Hispanic officers granted asylum more often to *unrepresented* applicants (figure 10-4).[20] Black officers granted 24 percent more often to unrepresented applicants. In contrast, White officers granted 9 percent more often to represented applicants. Because there were more White officers than nonwhite officers, the overall grant rate was nearly the same for represented (46 percent) as for unrepresented (47 percent) applicants.

Officer's Ethnicity and Applicant's Dependents

We also discovered surprising differences with regard to whether or not applicants had dependents, as shown in figure 10-5.[21] Most officers granted asylum at about the same rates to applicants with or without dependents, but Hispanic officers' grant rate was 23 percent higher for applicants with dependents than for those who did not have dependents.

Fig. 10-5. Grant Rates by Ethnicity of Officer and Whether or Not Applicants Had Dependents

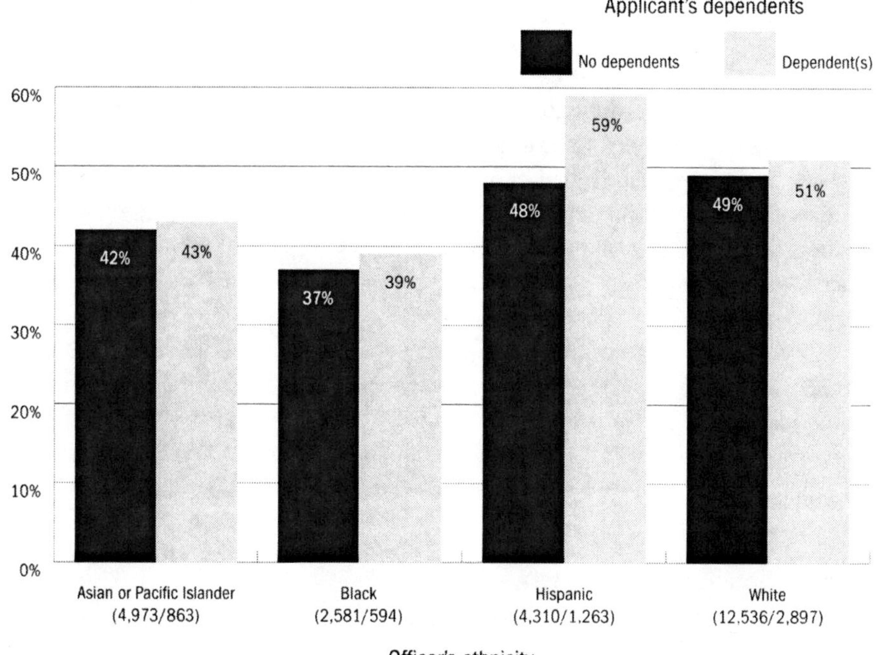

Fig. 10-6. Grant Rates by Ethnicity of Officer and Whether or Not Latin American and Caribbean Applicants Had Dependents

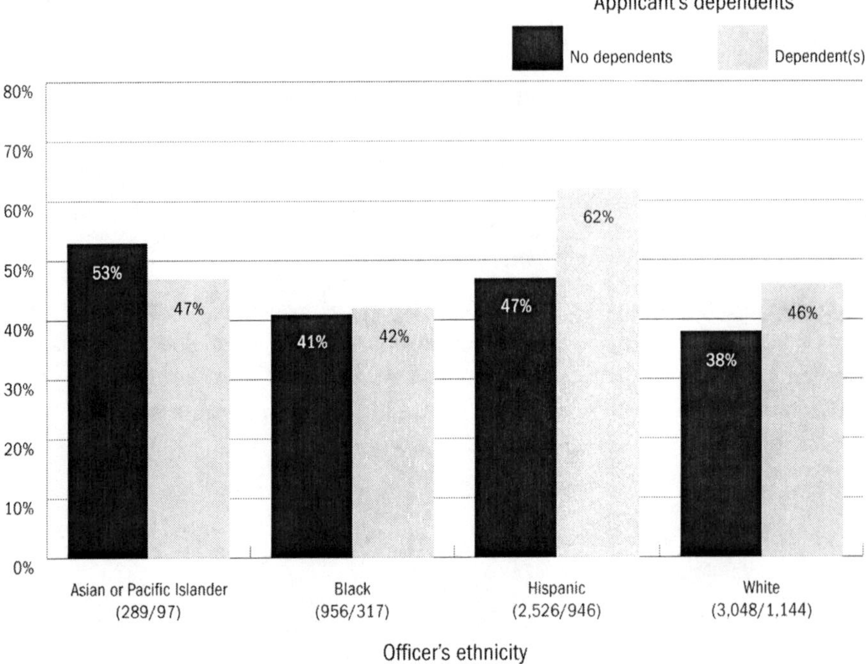

The differences in the outcomes for applicants with and without dependents was greatest for applicants from Latin America and the Caribbean whose cases were adjudicated by Hispanic asylum officers, as shown in figure 10-6.[22] These officers granted asylum to applicants with dependents at a rate 32 percent higher than they granted asylum to applicants without dependents. Among officers of other ethnicities adjudicating claims from the same region, the differences were much smaller.

By contrast, Hispanic officers granted asylum only 17 percent more often to applicants from East Asia and the Pacific with dependents than to applicants from East Asia and the Pacific without dependents.[23] But Asian or Pacific Islander officers granted asylum to East Asian and Pacific applicants with dependents at a rate 27.2 percent higher than to East Asian and Pacific applicants without dependents.[24]

Legal Education of the Officers

Asylum law is quite complex; officers must apply dense and often opaque rules from many sources including their training manuals, federal

Fig. 10-7. Grant Rates by Applicant Representation and Officer's Education

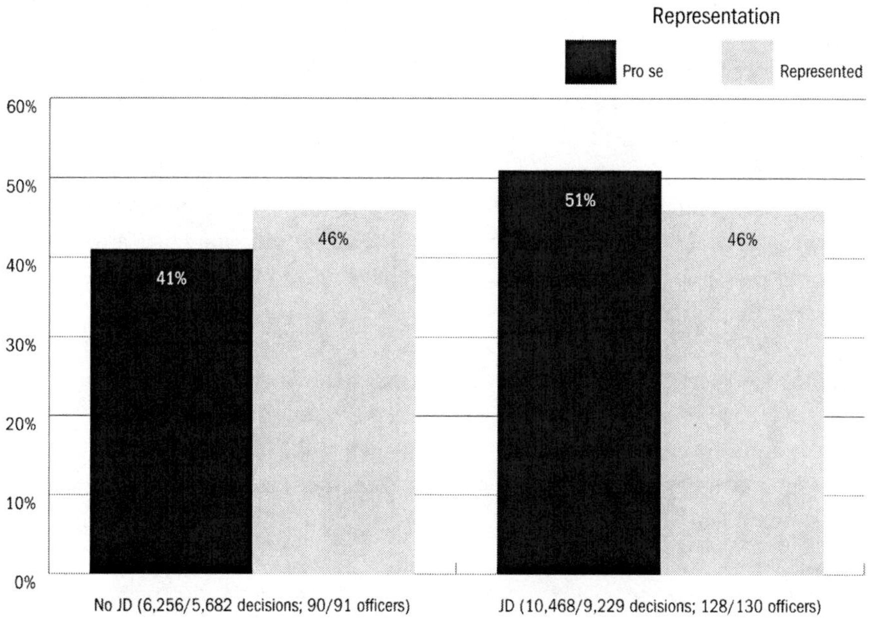

regulations, the Immigration and Nationality Act, decisions of the Board of Immigration Appeals, decisions of federal courts of appeals, and on occasion, treaties ratified by the United States and interpretations of those treaties by sister agencies in other countries such as Canada and Great Britain. We therefore explored the asylum officers' education to see whether having received a legal education correlated with grant rates.

We first examined the impact of having a juris doctor (JD) degree on case outcomes. Of the 221 asylum officers in our study, 130 reported that they held a JD degree. Asylum officers with a law degree granted asylum at a rate of 48.7 percent, 12.5 percent higher than the grant rate of 43.3 percent for officers without a law degree. The regression analyses confirmed that, with all other variables in the model held constant, for asylum officers, holding a law degree correlated with higher grant rates.

The graph in figure 10-7, however, tells an interesting story about the difference between officers with a law degree and those without.[25] For legally educated officers, pro se applicants had a grant rate 11 percent higher than represented applicants. In contrast, for officers without a legal education, represented applicants won asylum more often, with a grant rate 12 percent higher than pro se asylum seekers.

If we look at this differential from another angle, we see that represented applicants had basically the same grant rate regardless of whether the deciding officer had a law degree. But officers with a law degree granted asylum to pro se applicants at a rate 24 percent higher than did officers without law degrees (figure 10-8).[26]

The asylum officers with whom we spoke were not surprised by our finding. They pointed out that an officer with a JD degree in a nonadversarial interview could perform some of the investigative functions that a lawyer would have undertaken had the applicant been able to afford representation. One of them explained:

> With somebody who has a law degree, they are trained in issue spotting, and the legal analysis part of adjudicating the cases—they have the ability to evaluate and balance multiple factors whereas the nonlawyer adjudicator, when they see a difficult or complex case, they may say, well, it's safer

Fig. 10-8. Grant Rates by Officer's Education and Applicant Representation

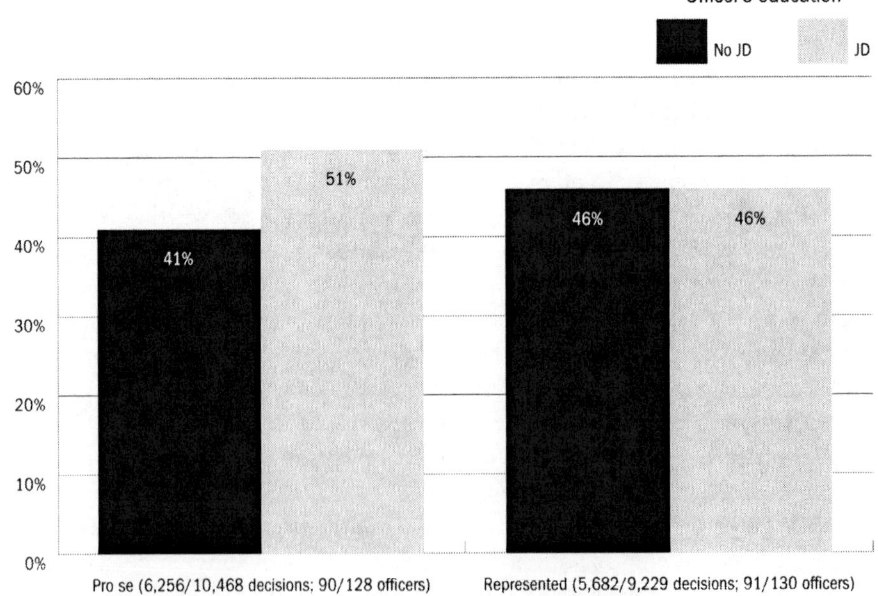

> just to refer and have them take it up with the judge because they don't understand it or see [the issue]. When I was doing the training, the issue-spotting part is very difficult for nonlawyers. Personally, I think every asylum officer should be a lawyer or have a legal background; you're dealing with the law and have to read cases all day long. Many times when I was an asylum officer and had a hard time deciding a case, [I would] go on Westlaw and look at precedent to see how a case was approached. I did this often before the interview to figure out how to formulate questions; if you don't formulate questions right, you can't write it up correctly—in a difficult case there might be a nexus but [a nonlawyer] might deny or refer a case. . . . They should revise the job description to make a JD requirement to do this kind of job.

Another asylum officer who was not a lawyer gave us a concrete example:

> Those who have a law degree, it's just more nuanced, it's more informed by caselaw. There was a [Court of Appeals] case that threatening phone calls can amount to persecution. If I didn't have my Westlaw password, I probably wouldn't know that. . . . You have to be willing to say, hmm, what does the [Court of Appeals] have to say about this? And I think if you have a legal background, that's your natural inclination.

Still another officer connected the difference between lawyer adjudicators and nonlawyer adjudicators to the different pools from which the asylum office hires its personnel:

> The asylum corps pulls from two pools: immigration advocates and CBP and ICE [border patrol officers and immigration enforcement personnel]. And with the unrepresented people, the former CBP and ICE people don't go digging deep into the story, whereas the advocates dig deeper. The advocates are more likely to be lawyers. To be in CBP or ICE you started at a young age and generally if you had a law degree you wouldn't be there, and if you did have a law degree you wouldn't go to the asylum office, you'd go be a trial attorney [arguing for the government in immigration court]. That's generally a higher pay grade.

DHS's survey of asylum officers did not ask the extent to which the officers probed the cases for facts and law that might warrant a grant. But DHS did ask how often officers developed a possible exception to the one-year deadline that the asylum applicant had not offered on her own. Only

8 percent of the 77 respondents with four-year college educations reported that they did so 75 percent to 100 percent of the time, compared to 17 percent of the 127 officers with law degrees. This sizable, though self-reported, difference may suggest that those with law degrees probe the applications more carefully, particularly with respect to highly technical issues, such as those presented in the regulations defining acceptable exceptions to the one-year deadline.

The difference between officers with and without law degrees was particularly marked for Hispanic and Black officers. Hispanic officers with JDs granted at a rate 29 percent higher than those without, and for Black officers, the JD–non-JD differential was even greater, at 47 percent (figure 10-9).[27]

A senior headquarters official suggested that "individuals with law degrees have wider opportunities for careers, so they have more choices—those who choose this part of the profession are people interested in human rights, and this effect could be even more pronounced with minority attorneys."

Fig. 10-9. Grant Rates by Ethnicity and Legal Education of Officers

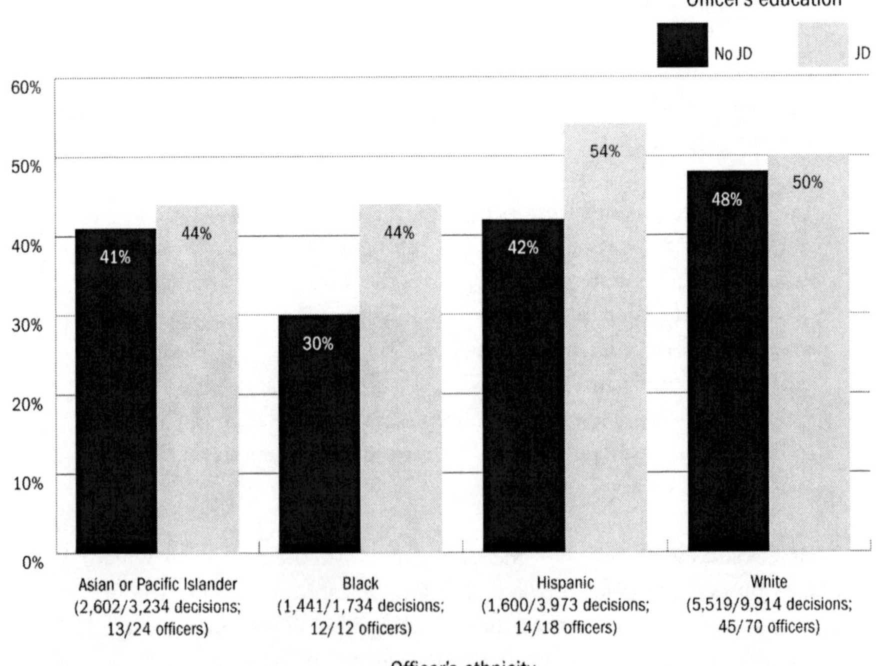

Number of Asylum Cases Previously Decided

Before we began our research for this book, we supposed, consistent with an idea prevalent among many practitioners, that the more cases an officer decided, the more jaded the officer became, both because the officer would become inured to stories of persecution and torture and because he or she would encounter cases of fraud that would make the officer more suspicious of applicants in general, and less likely to accept their stories as true. The asylum officers as a group shared our assumption. In DHS's survey of asylum officers, 61.2 percent of respondents, or 131 officers, believed that as asylum officers amassed more experience, their grant rate decreased. Only 2.3 percent, or 5 officers, believed that as asylum officers adjudicated more cases, their grant rate increased.[28] We measured experience by number of cases decided prior to the current case. As illustrated in figure 10-10, in contrast to our assumption and the expectations of the asylum officers surveyed, the grant rates of asylum officers in our study increased steadily with experience.[29]

The few asylum officers who predicted this outcome had a variety of explanations. On the more positive side, officers believed that those with

Fig. 10-10. Grant Rates by Number of Asylum Cases Previously Decided by Officers

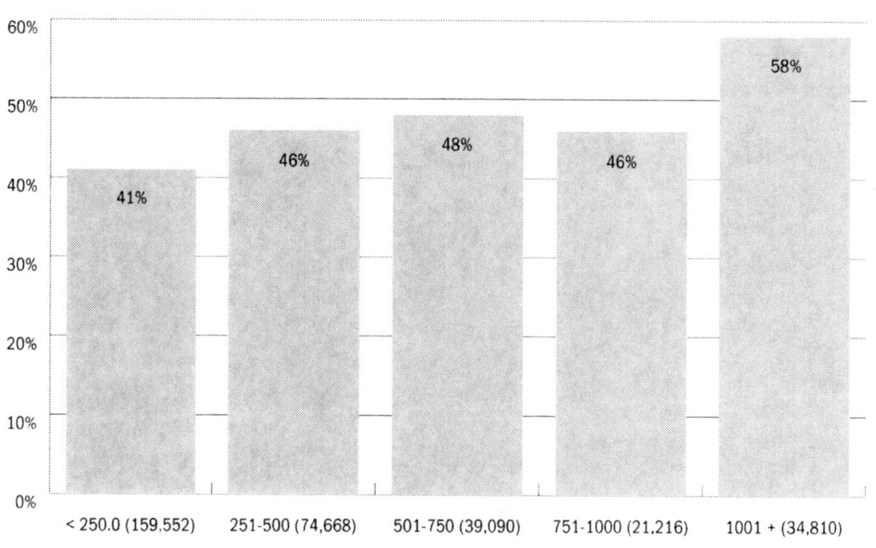

more experience "become more comfortable interviewing"; in particular, they "learn to ask better questions to tease out information." One officer thought that asylum officers with more experience have a "greater knowledge of the various issues and the law." An alternative and more negative explanation was that asylum officers with more experience "probe credibility less, since credibility assessments are difficult and time-consuming to write." Another officer noted that "the emphasis on numbers [of decisions per week or month] incentivizes" higher grant rates, since it takes less time to grant a case than to develop enough facts to justify ruling against the applicant.

Many of the asylum officers who assumed that grant rates decreased with experience similarly thought that more experience produced better interviewing skills (in particular probing credibility), knowledge of country conditions, and familiarity with the law, but that more skill would lead to lower grant rates. In the words of one, "Better interviews, better research = better decisions." Another said, "More knowledge, more experience = better questioning and probing of relevant issues." These officers believed that such experience would lead officers to be more attuned to fraud and more skeptical in credibility determinations. Several thought that more experienced officers become jaded or burned out. In the words of one, with experience, officers become "cynical, [and] lose the ability to relate to the horror that many refugees endure." The data, however, appear to belie this belief.

Asylum officers we interviewed had several explanations for the data we reported to them. One said, "Perhaps the more cases you see the more likely what they are saying is true. You become more expert and see that the situation is as bad as is being painted." Another had a darker theory:

> For your first five hundred or so cases, you are still figuring out [what is going on in each case]. Then you start denying because you see that certain documents are being submitted over and over and you start seeing fraud. But then, at a certain point, you say that they are all being granted by the immigration judges anyway so you just grant all the Chinese cases and move on. Most everyone from China has some sort of population control story or religious persecution. You can ask about their house church but every house church has a different procedure so that doesn't prove anything. They have learned to keep the case simple, with no documents that can reveal a fraud. You get beaten down from seeing what the judges are doing. You know it's going to be granted anyway.[30]

Similarly, one asylum officer explained:

> The way that I would classify this job, the first year asylum officers are overwhelmed by everything and really become aware of the time constraints. The second year, that's probably the most rewarding, because you know enough about the job that you know how to do it and you're working out your system and your routine but you're not so burned out by it that it doesn't romance you anymore. And then the third year, you either move on to a job in DC, you get promoted to Quality Assurance Trainer or Supervisory Asylum Officer or you move out. If you stay beyond the third year, it just becomes, you're the cog in a machine.

A senior headquarters official had this explanation: "People who stay a long time are either those who are trapped, they can't get another job, or those who like what they are doing. In either event, they are more likely to grant than to refer, because it's more pleasant to grant than to deny. Nobody wants to feel miserable in a job they are in for the rest of their lives."

We discovered, however, that Chinese cases showed a different pattern relating experience to grant rates. For the universe of all cases, there was a very slight (4 percent) dip in grant rates for officers who had decided 751–1,000 cases; then grant rates rose by 26 percent for the most experienced adjudicators (those who had decided more than 1,000 cases). But, as figure 10-11 shows, in Chinese cases,

Fig. 10-11. Grant Rates by Officer's Experience, Chinese Cases Only

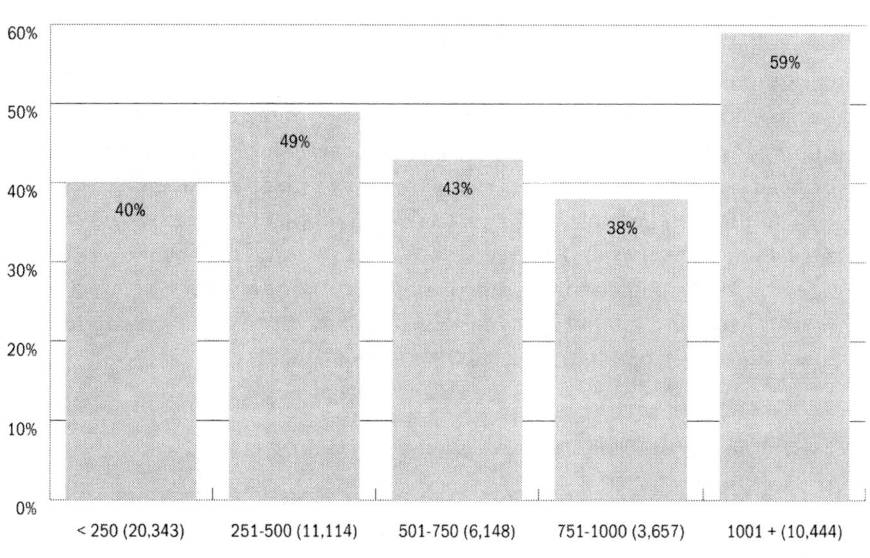

grant rates dropped by 12 percent for officers who had decided 501-750 cases and by another 12 percent for officers who had decided 751–1,000 cases.[31] Grant rates shot up by 55 percent for the most experienced adjudicators.

Further narrowing the focus, we found that the pattern in Chinese cases was especially pronounced among officers in Los Angeles (figure 10-12).[32]

Avenues for Future Research

In addition to the more robust variables described above, DHS provided us with information about asylum officers' marital status at the time of the FLETC training and about officers' states of birth. We describe below the limitations of these variables and the nonetheless interesting findings that resulted from our exploration of their relationship with grant rates. In future studies, we hope that these biographical characteristics of asylum officers can be measured more accurately. In chapter 11, we offer a description of other data that we hope DHS will begin to collect for future empirical studies of the asylum system.

Officer's Marital Status

DHS also provided us with information about asylum officers' marital status at the time of their FLETC training. Marital status is a social characteristic that can change, so we present these data with the caveat that they are not perfectly accurate—that is, some asylum officers were married or divorced after their training but before the end of the study. The decisions made by these officers after any change in their marital status are not accurately recorded in the data. So, for example, if an officer was married at the time of the FLETC training and was divorced a year later, all of the decisions she made after being divorced would be classified as decisions made by a married officer.

With that concern in mind, figure 10-13 shows that married asylum officers had the lowest grant rate and separated or divorced asylum officers the highest.[33] Perhaps those who ended unhappy marriages were happier, or perhaps had more time to spend in the office than those who were married. Either situation might have affected their decision making.

Officer's Region of Birth

We also see an interesting pattern of disparities based on the region of the asylum officers' state of birth.[34] This variable must of course be taken with a grain of salt, given that region of birth means only that. It does not mean that

Fig. 10-12. Grant Rates by Officer's Experience, Chinese Cases in the Los Angeles Regional Office

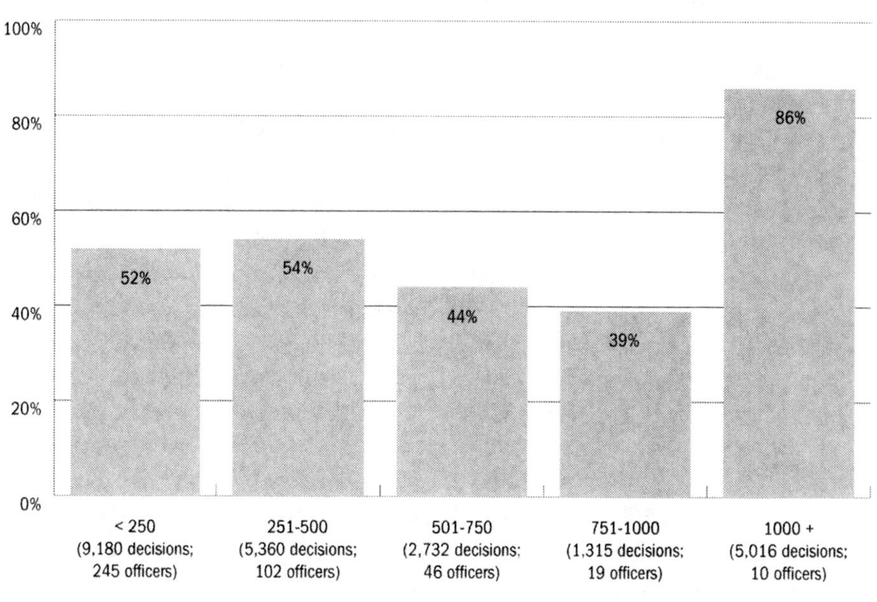

Fig. 10-13. Grant Rates by Officer's Marital Status

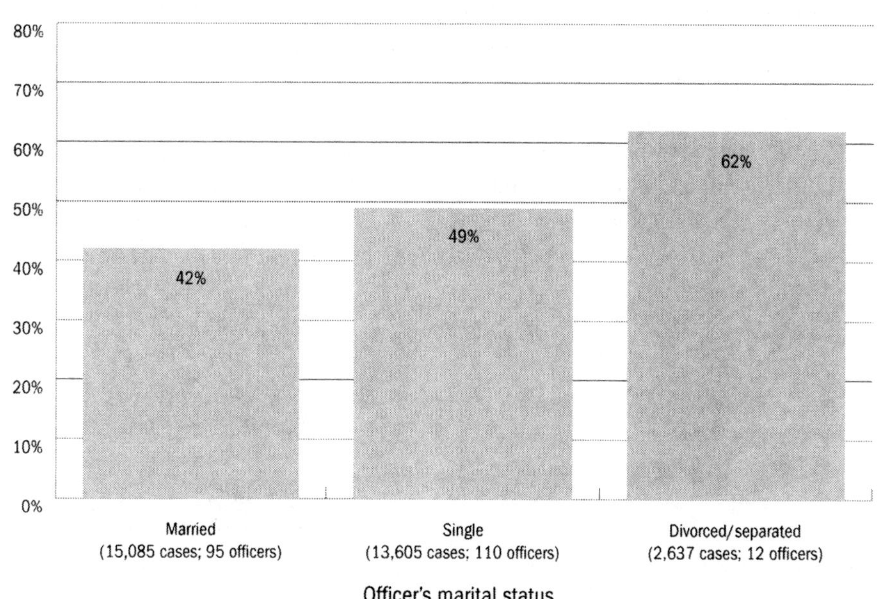

the officer grew up in that region, that the officer's parents came from that region, or that the officer identifies in any way with that region. With that caveat noted, however, figure 10-14 shows that the thirty-four officers born in the West granted asylum at a rate 40 percent higher than the thirty-four officers born in the South.[35] The forty asylum officers born in the Midwest granted asylum at a rate 20 percent higher than the forty-five officers born in the Northeast.

We were aware that some asylum officers work in the same region in which they were born, so the fact that the San Francisco and Los Angeles asylum offices had higher grant rates than the Miami and Houston asylum offices could have accounted to some extent for the substantial difference between the grant rates of officers born, respectively, in the West and the South. We therefore looked at the grant rates only of officers who were *not*, at the time of their FLETC training, working in the same region as their region of birth.[36] Even when we accounted in this way for possibly cultural differences among regions in which asylum officers worked, the region of birth seemed to matter. Whereas the overall grant rate for officers born in the West was 40 percent higher than that for officers born in the South, as figure 10-15 shows, the corresponding increase, for officers working outside of their own region of birth, was still 29 percent.[37]

The asylum officers we interviewed suggested the obvious explanation for this disparity among adjudicators: that people absorbed the cultures of the regions in which they were born, assuming that they grew up there, and different regions of the United States (and of other countries) continue to have different cultures. One officer said,

> Southerners may have had less multicultural contact where they grew up and less cultural awareness. Southerners may also be more conservative in general. In the northeast they may be multicultural but also jaded because they are surrounded by immigrants. They may themselves be third or fourth generation immigrants and may have the attitude "we don't let just everyone into the US."

Another commented, "We all have hidden prejudices. I lived in the South for a while . . . it's a different kind of mentality." Another put it this way: "In California, just look at the 9th Circuit [a U.S. Court of Appeals often regarded as liberal]. It's because of the background of the area. It's ingrained in your outlook. And in the Midwest, they aren't as affected by policies that bring in immigrants en masse. Whereas in Texas they are very affected."

Fig. 10-14. Grant Rates by Officer's Region of Birth

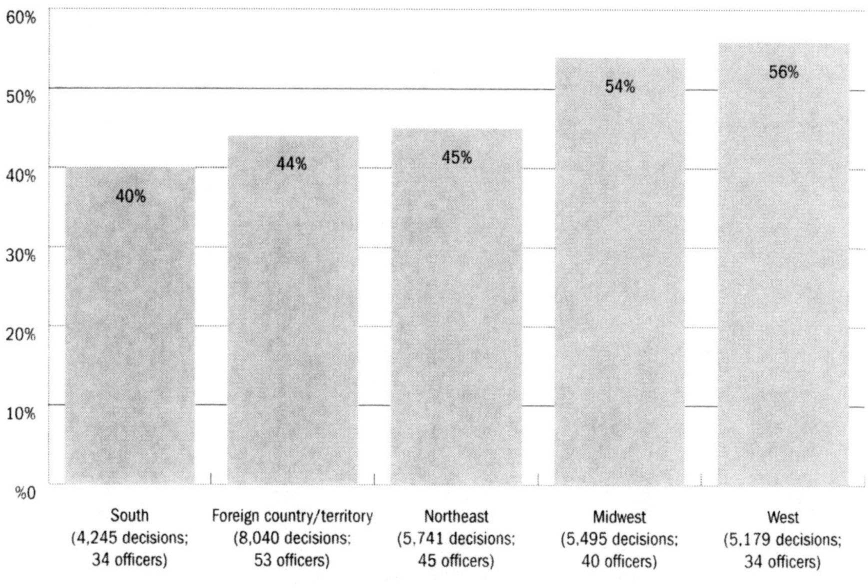

Fig. 10-15. Grant Rates by Officer's Region of Birth, Excluding Cases Decided by Officers Working in the Region in Which They Were Born

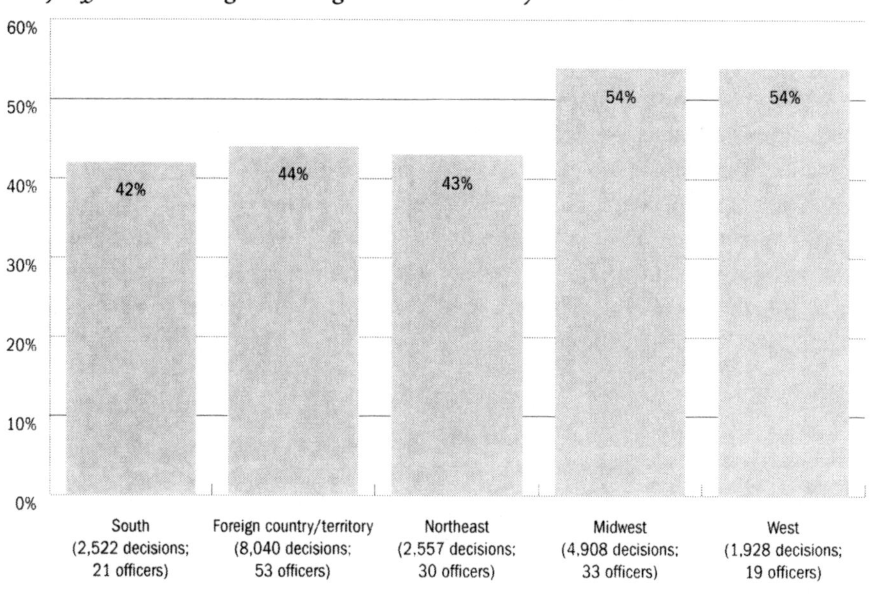

Fig. 10-16. Grant Rates by Officer's Region of Birth and Officer's Education

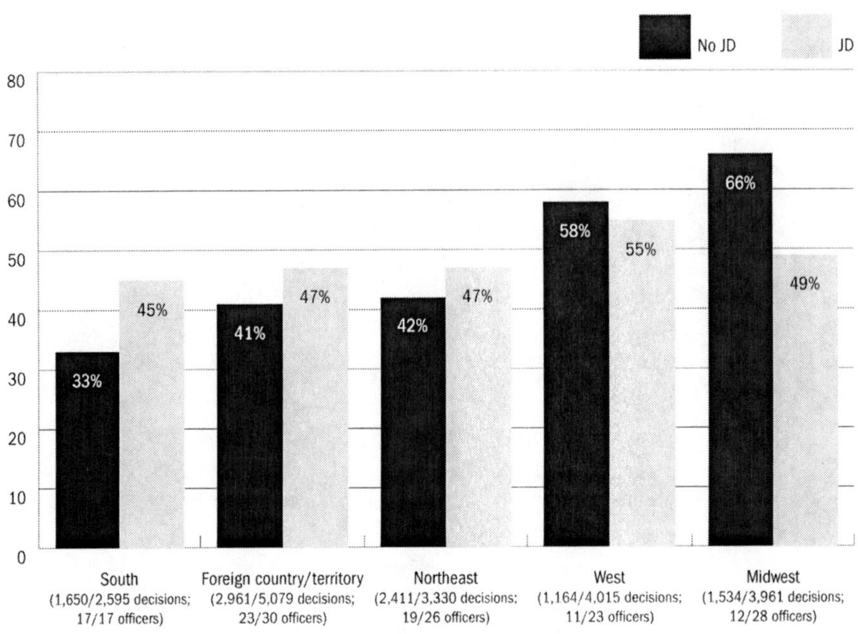

We also found an interesting phenomenon when we looked at variations based on both the state of birth of officers and whether or not they had JD degrees (figure 10-16).[38]

The graph in figure 10-16 shows that while, even for the lawyers, grant rates were higher for those born in the west and Midwest than for those born in the South or abroad, the differences among the lawyers were much smaller than for the nonlawyers. As a senior asylum official put it, regarding this figure, "Law degrees are the equalizer. They correct for a lot of other disparities."

11

Conclusions

By enacting the asylum provisions of the Refugee Act of 1980, Congress gave hope to tens of thousands of people who must flee their countries every year to escape persecution and find safety in the United States. The asylum provisions of the Refugee Act are administered, in the first instance, by a corps of civil servants who remain dedicated to fair adjudication despite overwhelmingly heavy caseloads that require them, day after day, to hear gruesome tales of torture and repression.

These men and women have nearly impossible jobs. Subject to approval by supervisors, they have the power to change for the better the lives of every applicant who sits across the interview table, and all of their descendants, because a grant of asylum is often the first step toward American citizenship. On the other hand, a negative decision is the beginning of a process that may well lead to a removal order by an immigration judge. To separate the bona fide cases from those that have no merit, the asylum officers must rely on oral testimony (often delivered through the volunteer interpretation services of the applicant's friend or relative) and only a scanty paper record, as most asylum applicants do not have and cannot be expected to have official records of imprisonment or official beatings, much less records that explicitly state that the reason for such treatment was the applicant's religion or her membership in an opposition political party or a labor union.

An adjudication error in either direction can be harmful. An erroneous grant of asylum to a person who is not actually eligible degrades a precious privilege and, if publicized, undermines confidence in the integrity of the asylum law and its associated administrative processes.[1] An erroneous rejection, unless reversed by an immigration judge, can lead to removal and an unjust imprisonment or death.

No adjudication system can be perfectly accurate, but officials strive to make them as accurate as possible, eliminating institutional or other factors that introduce arbitrary elements into the system. The first step in that process is ascertaining whether such elements exist. With respect to United States asylum determination procedures, this book is an effort to do so.

Grant Rates, Human Rights Violations, and Officer Gender Neutrality

A central conclusion of this book is that in some important ways, asylum adjudication is working fairly well. Two of our findings strongly suggest that grant rates meaningfully correspond to the statutory standard for asylum. First, and most important, in every period that we studied, asylum officers had substantially higher grant rates for applicants from countries that had the worst human rights records (figure 6-3).[2] Second, male and female asylum officers had virtually the same grant rates during the fourteen-year time frame of this study. This contrasts favorably with our finding in a prior study that immigration judges' grant rates over a five-year period strongly correlated with the gender of the judge.

Employment Authorization Reforms and Greater Sensitivity to Persecution of Women

Two other findings should also increase public confidence in our asylum adjudication system. First, our data confirm other accounts that suggest that the reforms that the former Immigration and Naturalization Service put into place in 1995 were effective in reducing fraud. Not only did applications decline precipitously in the years immediately after the rules were changed so that asylum seekers no longer received work authorization upon application, and cases began to be adjudicated promptly, but grant rates increased as a result, as one would expect if fewer nonmeritorious applications were being filed.

Second, a series of events that began in the mid-1990s with the Service's issuance of guidelines for adjudicating gender-related claims apparently resulted in a substantial increase in the rate at which female applicants were granted asylum.[3] This effort to deepen officers' understanding of the types of persecution that women face offers a useful model of altering institutional culture and approaches to decision making.

The One-Year Filing Deadline: An Arbitrary Imposition on an Otherwise Reasonable Adjudication Process

On the other hand, the goal of matching asylum grants precisely to those individuals who have a well-founded fear of persecution (and are not barred on other rational grounds, such as serious criminal records) has been substantially undercut by Congress's 1996 enactment of a one-year filing deadline on asylum applications. Some members of Congress believed the deadline would reduce the volume of nonmeritorious applications; they may have legislated without realizing that this problem had already been solved by the 1995 reform. As a result of the deadline, DHS has rejected many genuine refugees.

Costs and Benefits of the Deadline

The one-year bar on asylum applications has apparently had at least one salutary effect common to all statutes of limitations: the deadline seems to have pushed many applicants to file morepromptly than they would have without a deadline. In FY 1996, which ended just as Congress was passing the deadline, only 39.6 percent of asylum applicants filed within one year of arrival, but of those who filed since the deadline took effect, at least 69.5 percent did so within one year of entry.[4] We regard this development positively, because as a result, asylum officers and immigration judges are on the whole adjudicating cases in which memories of the details of past persecution are fresher and corroborating evidence is more readily obtainable.

On the other hand, we say that the deadline has only "apparently" had this effect because we have no way of knowing how many genuine refugees fail to file at all because they missed the deadline. That is, in a world without a deadline, a person with a strong asylum claim who was, for example, unaware for three years of the right to seek asylum would be likely to file upon learning of it. In a world with a deadline, such a person might instead decide never to file for asylum, because the act of applying would bring her to the government's attention, thereby risking deportation. The deadline, therefore, might not be prompting as much early filing as these percentage comparisons appear to show, because they do not take into account the people who filed late in the world as it existed before the deadline became law, but who do not file in the world as it now exists.

Against any positive benefits of a one-year filing deadline, members of Congress must also examine the costs, some of which we do not have sufficient data to quantify. First, there is the cost to the taxpayers of determining, in tens of thousands of cases every year, whether the applicant met the deadline—an investigation that asylum officers and, in the cases that they refer, immigration judges did not have to undertake before 1998. Second, to the extent that those who miss the deadline no longer apply and identify themselves to the government by so doing, the United States has a larger population of long-term undocumented foreign nationals than it would otherwise, an outcome that serves no one well.

In our view, however, the principal cost of the one-year deadline is its impact on genuine refugees who are excluded from a grant of asylum by this restriction, which is unrelated to the merits of their claims. We identify this as the "principal" cost because human life is potentially at stake. Those genuine refugees who are actually deported for failure to meet the deadline are at risk of being imprisoned, tortured, or murdered in their home countries.[5] Others, who meet the higher standard for withholding of removal but are barred from asylum, lose the opportunity to obtain permanent protection in the United States. They are also unable to obtain any protection at all for their spouses and children, who either remain abroad, separated from the refugee and possibly at risk precisely because their refugee relative has fled, or, after having accompanied their refugee relative to the United States, must quickly find a route to lawful immigration status or risk deportation. Even those refugees who are rejected because of the deadline by the Asylum Office but are eventually granted asylum in the immigration court or on appeal suffer unnecessarily long asylum procedures during which they are not authorized to work to support themselves. We do not know how frequent any of these outcomes are because data on immigration judges' one-year deadline determinations are not systematically collected. But we were able to investigate the very first stage of the chain, the adjudication of asylum applications by DHS, and the findings of our study warrant serious concern.

Implementation of the Deadline

During the time frame studied, asylum officers determined that more than 30 percent of asylum applicants filed more than a year after entry. To what extent these determinations of untimely filing were accurate, and to what extent they simply reflected an applicant's inability to produce official documentation of entry within a year of filing, we do not know, but we do know that almost 93,000 asylum claims fell within the scope of this procedural bar in the first eleven years of its implementation.

Many of those who missed the filing deadline did not miss it by much; nearly a third of those who filed untimely did file within two years of entry to the United States, though approximately another quarter filed four or more years after entry. Moreover, the percentage of cases with blank entry dates grew significantly over time, even though the percentage of applicants who entered without inspection remained fairly consistent. These data suggest that asylum officers may have applied stricter evidentiary standards over time in determining applicants' dates of entry.

Perhaps one of the most counterintuitive findings of our study was that late asylum seekers were more often represented than asylum seekers who filed timely. As discussed more fully in chapter 4, this phenomenon may have multiple causes. It may be that many who missed the deadline perceived a greater need to obtain counsel to overcome this bar to asylum. It may also be that asylum seekers miss the deadline because they face a multitude of barriers to securing representation, including lack of knowledge about the deadline and its exceptions as well as about the US legal system and procedures generally, very limited financial resources, lack of time and knowledge to search for counsel, and language and cultural obstacles. The inability to obtain representation within a year of entry is not an enumerated exception to the one-year bar. The deadline thereby fails to account for a legitimate ground for delay, rendering some genuine refugees ineligible for asylum because they could not obtain representation rather than because their claims lacked merit.

Exploring the nationalities of asylum seekers, we uncovered further reason for concern. Looking at the six most frequent nationalities of affirmative asylum filers since April 1998 (Armenian, Chinese, Colombian, Ethiopian, Haitian, and Indonesian applicants), we found some uneven relationships, confirmed by the regression analysis, between nationality and late filing. This led us to suspect that other variables, such as community networks and cultural obstacles, may account for different rates of timely filing. Some of the asylum officers with whom we spoke agreed that applicants of certain nationalities, such as Armenians and Haitians, had higher rates of on-time filing because they settled in areas where organizations of co-nationals advised new arrivals about how and when to seek asylum.

Female asylum seekers filed later than male asylum seekers in general and filed significantly later (four or more years after entry) in much higher numbers, perhaps because the nature of persecution suffered by women made it more difficult for them to share their stories with anyone, let alone a government official. Older applicants more often entered through official means and filed timely in comparison to younger applicants. This may have happened because older applicants have more experience navigating bureaucratic systems, but it is not clear that such skills bear any relationship to an asylum seeker's risk of persecution.

Applicants who entered without inspection not only filed later than inspected entrants but were also increasingly deemed late filers in recent years. This last finding gives rise to concern that asylum officers may have increasingly applied stricter evidentiary standards over time, rendering proof of timely filing more and more difficult for those without official documentation of entry, despite instructions from Asylum Headquarters that testimony alone can be sufficient evidence of timely filing.

We also learned that the eight regional asylum offices determined that asylum seekers filed late at very different rates. The regression analysis confirmed that, holding other variables such as nationality constant, different asylum offices had different rates of determining timeliness, leading us to worry that differences in management styles and procedures in the different asylum offices caused these variations.

Who Was Rejected?

After examining the patterns in the data describing groups of applicants who did not prove timely filing, our analysis next turned to the Department of Homeland Security's application of the statutory exceptions to the deadline. That is, we compared untimely cases that asylum officers rejected because of the deadline with untimely cases that such officers excepted from the deadline because of changed or extraordinary circumstances. We cannot tell from the data whether cases were rejected because no exceptions existed, because potential exceptions were not proved, or because one or more exceptions applied but the applicant failed to file within a reasonable period. Despite this shortcoming, the data reveal interesting and at times surprising relationships between the variables examined and rejection rates.

Our first finding in the rejection analysis was that nearly 60 percent of all asylum applicants deemed untimely filers were actually rejected because they had not met the deadline. To slice the data a different way, from April 1998 through mid-June 2009, 54,141 people, almost 18 percent of all asylum applicants in our database, were determined to be ineligible for asylum because they did not file on time.

We found that rejection rates varied by year of filing. For example, FY 2003 saw an increase in rejections on the deadline accompanied by a drop in referrals on the merits, while grant rates remained about the same. We believe that this growth in deadline rejections was due to stricter enforcement of the deadline that began in that year. This higher rejection rate has remained fairly constant since it peaked in FY 2003.

Rejection rates also varied by magnitude of lateness; that is to say, asylum seekers who filed more than a year but less than two years after entry were much less often rejected than those who filed more than two years after entry. Applicants who could not prove any date of entry faced particularly high rates of rejection. Generally, the later an applicant filed, the greater the chance that she was rejected based on the deadline.

We next explored characteristics of asylum seekers and their relationship to rates of rejection based on the one-year filing deadline. Our findings concerning representation confirmed those of numerous prior studies about the effects of representation on asylum outcomes; unrepresented late applicants were rejected more often than represented late applicants.

Exploring the applicants' regions of origin, untimely Latin Americans and East Asians faced the highest rejection rates, even when we looked only at those applicants who were inspected at entry. Of the inspected population, late North Africans and Middle Easterners were least often rejected on the deadline. We wonder whether these statistics might be explained to some degree by the significantly greater numbers of uninspected entrants from Latin America and East Asia, which may contribute to negative perceptions of *all* applicants from these regions in some asylum offices.

Perhaps the most dramatic finding of our rejection rate analysis was the enormous disparity in rejection rates across nationalities. While 17 percent of untimely Iraqis were rejected, 77 percent of late Gambians were barred from asylum by the deadline. Looking only at inspected entrants, the disparity across these two nationalities is similarly striking: only 20 percent of untimely Iraqis were rejected but 75 percent of late Gambians were barred from asylum by the deadline. Moreover, an exploration of the impact of the deadline on *all* (not just untimely) applicants by nationality demonstrates that, because some nationalities had a higher percentage of late filers than others, some national groups were much more affected by the deadline than others. For example, while *late* Haitians and Gambians faced a similar rate of rejection, just over 10 percent of *all* Haitians were rejected on the deadline compared to nearly 60 percent of *all* Gambians. These data gave rise to concern that, in practice, groups of refugees are rejected due to attributes that have little or no relationship to the degree of persecution in their home countries.

We discovered a particularly striking dynamic relating to religion. We present our religion data with the caveat that they are self-reported and must therefore be treated as tentative.[6] Late applicants who self-identified as Muslim and Sikh were more often denied on the deadline than applicants who reported practicing other religions. Exploring the data further, we discovered that untimely self-identifying Muslim applicants from sub-Saharan Africa faced particularly high rejection rates, in contrast with self-identified Muslims from other parts of the world and self-identified Christians from sub-Saharan Africa. Again, we do not know what caused this disparity, but given that self-reported Muslims and Christians from outside of sub-Saharan Africa faced nearly identical rates of rejection, these data raised additional concerns about whether the one-year deadline and its exceptions have been and can be applied fairly.

We also found significant disparities in rates of rejections across and within asylum offices. The mean rejection rates at the eight asylum offices were quite different; notably, these rejection rates showed a relationship with the percentage of uninspected applicants in each region. This finding gave rise to concern about the impact of asylum officers' or supervisory asylum officers' perceptions of immigrants on the deadline determination process. The range of variation between asylum officers also varied by region, with some regions showing remarkable consistency across officers and others showing disturbingly low levels of consistency.

Of course, none of this would matter if all of the rejected asylum applicants had weak cases on the merits. We began to explore this question by comparing grant rates and demographic characteristics of timely applicants, late but excepted applicants, and rejected applicants. We saw remarkable consistency in grant rates between the first two groups, even when broken out by each demographic characteristic, and striking similarities in these characteristics across all three groups.

We then performed an out-of-sample prediction, which provided the most important finding of our study of the effects of the deadline: about 44 percent of rejected asylum cases, or an additional 15,792 claims, would likely have been granted had the one-year deadline not existed over the time period studied. Moreover, these denials impacted an additional 5,843 refugees whose asylum claims were subsumed under those of their parents or spouses.[7]

While the limitations of the data collection practices of the Department of Homeland Security and the Department of Justice make it impossible for us to know whether these applicants were eventually granted withholding of removal or even asylum or actually deported, we are deeply troubled that the deadline has operated to bar genuine refugees from asylum. And though there are no data that would allow us to determine scientifically what has happened to refugees who have been returned to the country in which they fear persecution, our study of the application of the deadline warrants serious concern that the one-year filing bar has resulted in the deportation of a significant number of refugees, who may have faced beatings, sexual assault, torture, and even death in their home countries.

Effectiveness of the Deadline

In addition to these serious problems with the deadline in practice—its uneven application to different groups and uneven administration even to those in the same group—we have two very profound concerns about the deadline even as an ideal type. First, the deadline is ineffective in its goal of deterring fraud. It is both over- and underinclusive, in that it requires DHS to reject otherwise meritorious applicants who did not file within a year while imposing no barrier to the full evaluation of fraudulent applications if they were filed within a year.[8] Second, the deadline is a waste of government time and resources. We detail these concerns below.

Table 11-1. Problems with an Asylum Deadline

Proof of entry within a year of filing	Strength of asylum claim on the merits	Problem
Clear and convincing Evidence	Strong	Waste of government time and resources; additional hurdle for genuine refugee
Clear and convincing evidence	Weak	Waste of government time and resources
None or insufficient	Strong	Genuine refugee denied asylum and possibly returned to persecution
None or insufficient	Weak	Waste of government time and resources
Doesn't apply for fear of deadline	Strong	Genuine refugee without access to asylum and increased undocumented population
Doesn't apply for fear of deadline	Weak	Increased undocumented population

Consider the various categories of people who seek asylum. For those who have proof of entry within a year of filing, an estimated 69.5 percent of asylum applicants, the inquiry into whether they can establish timely filing by clear and convincing evidence is simply a waste of time and government resources. Genuine refugees in that situation are forced through an additional procedural hurdle that consumes their energy and resources, and asylum officers must waste time and taxpayers' money to determine when they entered the United States and whether they qualified for an exception. As to those who have a strong claim on the merits but either did not file timely or cannot prove that they filed timely, and to whom no exceptions are applied, the asylum officer must reject the application. Then, if the immigration judge does the same, these genuine refugees are denied asylum and possibly face beatings, torture, or death simply because of the deadline unless they meet the high burden of proof for withholding of removal.

For those with a weak case on the merits who cannot establish timely filing and to whom no exception is applied, the asylum officer must also reject the case. But if the one-year bar did not exist, the asylum officer would have referred the case anyway, on the merits rather than because of the deadline. Because of the deadline, the asylum officer must waste government resources to inquire into the timeliness of the application and write up a thorough explanation of why the applicant was found ineligible for an exception to the deadline.[9] Finally, there are those applicants who do not apply for asylum because they cannot prove that they filed within a year of entry. We have no way of knowing how many such individuals exist, but we suspect that the deadline forces many potential refugees underground. If the one-year bar did not exist, these individuals would have come forward to claim asylum, thereby revealing their presence in the United States to the Department of Homeland Security.

The deadline is surely counterproductive in these instances in that it bars access to asylum for genuine refugees and increases the undocumented immigrant population. The argument applies with even more force to someone with a plausible but weak claim who would have lost on the merits. That person is someone who should be encouraged to file an asylum application. If the claim is considered and denied, the person should be ordered deported. That person is now likely not to file a claim at all, and to go underground instead.

Moreover, the deadline adds unnecessary expense to the asylum process. Record-keeping limitations at the Department of Justice and the Department of Homeland Security prevent us from knowing what proportion of immigration courts' denials of asylum are based on failure to meet the deadline. Nor do these agencies publish data on what proportion of asylum officers' deadline-based referrals are affirmed or overturned by immigration judges. We do know that if this turned out to be a high proportion, it would show that many errors by the asylum officers were being corrected by the immigration judges, but at a very high cost to both the applicants and taxpayers.[10] Preparing for adversarial immigration court hearings often requires months of time by lawyers and thousands of dollars for applicants who have to pay legal fees. In addition, the hearing itself usually requires several hours of the time of the DHS lawyers who advocate for removal of the applicant, immigration judges, court interpreters (who at this stage of the asylum process are paid for by the government), and supporting staff members.

In short, the only benefit of the deadline is that it ensures that some evidence is fresher for the adjudicators. We believe that this positive benefit is outweighed by the very severe problems with the deadline. Indeed, our study demonstrates that the deadline is impossible to administer fairly and serves as a technical bar to many meritorious asylum claims.

Merits Determinations: Factors Other Than Those Specified by the Refugee Act That Appear to Affect Adjudication Outcomes

Although the relationship between human rights conditions in applicants' countries and grant rates suggests that the asylum adjudication system is fairly accurate in separating valid from unwarranted claims, our data indicate that factors other than an applicant's well-founded fear of persecution have some correlation with asylum officers' decisions. A goal of the system should be to make determinations in asylum cases track, as much as possible, the statutory definition of a genuine refugee; extraneous factors, such as the method by which the applicant entered the United States or the educational attainments of the adjudicator should not enter into the decision.

Human nature being what it is, we cannot expect asylum officers to achieve perfect objectivity. For example, sympathy for applicants with small children may inevitably influence decisions, causing otherwise very similar cases to have different results. We doubt that these factors powerfully affect overwhelmingly strong or impossibly weak asylum claims, but many applications fall in a middle ground and are subject to considerable subjective judgment of the adjudicator, particularly with respect to credibility decisions—the most difficult assessments that officers are required to make.[11] Still, we are troubled that certain nonmerits factors appear to creep into decisions made on applications that make it past the hurdle of the deadline, and we recommend some modest procedural steps that might alleviate some of the resulting distortions. Since several of those recommendations apply to more than one of the factors causing disparities, we defer those recommendations until the end of this section.

Differences in Regional Asylum Offices

Perhaps the strongest nonmerits factor that affects asylum grant rates is the region of the country in which the applicant happens to settle, and therefore the region that will adjudicate the applicant's case. As we show in chapter 8, even when we examine the cases of applicants of a single nationality (thereby excluding effects that might be caused by nationals of more severe human rights abusers settling in one region more than in another), we see very large disparities. For example, Colombians who settled in southern states other than Florida (and were therefore interviewed in Houston) won at a rate of 36 percent, while those who settled in Florida (and were interviewed in Miami) won at a rate of 56 percent. Somalis who settled in the center of the country and were interviewed in Chicago won at a rate of 34 percent, while those who went to Northern California or the northwestern states and were interviewed in San Francisco won at a rate of 89 percent. And Indonesians who settled in New England, Manhattan, the Bronx, New Jersey, or Pennsylvania and were interviewed in the Newark office won at a rate of 20 percent, while those who went west fared much better (53 percent if interviewed in Los Angeles, 54 percent in San Francisco). Russian applicants succeeded more than twice as often in San Francisco than in New York.

It is theoretically possible that some of this disparity results from applicants' gaming the system. For example, some might speculate that those Somalis who are better educated, and therefore more able to articulate their asylum claims, learn (as a result of that education) that the San Francisco office is more likely to grant their cases and therefore settle in Northern California, further raising the Somali grant rate there. But we doubt that this is a significant factor. For one thing, it could as easily be argued that those with the weakest cases would have the strongest incentive to go to the highest-granting office. Second, the calculation of where to settle to enhance a claim would be exceedingly complex. The refugee would have to take into account not only where the best asylum office was located but also (in case she lost at that level) where the immigration court was best for applicants of her nationality, and (in case she lost in immigration court), which federal circuit's U.S. Court of Appeals would be most likely to reverse a denial of asylum. But more important, all three authors have worked in an asylum clinic, supervising the representation of asylum seekers. Except in rare cases, asylum applicants are not allowed to work while their applications are pending at the asylum office. Unless they arrived with substantial assets (which is very unusual), they are therefore dependent for their subsistence on the kindness of relatives or friends of relatives, who often house and feed them. We know from experience that nearly all applicants settle where they have such support systems, even traveling across the country to be housed with someone who will take them in. Furthermore, we have never met an asylum applicant who was aware of statistics about the asylum offices such as those reported in this book. The availability of free shelter and food, rather than the statistical record of the eight regional offices, determines where an asylum seeker lives.

Instead, something about the regional office itself seems to affect the grant rate. We don't know what that is, and in fact the cause could be a combination of factors, such as the hiring preferences of office directors, the management styles and approaches of particular supervisors, the cultures of the communities in which the offices are located or in which the plurality of officers grew up, the experience of certain offices with claims that turned out to be fraudulent, or suspicions of supervisors or officers in particular regions about lawyers or others who frequently prepare applications for those of particular ethnic groups. In response to DHS's 2011 survey, a plurality of respondents (48 of 194 responding) gave "different management" as the reason for disparities in grant rates among the regional offices, and some who did not check that reason offered a variant of it as an open-ended comment.[12] Whatever the cause, it is not a just or desirable outcome for applicants or citizens' confidence in government processes for there to be large disparities in similar cases depending on the happenstance of where a refugee settles before making a claim.

Officer's or Supervisor's Experience and Personal Characteristics

The data presented in chapters 9 and 10 are the second most troubling finding of our study. Even within individual offices, and even controlling the data by selecting cases involving single nationalities, the outcome for an individual applicant appears to depend, to a large extent, on the identity of the asylum officer to whom the case is randomly assigned.

It is possible that these disparities are to some extent largely caused not by differences among asylum officers but by differences among the supervising asylum officers to whom they report. We can't tell, because DHS does not code for the supervisor who reviews the case. To the extent we have information about this, it supports the view that supervisors' attitudes matter. Several asylum officers told us that supervisors' attitudes—lenient or strict—strongly influenced how they decided cases that were marginal in terms of credibility or legal sufficiency. In addition, although DHS's 2011 survey of its officers did not ask about supervisors' influence on merits decisions, it did ask about their influence on decisions about applying the one-year deadline. Of the 197 officers who responded, 88 stated that supervisors told them to apply the deadline more or less strictly, and 48 of those 88 said that supervisors had at various times given them opposite instructions in that regard.

Whether the cause is differences among the officers themselves or among their supervisors, they are substantial. Among asylum officers in San Francisco who adjudicated at least one hundred cases of Indian nationals, grant rates ranged from 6 percent to more than 90 percent. Among Miami officers who interviewed at least one hundred Haitians, grant rates ranged from 5 percent to 85 percent. Among Los Angeles officers who handled at least one hundred Chinese cases, grant rates ranged from 1 percent to 99 percent. In none of these cases did any degree of consensus develop within any regional office—officer grant rates simply ranged widely between these extremes.

Based on our smaller database of 31,635 cases decided by officers who provided biographical information during DHS training, we were able to explore some of the characteristics of officers that might account for at least some of the disparities.[13] The form that officers completed at their training session did not include some relevant sociological information, such as political party affiliation, income, and religion, so our investigation is not as thorough as we would have liked. And some characteristics, such as the gender of the officers, did not have a large impact on grant rates.

Nevertheless, the personal data did offer some interesting and very surprising results. Like most observers of asylum, we assumed at the outset that asylum officers became jaded over time by hearing similar stories of persecution and torture and by learning through newspaper articles and criminal prosecutions of application preparers that some individuals to whom they granted asylum had committed fraud. We therefore surmised that the more cases an officer had decided, the lower that officer's grant rate would be. The data showed quite the opposite, that grant rates were highest for officers who had decided more than one thousand cases.[14] A senior asylum official suggested that those who had settled into long careers with the asylum office might be those who loved their work, and that they stayed in part because it gave them great satisfaction to be able to enable persecuted people to enjoy American freedom. We don't know whether this psychological factor was at play, but it is a plausible explanation for the positive correlation between experience and higher grant rates.

A second surprising result was the relationship between officers' ethnicities, as self-reported on the personal information form, and grant rates. The regressions showed that Asian or Pacific Islander officers had lower grant rates than Black, Hispanic, and White officers. Again, we have no idea why ethnicity matters.

We also discovered ways in which the ethnicity of the officers interacted with other variables. Asylum law makes no distinction between inspected and uninspected applicants, and Black and Asian/Pacific Islander officers made little differentiation between applicants in these two categories. But White and Hispanic officers granted asylum to inspected applicants at much higher rates than to uninspected applicants (figure 10-3).

Similarly, whether an applicant has dependents in the United States is legally irrelevant, and there was little difference in how applicants with and without dependents were adjudicated by Asian/Pacific Islander, Black, and White officers, but Hispanic officers granted asylum to applicants with dependents 23 percent more often than to those without dependents (59 percent versus 48 percent) (figure 10-5).

Over the time frame studied in the smaller database of decisions by adjudicators with biographical information, officers from all minority groups had higher grant rates for pro se applicants, while White adjudicators had higher rates for represented applicants (figure 10-4). We can't be certain, however, whether the ethnicity of officers correlated with the substantial advantage for represented applicants over the whole fourteen-year period of the study, as we don't know the ethnicity of all of the officers who served during that period.

The level of education of the officer should be irrelevant to a decision on whether or not to grant asylum, and indeed the difference overall in grant rates between the officers with law degrees and those without was relatively small (12 percent). However, when we dug a little deeper, we found a much larger education-driven disparity, a 25 percent grant rate differential between officers with and without law degrees, with respect to unrepresented applicants. Moreover, there was a pronounced disparity for Black and Hispanic officers with law degrees, who granted asylum at rates 47 percent and 29 percent higher, respectively, than officers from their racial group without law degrees.

The Effect of the 9/11 Terrorist Attacks

We were not surprised to learn that asylum grant rates dropped in the wake of the terrorist attacks of September 11, 2001. Most Americans, and particularly government officials, became substantially more concerned that some foreign nationals who entered the United States with visas or without inspection were in fact terrorists. Seeking asylum was an unlikely route for a terrorist trying to remain in the United States, because applicants for asylum must provide biometric and voluminous documentary evidence to asylum officials. Nevertheless, increased scrutiny and security checks led to many delayed asylum decisions and apparently also to more frequent denials in cases that were fully adjudicated.

Between FY 2001 and FY 2003, the grant rate for actually adjudicated cases fell from 59 percent to 43 percent, and it has never since reached a level close to the FY 2001 level (figure 6-1). It may have been too high in FY 2001, or it may have been too low in subsequent years; we have no way to measure the "correct" level. As asylum officers explained to us, some of the decline may be due to increased information about applicants' previous efforts to obtain visas to the United States and other consular interactions that were inconsistent with their asylum claims. We are concerned, however, that a single event, external to the asylum process (that is, not mandated by a change in the law) had such a severe and long-lasting effect on asylum adjudication. In particular, we worry that the attacks permanently changed asylum adjudication, from an earlier era in which officers were instructed to give asylum seekers the benefit of the doubt to a "when in doubt, refer to immigration court" approach. We are also troubled by the facts that grant rates for applicants from countries suffering some of the world's worst human rights abuses fell very markedly (figure 6-8).

Characteristics of Applicants

Finally, our study of all cases adjudicated on the merits over a fourteen-year period revealed that certain characteristics of applicants were associated with higher or lower grant rates. Despite the legal irrelevance of whether an applicant had dependents in the United States, those with dependents won 18 percent more often than those without dependents, and this gap was much greater for those from certain countries, such as Haiti and China (figure 7-1).

Although the law does not distinguish between those who entered with and without inspection, among applicants who met the deadline requirements (or who applied before it became the law), those who entered with inspection won asylum at a rate much higher (45 percent higher) than those who were not inspected at entry. This factor probably favored wealthier and more educated applicants, as they were more likely to have been granted tourist, business, student, or other visas by U.S. consular officers and had no need to evade border inspection. The gap between grant rates for inspected and uninspected applicants was particularly great for younger applicants (51 percent versus 33 percent for eighteen- to twenty-nine-year olds), who may have been perceived by some officers as economic migrants (figure 7-3), and for those from Latin America and the Caribbean (figure 7-4).

Representation

We think it unfortunate that in the United States, unlike some other countries, the government does not supply representatives for indigent asylum applicants. It would make no difference if pro se applicants won asylum at the same rate as represented applicants, but over the period of the study, represented applicants won 50 percent of the time, compared with pro se asylum-seekers who won 42 percent of the time. Fortunately, the size of this gap has appeared to diminish over time.

With respect to representation, age made a difference; the disadvantage for pro se applicants was greatest for younger adult applicants (figure 7-6). Representation mattered less for those who had entered with passports and visas than for those who were uninspected (figure 7-8), and it mattered only for the 82 percent of applicants who lacked dependents in the United States; there was no appreciable difference for those with dependents (figure 7-7).

Recommendations

Repeal the Arbitrary Deadline on Asylum Applications

Our first recommendation is that the deadline should be repealed to protect genuine refugees, to improve the efficiency and accuracy of asylum adjudication, and to reduce unnecessary government expenditure.

It should be clear that we believe that responsibility for the problems of efficiency and fairness that result from the deadline lies with Congress, not with the asylum officers who are tasked with administering it. We have met many asylum officers and greatly admire their commitment to making accurate judgments, their willingness to listen on a daily basis to testimony of persecution and torture that few of us would ever want to know about, and their pride in doing a difficult job for which the public gives them scant reward and little credit. The one-year deadline not only burdens their work but forces them to reject otherwise valid claims for asylum, putting many of them under the strain of having to turn away some whose experiences were traumatic and heartbreaking. We suspect that if members of Congress had done the work of asylum officers for even a week, they would never have imposed a one-year deadline on asylum applications. When the deadline was first adopted, Senator Orrin Hatch, the floor manager of the legislation in which it was included, pledged that "if the time limit and its exceptions do not provide adequate protection to those with legitimate claims of asylum, I will remain committed to revisiting this issue in a later Congress."[15]

Seventeen years later, that time has come. In 2010, a provision to simply repeal the deadline was proposed in four legislative vehicles: the first comprehensive immigration reform bill introduced during the Obama administration; the Refugee Protection Act introduced by Senator Patrick Leahy; a stand-alone deadline repeal bill introduced by Representative Pete Stark; and the Senate's FY 2011 State Department appropriations bill.[16] Despite White House support for eliminating the deadline, none of these proposals were adopted.[17] In November 2013, the bipartisan comprehensive immigration reform bill passed by the Senate includes repealing the one-year deadline.[18] It is too early to predict whether the House of Representatives will enact any comprehensive immigration reform during the 113th Congress or, if so, whether repeal of the one-year bar will be included in the final bill that is sent to the President for signature. But the filing deadline is a problem that Congress created and needs to address.

While awaiting congressional repeal of the deadline, the executive branch should adopt several policies to minimize its dangers. First, DHS should amend its regulations to expand the list of "exceptional circumstances" that asylum officers should recognize as legitimate reasons for missing the deadline. The list that is currently in the regulations consists of only six such reasons, although the regulations explicitly state that the list is not exclusive, and less formal DHS training materials reiterate its nonexclusivity.[19] These training guidelines further advise that "other circumstances that are not specifically listed in the nonexclusive list in the regulations, but which may constitute extraordinary circumstances, depending on the facts of the case, include, but are not limited to, severe family or spousal opposition, extreme isolation within a refugee community, profound language barriers, or profound difficulties in cultural acclimatization."[20] This advice is commendable, but it is vague and still incomplete. The list in the regulations should remain nonexclusive, but it should be expanded to include the factors listed in DHS's guidance (severe family or spousal opposition, extreme isolation, profound language barriers, and profound difficulties in acclimatization) and several other common circumstances that cause late filing. These additional circumstances are unawareness of the existence of the right to seek asylum, unawareness of the time limit on applications, detention within the United States, fear that efforts to obtain the corroborating evidence necessary for a successful asylum application will endanger family members in the applicant's home country, victimization by a person other than an attorney (including a person pretending to be an attorney) who purported to be helping the applicant to file an application, and inability, despite genuine and timely effort, to obtain a representative who could help to compile the supporting evidence and file the application.[21] Expanding the list as suggested could help reduce the degree of disparities in the application of the exception and reduce some of the differential impact of the deadline on particular groups, as documented in chapters 4 and 5.

The Department of Homeland Security should expand its training course and manual to require that asylum officers consider a broader range of evidence in determining the entry date for uninspected applicants. According to DHS policy, testimony alone, if clear and convincing, is sufficient to prove an asylum applicant's date of entry.[22] Yet some advocates report that asylum officers are unwilling to consider either affidavit evidence or several pieces of circumstantial evidence that, in combination, support an approximate date of entry into the United States.[23] Circumstantial evidence of these types need not be dispositive but should always be considered.

The Department of Homeland Security should develop exercises and simulations to help train its officers to take into account the unique challenges faced by asylum applicants when the officers decide whether the deadline was met and whether a late applicant qualified for an exception. Genuine refugees may have legitimate reasons for their inability to produce documentation of entry. In cases in which an application is deemed late, training and supervision should also ensure that asylum officers not be passive listeners but rather dig for all possible exceptions for which an asylum seeker might be eligible, as provided for in regulation, BIA precedent and DHS's own asylum training manual.[24] Asylum seekers unfamiliar with the system and the law might not come up with such exceptions on their own.

Finally, DHS should ensure that asylum officers are assessing appropriately, on a case-by-case basis, the "reasonable period" for filing after an exception is applied. In particular, the department should ensure that asylum officers understand that a delay of more than six months might be reasonable.[25]

We know from the study reported in our previous book, *Refugee Roulette* and from the research reported in this volume that the asylum adjudication process is deeply affected by random factors such as the identity of the adjudicator and the location of the regional asylum office deciding the case. The one-year filing deadline is an important random factor contributing to refugee roulette, because it is not, and cannot be, evenly applied to all applicants. First, various groups of applicants are deemed timely in differing degrees, probably reflecting not only differences in immigrant support systems that advise applicants to file promptly but also the extent to which different asylum officers or their supervisors apply strict or generous evidentiary standards in determining entry dates. The asylum officers grant exceptions to late applicants at rates that are different for different groups, and different officers even within regional offices grant exceptions to late applicants at very different rates. Thus, even aside from the inherent unfairness of refusing asylum to people for reasons beyond their control, the deadline introduces irrelevant sociological factors such as the existence of co-ethnic support groups in the applicant's community, and factors related to the attitudes of the adjudicators, into the determination of who obtains refuge in America. The deadline has not been and probably cannot be administered in a way that treats applicants either fairly or in ways that treat all late applicants alike. The best solution to the problem of the deadline is its total repeal by the Congress of the United States.

Make a Law Degree a Job Requirement for Asylum Officers Hired in the Future

Our study of how the personal characteristics of asylum officers affected grant rates showed that officers without a law degree granted asylum more often to represented applicants than to those without representation. In contrast, officers with a law degree granted asylum more often to pro se applicants than to represented applicants (figure 10-7).

It may be that interviewers who were lawyers probed the cases of pro se applicants in greater depth. Such applicants often cannot know which aspects of their histories are legally relevant to their asylum claims and can rarely show how a case that is legally novel fits into the rules printed in the Code of Federal Regulations or the case law promulgated by the Board of Immigration Appeals. Since the asylum officer corps was created in 1990, asylum law has become more and more complex.[26] Legal knowledge, not only of the substance of the law but also of legal research tools and methods, is more than ever necessary to adjudicate claims accurately.

One supervisory asylum officer noted that asylum officers with law degrees are able to complete cases much more quickly than officers without law degrees. Again, this may be a function of the analytical training received in law school, facility with research tools and methods, and heightened interviewing skills.

While the most effective way to eliminate disparities would be to require the government to provide legal counsel to all applicants who could not afford it, the substantially less expensive approach of requiring all future asylum officers to have law degrees would be a significant step towards leveling the playing field. As of this writing in September 2012, 64 percent of the asylum officers did have law degrees.[27] As we noted in chapter 10, a senior official put it to us, "Law degrees are the equalizer. They correct for a lot of other disparities."

Until the Office of Personnel Management reclassifies the position of asylum officer to require a law degree (or if not a law degree, then some advanced degree beyond a bachelor's degree), we suggest the asylum office modify its random assignment of officers to cases by assigning officers with law degrees to pro se applicants.[28] Perhaps this will provide a greater degree of fairness to those least fortunate now: those who can't afford lawyers and are assigned to interviewers who are themselves not lawyers.[29]

Provide Free Legal Services for Indigent Asylum Seekers

High-quality representation is crucial to a fully functioning asylum process. Representatives can present asylum officers with cases that are focused on the relevant factual and legal questions, providing documentary evidence to address any gaps in the applicant's testimony. A good representative spends many hours with her client discussing their story of persecution, clarifying perceived inconsistencies, and probing for additional details and sources of evidence. Cases prepared by high-quality representatives can therefore be decided more quickly and more accurately than pro se cases.

Moreover, a high-quality representative can weed out fraudulent applicants from the asylum process. An asylum officer spends only an hour or two with each applicant and only an average of four hours working on each case; it is very difficult to determine whether an applicant is credible in such a short period of time. A good representative spends at least ten times as many hours meeting with her client and asking detailed questions about the claim, not to mention the hours spent speaking with family and friends in the applicant's home country to prepare affidavits. It is much harder to maintain a fraudulent story faced with this level of scrutiny, and each of the authors has had the experience of seeing a claim "wash out" when the client balked at being asked one too many questions. High quality representation makes the process more accurate from both ends.

In an ideal world, all indigent asylum seekers would be provided with free counsel, subject only to an income test. This is an expensive proposition, however, and one that is not likely to become a reality in the near future. In the meantime, funding could be provided to specific groups. One option might be to focus on vulnerable groups, such as unaccompanied minors or persons with mental disabilities.[30] Another might be to screen cases and triage, focusing funds on those with the most obviously meritorious or perhaps the most challenging cases. In either case, law students or recent law graduates should be considered as groups able to provide excellent representation at relatively low cost, perhaps through a government-funded fellowship position.

Allow Asylum Officers More Time to Make Decisions

DHS should allot more time to asylum officers to hear cases in order to account for increased time spent on procedural requirements. Asylum officers repeatedly told us that since September 11, 2001, they have had less time to interview applicants because they have had to spend significantly more time on pre-interview screening of applicants, including security checks. Despite these increased process requirements, officers have not been given more time to adjudicate asylum claims.

We are deeply concerned that these greater time pressures have made it more difficult for asylum officers to decide cases accurately. Social psychology research shows that adjudicators with less time to decide cases are more likely to make decisions based on instinct rather than through careful processing.[31] Instinctual adjudication is less likely to be accurate and more likely to be biased. In the asylum process, this likely means that more improperly denied asylum claims will be renewed in immigration court, thus increasing the systemic cost of adjudication.

Allowing asylum officers sufficient time to take breaks is also important in ensuring the accuracy of their decision making. Social science studies have suggested that "making repeated judgments or decisions depletes individuals' executive function and mental resources, which can, in turn, influence their subsequent decisions."[32] In particular, judges have been found to decide more often in favor of the status quo, or the path of least resistance after making repeated decisions.[33] This problem may be overcome "by taking a break to eat a meal, consistent with previous research demonstrating the effects of a short rest, positive mood, and glucose on mental resource replenishment."[34]

Increase Opportunities for Interaction among Asylum Officers

There are several low-cost opportunities to improve the quality of decision making at the Asylum Office by exposing officers to other adjudication styles and office cultures. By increasing opportunities to work in different regional asylum offices, a process that already happens on a more limited scale, DHS can expose officers to different management styles and cultures. Within offices, DHS can address disparities by assigning officers to work together with peers with different grant rates and with different biographical characteristics.

One way to reduce disparities among regional offices may be to encourage officers to experience the cultures of offices other than their own. We recommend visiting exchanges, of a few weeks duration, among the regional offices, particularly exchanges between traditionally high-granting offices, such as San Francisco, and low-granting offices, such as New York and Newark. Supervising asylum officers, too, should exchange places with each other in different regions.

A more inexpensive approach might be to have officers from different regional offices discuss cases with each other over the telephone or using video calling technology. Supervisors could create time for such discussions during training sessions, matching up each officer with a partner from a different office to discuss a particularly vexing case. In conversations about our book *Refugee Roulette*, we learned from federal courts of appeals judges that such discussions not only improve the quality of adjudication but may also help to increase consistency in decision-making.

The single-nationality disparities revealed in chapter 9 must be addressed. We strongly counsel against imposing grant rate quotas or limits of any kind on asylum officers.[35] Education is a better way to address extreme disparities. We recommend that within regional offices, the five officers with the highest grant rates and the five officers with the lowest grant rates should be assigned to handle twenty or thirty cases jointly. Each of them would read the file in these cases, and they would together interview the applicant and then discuss what decision to make. If they could not reach consensus, either the supervisor could break the tie or the tie could be resolved in favor of the applicant. The process of discussion might open each of them to the viewpoint of the other and in the process reduce the extreme disparities in each office. Moreover, to the extent that the ethnic disparities presented in chapter 10 are due to what contemporary sociologists call "implicit" or "unconscious" bias, this process might offer a useful corrective.[36]

Expose Asylum Officers and Their Supervisors to Data Such as the Findings of Our Study

Merely raising the consciousness of asylum officers to the patterns that are visible only through statistical analysis may solve some of the problems addressed by this book. Asylum officers who are aware, for example, that they may be more suspicious of the bona fides of uninspected applicants than inspected applicants, or of those without dependents than of those who bring their children to the interview, may change their modes of thinking after learning of how grant rates are affected by these factors. In addition, having learned how the reactions to the 2001 terrorist attacks appear to have influenced outcomes, particularly with respect to those fleeing the most abusive countries, officers may become more sensitive to the potential effects of national or international events unrelated to the merits of particular asylum claims.

Keep Additional Statistics

Statistical information is far better than intuition or anecdote as a prescription for reform. DHS deserves commendation for the extensive statistical database that it maintains and for its interest in learning from statistical information how it can improve its practices. For the benefit of future studies that could help to pinpoint desirable reforms, we recommend that DHS add a few categories to its databases. DHS informed us that RAPS will be replaced in a few years' time with the Electronic Immigration System (ELIS). The changeover between databases offers DHS an ideal opportunity to make the coding changes we suggest below.

First, we suggest that it collect more information about the representatives and interpreters who appear before it. DHS already assigns and enters into RAPS a code number to each person who represents an applicant. However, only the representative's name, organization, and address are recorded, so RAPS does not reflect whether the representative is a lawyer, a law student, a law graduate who is not yet a member of the bar, an accredited nonlawyer representative, or a nonlawyer appearing at the applicant's request. We recommend that RAPS should reflect the type of representative who is assisting the applicant, as well as whether that person helped to fill out the written application, appeared in person at the interview, or both.[37] There should also be a code for the type of the representative's employer, distinguishing between nonprofit organizations, clinical programs at accredited law schools, pro bono work, and fee-charging work at for-profit law firms.[38]

This information would allow DHS to learn whether particular lawyers, or types of lawyers, were especially successful or especially unsuccessful. DHS, and in particular its fraud detection branch, FDNS, might use the information on representatives with spectacularly low grant rates to investigate whether they specialized in hard cases and provided vigorous if unsuccessful advocacy or whether, to the contrary, they were simply taking money from clients with hopeless cases, further victimizing the victims (and in some cases, not even showing up for the interview).

We think it particularly important that DHS code for legal representation and appearance given the comments we received from asylum officials about the declining quality of representation in many cities. Asylum officers have told us that the roles lawyers play in the proceedings vary considerably from region to region. In some regions, lawyers typically help applicants with their written applications, attend the interviews, and clarify testimony that seems unclear because of poor interpretation or disabilities of the applicant. In other regions, however, lawyers often help applicants with their written submissions but send their clients to fend for themselves at the interviews (possibly expecting them to be referred to immigration court, where the lawyers can collect additional fees for representation at that stage). And in at least one region, it is common for nonlawyer "preparers" to help the applicants with their written submissions and to pass the applicants along to lawyers who meet their "clients" for the first time in the asylum office parking lot. The lawyers then attend the interviews (charging fees for this service) but ask no questions and make no statements, as they have insufficient knowledge of their clients' cases.

DHS should also code for whether there was an interpreter present at the interview or participating telephonically. Similar to representatives, different interpreters should be given different codes and should be classified according to whether they are family members or professional interpreter, and whether they provided their services free of charge or for a fee. With these data, researchers could learn more about whether fluency in English is an advantage in asylum interviews and could gauge the effectiveness of different types of interpreters. This would also enable DHS to track interpreters who appeared repeatedly, some of whom may have participated in fraud schemes.

Second, DHS should collect more biographical information on both officers and applicants. All officers should be required to fill out biographical information profiles like those completed by those who were trained at the Federal Law Enforcement Training Center between 2003 and 2008. Without such information, it is not possible to learn whether differences in grant rates are associated with differences in age, gender, ethnicity, education, prior government service, marital status or other sociological factors. If DHS had been recording such information systematically starting in 1991 rather than 2003, our analysis of the effect of such factors would have encompassed nearly ten times as many cases and would have been more robust.

DHS should also code information that they already collect about applicants that might further inform research on the asylum system. DHS should code for the education level of applicants to learn whether better-educated applicants have an advantage in presenting their claims, and if so, possibly take action to assist less well educated asylum seekers who may have equally valid claims but are simply less able to articulate them.[39] Similarly, DHS should code for the prior occupation of asylum seekers in their home countries. This recommendation simply seeks to code existing data, as asylum seekers must disclose all of this information on their application.

Third, RAPS should be expanded to include more data about the decision-making process. Far more useful information could be collected about the application of the one-year filing deadline, the grounds for the applicant's claim for asylum, and the reasons for not accepting the claim. Without this information, it is not possible for DHS to understand in any systematic way the nature of its caseload or to understand how its officers go about making their decisions.

For applicants rejected due to the one-year filing deadline, DHS should create separate codes to distinguish between late asylum seekers (1) for whom no exception is applicable, (2) who might be eligible for an exception but cannot meet the evidentiary standard required to prove that such an exception applies, and (3) who establish eligibility for an exception but fail to apply within a reasonable period of the end of the condition giving rise to the exception. In cases of late applicants who are found to meet one of the exceptions to the deadline, DHS should code the type of exception applied so that analysts can understand how wedded asylum officers are to the enumerated exceptions and determine which obstacles most commonly prevent asylum seekers from applying on time. For all applicants, DHS should code the time period between the end of the condition giving rise to the exception and the date of filing, thereby enabling a reliable assessment of the "reasonable period" requirement and its implementation by asylum officers.

For applicants rejected because of the one-year filing deadline, DHS should code whether the officer found the applicant to be credible or not. Asylum officers reported to us that they are required to code in RAPS for credibility in merits decisions. If analysts and members of Congress had credibility information about deadline-based rejections, they would be better able to determine how many meritorious cases were being rejected for reasons other than the merits of the asylum claim.[40]

As discussed in chapter 8, several asylum officers told us that the identities and outlooks of the supervisory asylum officers contributed significantly to the cultures of the regional offices and accordingly had a strong impact on grant rates. One officer even told us that in past years, certain supervisors in two regional offices would not approve any grants of asylum, in response to which asylum officers waited until those supervisors were on vacation to submit proposed grants to the supervisors who were substituting for them. We could not test the hypothesis that supervisors' personalities and histories strongly influenced outcomes because RAPS does not code the identity of the supervisory asylum officer. DHS should record which supervisory asylum officer approved each case so that future research could evaluate the impact of the different supervisors.

DHS currently uses a crude coding system to identify the grounds on which cases were decided on the merits. DHS records only six grounds: race, religion, nationality, political opinion, social group, and coercive family planning.[41] These categories match the statutory criteria but are overbroad for purposes of policy analysis as officers decide many cases based on subcategories that have been recognized in case law decided within the past quarter century.

DHS should create new categories to code the grounds of asylum decisions. These categories should be designed very carefully.[42] We tentatively suggest that the categories include claimed fear of persecution on account of: race; nationality; religion (including Falun Gong); forced abortion or sterilization; political or union activities (including opposition to corruption); forced military service; membership (but not activities) in a political organization (including a union); imputed political opinion; clan or tribal membership; homosexuality; genital cutting; domestic violence; other gender-related claims; and other membership or imputed membership in a particular social group; and any other basis (described briefly by the officer). The categories should also delineate between claims of severe past persecution only, of past persecution that has led to a well-founded fear of future persecution, or of a well-founded fear of future persecution without past persecution. Finally, DHS should code whether the persecutor was a government official or a nonstate actor.

As one asylum officer suggested, RAPS also should include information about the reasons that asylum claims were referred or denied. These categories should include, at a minimum not only the one-year filing deadline (which already has a special code) but also credibility; internal inconsistency; inconsistency with external country conditions reports; ineligibility as a matter of law; criminal, persecutor or terrorist bar;[43] danger to the public, other bar; and the officer's discretion. Supervisors can access this information on a case-by-case basis, but unless the information is coded and available for statistical analysis, either by DHS or by independent researchers, it becomes impossible to understand how, in the aggregate, asylum officers are applying the law and deciding cases.

Finally, DHS should, along with the Department of Justice, institute a record-keeping system that can track cases accurately as they move from the asylum office to the immigration courts to the Board of Immigration Appeals. A senior official informed us that the Department of Justice does report to DHS the ultimate result of adjudication of cases that were referred to immigration court, but that these reports are not sufficiently accurate. A reliable unified asylum record-keeping system could be a source of useful feedback to asylum officers and their supervisors on the outcomes of their cases in immigration court. It is also the only way that researchers can understand the true impact of the one-year filing deadline. A unified system could also provide useful information on similarities and differences in adjudication among the different levels of the asylum process.

In short, more data in each of these areas would enable government officials and researchers to make recommendations for systemic reform based on evidence rather than inference or impressions.

Conclusion

This study demonstrates that in adjudicating claims, DHS asylum officers have generally granted protection to refugees according to the severity of the human rights situation in their home countries. This is a central priority of asylum law, and this study shows that DHS officers are generally implementing the law in this respect as it was intended. At the same time, factors other than the merits of the claim, such as the procedural filing deadline and the education of the adjudicator, matter in terms of outcomes. We all desire implementation of the Refugee Act in a way that works fairly for those fleeing persecution, for in the adjudication of asylum applications, there are often lives in the balance. We hope that the findings and recommendations articulated in this book help to achieve that goal.

APPENDIX

Catchment Areas of the Eight Regional Asylum Offices

Arlington

Alabama, Georgia, Maryland, North Carolina, South Carolina, Virginia, West Virginia, the District of Columbia, and these counties in Pennsylvania: Allegheny, Armstrong, Beaver, Bedford, Blair, Bradford, Butler, Cambria, Clarion, Clearfield, Crawford, Elk, Erie, Fayette, Forest, Greene, Indiana, Jefferson, Lawrence, McKean, Mercer, Somerset, Venango, Warren, Washington, Westmoreland.

Chicago

Illinois, Indiana, Ohio, Michigan, Wisconsin, Minnesota, North Dakota, South Dakota, Montana, Idaho, Nebraska, Kansas, Iowa, Missouri, Kentucky.

Houston

Arkansas, Colorado, Louisiana, Mississippi, Oklahoma, New Mexico, Tennessee, Texas, Utah, Wyoming.

Los Angeles

Arizona, Hawaii, and the Territory of Guam; and these counties in California: Imperial, Los Angeles, Orange, Riverside, San Bernardino, San Diego, San Luis Obispo, Santa Barbara, Ventura, and the following counties in the state of Nevada: Clark, Esmerelda, Lincoln, Nye.

Miami

Florida, the Commonwealth of Puerto Rico, the United States Virgin Islands.

Newark

Connecticut, Delaware, Maine, Massachusetts, New Hampshire, New Jersey, Rhode Island, Vermont, and these counties in New York: Albany, Allegany, Bronx, Broome, Cattaraugus, Cayuga, Chautauqua, Chemung, Chenango, Clinton, Columbia, Cortland, Delaware, Erie, Essex, Franklin, Fulton, Genesse, Greene, Hamilton, Herkimer, Jefferson, Lewis, Livingston, Madison, Monroe, Montgomery, New York (Manhattan), Niagara, Oneida, Onondaga, Ontario, Orleans, Oswego, Otsego, Rensselaer, Saint Lawrence, Saratoga, Schenectady, Schoharie, Schuyler, Seneca, Steuben, Tioga, Tompkins, Warren, Washington, Wayne, Wyoming, Yates; and these counties in Pennsylvania: Adams, Berks, Bucks, Cameron, Carbon, Centre, Chester, Clinton, Columbia, Cumberland, Dauphin, Delaware, Franklin, Fulton, Huntingdon, Juniata, Lackawanna, Lancaster, Lebanon, Lehigh, Luzerne, Lycoming, Mifflin, Monroe, Montgomery, Montour, Northampton, Northumberland, Perry, Philadelphia, Pike, Potter, Schuylkill, Snyder, Sullivan, Susquehanna, Tioga, Union, Wayne, Wyoming, York.

New York

These counties in New York: Dutchess, Kings (Brooklyn), Nassau, Orange, Putnam, Queens, Richmond (Staten Island), Rockland, Suffolk, Sullivan, Ulster, Westchester.

San Francisco

Alaska, Oregon, Washington, and these counties in California: Alameda, Alpine, Amador, Butte, Calaveras, Colusa, Contra Costa, Del Norte, El Dorado, Fresno, Glenn, Humboldt, Inyo, Kern, Kings, Lake, Lassen, Madera, Marin, Mariposa, Mendocino, Merced, Modoc, Mono, Monterey, Napa, Nevada, Placer, Plumas, Sacramento, San Benito, San Francisco, San Joaquin, San Mateo, Santa Clara, Santa Cruz, Shasta, Sierra, Siskiyou, Solano, Sonoma, Stanislaus, Sutter, Tehama, Trinity, Tulare, Tuolumne, Yolo, Yuba; and these counties in Nevada: Carson City, Churchill, Douglas, Elko, Eureka, Humboldt, Lander, Lyon, Mineral, Pershing, Storey, Wash, White Pine.

NOTES

NOTES TO THE ACKNOWLEDGMENTS

1. Philip G. Schrag, Andrew I. Schoenholtz, Jaya Ramji-Nogales and James P. Dombach, "Rejecting Refugees: Homeland Security's Administration of the One-Year Bar to Asylum," 52 *William and Mary Law Rev.* 651 (2010).

NOTES TO THE INTRODUCTION

1. National Academy of Public Administration, Department of Homeland Security Executive Staffing Project (2007), http://www.napawash.org/pc_management_studies/dhs.html (accessed May 15, 2011).
2. As of 2007, 291 asylum officers were authorized to be employed, and 215 were available for duty (not in training, assigned for overseas refugee adjudications, or on leave). Government Accountability Office, U.S. Asylum System: Agencies Have Taken Actions to Help Ensure Quality in the Asylum Adjudication Process, but Challenges Remain, GAO 08-935 at 150 (2008). These asylum officers are distributed among eight regional offices. The staff of the entire Department of Homeland Security includes more than 200,000 employees. Government Accountability Office, Department of Homeland Security: Progress Made and Work Remaining in Implementing Homeland Security Missions 10 Years after 9/11, GAO 11-881 (2011).
3. United Nations Protocol Relating to the Status of Refugees, 606 U.N.T.S. 267 (1967).
4. George W. Bush, Proposal to Create the Department of Homeland Security (2002), http://ipv6.dhs.gov/xabout/history/publication_0015.shtm (accessed August 14, 2012).
5. Gregg A. Beyer, "Establishing the United States Asylum Officer Corps: A First Report," 4 *Int'l. J of Refugee L.* 455 (1992).
6. The Social Security adjudication system, probably the largest such system in the country, handles about twice as many cases. In FY 2010, the latest year for which statistics are available on line, the Social Security administrative law judges disposed of 50,470 cases. Social Security Online, FY 2010 Hearing Office Workload Data, http://www.ssa.gov/appeals/DataSets/Archive/02_FY2010/02_September_HO_Workload_FY2010.html (accessed November 29, 2011). Our data show that the Asylum Office interviewed 20,324 applicants who filed in FY 2008, down from a high of 44,624 cases in FY 2001.
7. See, for example, Suketu Mehta, "The Asylum Seeker," *New Yorker*, August 1, 2011; Jon Swaine, "Dominique Strauss-Kahn Accuser Could Face Perjury Charges," *London Telegraph*, July 3, 2001, http://www.telegraph.co.uk/finance/dominique-strauss-kahn/8614282/Dominique-Strauss-Kahn-accuser-could-face-perjury-charges.html) (accessed November 29, 2011).
8. http://www.law.georgetown.edu/humanrightsinstitute/LivesInTheBalance/.
9. Id.

NOTES TO CHAPTER 1

1. 606 U.N.T.S. 267.
2. Refugee Act of 1980, P.L. 96-212 (1980).

3. In 1990, 120,000 refugees were admitted. The number of annual admissions gradually fell during the 1990s, reaching a low of just over 20,000 in 2002, after the terrorist attacks in 2001. It increased thereafter, reaching nearly 80,000 in 2009. U.S. Department of Homeland Security, 2009 *Yearbook of Immigration Statistics*, Refugees and Asylees 2009, figure 1, http://www.dhs.gov/xlibrary/assets/statistics/publications/ois_rfa_fr_2009.pdf . For FY 2012, President Barack Obama authorized the admission of 76,000 refugees. Presidential Determination 2011-17 (September 30, 2011), http://www.whitehouse.gov/the-press-office/2011/09/30/presidential-memorandum-fiscal-year-2012-refugee-admissions-numbers-and- (accessed December 1, 2011).
4. For an outstanding analysis of the U.S. program for refugee admissions, see David A. Martin, *The United States Refugee Admissions Program: Reforms for a New Era of Refugee Resettlement* (Washington, DC: Migration Policy Institute, 2005).
5. 8 U.S.C. Secs. 1101(a)(42), 1158. Unlike a candidate for resettlement by the State Department, an applicant for asylum must already be in the United States or at its borders. In addition, a grant of asylum to an otherwise eligible applicant is considered "discretionary," although in practice, the exercise of discretion may not be arbitrary. Thus it is possible that asylum would be denied to an otherwise eligible applicant because the applicant was found to be a spouse-abuser, or to have committed crimes that are so minor that they would not legally preclude a grant of asylum. See Asylum Officer Basic Training Course: Mandatory Bars to Asylum and Discretion, March 25, 2009, at 34, http://www.uscis.gov/USCIS/Humanitarian/Refugees%20&%20Asylum/Asylum/Bars-to-Asylum-Discretion-31aug10.pdf. Using fraudulent documents to enter the United States is generally not by itself a discretionary basis for refusing asylum, because victims of persecution must often resort to using such documents to escape from their home countries. Id. at 36—37. In practice, "discretionary" denials are rare; the vast majority of refusals to grant asylum occur because the applicant is found ineligible.
6. 8 CFR § 208.4(b)(1).
7. Almost exclusively, DHS adjudicates only these "affirmative" applications for asylum. See 8 C.F.R. § 208.4(a). Affirmative applications are those filed by persons who come forward on their own and identify themselves to DHS when they request asylum. Executive Office for Immigration Review, Department of Justice, FY 2008 *Statistical Year Book* I1, available at http://www.justice.gov/eoir/statspub/fy08syb.pdf [hereafter DOJ FY 2008 *Statistical Year Book*]. Aliens who file affirmatively have not been apprehended by immigration authorities either at the border or after entering the United States.

   Persons who are apprehended and placed into removal (that is, deportation), proceedings may apply for asylum in those proceedings, which are presided over by immigration judges of the Department of Justice; DOJ FY 2008 *Statistical Year Book*, at I1. These individuals do not have an opportunity to have their asylum claims determined first by DHS, and they are known as "defensive" applicants. Id.

   Affirmative applicants who lose before the Asylum Office and do not maintain an alternative lawful immigration status are then placed into removal proceedings, where they can present their asylum claims anew. Id. These asylum seekers continue to be known as "affirmative" applicants. See id. Affirmative cases also include those granted asylum by DHS, as well as those denied asylum by DHS who continue to maintain a legal immigration status. See 8 C.F.R. § 1240.11(a). Affirmative cases significantly outnumber defensive cases. Office of Immigration Statistics, Department of Homeland Security, 2008 *Yearbook of Immigration Statistics (reporting FY 2008 statistics) (hereafter FY 2008 DHS*

Statistical Yearbook), 43 table16, available at http://www.dhs.gov/files/statistics/publications/YrBk08RA.shtm.

In FY 2008, the DHS granted asylum to 12,187 applicants and their dependents, id., and referred another 32,946 to immigration courts after deciding not to grant asylum, either because of the one-year deadline discussed in chapters 3 through 5 or because of the merits of the cases. FY 2008 DHS *Statistical Yearbook, Table 17;* DOJ FY 2008 *Statistical Year Book* at I1. That year, DHS also denied asylum to 6,158 individuals who maintained their legal status. E-mail from Michael Hoefer, Director, Office of Immigration Statistics, Department of Homeland Security, to Andrew I. Schoenholtz (February 24, 2010) (on file with author) (attaching "Asylum Applications FY 2008" and explaining that the table refers to applications or cases, not persons, and recommending the use of a 1.4 historical ratio of 1.4 persons per application or case to convert the figures from cases to persons). The immigration court received defensive applications regarding 14,067 individuals. DOJ FY 2008 *Statistical Year Book*, I1. So in 2008, affirmative asylum seekers and their dependents constituted about 79 percent of the total. In March 2009, the DHS Asylum Office began adjudicating asylum applications filed by unaccompanied minors in removal proceedings, as mandated by Congress through the William Wilberforce Trafficking Victims Protection Reauthorization Act of 2008. http://www.uscis.gov/portal/site/uscis/menuitem.5af9bb95919f35e66f614176543f6d1a/?vgnextoid=b3b6040faa930210VgnVCM1000004718190aRCRD&vgnextchannel=f25faca797e63110VgnVCM1000004718190aRCRD.

8. 8 CFR § 1240.11(c).
9. Defensive applications include those that are filed by persons who are arrested in DHS raids or who are placed in DHS custody after being arrested for crimes that are not related to immigration. They also include so-called "credible fear" cases: those in which applications are filed by persons who arrive at airports or seaports without U.S. visas, or who are apprehended within the U.S. near a land border, claim to fear returning to their countries, are detained by DHS, and are found to have credible fear of being returned involuntarily. See U.S. Commission on International Religious Freedom, Report on Asylum Seekers in Expedited Removal, http://www.uscirf.gov/images/stories/pdf/asylum_seekers/Volume_I.pdf (2005).

   DHS asylum officers do play a small role in "credible fear" cases, in that they make an initial screening decision to determine whether the applicant has a credible fear of persecution, a lower standard than the "well-founded fear" standard that must be met to obtain asylum. Once a DHS officer determines that such an applicant has credible fear, the applicant is scheduled for a hearing before a DOJ immigration judge to determine whether he or she qualifies for asylum. Defensive applications also include asylum claims asserted by unaccompanied minors before the immigration court.
10. U.S. Citizenship and Immigration Services, Form I-589, Applicant for Asylum and for Withholding of Removal, available at http://www.uscis.gov/files/form/i-589.pdf
11. Id. at 5–6.
12. Id. at 5.
13. Id. at 9.
14. Id. at 5.
15. U.S. Citizenship and Immigration Services, Form I-589 Instructions, Application for Asylum and Withholding of Removal 8, available at http//www.uscis.gov/files/form/i-589instr.pdf.
16. U.S. Citizenship and Immigration Services, Affirmative Asylum Procedures Manual 7, 133-36 (2007, revised 2010), available at http://www.uscis.gov/USCIS/Humanitarian/

Refugees%20&%20Asylum/Asylum/2007_AAPM.pdf (hereafter referred to as USCIS Asylum Manual).

17. See id. at 10.
18. There are eight regional asylum offices: Arlington, Virginia; Chicago, Illinois; Houston, Texas; Los Angeles, California; Miami, Florida; Newark, New Jersey; New York, New York; and San Francisco, California. Id. at 9–10. See catchment map on p. ii of this book.
19. For an explanation of the veterans' preference in civil service hiring, see USA Jobs, Veterans' Preference, http://www.fedshirevets.gov/job/vetpref/index (accessed January 26, 2013).
20. For a more detailed description of the training that asylum officers receive, see U.S. Citizenship and Immigration Services, Asylum Division Training Programs, http://www.uscis.gov/portal/site/uscis/menuitem.5af9bb95919f35e66f614176543f6d1a/?vgnextoid=2a1d1a877b4bc110VgnVCM1000004718190aRCRD&vgnextchannel=f39d3e4d77d73210VgnVCM100000082ca60aRCRD (accessed August 14, 2012).
21. From FY 2003 to FY2009, the number ranged between 268 and 334, with a high mean of 308 and a low mean of 286. E-mail from Jedidah Hussey, Deputy Chief, Asylum Division, U.S. Citizenship and Immigration Services, to Jaya Ramji-Nogales (August 26, 2010). The primary database on which this book draws includes cases decided by many more officers because it spans more than a decade.
22. In this book, we treat asylum decisions as though they were the decisions of individual asylum officers, which is in practice usually the case. However, as a formal matter, the asylum officer is making a recommended decision which, after supervisory review, is actually issued by the regional office director, acting on behalf of the Secretary of Homeland Security. 8 U.S.C. Sec. 1158(b)(1)(A).
23. Each supervising asylum officer oversees the work of five to seven asylum officers.
24. See U.S. Government Accountability Office GAO-08-935, U.S. Asylum System: Agencies Have Taken Actions to Ensure Quality in the Asylum Adjudication Process, But Challenges Remain 61-62 (2008) (hereafter referred to as GAO Asylum Study) (noting that asylum officers are faced with increased adjudication requirements without any corresponding increase in time to adjudicate their cases).
25. See USCIS Asylum Manual, at 17 (describing the random assignment of cases). In some of the regional offices, asylum officers occasionally "ride circuit" to conduct interviews in cities other than the one in which they normally work. Although the USCIS Manual calls for strictly random assignment of cases to officers, purely random assignment may have been compromised at times by a degree of self-selection in circuit ride assignments. According to the national agreement between DHS and the union to which asylum officers belong, regional office directors must rely largely on volunteers when assigning officers to go on circuit rides. Local offices and unions specify their own selection procedures, which likely consider seniority in the first instance. Certain officers may routinely volunteer for and travel to particular cities, though individual cases at those circuit ride locations are randomly distributed. Some of the cities on the circuits may have had applicant populations from more abusive countries than the applicant populations in other cities, so certain officers who ride circuit frequently may have had somewhat higher or lower grant rates depending on the frequency of their travel and the applicant populations in their destinations. However, several variables counteract any self-selection problem caused by circuit riding. The extent to which officers may view these travel opportunities as perks or burdens varies, depending upon perceptions of the caseload in

a given city (examples include the straightforwardness of cases and quality of representation, the desirability of the city as a tourist destination, and the personal preferences of officers, such as the location of family members or friends). These location priorities likely change over time and vary by officer. Moreover, senior officers advance routinely within the federal government, or move on to other opportunities, so individuals with the ability to select destinations change over time as well. Two other procedures also modify, to a minor degree, the strictly random assignment of cases to officers. First, in some offices, particular asylum officers were, during certain periods, assigned to interview all child applicants. However, only 1 percent of the applicants during the period of our study were children. Second, in some offices, certain officers were assigned for periods of months to complete and sign off on groups of cases where other officers had conducted interviews but the cases had been put on hold due to delayed background checks; these officers made the recommended final approvals, and RAPS reflected their code numbers rather than those of the officers who conducted the interview. Most of those closeouts tended to be grants, which could cause the approval rates of such officers to be inflated. These deviations from the random assignment of cases are discussed further in chapter 9, note 1.

26. See GAO Asylum Study, supra n. 24, at 58–59 (reporting that time constraints caused asylum officers to "rush through their work").
27. Id. at 57–63. The four-hour standard was adopted in 1999 with no empirical data to support it. Id. at 61. But 65 percent of asylum officers and 73 percent of supervisors believe that asylum officers need more than four hours to complete a case, 39 percent of asylum officers say that they rush through their work, and 43 percent say that the standard "hindered their ability to properly adjudicate" in about half or more of their cases. Id. at 58.
28. 8 U.S.C. Sec. 1158(b)(1)(B).
29. 8 C.F.R. § 208.9(e).
30. 8 C.F.R. § 208.9(g). For examples of serious errors caused by poor, nonprofessional interpretation at asylum office interviews, see Shari Robertson and Michael Camerini, *Well-Founded Fear* (PBS television broadcast June 5, 2000), available at http://www.pbs.org/pov/wellfoundedfear/. In recent years, the Asylum Office has contracted with "interpreter monitors" who listen by telephone to some but not all asylum office interviews with applicants who provide their own interpreters. These monitors are not permitted to act as interpreters; they notify officers when they detect errors of interpretation and "may assist the applicant's interpreter when he or she asks for assistance but only if it involves the interpretation of a word (or two) or phrase." Asylum Officer Basic Training Course, Lesson Plan Overview, Interviewing Part VI: Working with an Interpreter (2006).
31. 8 C.F.R. § 208.9(b). For a critique of the law prohibiting the government from supplying counsel to indigent asylum seekers, even in immigration court where the result could be deportation followed by murder at the hands of the applicant's government, see John R. Mills, Kristen M. Echemendia and Stephen Yale-Loehr, "'Death Is Different' and a Refugee's Right to Counsel," 42 *Cornell Int'l. L. J.* 361 (2009).
32. 8 C.F.R. § 208.9(b).
33. 8 U.S.C. §1158 (b)(1)(a) renders the applicant eligible if she is a "refugee," a term defined in 8 U.S.C. § 1101(a)(42)(A) as a person who is "unable or unwilling to return to [the applicant's home] country because of persecution or a well-founded fear of persecution on account of race, religion, nationality, membership in a particular social group, or political opinion."
34. 8 C.F.R. § 208.13(b).

35. See 8 U.S.C. Sec. 1158(a)(2)(B).
36. Similarly, applicants who entered with false passports that they then returned to smugglers must use alternative evidence of their date of entry. This evidence may consist, among other things, of bus tickets from the border, airline tickets, or witness testimony. It may also consist of proof that they were in another country less than a year before applying for asylum; if so, they had to have entered the United States within a year before applying.
37. For example, for some years it was uncertain whether a person who was persecuted because he was gay qualified as persecution on account of membership in a particular social group, but this was resolved in favor of gay applicants in 1994. Matter of Toboso-Alfonso, 20 I & N Dec. 819 (BIA 1990), made a precedential decision by Attorney General Janet Reno on June 14, 1994. Similarly, the question of whether fear of female genital cutting qualified was resolved (again in favor of asylum) in 1996. Matter of Kasinga, 21 I & N Dec. 357 (1996).
38. For an account of coaching to tell a false story, see Suketu Mehta, "The Asylum Seeker," *New Yorker*, August 1, 2011.
39. 8 U.S.C. Sec. 1158(b)(1)(B)(iii) (2006) (providing that a trier of fact may base a credibility determination on, among other things, the internal consistency between an applicant's written and oral statements, even with respect to statement that are not material to the applicant's asylum claim).
40. 8 U.S.C. Sec. 1158(b)(1)(B)(ii) (2006).
41. See supra n. 39. The reports are available at http://www.state.gov/g/drl/rls/hrrpt/.
42. 8 C.F.R. § 208.9(d).
43. USCIS Asylum Manual at 33–35.
44. Interview with three former asylum officers by Philip Schrag, July, 2009.
45. The asylum officers' manual directs them to delete a purported date of entry if it has not been proved by the asylum applicant by clear and convincing evidence. USCIS Asylum Manual at 124. But as noted in the text at n.44, not all officers make this change in RAPS.
46. See 8 C.F.R. §208.19.
47. "No applicant is to be denied a full asylum interview based solely on one-year filing deadline issues. A full and thorough asylum interview includes a pre-interview check of country conditions and post-interview research where necessary." Asylum Officer Basic Training Course, Lesson Plan Overview, One-Year Filing Deadline (2009).
48. USCIS Asylum Manual at 126.
49. USCIS Asylum Manual at 124 ("Regardless of the filing date of an application, Asylum Officers are to give all applicants an asylum interview"; also noting that referral based on the deadline is mandatory for applicants who don't meet the deadline or establish an exception and filing within a reasonable time). The precedence given to deadline determinations may stem from the peculiar wording of the 1996 law that established the deadline. Instead of providing that an application should be denied if it was not filed on time, it says that the provisions allowing a person to apply for asylum "shall not apply" to an alien who does not prove entry within a year of the application. 8 U.S.C. §1158(a)(2)(B), suggesting that a late application does not get far enough along in the process to be turned down based on the merits of the claim.
50. USCIS Asylum Manual at 125 (assessment must contain (1) biographical information about the applicant, his entry into the United States, and the date of application; (2) identification of the protected characteristics of the applicant relevant to his claim on the merits and a brief description of the harm feared; (3) a statement and supporting analysis of the finding that the applicant was ineligible for an exception based on changed

circumstances, supported by a "specific description, with citations, of country conditions pertinent to the protected characteristic" for the period from twenty-four months before the date of filing until the date of decision; and (4) a statement demonstrating that other possible changed and extraordinary circumstances relating to the applicant's case were examined, and showing why the applicant was nevertheless deemed ineligible).

51. If the applicant has some other lawful immigration status, such as a student visa, when DHS decides the case, DHS "denies" the application rather than referring it because the applicant is not subject to removal at that time. 8 C.F.R. Sec. 208.14(c)(2). But fewer than 15 percent of applicants have another lawful status at the time of DHS's adjudication. (A higher percentage apply before their lawful status expires but fall out of lawful status while DHS is adjudicating the claim). In FY 2008, for example, DHS granted asylum in 12,187 cases and referred 32,946 cases to immigration court but "denied" only 6,158 cases—12 percent of the total. Hoefer e-mail, supra n. 7. Some of the applicants who were granted asylum were likely also persons in lawful status, so the total percentage in lawful status is likely to be slightly higher than 12 percent.
52. 8 U.S.C. §1229(b)(5).
53. Occasionally, after reviewing the applicant's file, hearing the applicant's testimony in court, and cross-examining the applicant, DHS attorneys state on the record that the government has no objection to a grant of asylum by the immigration judge. But in the vast majority of cases, DHS attorneys challenge applicants' corroborating evidence, cross-examine applicants to elicit contradictions, argue that applicants do not meet the statutory standards for asylum, and in other ways try to show that the applicant should be deported rather than granted asylum. In many ways, immigration court hearings are like trials in civil or criminal cases, though they differ from those cases in that the rules of evidence do not apply, there is no right to trial by jury, the foreign national who is subject to deportation has the burden of proving entitlement to asylum, and cases cannot be settled or plea-bargained for a compromise outcome. In addition, in deportation proceedings, unlike criminal cases, an indigent respondent is not entitled to the assistance of a lawyer at government expense. For a book-length description of an asylum case that proceeded through all four levels of the asylum adjudication process (DHS, immigration court, and two appeals), see David A. Kenney and Philip G. Schrag, *Asylum Denied: A Refugee's Struggle for Safety in America* (Berkeley: University of California Press, 2008).
54. 8 C.F.R. §1240.7(a).
55. Applicants can get nearly immediate hearings in immigration court if they accept the "next available" hearing date. But the proffered date is often within weeks—too soon for the applicant to obtain counsel, and too soon for counsel to be able to collect the corroborating evidence needed to succeed in court. An applicant who rejects that date goes to the back of the line and is not permitted to work while awaiting a hearing.
56. USCIS Asylum Manual at 45.
57. Such an apprehension is at the heart of the popular 2007 film *The Visitor.*
58. A person who is removed, or who leaves the United States while under an order of removal, is not allowed to reenter the United States for ten years. 8 U.S.C. Sec. 1182(a)(9)(A).

NOTES TO CHAPTER 2

1. "FY" refers to the U.S. government's fiscal year, which runs from October 1 through the following September 30. The number of the fiscal year refers to the calendar year in which the fiscal year ends. In some of our studies (those pertinent to the one

year filing deadline), we divide "FY 1998" into two portions. In those instances, "FY 1998" refers to the period before April 16, 1998, when the deadline went into effect, and "1998.5" refers to the rest of that fiscal year. The database was provided to us as a series of Excel files (generally, one for each cohort of applicants who filed in a particular fiscal year), which we combined and converted to an SPSS file that could encompass all of the data. These data are available to the public at http://www.law.georgetown.edu/humanrightsinstitute/LivesInTheBalance

2. The largest group of cases that we excluded from our data set consisted more than 100,000 cases that were administratively closed (for example, terminated by DHS because the asylum seeker discontinued the application). The second-largest group consisted of 62,568 applications filed by Mexican nationals. As explained in the Methodological Appendix, available at http://www.law.georgetown.edu/humanrightsinstitute/LivesInThe-Balance, most of these Mexican claims were filed only to enable the applicants to seek "cancellation of removal" (a type of immigration relief based on good conduct and long-term residence in the United States) rather than asylum, after the Asylum Office referred them to immigration court.
3. The Methodological Appendix is available on our website at http://www.law.georgetown.edu/humanrightsinstitute/LivesInTheBalance.
4. This is a unique and confidential identifier for the case. The serial number is not the same as the "A" number that DHS assigns to applicants.
5. This is generally the date of entry claimed by the applicant, unless the asylum officer found that the applicant had entered on a different date. See the Methodological Appendix, available at http://www.law.georgetown.edu/humanrightsinstitute/LivesInTheBalance, for more detail.
6. The code number was completely confidential and was different from the same code number that the asylum officer uses on DHS documents.
7. The eight regional offices are in Arlington, Virginia, Chicago, Illinois; Houston, Texas; Los Angeles, California; Miami, Florida; Newark, New Jersey; New York, New York; and San Francisco, California. See map on p. ii of this book.
8. Our database of cases before the deadline went into effect on April 16, 1998, includes only those cases filed from October 1, 1995 (the beginning of FY 1996), through April 15, 1998. We did not ask DHS for information on cases in FY 1995 or earlier,because many cases during that period were likely filed for the purpose of obtaining temporary work authorization while an asylum application was pending. Work authorization was rarely granted to asylum applicants who filed on or after January 4, 1995. Therefore all of the cases in our pre-deadline sample were filed by applicants who should not have expected to obtain work authorization before their asylum cases were adjudicated. See Methodological Appendix, available at http://www.law.georgetown.edu/humanrightsinstitute/LivesInThe-Balance, for further discussion of these variables and how we used them in our analysis.
9. The increase in applications by Chinese may have been due to a change in U.S. law in 1996. Congress stipulated that people who were fleeing China's "one-child" policy were deemed to be refugees eligible for asylum. For a description of how the "abortion wars" in the United States affected immigration and asylum policy, see Patrick Radden Keefe, *The Snakehead* (New York: Doubleday, 2009), 186–191, 258. The 1996 law is codified at 8 U.S.C. 1101(a)(42)(B).
10. Asylum is available not only to people who fear persecution from governments but also to those who seek refuge from persecuting groups that their governments are unwilling or unable to control. See Matter of O.Z. & I.Z., 22 I & N Dec. 23 (BIA 1998).

11. Among the Haitian applicants were probably those fleeing food insecurity; food prices rose rapidly in 2007-08, resulting in rioting and the ouster of the prime minister. Associated Press, "Haiti Votes to Oust PM after Deadly Food Protests," *USA Today*, April 12, 2008.
12. U.S. Department of State, 2005 Country Reports on Human Rights Practices, Ethiopia, http://www.state.gov/g/drl/rls/hrrpt/2005/61569.htm
13. Several thousand Sikhs were slaughtered by Indian security forces in the period beginning with the Gandhi assassination in 1984 and continuing into the 1990s. See Barbara Crossette, "India's Persecuted Christians," *The Nation*, October 29, 2008.
14. In 1996, the Illegal Immigration Reform and Immigrant Responsibility Act of 1996 amended the Immigration and Nationality Act not only by adding the bar to asylum based on the deadline (with its complex exceptions) but also bars that were based on an expanded list of prior crimes. After the attacks in 2001, Congress also imposed more severe bars on applicants who had provided "material support" to a terrorist organization (which was interpreted to apply even to cases in which aid was de minimis or had been provided under duress). Uniting and Strengthening America by Providing Appropriate Tools Required to Intercept and Obstruct Terrorism (USA PATRIOT) Act of 2001, P.L. 107-56, 115 Stat. 272, § 411(a). Beginning in 2005, the law required asylum applicants in many cases to provide corroborating evidence to support even credible testimony of persecution. This requirement is now codified at 8 U.S.C. §1158(b)(1)(B)(ii).
15. Our calculation of those who entered with and without inspection is based on the data provided by DHS, which in turn reflects the method of entry that the applicant claimed to have used. In some cases, the applicant may have lied. For example, an applicant who entered without inspection by crossing a land border may present a false passport, with a visa stamp, belonging to a friend or relative whose picture is similar to the applicant. But fingerprints would ordinarily reveal the fraud, and DHS would report that entrant as uninspected. Slightly more frequently, but still rare in our experience, an applicant who entered with a visa might claim to have entered without inspection by crossing a land border. For example, an applicant might have entered at an airport by "borrowing" the passport and visa of a relative, in a desperate maneuver to seek safety abroad. This applicant might claim to have come across a land border without inspection to avoid possible prosecution of the relative for "lending" the passport. In this scenario, DHS would have a more difficult time rebutting the applicant's claim to have entered without inspection. But inspection documents provide the best way of proving a date of entry to satisfy the one-year deadline, so we do not think that many applicants falsely claim an uninspected entry.
16. In each year from FY 1998 through FY 2001 (which ended on September 30, 2001, just after the 9/11 terrorist attacks), Muslims constituted between 13 percent and 22 percent of the asylum applicants who stated a religion. In each year starting with FY 2002, they constituted only 10 percent or 11 percent of the applicants, perhaps reflecting a greater difficulty in obtaining visas to come to the United States. In FY 2009, for which we have only partial data, the percentage of Muslims was 8.5 percent.
17. All but twenty-five of these officers were recently hired. See Government Accountability Office, U.S. Asylum System, Agencies Have Take Actions to Help Ensure Quality in the Asylum Adjudication Process, but Challenges Remain, Report GAO-08-935 (2008), http://trac.syr.edu/immigration/library/P2869.pdf, at 19.
18. See preamble to Pre-AOBTC #29 Student Information Questionnaire (on the companion website to this book, http://www.law.georgetown.edu/humanrightsinstitute/LivesInTheBalance).

19. For example, the standard FLETC survey instrument did not ask how many languages the respondent spoke.
20. The 68 percent figure may actually understate the officers' international experience, as 9 percent of them did not answer the question and are not included in this figure. Seventy-five percent of those who responded had lived abroad.
21. Of the 214 respondents, 201 answered the question about languages spoken.
22. The questionnaire and the raw results of this survey are available on the companion website to this book. See supra n. 18.
23. See memorandum to Asylum Office Directors from Joseph E. Langlois, Chief of the Office, April 15, 2011 (stating that "while the survey is voluntary, we request that you encourage maximum participation"). The chief's office reminded the regional directors of the importance of maximum participation in two e-mails during the survey period. E-mail to Philip G. Schrag from Ted H. Kim, Asylum Office Deputy Chief (June 14, 2011).
24. At the time of the survey in May 2011, 278 asylum officers and supervising asylum officers served in the eight regional offices; 213 of them responded to the survey. Of those, 194 (70 percent of the 278 officers) completed the survey.
25. See Government Accountability Office, U.S. Government Accountability Office GAO-08-935, U.S. Asylum System: Agencies Have Taken Actions to Ensure Quality in the Asylum Adjudication Process, But Challenges Remain 61–62 (2008) at 3, available at http://www.gao.gov/products/GAO-08-935.
26. The larger proportion of individuals who did not to answer this question when responses were explicitly voluntary makes the comparison difficult.
27. See, for example, In re: O- Z- and I- Z-, 22 I. & N. Dec. 23 (1998); Deborah Anker, *The Law of Asylum in the United States*, 3d ed. (Boston: Refugee Law Center, 1999), 191.
28. These differences among asylum officers may be attributed in part to the fact that they worked in different regional offices, but apparently differences among regions are not the entire explanation. Even within certain regional offices, there was a striking lack of consensus with regard to the proportion of applicants who had suffered past persecution. Among the forty respondents who answered the question and had spent most of their careers as asylum officers in the New York office, 15 percent believed that past persecution cases accounted for 30 percent or fewer of their grants, while 53 percent believed that they accounted for at least 80 percent of their grants. Thirty-six percent of the twenty-eight respondents who answered this question and had worked primarily in the Miami office thought that past persecution cases constituted 50 percent or less of their grants, while 57 percent thought that such cases comprised at least 75 percent of their grants. On the other hand, in several other regional offices, there was much greater agreement about the percentage of applicants who had been persecuted in the past.
29. Fifty-three percent stated this was "very often" the reason.
30. Only 66 percent of the officers gave any of these reasons as being "very often" the cause of an applicant being turned down.

NOTES TO CHAPTER 3

1. This standard is codified 8 U.S.C. §1158(a)(2)(B).
2. 8 U.S.C. §208(a)(2)(D).
3. 8 C.F.R. §208.4(a)(4)(C)(ii).
4. 8 C.F.R. § 208.5.
5. 8 U.S.C. §241(b)(3).
6. INS v. Cardoza-Fonseca, 480 U.S. 421 (1987).

7. 8 C.F.R. §208.16(a). A late-filing applicant who is in a lawful immigration status when applying for asylum would ordinarily qualify for one of the exceptions to the deadline. 8 C.F.R. §208.4(a)(5)(iv).
8. The history of the adoption of the one-year deadline is related in Philip G. Schrag, *A Well-Founded Fear: The Congressional Battle to Save Asylum in America* (New York: Routledge, 2000). The sole exception in the original proposal would have protected applicants who filed more than thirty days after entry because human rights conditions in their home countries had subsequently deteriorated.
9. Senator Simpson opined that "if you are truly a refugee, you need to seek refuge [and] you don't need to sort it out." Telephone interview with former Senator Alan K. Simpson by Philip G. Schrag, July 1, 1998. Representative McCollum thought that those who had fled persecution "have a duty to come forward. There should be some responsibility to make themselves known." Telephone interview with Carmel Fisk, former legislative assistant to Representative McCollum by Philip Schrag, May 19, 1998. McCollum told the House Judiciary Committee, "I believe this, that, by far and away, the vast majority of those who come here seeking asylum will know when they set foot on the soil that's what they want . . . and opening the door for [an exception to the deadline based on] any change in circumstance opens the door for a lot of mischief." Transcript of House Judiciary Committee Mark-up of H.R. 2202 (104th Cong.), October 11, 1995, quoted in Schrag, supra n. 8, at 83.
10. Before 1995, applicants were permitted to work in the United States while their applications were pending. Some people filed nonmeritorious claims simply to be allowed to work. As more people did so, the nonmeritorious applications clogged the adjudication system, increasing the amount of time before applications were adjudicated. As the delays grew longer, the incentive to file non-meritorious cases increased, further increasing the lag between application and decision. David A. Martin, "Making Asylum Policy: The 1994 Reforms," 70 *Wash. L. Rev.* 725 (1995). The system was changed in January 1995, a few months before Simpson and McCollum introduced the proposal for a deadline on applications. Since January 1995, applicants have not been allowed to work until asylum is granted unless, through no fault of the applicant, the government fails to adjudicate the application within 180 days after it is filed. 8 C.F.R. §208.7(a). The 180-day period includes approximately two months for an initial decision by DHS and, if asylum is denied and the applicant is referred for a removal hearing, four more months for a final decision by a DOJ immigration judge. Any delay caused by the applicant, including a delay granted at the request of the applicant for securing an interpreter at the DHS interview or for obtaining counsel at any stage, stops the 180-day clock until the applicant secures an interpreter or counsel (if the applicants desires counsel) and appears at a rescheduled asylum office interview (or hearing, if the applicant requests a delay after referral to immigration court). The applicant does not receive work authorization unless asylum is granted or the full 180-day clock runs down, not counting any periods during which the clock was stopped because the applicant requested a delay. If asylum is not granted by DHS and is then denied by an immigration judge, the applicant is barred from working in the United States during the pendency of any appeals. The operation of this employment clock causes severe hardship for many asylum applicants, particularly those who miss the one year deadline and are referred to immigration courts, where many judges stop the clock for reasons that are not always the fault of the applicant. For recent criticism of how the clock works in practice, *see* Center for Immigrants' Rights, Penn State Dickinson School of Law, *Up Against the Asylum Clock: Fixing the Broken Employment Authorization Asylum Clock* (February 2010), 15–23, available at http://law.psu.edu/_file/Immigrants/Asylum_Clock_Paper.pdf.

11. McCollum himself was reportedly unaware, even two months after the subcommittee vote, that INS had changed its rules on work authorization for asylum applicants. Schrag, supra n. 8, at 71–72. But being briefed by the agency, he refused to retreat from his proposal to impose a thirty-day deadline. Id. at 82.
12. On the connection between several terrorist attacks from 1993 through 1995 and the impetus to restrict immigration, see Schrag, supra n. 8, at 38–42, 50–51, 62, 152–154.
13. "Our borders leak like a sieve," the president had proclaimed. Remarks and an Exchange with Reporters on Immigration Policy, 1 Pub. Papers 1196 (July 27, 1993).
14. See "House Immigration Subcommittee Approves Reform Bill," 72 Interpreter Releases 973, 974 (1995); "House Committee Approves Major Reform Bill, Floor Action Next," 72 Interpreter Releases 1503 (1995); "Senate Subcommittee Approves Legal Immigration Reform Measure," 72 Interpreter Releases 1605 (1995).
15. See, for example, Philip G. Schrag, "Don't Gut Political Asylum," *Washington Post*, November 12, 1995, reprinted at 10 *Geo. Immig. L. J.* 93 (1996); Michele R. Pistone, "Asylum Filing Deadlines: Unfair and Unncessary," 10 *Geo. Immig. L.J.* 95 (1996).
16. 142 Cong. Rec. S. 11491, 11492 (September 27, 1996).
17. For a history of the evolution of the regulations interpreting the exceptions, see Michele R. Pistone and Philip G. Schrag, "The 1996 Immigration Act: Asylum Application Deadlines and Expedited Removal—What the INS Should Do," 73 Interpreter Releases 1565 (1996); Philip G. Schrag and Michele R. Pistone, "The New Asylum Rule: Not Yet a Model of Fair Procedure," 11 *Geo. Immig. L. J.* 267 (1997); Michele R. Pistone and Philip G. Schrag, "The New Asylum Rule: Improved but Still Unfair," 16 *Geo. Immig. L. J.* 1 (2001).
18. The training manual has gone through several iterations, the latest of which at this writing is United States Citizenship and Immigration Services, Asylum Officer Basic Training Course, Lesson Plan Overview: One-Year Filing Deadline (March 23, 2009), available at http://www.uscis.gov/USCIS/Humanitarian/Refugees%20&%20Asylum/Asylum/AOBTC%20Lesson%20Plans/One-Year-Filing-Deadline-31aug10.pdf .
19. 8 C.F.R. § 208.4(a).
20. Asylum Officer Basic Training Course, supra n. 18, at 10.
21. Id. at 14.
22. Id. at 12.
23. Asylum Officer Basic Training Course, supra n. 18, at 20.
24. Id. at 22–25.
25. Id. at 22.
26. Id. at 24.
27. Matter of T-M-H- & S-W-C-, 25 I&N Dec. 193 (BIA 2010), http://www.justice.gov/eoir/vll/intdec/vol25/3673.pdf (remanding the case to the immigration judge for an evaluation of the applicant's particular circumstances and noting the six month requirement in cases in which the applicant qualified for the exception based on prior lawful status).
28. See, for example, Human Rights First, "The Asylum Filing Deadline: Denying Protection to the Persecuted and Undermining Governmental Efficiency" (2010), http://www.humanrightsfirst.org/pdf/afd.pdf; Leena Khandwala et al., "The One-Year Bar: Denying Protection to Bona Fide Refugees, Contrary to Congressional Intent and Violative of International Law," *Immig. Briefing* (Augus 2005) at 1; Karen Musalo and Marcelle Rice, "The Implementation of the One-Year Bar to Asylum, "31 *Hastings Int'l & Comp. L. Rev.* 693 (2008); Heartland Alliance Nat'l Immigrant Justice Ctr. et al., "The One-Year Asylum

Deadline and the BIA: No Protection, No Process" (2010), available at http://www.immigrantjustice.org/policy-resources/oneyeardeadlinereport/oneyear deadline.html;

29. E-mail to Philip G. Schrag from Karen Musalo (August 26, 2009).
30. Musalo and Rice, supra n. 28, at 722.
31. Asylum Officer Basic Training Course, supra n. 18, at 22.
32. Human Rights First, "The Asylum Filing Deadline: Denying Protection to the Persecuted and Undermining Governmental Efficiency," supra n. 28, at 1.
33. Musalo and Rice, supra n. 28, at 704. The asylum officer in this case may have overlooked the fact that victims of trauma can sometimes perform ordinary life functions, but applying for asylum requires them to relive and put on paper an account of the horrendous events of their persecution, and dredging up these memories may trigger nightmares, flashbacks, and physical symptoms associated with re-experiencing the trauma.
34. Gomis v. Holder, 571 F. 3d 353 (4th Cir. 2009) *cert. denied*, 2010 WL 58386 (Jan. 11, 2009). DHS's rejection of Ms. Gomis because of the deadline was confirmed by Ms. Gomis's attorney. Telephone interview of Kell Enow by Philip G. Schrag, February 23, 2010.
35. In immigration court, the DHS attorney stated that she found the respondent credible and offered the lesser relief withholding of removal. His representatives asked the judge to grant asylum. In the alternative, if the judge thought that the deadline was a bar, they asked for an arrangement in which (1) the judge would grant withholding and deny asylum, (2) the government would waive appeal as to withholding, and (3) the applicant would appeal the denial of asylum. The DHS attorney said that if the applicant did not accept the offer of withholding she would appeal any grant of relief that the judge awarded. Under this pressure, the applicant accepted the offer of withholding and abandoned his application for asylum.
36. Human Rights First," Renewing U.S. Commitment to Refugee Protection," http://www.humanrightsfirst.org/asylum/refugee-act-symposium/30th-AnnRep-3-12-10.pdf, at 12 (citing interview by Human Rights First with Lynette Tonin Esq. on May 14, 2009).
37. Id. This Burmese case is reported as Soe v. Gonzales, 227 Fed. Appx. 468 (6th Cir. 2007), with additional details taken by Human Rights First from Soe's brief to the Board of Immigration Appeals.
38. Our study is limited, of course, by the fact that we understandably have no access to the actual legal records of even a random sample of the hundreds of thousands of cases on which we have statistical information. Those records contain the asylum officers' notes on their interviews with the applicants, which might enable observers to assess independently whether deadline-based rejections of the applications were warranted. But this information was provided to the government confidentially and is not revealed to researchers. See 8 C.F.R. §208.6(b). The study's lack of transcripts or notes from asylum interviews is offset by the very large size of the database. Moreover, because the database includes the complete universe of asylum cases decided by DHS in the time frame studied, all of the findings that we present are based on actual cases in the database, and are not merely predictions from a random sample.

NOTES TO CHAPTER 4

1. Our count of "late" asylum seekers includes those who may have filed within a year but could not prove their date of entry to the asylum officer by clear and convincing evidence.

2. The regression model contained the following independent variables: asylum office in which the applicant's case was heard, whether the applicant entered lawfully, the applicant's geographic region of origin, the applicant's religion, the applicant's gender, whether the applicant had dependents, whether the applicant had representation, the applicant's age at filing, and the fiscal year during which the applicant filed. The Methodological Appendix, available at http://www.law.georgetown.edu/humanrightsinstitute/LivesInThe-Balance, discusses how we measured and coded these variables and how we created the "timely filing" database. In the text, we reference the regression run with the independent variable of asylum applicants' nationalities recoded into geographic regions, with the sole exception of the section on nationality, for which we used the results of the regression run with the independent variable of asylum applicants' nationalities.
3. The variables were statistically significant at the 0.01 level.
4. For nominal variables, all of the variables that we report in the text had a statistically significant effect on the likelihood of timely filing. However, in some cases, there were some statistically insignificant variables that we did not report. For example, for asylum seeker geographic region of origin, North America was statistically insignificant (because Mexicans were excluded from the database and a negligible number of Canadians applied for asylum); we did not report the relevant cross-tabulation result in the text.
5. The database contains 24,819 applicants with blank dates of entry. When an applicant fails to prove a date of entry by clear and convincing evidence, asylum officers are instructed to delete any asserted date of entry from the RAPS record and leave that field blank. DHS, Affirmative Asylum Procedures Manual 129 (2003), http://www.uscis.gov/files/article/AffrmAsyManFNL.pdf So it is likely that most of the blank records represent applicants who were determined to be late, though how late they were cannot be assessed. Our survey of officers confirmed that the directions in the manual are often, but not always, followed. Ninety-three officers stated that they always deleted the date of entry that the applicant had listed and entered a blank, thirty officers said that they always left the applicant's asserted date in the RAPS record, and six officers always entered a date that was more than a year before entry. A few officers reported different actions depending on the case.
6. In 1998, the percentage of applications four or more years after entry was quite high (nearly 15 percent), but we consider this an anomaly caused by the start of the deadline's implementation that year. In subsequent years, from 1999 through 2003, the number hovered consistently around five percent.
7. We will return to this hypothesis in chapter 5, where we examine a corresponding increase, over time, in the percentage of late applicants who were found not to qualify for an exception.
8. While we know that instructions on leaving entry dates blank were not incorporated into the asylum officers' procedural manual until 2003, the drop in blank entry dates in 2006 and increase in 2008 and 2009 leads us to believe that additional factors were at play. See Methodological Appendix, available at http://www.law.georgetown.edu/humanrightsinstitute/LivesInTheBalance.
9. In 2005, 35 percent of applicants entered without inspection and in 2003, 31 percent entered without inspection; in all other years from 2002 to 2009, the percentage was 30 percent.
10. Some characteristics that we analyzed did not reveal noteworthy differences in the rates at which asylum officers determined that the applicants filed late. These included whether applicants applied with dependents or identified with particular religions.
11. Felinda Mottino, "Moving Forward: The Role of Legal Counsel in New York City Immigration Courts," at 24, Vera Institute of Justice (July 2000), available at http://www.vera.

org/content/moving-forward-role-legal-counsel-new-york-city-immigration-courts (noting that the "search for counsel is often a time-consuming and frustrating experience" and that "language barriers, cultural misunderstandings, and lack of familiarity with U.S. systems and procedures compound the problem"). This is the only major study of representation in U.S. immigration courts that examines the challenges of finding counsel based on interviews with noncitizens in removal proceedings. Arnold & Porter LLP, Study Conducted for the American Bar Association Commission on Immigration, "Reforming the Immigration System: Proposals to Promote Independence, Fairness, Efficiency, and Professionalism in the Adjudication of Removal Cases," Part 5, 13–14 (2010).

12. In some areas of the country, free legal services for some applicants are available from charitable organizations, law school clinics, or large law firms that do pro bono representation. The demand for such service far outstrips supply, however, and many immigrants do not know about the existence of these services.
13. According to the New York Representation Study, private sector attorneys are viewed as particularly deficient by surveyed immigration judges: "New York immigration judges rated nearly half of all legal representatives as less than adequate in terms of overall performance; 33 percent were rated as inadequate and an additional 14 percent were rated as grossly inadequate. The epicenter of the quality problem is in the private bar, which accounts for 91 percent of all representation and, according to the immigration judges surveyed, is of significantly lower quality than pro bono, nonprofit, and law school clinic providers." The Steering Committee of the New York Immigrant Representation Study Report, "Accessing Justice: the Availability and Adequacy of Counsel in Immigration Proceedings," 4 (2011), http://www.cardozolawreview.com/content/denovo/NYIRS_Report.pdf.
14. Most asylum seekers are either undocumented or present in the United States on visitor, business, or student visas; they are not permitted to work if they are in any of these categories. However, many of them do work, if only to survive. Because they are working without authorization, they are more likely to be exploited than other workers, and it may take them a long time to earn the thousands of dollars that most immigration lawyers charge to represent an asylum applicant, even in the initial stage of an application (representation at the asylum office).
15. For example, U.S. case law and an order of the attorney general established that persecution on the basis of homosexuality is persecution on account of membership in a social group, and that a victim is therefore eligible for asylum. In re Toboso-Alfonso, 20 I. & N. Dec. 819 (B.I.A. 1990); Att'y Gen. Order 1895-94 (June 19, 1994) (designating *Toboso-Alfonso* as a precedent binding the immigration courts and the Board of Immigration Appeals). But this proposition is not necessarily self-evident to the victims who flee to the United States, and they may not learn of their eligibility until they consult an attorney, perhaps years after entering the country.
16. The regression analysis found that, with all other variables in the model held constant, Indonesian nationality was associated most with late filing, followed by Chinese, Colombians, Armenians, Haitians, and Ethiopians.
17. The regression analysis shows that, with all other variables in the model held constant, Armenian nationality was more correlated with late filing than Ethiopian and Haitian nationality. In other words, one or more variables other than nationality drove down the rate of late filing by Armenians.
18. See notes 15 and 16 with regard to the Colombian rate of late filing.

19. *See* Aaron Terrazas, "Haitian Immigrants in the United States," Migration Information Source (January 25, 2010), available at http://www.migrationinformation.org/USFocus/display.cfm?ID=770.
20. Id.
21. United States Census Bureau, United States Foreign Born Population Data Tables: Haiti (2000), available at http://www.census.gov/population/www/socdemo/foreign/datatbls.html; Terrazas, "Haitian Immigrants in the United States," supra n. 19.
22. Graeme Hugo, "Indonesia's Labor Looks Abroad," Migration Information Source (Apr. 2007), available at http://www.migrationinformation.org/Profiles/display.cfm?ID=594.
23. United States Census Bureau, United States Foreign Born Population Data Tables: Indonesia (2000), available at http://www.census.gov/population/www/socdemo/foreign/datatbls.html.
24. Id.
25. U.S. Census Bureau, Table FBP-1, Profile of Selected Demographic and Social Characteristics: 2000, http://www.census.gov/population/foreign/files/stp-159/STP-159-Armenia.pdf
26. U.S. Census Bureau, Table FBP-1, Profile of Selected Demographic and Social Characteristics: 2000, http://www.census.gov/population/foreign/files/stp-159/STP-159-Colombia.pdf
27. The regression confirms that, with all other variables in the model held constant, female gender correlated with lower rates of timely filing.
28. Diana Bogner, Jane Herlihy, and Chris R. Brewin, "Impact of Sexual Violence on Disclosure During Home Office Interviews," 191 *Brit. J. Psychiatry* 75 (2007).
29. The data reveal that 62.5 percent of the 11,184 women who filed four or more years after entry were represented, compared with only 51 percent of the 10,702 men who filed four or more years after entry.
30. See figure 4-16, (showing correlation between entry without inspection and late filing).
31. If we consider only inspected applicants, the differences were smaller, but older applicants still filed timely more often than younger applicants. In all, 29 percent of those who were under age eighteen and 29 percent of those who were eighteen to twenty-nine years old filed late, whereas 26 percent of those between thirty and thirty-nine and 24 percent of those age forty and over were late.
32. The regression analysis confirms that, with all other variables in the model held constant, inspected entry correlated with timely filing.
33. The regression analysis found that, holding all of the other variables in the model constant, applicants before the Asylum Office in Newark were most often correlated with untimely filing, followed by New York, Chicago, Houston, Arlington, San Francisco, Los Angeles, and Miami. The graph in figure 4-14, based on crosstabs of the data, reflects this order with one slight difference: according to the crosstabs, applicants in Miami, San Francisco, and Los Angeles filed untimely at virtually identical rates.

NOTES TO CHAPTER 5

1. Here, as elsewhere, we use the shorthand terms "late," "rejectable," and "untimely" interchangeably. We use the term "timely" to mean that the applicant was found to have filed within a year of entry.
2. Of course the database for our studies of rejectable cases includes only cases that were filed after April 15, 1998, the date the one-year filing bar went into effect.
3. See chapter 3 for a more detailed description of the exceptions.

4. For example, during the period of the study, DHS apparently followed advice from the Department of Justice to the effect that waiting more than six months to apply for asylum after lawful status (under a visa) expired was unreasonable. DHS, Asylum Officer Basic Training Course, One-Year Filing Deadline, http://www.uscis.gov/files/article/One-Year-Filing-Deadline.pdf at 24. DHS did not deem waiting more than six months per se unreasonable in other situations, but some asylum officers may have applied the six-month rule in other contexts (for example, where the applicant filed more than six months after learning that human rights conditions in her country had deteriorated). *See* letter to Joseph Langlois, Chief of the Asylum Division of U.S. Citizenship and Immigration Services, from Tori Andrea, on behalf of Human Rights First and many other human rights organizations and experts, December 7, 2009 (on file with the authors).
5. We regarded three types of applicants as having qualified for an exception and having filed for asylum while the exception applied or within a reasonable period of time thereafter: (1) those whose date of entry was more than a year before their applicant, or was blank, and who were granted asylum,;(2) those whose date of entry was more than a year before their date of application, or was blank, and who were referred to immigration court for a reason other than late filing; and (3) those whose date of entry was more than a year before their date of application, or was blank, and who were denied asylum for a reason other than late filing. (The third category refers only to the small number of individuals who were in a lawful status when DHS reached decisions on their applications.)
6. 8 U.S.C. Sec. 1158(a)(2)(D).
7. Asylum Officer Basic Training Course, One-Year Filing Deadline Lesson Plan, at 18 (Sept. 14, 2006), citing UNHCR Handbook, para. 196; Matter of S-M-J-, 21 I&N Dec. 722 (BIA 1997); 8 C.F.R. § 208.9(b).
8. A typical comment was, "Maintaining legal status is the most common exception. It probably accounts for about 50–60 percent of all exceptions."
9. The regression model contained the following independent variables: asylum office in which the applicant's case was heard, the number of cases previously decided by the asylum officer who heard the applicant's case, whether the applicant entered lawfully, the applicant's geographic region of origin, the state of political and civil rights in the applicant's nation of origin, the applicant's religion, the applicant's gender, whether the applicant had dependents, whether the applicant had representation, the applicant's age at filing, the length of time elapsed between the applicant's date of entry and date of filing, and the fiscal year during which the applicant filed. The Methodological Appendix, available at http://www.law.georgetown.edu/humanrightsinstitute/LivesInTheBalance, discusses how we measured and coded these variables and how we created the "rejected" database. In the text, we reference the regression run with the independent variable of asylum applicants' nationalities recoded into geographic regions, with the sole exception of the section on nationality, for which we used the results of the regression run with the independent variable of asylum applicants' nationalities without recoding.
10. The variables were statistically significant at the 0.01 level.
11. Through FY 2004, DHS's *Yearbook of Immigration Statistics* showed the asylum grant rate by year—the Bush administration ended that practice starting with the FY 05 statistics. DHS, 2004 *Yearbook of Immigration Statistics*, table 18, http://www.dhs.gov/files/statistics/publications/YrBk04RA.shtm. DHS's FY 2004 grant rate table reports grant rates from FY 1996 through FY 2004, and those rates show significantly lower grant rates (particularly for FY 1997, FY 1998 and FY 1999), compared to those computed from the database that

DHS provided to us. The most likely explanation of the difference is that DHS's computations included a substantial number of cases filed by Mexican nationals, who were excluded from our database. See the Methodological Appendix, available at http://www.law.georgetown.edu/humanrightsinstitute/LivesInTheBalance, for an explanation of the exclusion. In addition, the yearbook statistics are based on the date of completion, so they include many cases from the backlog of over 400,000 cases filed from the late 1980s through December 1997; our data are based only on the fiscal year of filing.

12. More stringent application of the deadline could have taken any of three forms: giving applicants less benefit of the doubt with respect to their uncorroborated testimony about when they entered the United States; becoming less accepting of proffered justifications for exceptions to the deadline; or becoming more strict about the definition of a "reasonable" time in which to file after an exception no longer justified a late application.
13. Of those who had been given guidance to become more or less strict, whether in only one direction or in both directions at different times, 31 percent reported being given it in connection with one or more specific cases, 22 percent in general feedback about their work, and 47 percent in both contexts.
14. The percentages are higher in this figure than in figure 4-1 because the baseline is rejectable cases rather than all cases.
15. The regression analysis confirmed that, with all other variables in the model held constant, later fiscal years correlated with higher rejection rates.
16. As we noted in chapter 3, the deadline is subject to exceptions, and the exceptions are themselves subject to a requirement of filing within a reasonable period of time after the exception is no longer applicable. We do not think that the "reasonable time" rule accounts for the sliding scale demonstrated by the graph, however. The "reasonable time" rule applies only if an exception is involved, and the exceptions involve events that would ordinarily produce substantial delays (that is, months if not years), including changed country conditions, posttraumatic stress disorder, and the expiration of lawful status. Figures 5-4 and 5-5 show that the rejection rate climbs steadily even within the first sixty days of late filing.
17. The regression analysis confirms that, with all other variables in the model held constant, female gender of the asylum seeker correlated with lower rejection rates.
18. The regression analysis confirms that, with all other variables in the model held constant, having dependents correlated with lower rejection rates for asylum seekers.
19. Cf. Jaya Ramji-Nogales, Andrew I. Schoenholtz, and Philip G. Schrag, *Refugee Roulette: Disparities in Asylum Adjudication and Proposals for Reform* (New York: NYU Press, 2009), 46 (finding that immigration judges granted asylum 48.2 percent of the time to applicants with dependents but only 42.3 percent of the time to applicants without dependents).
20. As noted in chapter 2, representation does not necessarily mean representation by an attorney.
21. The regression confirms that, with all other variables in the model held constant, representation correlated with lower rejection rates.
22. *See Refugee Roulette*, n. 19, supra, at 44–45; Donald Kerwin, "Revisiting the Need for Appointed Counsel," in *Insight*, at 1 (Migration Policy Institute, No. 4, 2005), available at http://www.migrationpolicy.org/insight/Insight_Kerwin.pdf; Charles H. Kuck, "Legal Assistance for Asylum Seekers in Expedited Removal: A Survey of Alternative Practices," in II *Report on Asylum Seekers in Expedited Removal* 232, 239 (2005), available at http://www.uscirf.gov/countries/global/asylum_refugees/2005/february/index.html.; Andrew

I. Schoenholtz and Jonathan Jacobs, "The State of Asylum Representation: Ideas for Change," 16 *Geo. Immigr. L. J.*739, 742 (2002). We were not surprised that the magnitude of the difference was fairly small—much smaller, for example, than the difference in the success rates of represented and unrepresented asylum applicants in immigration court. See *Refugee Roulette*, supra n. 19, at 45–46. The Asylum Office interview is nonadversarial, and asylum officers are likely to take special care, in that setting, to bring out whatever facts may help an unrepresented applicant, even if the applicant, because of the lack of representation, does not know the relevance of those facts or the need to present them. See, for example, "Legal Assistance for Asylum Seekers in Expedited Removal," supra, at 239 (describing the interview process as nonadversarial); *Refugee Roulette*, supra n. 19, at 12.

23. The number in parentheses on the x axis of the figure is the number of inspected, rejectable applicants from the region. We looked only at inspected applicants for this regional analysis because otherwise the differing percentages of persons who entered without inspection from each region would strongly influence the reported percentage of rejections. The figure excludes 10 Canadian cases and 833 cases that DHS coded as persons of "unknown" origin among the 96,622 late applicants. Africa refers to sub-Saharan Africa. A full description of geographic regions broken down by nationalities is provided at our website, http://www.law.georgetown.edu/humanrightsinstitute/LivesInTheBalance/
24. If we look at all inspected applicants (including those who filed timely), the relationship similarly holds. Latin Americans and East Asians faced rejection rates of 15 percent and 12 percent, respectively; North Africans and Middle Easterners had the lowest rejection rates, at 8 percent. In between we see Europeans at 12 percent, sub-Saharan Africans at 11 percent, South Asians at 10 percent, and Central Asians at 9 percent. Looking at all rejectable applicants (including those who entered without inspection), the relationship is also similar. Latin Americans and East Asians are most likely to be rejected, at 64 percent and 62 percent, respectively, and North Africans and Middle Easterners are least likely to be rejected, at 34 percent. We do, however, see some shifting in the middle: inspected Central Asian applicants were less often rejected than inspected African and South Asian applicants.
25. This generally tracks the findings of the regression analysis, with the exception that the East Asian region of origin was most often correlated with rejection, followed by Central and Latin America, Africa, Europe, South Asia, and North Africa and the Middle East. These findings suggest that one or more variables other than nationality and inspected entry impacted outcomes.
26. There were thirty-seven countries from which more than five hundred rejectable cases were decided during the timeframe of our study. The results of the regression analysis run with the independent variable of nationality showed that seven of those nationalities——Belarus, Mali, Somalia, Ukraine, Uzbekistan, Venezuela, and Zimbabwe——were not statistically significant to the .05 level. We excluded these countries from figure 5-8. For the thirty nationalities that were significant to the .05 level, with all other variables held constant, the order of likelihood of rejection was different than in figure 5-8. The significant nationalities were arrayed, from largest to smallest correlation with rejection, in the following order: Mauritania, the Gambia, Cote d'Ivoire, Indonesia, Haiti, Guinea, China, Guatemala, Russia, Colombia, Pakistan, Kenya, Burma, Egypt, Armenia, Eritrea, India, Peru, Democratic Republic of Congo, Albania, Yugoslavia, Togo, Sierra Leone, Nepal, Iran, Cameroon, El Salvador, Ethiopia, Iraq, and Liberia. The major differences between the regression and the cross-tabulation analysis displayed in figure 5-8 are that nationals of Burma, Colombia, Egypt, Eritrea, Indonesia, Kenya, Pakistan, and Russia were more

frequently rejected than the cross-tabulation analysis indicated, and nationals of Albania, El Salvador, Guatemala, India, Sierra Leone, and Yugoslavia were less frequently rejected than the cross-tabulation analysis indicated. Other differences were a matter of five or fewer percentage points on the graph.

27. Eighty-two percent of Haitians but only 24 percent of Gambians were determined to have filed on time.
28. Only 54 percent of Sierra Leoneans were determined to have filed on time, compared with 82 percent of Indians.
29. Haitians and Indians are present in the United States in far greater numbers than Gambians and Sierra Leoneans. The 2000 census numbers for individuals born in those countries are: Haitians: 419,315; Gambians: 5,765; Indians: 1,022,550; Sierra Leoneans: 20,830 . U.S. Census Bureau, United States Foreign-Born Populations, Foreign-Born Profiles, available at http://www.census.gov/population/www/socdemo/foreign/STP-159-2000tl.html. See Aaron Terrazas, "Haitian Immigrants in the United States," Migration Info. Source, January 2010, http://www.migrationinformation.org/USFocus/display.cfm?ID=770 for further discussion of the characteristics of the foreign born from Haiti in the United States. As we noted in chapter 4, furthermore, we believe that the number of recent immigrants from a particular country to the particular locality in which an asylum applicant settles is more important than the total number of co-nationals in the United States. We do not mean to suggest that the relationship between the impact of the deadline and the prevalence of co-ethnic persons in a town, city, or region is as simple as comparing these numbers would suggest. Support systems are not measured by numbers alone, as they involve the degree of organization of the community; its mean age, education, wealth, and social cohesion; how well the community has already adapted to American life; and other factors. Nevertheless, we think that our hypothesis suggests that there is some relationship is worthy of further study.
30. Not all religions were significant to a .05 significance level; the religions that were significant are Christian, Buddhist, Jewish, Other, Muslim, Sikh, and Unknown. Bahai, Druze, Jain, Jewish, and Zoroastrian were not significant at the .05 level and were not included in the figures. We also excluded Other and Unknown from figure 5-11.
31. *Refugee Roulette*, supra n. 19, at 310–325.
32. The median rejection rates in figure 5-15 are slightly different from the rejection rates shown in figure 5-13 for two reasons. First, figure 5-15 takes into account only the asylum officers in each region who decided at least 100 rejectable cases. Second, figure 5-13 shows mean rather than median rejection rates.
33. While the grant rate was the same overall, six of the eight regional asylum offices had slightly higher grant rates for those who were excused than for those who filed within a year; one office granted at the same rate for both groups; and one office granted at a lower rate to those who were excused than to those who were timely (55 percent compared to 62 percent). The overall grant rate for late filers was much lower, because it was of course zero for late filers who did not qualify for an exception, resulting in a grant rate of only 20 percent for all late filers, both those who qualified for and those who did not qualify for an exception
34. As noted in chapter 2, the database contained only small numbers of Sikhs and Jews, and many applicants in the study did not state a religion.
35. To perform the prediction, the toughest methodological question was the determination of the comparison group. There were three possible choices: (1) timely applicants, (2) untimely and excepted applicants, and (3) pre-deadline cases. We decided against

pre-deadline cases because of the changes in world conditions since the enactment of the deadline and the uncertainty of comparing two sets of data with relatively little in common. Because we were concerned about selection effects between timely and untimely applicants, we chose the untimely and excepted as our comparison group. The predicted grant rate using timely applicants as the comparison group was 39.36 percent, slightly lower than the number we report below that relies on untimely but excepted applicants as the comparison group.

36. One could object that the number of rejected applicants who would have been granted asylum cannot be estimated by comparing their personal characteristics to those of applicants who filed untimely but were excepted because DHS only collected data on some of those personal characteristics, such as age, gender, nationality, representation, religion, and so forth. It might be argued that some other characteristic, as to which DHS did not collect and code data, would distinguish late-but-excepted from rejected applicants. For example, perhaps a very high proportion of late-but-excepted applicants smiled at their interviewers, which influenced the interviewers positively, but only a few rejected applicants smiled at their interviewers. This objection, based on potential variables that nobody thought important enough to consider, applies to all statistical social science projections. It is, of course, worth pausing to consider whether it is valid in the context of our study. We think not, for two reasons. First, we have a very large database, so factors other than those for which coded data was available are less likely to influence one population more than another, as compared to an analysis based on a small database. Second, we have not been able to think of any plausible uncoded variable that would cause the merits of the cases of rejected asylum applicants to be radically stronger or weaker than the merits of the cases of late-but-excepted filers.
37. The precise percentage was 43.62 percent. The prediction generated standard error values for each rejected case, which were used to calculate confidence intervals. The standard errors ranged from .0115 to 1.121 with an average standard error of .0266. For further discussion of the confidence intervals, see the Estimation Appendix on this book's website.
38. This number is artificially low because asylum would likely have been granted to at least some of the 17,921 individuals with blank entry dates, some of whom surely would have qualified for an exception and then would have been found to have meritorious cases. In fact, 3.5 percent of those who had blank entry dates and sought asylum between October 1, 1995, and April 15, 1998, were granted asylum, and 19.9 percent of those who had blank entry dates and qualified for exceptions after the deadline became effective won asylum. Applying these percentages to the 17,921 applicants after April 15, 1998, who were not excepted, we might guess that between 627 and 3,566 additional applicants could have won asylum if there had been no deadline. But we could not subject this estimate to the rigorous regression analysis described in the text, so we made the extremely conservative assumption that none of these 17,921 applicants would have won asylum. See Methodological Appendix, available at http://www.law.georgetown.edu/humanrightsinstitute/LivesInTheBalance, for further explanation.
39. In *Rejecting Refugees*, we provide, in graphical format, 95 percent confidence intervals for this out-of-sample prediction. 97.6 percent of all cases rejected on the one-year deadline had at least a 20 percent probability of being granted asylum on the merits, and just over 80 percent had at least a 30 percent probability of being granted asylum. Even with an extremely conservative estimate that relies on the lower bounds of the 95 percent confidence interval, more than 90 percent of all rejected cases had at least a 20 percent chance

of being granted asylum. Philip G. Schrag, Andrew I. Schoenholtz, Jaya Ramji-Nogales, and James Dombach, "Rejecting Refugees: Homeland Security's Administration of the One-Year Bar to Asylum," 52 *William and Mary L. Rev.* 651, 801–804 (2010).

40. An e-mail from Jedidah Hussey, Deputy Chief, Asylum Div., U.S. Citizenship & Immigration Servs., to Jaya Ramji-Nogales (August 26, 2010) (on file with author) provided raw numbers of 106,690 asylum applicants and 38,935 dependents with cases completed before the Asylum Office between FY 1998 and FY 2009, from which we calculated the applicant to dependent ratio of 1:1.37. This time frame is a close but inexact match with the time frame of our prediction, which analyzes cases filed between April 16, 1998, and June 9, 2009.

NOTES TO CHAPTER 6

1. By comparison, the overall grant rate for those who filed before the deadline took effect was 33 percent, the overall grant rate for the entire period of our study was 38.7 percent, and the grant rate for all who applied after the deadline took effect was 40 percent. The grant rate for all post-deadline applicants was lower than the 45 percent figure stated in the text as the rate for cases not affected by the deadline because DHS rejected the 54,141 applications that were filed late and did not qualify for an exception. The cases discussed in this chapter include those that were adjudicated before the deadline went into effect on April 16, 1998, as well as those that were filed after April 16, 1998, and were not rejected because of the deadline.
2. 8 U.S.C. Sec. 1158(b)(1)(B)(ii) and (iii).
3. Jaya Ramji-Nogales, Andrew I. Schoenholtz, and Philip G. Schrag, *Refugee Roulette: Disparities in Asylum Adjudication and Proposals for Reform* (New York: NYU Press, 2009), 44–53.
4. We ran two logistic regressions, including one with standard errors clustered by asylum officer, and one hierarchical logistic regression on the database of all merits cases, exploring the dependent variable of grant. The regression models contained the following independent variables: regional asylum office in which the applicant's case was heard, the number of cases previously decided by the asylum officer who heard the applicant's case, whether the applicant entered lawfully, the applicant's geographic region of origin, the state of political and civil rights in the applicant's nation of origin, the applicant's stated religion, the applicant's gender, whether the applicant had dependents in the United States, whether the applicant was represented, the applicant's age at filing, and the asylum era during which the application was decided. The Methodological Appendix, available at http://www.law.georgetown.edu/humanrightsinstitute/LivesInTheBalance, discusses how we measured and coded these variables and how we created the database. In the text, we reference the regressions run with the independent variable of fiscal year in which the application was decided recoded into four asylum eras, with the exception of discussions of specific fiscal years, for which we used the results of the regression run with the independent variable of fiscal year of decision without recoding.
5. Unless otherwise noted, the relationships between these variables and grant rates were statistically significant at the 0.05 level and confirmed the findings of the cross-tabulation analyses. The regression results appear on our website (http://www.law.georgetown.edu/academics/centers-institutes/human-rights-institute/lives-in-the-balance.cfm).
6. In chapters 4 and 5, we were concerned with the effects of the one-year deadline, which relates to the period between the date of an applicant's arrival and the date of *filing* an application. Our graphs of the grant rate over time in those chapters therefore are based on grant rates for cases filed in the fiscal years in question. The studies in chapters 6 through

10 do not relate to the periods between arrival and filing, so unless otherwise indicated, the studies in these chapters of changes over time use the fiscal year of *decision* as the operative date. There is not a great deal of difference between the two methods of assigning a case to a fiscal year, as most asylum decisions were rendered occur within 60 days after the applicant files. The exception is that in the relatively few cases in which the applicant was suspected of being a terrorist, the case was held in abeyance for a long time, possibly years.

7. The binary logistic regression and the hierarchical logistic regression confirmed that with all other variables in the model held constant, the fiscal years after September 11, 2001, correlated with lower grant rates. In other words, factors other than the fiscal year influenced the grant rate, but the regression confirms a pattern similar to the cross-tabulation analysis presented in figure 6-1 even with these other factors held constant. In the binary logistic regression, grant rates increased from FY 1997 to 2002, and then dropped in FY 2003, never again returning to the levels seen in FY 1992 to 2002. It appears that other variables contributed to lower grant rates in FY 1996-1998. The hierarchical logistic regression confirms a similar relationship between fiscal year and grant rates, with grant rates steadily increasing from FY 1997 through 2001, dropping in FY 2002 and 2003, and remaining fairly steady through FY 2009. The only difference is that the hierarchical logistic regression shows a drop in grant rates between FY 1996 and 1997.
8. The percentage of asylum claims decided on the merits from the most abusive countries rose from 34 percent in the first era to 41 percent in the second era but remained fairly constant thereafter. It was 42 percent in the third era and 43 percent in the fourth era.
9. Cases filed before October 1, 1995, were excluded from our database entirely, even if they were decided after that date.
10. See chapters 3 through 5.
11. As stated in note 9, cases filed before October 1, 1995, were excluded from our database entirely, even if they were decided after that date.
12. The binary logistic regression confirmed a small difference in grant rates among the three eras. In the logistic regression with standard errors clustered by asylum officer and the hierarchical logistic regression, we ran Era 4 as the control. Both of these regressions failed to confirm statistical significance for Eras 1 and 3.
13. Freedom House is a nongovernmental organization, independent of DHS, whose evaluations are frequently relied upon by social scientists in their empirical studies. See, for example, Dursun Peksen, and A. Cooper Drury, "Coercive or Corrosive: The Negative Impact of Economic Sanctions on Democracy," 36 *Int'l Interactions* 240–264 (2010); Mirjam Kunkler and Julia Leininger, "The Multi-Faceted Role of Religious Actors in Democratization Processes: Empirical Evidence from Five Young Democracies," 16 *Democratization* 1058–1092 (2009); Daniel Stockemer, "Women's Parliamentary Representation: Are Women More Highly Represented in (Consolidated) Democracies than in Non-Democracies?," 15 *Contemp. Pol.* 429–443 (2009). See also U.S. Government Accountability Office, GAO-09-993, Democracy Assistance: U.S. Agencies Take Steps to Coordinate International Programs but Lack Information on Some U.S.-Funded Activities (2009) (GAO Report using Freedom House scores to evaluate the effectiveness of U.S. democracy assistance foreign aid programs).
14. Freedom House scores every country every year, measuring deprivations of civil liberties and of political rights on a scale of 1 through 7, with 7 being the worst score. Therefore each country has a score from 2 through 14. We regarded countries with scores from 12 through 14 in the year before a person sought asylum in the United States as a "most

abusive" country, while we deemed countries with scores of 11 or lower as "less abusive" nations. To more accurately reflect country conditions at the time the applicant fled, we used the Freedom House score for the year *prior* to the year in which the asylum seeker filed her case. See the Methodological Appendix, available at http://www.law.georgetown.edu/humanrightsinstitute/LivesInTheBalance, for further explanation.

15. The regression analyses confirmed that, holding all other variables in the model constant, higher Freedom House scores correlated with higher grant rates.
16. A chi-square test confirmed the statistical significance of the cross-tabulation analysis reported in figure 6-3.
17. Several articles provide valuable information about the 1995 asylum reforms, including: Immigration and Naturalization Service, "Asylum Reform: 5 Years Later" (2000) [hereafter "Asylum Reform"], http://www.ailc.com/services/asylum/asylum_brochure.pdf; David A. Martin, "Making Asylum Policy: The 1994 Reforms," 70 *Wash. L. Rev.* 725 (1995); and Gregg A. Beyer, "Reforming Affirmative Asylum Processing in the United States: Challenges and Opportunities," 9 *Am. U. Int'l L. Rev.* 43 (1994).
18. In 1986, Congress enacted the Immigration Reform and Control Act requiring employers to hire only those who had permission to work and sanctioning those who knowingly hired unauthorized workers.
19. It is important to note that the figures for 1991 come from the 1999 Statistical Yearbook of the Immigration and Naturalization Service, table 25, available at http://www.dhs.gov/files/statistics/publications/YrBk99RA.shtm and the figures from 1992 to 1999 come from U.S. Department of Justice, Asylum Reform: 5 Years Later, at 5, available at http://www.ailc.com/services/asylum/asylum_brochure.pdf. As a result, they differ from the other figures in our study, which follow a different methodology (e.g. excluding Mexican cases). The INS and DOJ data are shown here to demonstrate the trends from FY 1991 to FY 1996, which we do not have in our database. These data exclude reopened cases and applications filed as a result of the 1991 settlement in the case of American Baptist Churches v. Thornburgh. That case challenged the allegedly discriminatory denials of applications by Salvadorans and Guatemalans during the 1980s; the plaintiffs claimed that the denials were based on ideological and political positions taken by the Reagan administration rather than on factors specified in the Refugee Act. The settlement allowed Salvadoran and Guatemalan individuals who had applied and been denied after 1980 to have their claims readjudicated. See Center for Constitutional Rights, American Baptist Churches v. Thornburgh, http://ccrjustice.org/ourcases/past-cases/american-baptist-churches-v.-thornburgh (accessed July 3, 2012).
20. A senior DHS official confirmed to us that it "took a while" for the information about the 1995 asylum reform to disseminate among foreign nationals in the United States.
21. "Asylum Reform,"supra n. 17, at 10.
22. Better training, resulting in increasing professionalization of the asylum officer corps may have been another factor contributing to higher grant rates over time. We have no way to test the degree to which such training contributed to the rate increase.
23. A chi-square test confirmed the statistical significance of the cross-tabulation analysis reported in figure 6-6.
24. The regression analysis shows that with all other variables held constant, female gender of the asylum seeker correlated with higher grant rates. In a study of over 66,000 refugee determination decisions by Canada's Immigration and Refugee Board between 2004 and 2008, women also won asylum more frequently than men; there the rate for females (55 percent)

was higher by 17 percent than the rate for males (47 percent). Sean Rehaag, "Do Women Refugee Judges Really Make a Difference? An Empirical Analysis of Gender and Outcomes in Canadian Refugee Determinations," 23 *Canadian J. of Women and the Law* 627, 642 (2011).

25. In FY 1996, the grant rate for male asylum seekers was 30.0 percent and the grant rate for female asylum seekers was 30.6 percent. A chi-square test failed to confirm statistical significance of the cross-tabulation analysis for FY 1996, possibly because the grant rates for males and females were so similar.
26. A chi-square test confirmed the statistical significance of the cross-tabulation analysis reported in Figure 6-7, except for FYs 1996, 1997, and 2004, likely because the difference in grant rates for male and female applicants was not statistically significant in these years.
27. Immigration and Naturalization Service, Considerations for Asylum Officers Adjudicating Asylum Claims from Women (2005), http://cgrs.uchastings.edu/documents/legal/guidelines_us.pdf.
28. See DHS, Asylum Officer Basic Training, Female Asylum Applicants and Gender-Related Claims, http://www.uscis.gov/USCIS/Humanitarian/Refugees%20&%20Asylum/Asylum/AOBTC%20Lesson%20Plans/Female-Asylum-Applicants-Gender-Related-Claims-31aug10.pdf. The version currently posted on the Internet is the 2009 revision, but according to a senior DHS official, asylum officers had been trained on gender-related claims by the end of FY 1996.
29. *In re: Fauziya Kasinga*, 21 I. & N. Dec. 357 (BIA 1996).
30. Pub. L. 104-208, Div. C (1996). The provision is codified as the last sentence of 8 U.S.C. Sec. 1101(a)(42).
31. The case was Matter of R- A-, 22 I&N Dec. 906 (BIA 1999). The *New York Times* story about the case typified reports of the controversy that erupted in its wake. Susan Sachs, "Fears of Rape and Violence; Women Newly Seeking Asylum," *New York Times*, August 1, 1999.
32. Some asylum officers suggested to us that another possible factor contributing to the higher grant rate for women was Congress's enactment of a new provision of the law, effective in April 1997, deeming victims of compulsory population control to be refugees and therefore eligible for asylum. However, our data suggests that this was not a significant factor. That new legal provision applied almost exclusively to Chinese asylum seekers, but the grant rate for Chinese women increased by only 8 percent during the years following enactment of that law. Further, the percentages of Chinese men and women who received asylum remained almost identical through FY 1999; only in FY 2000 did Chinese women receive asylum at rates higher than Chinese men, with the largest differential (61 percent vs. 44 percent) occurring in FY 2005. By contrast, non-Chinese women began qualifying for asylum at a rate greater than non-Chinese men as early as FY 1998 (40 percent versus 32.5 percent).
33. Though we measure fiscal years by date of decision, we see a similar drop after FY 2001 when we measure fiscal years by date of filing. Using the filing date measure, from a high of 56 percent in FY 2000, grant rates dropped to 55 percent in FY 2001, 49 percent in FY 2002, and 43 percent in FY 2003.
34. We measured the dates on which officers began to decide cases by determining the date of the tenth decision for each asylum officer (avoiding the risk that the date of what seemed to be the first decision might have been miscoded in the database).
35. Burma and Sudan had a score of 14 throughout the period. Iraq was at 14 from 1995 to 2003 and 12 from 2004 to 2009. Somalia scored 14 from 1995 to2000 and from 2007 to 2009, and a 13 from 2001 to 2006. China was at 14 from 1995 to 1998 and 13 thereafter.

Iraq's score was 12 or higher for all eras except the fourth, when its mean score was 11. A chi-square test confirmed the statistical significance of the cross-tabulation analysis presented in figure 6-8.

36. DHS, "Questionnaire for Asylum Officers," question 24. The choices were: "Security check requirements increased, delaying many approvals until later years and providing officers with negative information to which they did not previously have access"; "The law changed to make asylum more difficult to obtain"; "Applicants who arrived after 2001 were coincidentally less deserving of asylum;" "Supervisors encouraged asylum officers to apply a higher burden of proof"; "Independently of supervisors' guidance, asylum officers applied a higher burden of proof"; "Asylum officers with different background or experiences were hired"; "Other reasons (please explain below)"; "I don't know."
37. Of 71 asylum officers, 41 (55 percent) selected this answer as the most important reason for the decline in grant rates. Fifty officers identified this as either the most or second most important reason for the decline. A delay in approvals for security checks could have reduced the number of cases that would otherwise have been decided within a particular fiscal year, but we do not see how mere delay would have reduced the grant rate. More negative information as a result of the security checks could, however, negatively influence the grant rate.
38. Shankar Vedatam, "Scientist's Visa Denial Sparks Outrage in India," *Washington Post*, February 23, 2006.
39. Eric Schmitt, "A Nation Challenged: The Immigration Agency; 4 Top Officials Are Replaced," *New York Times*, March 16, 2002; Julia Malone, "INS Managers Bounced, Visas for Hijackers Get Bureaucrats Reassigned," *Atlanta Journal-Constitution*, March 16, 2002.
40. Memorandum from James W. Ziglar, Commissioner, Immigration and Naturalization Service, to All Regional Directors and All District Directors (March 22, 2002), available at www.nationofimmigrators.com/Zero%20Tolerance%20Policy.pdf.
41. Government Accountability Office, Agencies Have Taken Actions to Help Ensure Quality in the Asylum Adjudication Process, but Challenges Remain, GAO-08-935, September 25, 2008, at 13.
42. Uniting and Strengthening America by Providing Appropriate Tools Required to Intercept and Obstruct Terrorism (USA Patriot Act) Act of 2001, § 411. See Georgetown University Law Center, Human Rights Institute, "Unintended Consequences: Refugee Victims of the War on Terror" (2006), HRI Papers & Reports. Paper 1. http://scholarship.law.georgetown.edu/hri_papers/1 (showing how the material support bar prevented Colombian refugees who had suffered persecution by armed groups from being resettled in the United States); Human Rights First, "Denial and Delay: The Impact of the Immigration Law's 'Terrorism Bars' on Asylum Seekers and Refugees in the United States" (2009) (explaining that current law and legal interpretation regarding "material support" to "terrorism" mean that many innocent refugees and asylum seekers, who are themselves victims of violence or repression in foreign countries, have been stuck in limbo or denied entry to the United States), http://www.humanrightsfirst.org/our-work/refugee-protection/material-support/.
43. Pub. L. 109-13, Div. B, codified at 8 U.S.C. Sec. 1158(b)(1)(B).
44. Matter of Dass, 20 I&N Dec. 120 (BIA 1989); Matter of S-M-J-, 21 I&N Dec. 722 (BIA 1997); Matter of Y-B-, 21 I&N Dec. 1136 (BIA 1998).
45. The U.S. Court of Appeals for the Ninth Circuit had held that the Board's jurisprudence in these cases was not valid. Kataria v. INS, 232 F.3d 1107, 1113 (9th Cir. 2000). It ruled in that case that asylum adjudicators must accept the applicant's testimony as true in the absence of an explicit adverse credibility finding and that independent corroborative

evidence is not required from an asylum applicant who testifies credibly in support of their application.

46. As Representative Hostettler put it on the House floor, "The asylum provisions in H.R. 418 do not prevent aliens from seeking asylum. Those who truly have been persecuted for religious or political grounds will be allowed to present their cases just as they are able to now. These provisions merely overturn Ninth Circuit Court decisions saying that immigration judges cannot use inconsistencies in an alien's statement to determine if he or she is being untruthful." (Statement of Rep. John Hostettler, 151 Cong. Rec. 551, February 10, 2005). Representative Lamar Smith added, "Under a 9th Circuit decision, a judge can determine that an asylum applicant is lying and still be required to grant the applicant admission. The DOJ Inspector General reported that it was common for asylum applicants to make claims that they were falsely accused of being terrorists. In this situation, even if the judge believes that the applicant is lying and is a terrorist, the judge may still be required to approve the application. The REAL ID Act reverses this 9th Circuit decision and makes it harder for terrorists to exploit our asylum system." Id. at 552.
47. A chi-square test confirmed the statistical significance of the cross-tabulation analysis reported in figure 6-9.
48. As figure 6-6 shows, the grant rate for this group dropped from 38 percent to 29 percent between Era 3 and Era 4.
49. A chi-square test confirmed the statistical significance of the cross-tabulation analysis reported in figure 6-10.

NOTES TO CHAPTER 7

1. Jaya Ramji-Nogales, Andrew I. Schoenholtz, and Philip G. Schrag, *Refugee Roulette: Disparities in Asylum Adjudication and Proposals for Reform* (New York: NYU Press, 2009), at 46.
2. Chapter 9 includes a comment from a supervisory asylum officer who views time constraints as the biggest obstacle to achieving greater consistency.
3. Chris Guthrie, Jeffrey J. Rachlinski, and Andrew J. Wistrich, "Blinking on the Bench: How Judges Decide Cases," 93 *Cornell Law Rev.* 1, 35 (2007) ("Judges facing cognitive overload due to heavy dockets or other job constraints are more likely to make intuitive rather than deliberative decisions because the former are speedier and easier. Furthermore, being cognitively 'busy' induces judges to rely on intuitive judgment"), http://www.lawschool.cornell.edu/research/cornell-law-review/upload/Blinking-on-the-Bench.pdf
4. A chi-square test failed to confirm the statistical significance of the cross-tabulation analysis of applicants with and without dependents and grant rates for the geographic regions of origin of Central Asia and Europe. Given the high numbers of cases in these categories (17,346 and 26,916, respectively), we suspect that the lack of significance may be due to the similarities in grant rates among applicants with and without dependents in these geographical regions.
5. A chi-square test confirmed the statistical significance of cross-tabulation analysis of applicants with and without dependents and grant rates for the geographic regions of origin of Latin America.
6. A chi-square test confirmed the statistical significance of the cross-tabulation analysis reported in figure 7-1.
7. In 2010, Haiti ranked 158th in Human Development, just above the vast majority of sub-Saharan African nations, according to the United Nations Development Programme's 2011 Report. http://hdrstats.undp.org/en/countries/profiles/HTI.html Because of Haiti's

proximity and migration relationship to the United States, even regular newspaper reading would keep officers apprised of the very difficult conditions of life in Haiti, particularly in Miami, which received the largest share of Haitian claims. While such conditions may not directly address a persecution claim, it may be that such knowledge informs sympathies with families who claim they cannot return to Haiti.

8. The regression analyses confirmed that, holding all other variables in the model constant, female gender of the asylum seeker was correlated with higher grant rates.
9. In the 2011 survey conducted by DHS, 63 percent of the 194 respondents who stated their gender were female, and 67 percent of the 27 supervisors who stated their gender were female.
10. A chi-square test failed to confirm the statistical significance of the cross-tabulation analysis of applicant's gender and grant rates for applicants with dependents.
11. A chi-square test confirmed the statistical significance of the cross-tabulation analysis of applicant's gender and grant rates for applicants without dependents. This pattern can be seen in populations of applicants from countries that produced many applicants, as well as in the database as a whole. For example, among Chinese, women with dependents won asylum at a rate only 6 percent higher than men with dependents, but women without dependents won asylum at a rate 14 percent higher than men without dependents. Indonesian women and men with dependents won asylum at the same 44 percent rate, but Indonesian women without dependents won asylum at a rate 13 percent higher than their male counterparts.
12. Eighteen percent of male applicants with dependents were over the age of fifty, compared with only 5 percent of the male applicants without dependents. (Eight percent of the females with dependents were over fifty, compared with 11 percent of the females without dependents).
13. See the Methodological Appendix, available at http://www.law.georgetown.edu/humanrightsinstitute/LivesInTheBalance, for further explanation. In addition, the regression analyses failed to confirm a statistically significant relationship between grant rates and the category of applicants who self-identified as Muslim, possibly because the grant rates for these applicants were indistinguishable from self-identified Christians (the control, or comparison category) when all other variables in the model were held constant.
14. A chi-square test confirmed the statistical significance of the cross-tabulation analysis of gender and self-identified religion and grant rates for applicants who identified as Christian, Sikh, and Muslim. The test failed to confirm the statistical significance of the cross-tabulation analysis of gender and self-identified religion for applicants who identified as Buddhist, possibly because the grant rates for men and women were so similar.
15. Of the 41,763 applicants in our database who identified as Muslims on their applications, 6222 were from North Africa and the Middle East, 3133 were from South Asia, and 23,380 were from Sub-Saharan Africa.
16. A chi-square test confirmed the statistical significance of the cross-tabulation analysis of the relationship between male and female gender of the applicant and grant rates for applicants who self-identified as Muslims from South Asia.
17. A chi-square test confirmed the statistical significance of the cross-tabulation analysis of the relationship between male and female gender of the applicant and grant rates for applicants who self-identified as Muslims from sub-Saharan Africa.
18. A chi-square test failed to confirm the statistical significance of the cross-tabulation analysis of the relationship between male and female gender of the applicant and grant rates for applicants who self-identified as Muslims from North Africa and the Middle East, possibly because the grant rates for men and women were so similar.

19. See, for example, Rey Koslowski, "The Evolution of Border Controls as a Mechanism to Prevent Illegal Immigration," Robert Schuman Centre for Advanced Studies, European University Institute, Migration Policy Institute 2–3 (2011) http://www.migrationpolicy.org/pubs/bordercontrols-koslowski.pdf .
20. See Trevor J. Murphy, "Nearly 100 Countries Issue E-Passports," March 26, 2012, http://globalpapersecurity.com/100-countries-issue-epassports.htm; Transportation Security Administration, "Global Strategies," March 27, 2013 (latest revision), http://www.tsa.gov/stakeholders/global-strategies ("TSA has successfully vetted all airports with direct flights into the United States").
21. United Nations Convention Relating to the Status of Refugees, Article 31(1) "The Contracting States shall not impose penalties, on account of their illegal entry or presence, on refugees who, coming directly from a territory where their life or freedom was threatened in the sense of article 1, enter or are present in their territory without authorization, provided they present themselves without delay to the authorities and show good cause for their illegal entry or presence."
22. Holding all other variables in the model constant, the regression analyses confirmed that entry with inspection correlated with higher grant rates.
23. For the content of the CCD, see Department of State, Consular Consolidated Database Privacy Impact Assessment, http://www.state.gov/documents/organization/93772.pdf (accessed July 17, 2012).
24. A chi-square test confirmed the statistical significance of the cross-tabulation analysis of the relationship between inspected entry and grant rates for Haitian, Salvadoran, and Chinese applicants. A chi-square test run on all cases except those from China and Latin America and the Caribbean failed to confirm the statistical significance of the relationship between inspected entry and grant rates, possibly because the difference between grant rates for inspected and uninspected entrants was so small.
25. A chi-square test confirmed the statistical significance of the cross-tabulation analysis of the relationship between inspected entry and grant rates for applicants in the 18–29, 30–39, and 40–49 age range. A chi-square test failed to confirm the statistical significance of the cross-tabulation analysis of the relationship between inspected entry and grant rates for applicants in the 50–99 age range, possibly because there was little difference in grant rates between inspected and uninspected applicants in that age group. The number of minor children in the database is relatively small (4,564), but half of the child applicants entered lawfully, and they won asylum more than 60 percent more often than children who entered unlawfully (61 percent versus 38 percent). We believe that this differential relates particularly to the concentration of unaccompanied boys from Central America.
26. A chi-square test confirmed the statistical significance of the cross-tabulation analysis of the relationship between age of applicant, inspected entry and grant rates for applicants from Latin America and the Caribbean only. A chi-square test confirmed the statistical significance of the cross-tabulation analysis of the relationship between age of applicant, inspected entry, and grant rates for applicants from countries other than those in Latin America and the Caribbean.
27. One asylum officer suggested to us that the large gap between grant rates for inspected and uninspected Latin American applicants might have resulted from a relatively recent influx of uninspected applicants who, like many Mexican applicants (who were excluded from our database for this reason) did not have valid asylum claims and applied only so that they would be referred to immigration court, where they could apply for a different

immigration remedy based on their having lived in the United States for a long time without committing crimes. To test this hypothesis, we separately studied the grant rates for applicants from this region, excluding those from Era 4, but the results were similar: a 20 percent grant rate for those who were not inspected, and a 48 percent grant rate for those who were inspected.

28. Though this is a large gap, it is not nearly as stark as the grant rate differential in immigration court, where represented applicants win about three times as often (46 percent) as pro se applicants (16 percent). *Refugee Roulette*, supra n. 1, at 45.
29. A chi-square test confirmed the statistical significance of the cross-tabulation analysis presented graphically in figure 7-5.
30. "The Asylum Division has undertaken fraud prevention efforts and considered fraud risk and prevention when establishing basic program procedures since the 1990s. The Asylum Division designated Fraud Prevention Coordinators (FPC) in each of the Asylum Offices in the late 1990s. We have FPC reports on file going back to 1999, but the FPC had been in place for several years prior to that period. As a larger USCIS effort, the Fraud Detection and National Security Unit (now it is a Directorate) was established in 2004 to support the adjudication programs in fraud detection. In that same year, FDNS Immigration Officers were employed by all of the Asylum Offices." E-mail to Philip G. Schrag from Mary Margaret Stone, Chief of Operations, Asylum Division, Refugee, Asylum and International Operations Directorate, U.S. Citizenship and Immigration Services, Department of Homeland Security (September 24, 2012).
31. DHS publishes most of the "lesson plans" (training materials) for its asylum officers on the website of U.S. Citizenship and Immigration Services.
32. Among the 4,564 applicants who were under the age of eighteen, the difference was even greater: 60 percent of represented applicants prevailed, compared to only 43 percent of unrepresented applicants.
33. A chi-square test confirmed the statistical significance of the cross-tabulation analysis presented graphically in figure 7-6.
34. For applicants without dependents, a chi-square test confirmed the statistical significance of the relationship between representation and grant rates. For applicants with dependents, a chi-square test failed to confirm the statistical significance of the relationship between representation and grant rates, possibly because the difference in grant rates between represented and unrepresented applicants was so small.
35. A chi-square test confirmed the statistical significance of the cross-tabulation analysis presented graphically in figure 7-8.
36. A chi-square test run on the cross-tabulation analysis presented graphically in figure 7-9 failed to confirm the statistical significance of the relationship between female uninspected applicants with dependents and representation and grant rate. The test confirmed the statistical significance of the other aspects of the cross-tabulation analysis presented graphically in figure 7-9.

NOTES TO CHAPTER 8

1. Jaya Ramji-Nogales, Andrew I. Schoenholtz, and Philip G. Schrag, *Refugee Roulette: Disparities in Asylum Adjudication and Proposals for Reform* (New York: NYU Press, 2009) at 22 and 26–27. To qualify, in the year 2005, a country had to have generated at least five hundred applicants who must have had a grant rate of at least 30 percent,

in either the DHS asylum offices or the immigration court system. *Refugee Roulette* at 18.

2. Variations in those rates of rejection on the one-year deadline are reported in chapters 4 and 5.
3. The Freedom House scores are discussed in chapter 6. How we used them in our analyses is discussed in more depth in the Methodological Appendix, available at http://www.law.georgetown.edu/humanrightsinstitute/LivesInTheBalance.
4. This variation might also be caused by different workloads (asylum cases per officer per year) in different offices. Unfortunately, because asylum officers adjudicate not only asylum cases but also credible fear, reasonable fear, and NACARA cases, we were not able to include this variable in our study. The database we received from DHS included only asylum decisions by officer, and because the identities of the asylum officers were made anonymous in that database, it would have been far too burdensome for DHS to compile the actual workload (including credible fear, reasonable fear, and NACARA cases) by officer. We know that nonasylum workloads vary substantially by regional asylum office, so a simple count of asylum decisions by officer in each region cannot be used to create an accurate measure of actual workload.
5. The grant rates by office are ordered somewhat differently after regression than they are in the cross-tabulation analysis presented above, which means that some of the other independent variables in the regression models had some effect on the grant rates displayed in figure 8-1. With the other variables in the models held constant, the offices are ordered, from high to low, by grant rate: San Francisco, Miami, Los Angeles, Arlington, Chicago, Newark, New York, and Houston. But the regression confirms that, with the other factors in the models held constant, the offices can be divided into four offices that had much higher grant rates than the other four offices.
6. A chi-square test confirmed the statistical significance of the cross-tabulation analysis presented in figure 8-2.
7. Houston, Chicago, Los Angeles, San Francisco, and Arlington granted asylum 84 percent, 79 percent, 68 percent, 61 percent and 31 percent, respectively, more often to applicants from countries with high Freedom House scores than to countries with low Freedom House scores.
8. A chi-square test confirmed the statistical significance of the cross-tabulation analysis presented in figure 8-3.
9. For example, applicants from some provinces particularly complained of religious persecution, while applicants from other provinces complained of severe enforcement of the one-child policy through forced abortions and sterilizations.
10. More than 90 percent of the Salvadoran cases and more than 75 percent of the Guatemalan cases in our study were filed before FY 1999. Salvadoran applicants faced a grant rate of 6.4 percent and Guatemalans a grant rate of 18.5 percent over the entire time frame of our study.
11. Chi-square tests confirmed the statistical significance of the cross-tabulation analyses presented in figures 8-4 through 8-9.
12. As noted in the text above, we did not make a graph for Armenians, who settled primarily in California, because only two offices had substantial numbers of Armenian applications. But those who filed in San Francisco had a grant rate that was 40 percent higher than those who filed in Los Angeles. Similarly, the grant rate for Iranians was 33 percent higher in San Francisco than in Los Angeles.
13. 386 F. 3d 922 (9th Cir. 2004).
14. *See* U.S. Citizenship and Immigration Services, Asylum Division, Asylum Officer Basic Training Course, Asylum Eligibility Part II: Well-Founded Fear, at 8–9 (March 13, 2009).

15. Kho v. Keisler, 505 F.3d 50, 55 (1st Cir. 2007); Lie v. Ashcroft, 396 F.3d 530 (3d Cir. 2005) (finding that violence against the applicants, who were Chinese Christians in Indonesia, did not constitute a "pattern or practice" of persecution); Firmansjah v. Gonzales, 424 F.3d 598, 607 n. 6 (7th Cir.2005).
16. Paul Bradley, "Authorities Allege Immigration Fraud; Say Ring Based in N.Va. Helped Many Get Bogus Passports, ID Documents," *Richmond Times-Dispatch*, November 23, 2004, B-1.
17. Jon Ward, "ICE Mulls Fraud Case," *Washington Times*, April 28, 2005, B-1.
18. Bradley, supra n. 16.
19. Another asylum officer suggested that Indonesians who were political dissidents tended to settle in western states, while "peasant farmers" gravitated toward the East Coast. We had no way to test either supposition.
20. U.S. Government Accountability Office, Agencies Have Taken Actions to Help Ensure Quality in the Asylum Adjudication Process, but Challenges Remain, GAO 08-935 (September 2008) at 13. This standard assumes that each officer can decide 18 cases every two weeks as well as participate in four hours of training. As of the GAO's 2008 report, however, the Asylum Office lacked "empirical data on the time it takes to thoroughly adjudicate a case." Id. at Executive Summary.
21. *See* supra n. 4 for an explanation of why we were not able to include this metric in our study.
22. Of course, for some officers, more interview time could result in higher grant rates because the officer might uncover facts that would enhance an applicant's credibility.
23. See the citations collected in Deborah Anker, *The Law of Asylum in the United States*. The Court of Appeals for the Seventh Circuit (which covers the Midwest) had the highest rate of ruling in favor of asylum applicants between 2004 and 2005. See *Refugee Roulette*, supra n. 1, at 78. But most of those decisions overturned decisions of the Board of Immigration Appeals because the Board's decisions were not supported by sound reasoning or evidence rather than because the court disagreed with the Board's interpretation of the law.
24. The Court of Appeals for the Ninth Circuit, encompassing California, was not the court with the highest rate of reversing the Board of Immigration Appeals at least in 2004 and 2005. During those years, that distinction belonged to the Seventh Circuit, which covers Illinois, Indiana, and Wisconsin. See *Refugee Roulette*, supra n. 1, at 78. Asylum applicants residing in those states have their claims heard by the Chicago Asylum Office. An applicant seeking to game the system, then, would have to take into account the relatively low historical grant rate of the Chicago Asylum Office.
25. A chi-square test confirmed the statistical significance of the cross-tabulation analysis presented in figure 8-10.
26. Haitian applicants constituted 43 percent and Venezuelans 8 percent of the Miami caseload in Era 3.
27. Haitian grant rates in Miami were 24 percent in Era 2, just prior to September 11, and increased to 42 percent in Era 3. Venezuelan grant rates in Miami increased from 43 percent in Era 2 to 59 percent in Era 3.
28. A chi-square test confirmed the statistical significance of the relationships between grant rates and the Arlington, New York, and San Francisco regional asylum offices for asylum seekers who self-identified as Muslim in asylum eras three and four.
29. A chi-square test confirmed the statistical significance of the relationship between grant rates and asylum eras three and four for asylum seekers who self-identified as Muslim in the New York regional asylum office.

30. A chi-square test confirmed the statistical significance of the cross-tabulation analysis presented in figure 8-11.
31. We wondered whether this difference was due to a higher proportion of officers with law degrees in San Francisco than Chicago and Houston, but we were not able to explore this on the larger database of all cases decided on their merits because DHS was unable to provide us with biographical characteristics of all of the asylum officers. In the smaller database, which we discuss in further detail in chapter 10, 61 percent of asylum officers in San Francisco had law degrees, compared with 35 percent of officers in Chicago and 52 percent of officers in Houston.
32. A chi-square test confirmed the statistical significance of the cross-tabulation analysis presented in figure 8-12.

NOTES TO CHAPTER 9

1. In some of the graphs that follow, one or two officers appear to have had extraordinarily high grant rates, much higher than most of the officers who otherwise would have had the highest grant rates in the relevant regional offices. In some offices, the one or two bars at the right side of the graph may have been individuals who were assigned, for a period of several months, to be "final approval officers" who did nothing but grant final approvals in cases in which (as explained in a note to chapter 1) a different officer had interviewed the applicant but not made a final decision and the formal grant of asylum had been delayed for a period of time. We were told by officers in the field that the final approval officers entered their own code numbers into RAPS, replacing the code number of the officer who interviewed the applicant. Therefore, the grant rates of these few officers may have been artificially increased as a result of their temporary duties. Final approval officers were not used in all eight regions, and records were not made of which offices used them, and for what periods of time. Similarly, in a few instances, the officers represented by the bars at the extreme left and right sides of the graphs may reflect the grant rates of a small number of officers whose grant rates were artificially lower or higher than others because they were senior officers who were allowed, by virtue of their seniority, to choose to ride circuit to cities in which the applicants tended to come from countries whose emigrants had particularly weak or strong asylum claims. However, even if one were to disregard the one or two highest or lowest grant rates in the graphs in this chapter, the graphs still reveal a remarkable degree of disparity in grant rates among officers working in close proximity to each other and deciding randomly assigned cases.
2. We first briefed the national Asylum Office about our disparity findings in the fall of 2006, at about the same time that what we call "Era 4" began. Our findings received national attention after being reported on the front page of the *New York Times* on May 31, 2007. Julia Preston, "Big Disparities in Judging of Asylum Cases," *New York Times*, May 31, 2007. Our *Refugee Roulette* data were first set forth in full in the November 2007 issue of the *Stanford Law Review*. Jaya Ramji-Nogales, Andrew I. Schoenholtz, and Philip G. Schrag, "Refugee Roulette: Disparities in Asylum Adjudication," 60 *Stanford L. Rev.* 295 (2007). The Government Accountability Office studied disparities in the asylum decisions of the immigration court, and in September 2008, confirmed the lack of consensus that we had discovered. Government Accountability Office, U.S. Asylum System: Significant Variation Existed in Asylum Outcomes across Immigration Courts and Judges, GAO 08-940 (September 2008).

3. The median grant rates for each regional asylum office in figure 9-6 are slightly different from the grant rates shown in figure 8-1 for two reasons. First, figure 9-6 takes into account only the asylum officers in each region who decided at least one hundred rejectable cases. Second, figure 9-6 shows mean rather than median rejection rates.
4. Arlington decided 7,989 of 12,182 total Ethiopian cases.
5. San Francisco decided 12,455 of 14,832 Indian cases.
6. It is possible that there was less disparity among the officers deciding Indian cases in San Francisco after 2004, when the lawyers at the San Francisco law firm of Sekhon and Sekhon were indicted (and later convicted) of filing hundreds of fraudulent asylum applications on behalf of Indian nationals between 2000 and late 2004. See U.S. Department of Justice, Office of the U.S. Attorney for the Eastern District of California, "Three Attorneys Receive Lengthy Sentences for Asylum Fraud Scheme" (press release, September 24, 2010). The grant rate for Indian applicants in that office fell from 46 percent and 40 percent in FY 2003 and FY 2004, respectively, to 5 percent and 12 percent in FY 2005 and FY 2006.
7. Miami decided 30,536 of 32,448 Haitian cases.

NOTES TO CHAPTER 10

1. A fascinating recent study suggests that judges make decisions differently before and after meal breaks. Shai Danziger, Jonathan Levav, and Liora Avnaim-Pesso, "Extraneous Factors in Judicial Decisions," 108 (17) *Proc. of the Nat'l Acad. Sci. U.S.A.* 6889 (2011), available at http://www.ncbi.nlm.nih.gov/pmc/articles/PMC3084045/. Looking at parole board decisions at the four major prisons in Israel, the researchers found that "the likelihood of a favorable ruling is greater at the very beginning of the work day or after a food break than later in the sequence of cases. . . the likelihood of a ruling in favor of a prisoner spikes at the beginning of each session—the probability of a favorable ruling steadily declines from ≈0.65 to nearly zero and jumps back up to ≈0.65 after a break for a meal." DHS does not record in RAPS the time of day at which the asylum officer made a decision in the case, so we were not able to study whether grant rates were affected by the time of the decision.
2. DHS provided us with biographical data only for officers trained within this time frame because these were the only officers in our database for whom they collected this information. "Before 2003 [the FLETC] questionnaire was not given to AOBTC students. AOBTC moved from FLETC after the July 2008 class, and the questionnaire was not given to the two subsequent classes." E-mail from Sally Armstrong, Department of Homeland Security, to Philip G. Schrag (July 1, 2009). The FLETC questionnaire is described further in the next paragraph.
3. A copy of the FLETC questionnaire appears on this book's companion website, http://www.law.georgetown.edu/humanrightsinstitute/LivesInTheBalance.
4. The regression models contained the following independent variables: regional asylum office in which the applicant's case was heard, the number of cases previously decided by the asylum officer who heard the applicant's case, the asylum officer's prior government work experience, the asylum officer's ethnicity, the asylum officer's gender, whether or not the asylum officer had a law degree, whether the applicant entered lawfully, the applicant's geographic region of origin, the state of political and civil rights in the applicant's nation of origin, the applicant's stated religion, the applicant's gender, whether the applicant had dependents in the United States, whether the applicant was represented, the applicant's age at filing, and whether the application was decided during the first three or the fourth asylum era. The

Methodological Appendix, available at http://www.law.georgetown.edu/humanrightsinstitute/LivesInTheBalance, discusses how we measured and coded these variables and how we created the database. In the text below, we reference the regressions run with the independent variable of fiscal year in which the application was decided recoded into four asylum eras, with the exception of discussions of specific fiscal years, for which we used the results of the regression run with the independent variable of fiscal year of decision without recoding.

5. The variables were statistically significant at the 0.05 level.
6. The regression outputs appear on this book's companion website, http://www.law.georgetown.edu/humanrightsinstitute/LivesInTheBalance.
7. Jaya Ramji-Nogales, Andrew I. Schoenholtz, and Philip G. Schrag, *Refugee Roulette: Disparities in Asylum Adjudication and Proposals for Reform* (New York: NYU Press, 2009) at 47.
8. The logistic regression analysis confirmed that, with all other variables in the model held constant, female gender of asylum officers correlated with higher grant rates. The logistic regression analysis with standard errors clustered by asylum officers and the hierarchical logistic regression failed to confirm a statistically significant relationship between the asylum officer's gender and grant rates, perhaps because the differences in grant rates between male and female asylum officers was so small.
9. Chi-square tests confirmed the statistical significance of the relationships displayed in Figure 10-1 with one exception. The chi-square test failed to confirm a statistically significant difference between the grant rates of male and female asylum officers for female asylum seekers, possibly because the differences in grant rates between these two groups were so small.
10. *Refugee Roulette*, supra n. 7, at 48-52.
11. The logistic regression analysis confirmed that, holding all other variables in the model constant, prior government service of the asylum officer correlated with higher grant rates. The logistic regression analysis with clustered standard errors and the hierarchical logistic regression also confirmed this relationship but were statistically significant only at the $p<0.1$ level.
12. Twenty-six officers identified themselves as having worked for CBP, DHS, ICE, or INS, twenty-three officers for CIS, and thirty-one officers for an agency other than those listed above.
13. For the proportions and numbers of officers by ethnicity, see chapter 2, figure 2-13. Twelve officers left the entry blank. Because only one officer was Native American or Alaskan Native, we do not present outcomes for that ethnic group.
14. We use here the terms presented by the FLETC questionnaire to denote ethnic categories, namely Asian or Pacific Islander, Black (not of Hispanic Origin), Hispanic, and White (not of Hispanic Origin). The construction of these categories leaves open the possibility that some officers who self-reported as Hispanic may have also fallen within the Black ethnic group.
15. In a recent study, two scholars examined the voting records by race of U.S. Court of Appeals judges in 2000 cases involving deportation or asylum. They found that the African American judges were less likely to vote in a pro-alien manner than their white counterparts and that there were too few votes by Asian American or Hispanic judges to be statistically significant. Margaret S. Williams and Anna O. Law, "Understanding Judicial Decision Making in Immigration Cases at the U.S. Courts of Appeals," 33 *Justice System Journal* 97, 108 (2012).
16. The binary logistic regression analysis confirmed a statistically significant relationship between ethnicity of the officer and grant rate but found that Hispanic officers had the highest grant rates, followed by White, Black, and Asian or Pacific Islander officers.

17. The logistic regression with standard errors clustered by asylum officer and the hierarchical logistic regression failed to confirm a statistically significant relationship between ethnicity and grant rates for Black and Hispanic officers.
18. In the rest of this section, we report the results of clustered cross-tabulation analyses, checked with chi-square tests. Because it is not possible to test these slices of the data through a regression analysis, we do not know whether variables other than those reported contributed to the results.
19. For Hispanic and White officers, a chi-square test confirmed the statistical significance of the cross-tabulation analysis presented graphically in figure 10-3. But for Asian or Pacific Islander or Black officers, a chi-square test failed to confirm the statistical significance of the cross-tabulation analysis presented graphically in figure 10-3, possibly because the grant rates for inspected and uninspected applicants were so similar for officers of these two ethnic groups.
20. A chi-square test confirmed the statistical significance of the cross-tabulation analysis displayed graphically in figure 10-4.
21. For Hispanic and White officers, a chi-square test confirmed the statistical significance of the cross-tabulation analysis presented graphically in figure 10-5. For Asian or Pacific Islander and Black officers, a chi-square test failed to confirm statistical significance, possibly because the difference in grant rates for applicants with and without dependents was so small for officers of these two ethnicities.
22. For Hispanic and White officers, a chi-square test confirmed the statistical significance of the cross-tabulation analysis presented graphically in figure 10-6. For Asian or Pacific Islander and Black officers, a chi-square test failed to confirm statistical significance, possibly because the difference in grant rates for applicants (once all other variables are held constant) with and without dependents was so small for officers of these two ethnicities.
23. A chi-square test failed to confirm the statistical significance of the cross-tabulation analysis of the relationship between Hispanic ethnicity of the officer and dependents for applicants from East Asia and the Pacific, possibly because there was no statistically significant difference in grant rates for applicants (once all other variables are held constant) with and without dependents.
24. A chi-square test confirmed the statistical significance of the cross-tabulation analysis of the relationship between Asian or Pacific Islander ethnicity of the officer and dependents for applicants from East Asia and the Pacific.
25. A chi-square test confirmed the statistical significance of the cross-tabulation analysis presented graphically in figure 10-7.
26. Also, there was little difference between officers with law degrees and those without such degrees when assessing claims from countries with the most abusive human rights records (47 percent versus 45 percent). A much larger difference appeared in the adjudication of claims from countries whose Freedom House scores showed less abuse. In those cases, the lawyers granted at a rate of 50 percent, a figure 19 percent higher than the 42 percent rate of the lay adjudicators. Perhaps the cases from the most abusive countries involve so much torture and imprisonment that they are relatively easy to analyze, whereas the more subtle forms of persecution or more complex relationships between persecution and the five grounds for asylum present situations in which lawyers are more confident in their judgments to grant rather than passing the buck by referring the cases to immigration judges.

For pro se applicants, a chi-square test confirmed the statistical significance of the cross-tabulation analysis of the relationship between the asylum officer's law degree and grant rate. For represented applicants, a chi-square test failed to confirm the statistical significance of the cross-tabulation analysis of the relationship between the asylum officer's law degree and grant rates, likely because there was no difference in grant rates for officers with and without law degrees.

27. A chi-square test confirmed the statistical significance of the cross-tabulation analysis presented graphically in figure 10-9.
28. Seventy-eight officers, or 36.4 percent, believed that asylum officers' grant rates do not change appreciably over time.
29. The regression analyses confirmed that, with all other variables in the model held constant, officers who had heard more than 1,000 cases had the highest grant rates, followed by officers who had heard 501–750 cases, then 751–1,000 cases, then 251–500 cases, and that officers who had heard fewer than 250 cases had the lowest grant rates.
30. This officer may have had an incorrect understanding of immigration judges' grant rates in cases referred from the asylum office. They do grant many applications that have been referred by asylum officers, often after the applicant finally obtains a lawyer who compiles corroborating evidence on which a grant of asylum can be based. But they do not grant all such cases. In fact their collective grant rate (which varies very widely from judge to judge, as we showed in *Refugee Roulette*) ranged from 45 percent to 56 percent between FY 2005 and FY 2009. Executive Office for Immigration Review, FY 2009 *Statistical Year Book*, p. K5, figure 19-B. During most years of our study, it was considerably lower.
31. A chi-square test confirmed the statistical significance of the cross-tabulation analysis displayed graphically in figure 10-11.
32. A chi-square test confirmed the statistical significance of the cross-tabulation analysis displayed graphically in figure 10-12.
33. A chi-square test confirmed the statistical significance of the cross-tabulation analysis reported graphically in figure 10-13.
34. These categories use the U.S. Census Bureau's four regions, available at http://www.census.gov/geo/www/us_regdiv.pdf.
35. A chi-square test confirmed the statistical significance of the cross-tabulation analysis displayed graphically in figure 10-14.
36. The elimination of those cases reduced the total number of cases in the study from 31,635 to 22,890.
37. A chi-square test confirmed the statistical significance of the cross-tabulation analysis displayed graphically in figure 10-15.
38. A chi-square test confirmed the statistical significance of the cross-tabulation analysis reported graphically in this figure, except that it failed to confirm statistical significance of the relationship between grant rates and officer's education for asylum officers born in the West. This may be the case because the difference in grant rates between officers who were lawyers and officers who were not lawyers was not statistically significant for officers born in the West or it may be that the numbers of officers in the West, particularly those without law degrees, was too small to form a basis for statistically significant findings.

NOTES TO CHAPTER 11

1. In 2011, for example, the public learned of an asylum grant to an individual who had fabricated part of her life story and fooled asylum officers. Suketu Mehta, "The Asylum Seeker," *The New Yorker*, August 1, 2011. In another case, it was at first widely reported that the woman who accused Dominique Strauss-Kahn of attacking her had falsely claimed a gang rape in her native country in order to obtain asylum. However, it later turned out that she had not claimed a gang rape in her asylum application. Jim Dwyer, "With False Tale About Gang Rape, Strauss-Kahn Case Crumbles," *New York Times*, August 23, 2011, http://www.nytimes.com/2011/08/24/nyregion/housekeepers-false-tale-undid-strauss-kahn-case.html (accessed July 11, 2012).
2. We measured these human rights records with the Freedom House index, discussed in chapter 6.
3. The data are reported in chapter 6.
4. The percentage of those who applied within a year may be even higher, because 69.5 percent represents only the percentage of applicants able to prove by clear and convincing evidence that they entered within a year.
5. Although there are no statistically reliable data on the consequences of return for genuine refugees, and, to our knowledge, no systematic study of the fates of returned asylum seekers, there have been several journalistic reports of murders of unsuccessful asylum seekers after they were deported from the United States, Australia, Britain, and other countries. See Paul Bibby, "Deported Refugee Shot Dead," *Sydney Morning Herald*, August 2, 2008, at 1, available at http://www.smh.com.au/news/world/deported-refugee-killed/2008/08/01/1217097536265.html; Greg Campbell and Joel Dyer, "Death by Deportation," *Boulder Weekly*, May 27, 2004, available at http://archive.boulderweekly.com/052704/ coverstory.html; Krystel Rolle, "Haitian Political Asylum Seeker Killed: 37-Year-Old Shot in Dominican Republic," *Nassau Guardian*, May 1, 2009, at A5, available at http://archive.nassauguardian.net/ pubfiles/nas/archive/images_pages/05012009_A05.pdf; Anne Barrowclough, "Afghan Asylum Seekers Sent Home by Australia 'Killed by Taleban,'" *Times Online*, October 27, 2008, http://www.timesonline.co.uk/tol/news/world/article5025923.ece; "Darfur Asylum-Seeker Kicked Out of UK, then 'Murdered' in Sudan," *Huffington Post*, April 17, 2009, http://www. huffingtonpost.com/2009/03/17/darfur-asylum-seeker-kick_n_175730.html.
6. In particular, of 92,622 rejectable asylum applicants, 13,315 were classified as "other" religions and 10,230 were classified as being of an "unknown" religion. In other words, our study does not contain reliable religion data for nearly a quarter of the asylum seekers.
7. See chapter 5.
8. In our view, a person sophisticated enough to concoct a fraudulent application is more likely to be aware of the deadline and to file within the allowable period than to miss the deadline and have to jump his application over an additional hurdle.
9. U.S. Citizenship and Immigration Services, Affirmative Asylum Procedures Manual, *at* 121-24 (July 2010), *available at* http://www.uscis.gov/USCIS/Humanitarian/Refugees%20&%20Asylum/Asylum/2007_AAPM.pdf. (for example, when country conditions are relevant to the applicant's asylum eligibility, a finding of ineligibility for a changed country conditions exception "must be supported by a specific description, with citations, of country conditions pertinent to the protected characteristic(s) relevant to the applicant's claim, if any. . . .[T]he assessment must contain at least two country conditions citations to support a finding that the applicant has not established an exception based on changed circumstances. The time period covered by the citations is determined on a case-by-case

basis, but generally must cover the period beginning 24 months preceding the filing date, and ending on the date of the decision. It is preferable that the two citations be from different sources, however they may be from the same issuing organization or agency if another source cannot be found.")

10. If it turned out to be a low proportion, any valid critique of the deadline as adjudicated by asylum officers would also apply to the immigration judges.
11. Numerous authorities have commented that in the asylum context, credibility decisions are extremely difficult to make. See, for example, former immigration judge Bruce J. Einhorn, "Consistency, Credibility and Culture," in our book, Jaya Ramji-Nogales, Andrew I. Schoenholtz, and Philip G. Schrag, *Refugee Roulette: Disparities in Asylum Adjudication and Proposals for Reform* (New York: NYU Press, 2009) at 187–188; and similar views in the assessment of the British asylum system in Robert Thomas, "Refugee Roulette, a UK Perspective," in the same volume at 164, 169.
12. One respondent commented, "Inter-office inconsistency seems to mostly come from inconsistent application of the law amongst the offices, esp. regarding credibility standards and the 1-year rule, in a way that is not due to the minimal variations in federal circuit court law. The inconsistent legal analyses seem to come most importantly from insufficient oversight and guidance from a centralized HQ perspective regarding the legal issues (esp. credibility and 1 year) and a failure of management to actually examine inter-office inconsistencies via the QA [quality assessment] branch. But it also stems, in part, from the different office climates and norms regarding the prevailing cases in their jurisdiction, esp since each office is in essence its own fiefdom with surprising variations in both legal perspective and procedures." Another said, "Supervisors point of view- some more liberal than others, my office tends to liberal," and another said, "My office changes officer decisions due to supervisor opinion."
13. For this experience of the officer characteristic, we were able to construct a variable in the larger database.
14. This finding was based on the full database of more than 303,000 merits cases. There were not enough officers with more than 500 decisions in the smaller database for us to repeat the study on that database or to try to correlate the experience finding with other personal data such as the gender or ethnicity of the officers.
15. 142 Cong. Rec. S. 11491, 11492 (September 27, 1996).
16. Comprehensive Immigration Reform ASAP Act of 2009, H.R. 4321, §186; Refugee Protection Act of 2010, S. 3113, § 3; Restoring Protection to Victims of Persecution Act, H.R. 4800. The Senate Appropriations Committee approved a version of the FY 2011 appropriations bill (S. 3676) that included a provision (Sec. 7080) eliminating the one-year filing deadline for asylum applications. Senate Report 111-237, 111th Congress (2009–2010), http://thomas.loc.gov/cgibin/cpquery/?&dbname=cp111&sid=cp111FK1E5&refer=&r_n=sr237.111&item=&&&sel=TOC_285105&. The bill would also have authorized motions to reopen for those who in recent years were granted withholding of removal rather than asylum because they missed the filing deadline. The provision was struck before the bill reached the Senate floor.
17. In August 2010, in connection with S. 3676, the Obama administration communicated to the Senate its desire to eliminate the deadline (and to allow motions to reopen for those who had been granted withholding). E-mail to Andrew I. Schoenholtz from Scott W. Busby, former Director for Human Rights, National Security Staff, The White House (November 20, 2011).

18. Border Security, Economic Opportunity, and Immigration Modernization Act, S. 744, § 3401 113th Congress (passed by Senate, June 27, 2013).
19. 8 C.F.R. §1208.4(a)(5)(i)-(vi); Asylum Officer Basic Training Course, Lesson Plan Overview: One-Year Filing Deadline, at 12-20 (March 23, 2009), available at http://www.uscis.gov/USCIS/Humanitarian/Refugees%20&%20Asylum/Asylum/AOBTC%20Lesson%20Plans/One-Year-Filing-Deadline-31aug10.pdf
20. Asylum Officer Basic Training Course, supra n. 19, at 20.
21. See Michele R. Pistone and Philip G. Schrag, "The New Asylum Rule: Improved But Still Unfair," 16 *Geo. Immig. L. J.* 1, 23–30 (2001). We do not suggest that an asylum officer would have to accept the word of the applicant that any of these circumstances occurred. The applicant would have to prove the existence of one of these factors to the satisfaction of the officer, just as an applicant must now do with respect to one of the six extraordinary circumstances listed in the regulations.
22. The DHS training manual states that "testimony can be sufficiently clear and convincing to lead an asylum officer to a "firm belief" that the applicant arrived within one year before the filing date." Asylum Officer Basic Training Course, supra n. 19 at 8. But the large fraction of cases that are rejected based on the deadline leads us to recommend that the message be reinforced. This is also the law in determining asylum eligibility. 8 C.F.R. § 1208.13(a) ("The testimony of the applicant, if credible, may be sufficient to sustain the burden of proof without corroboration").
23. We recommend that DHS instruct its asylum officers to consider more carefully the following types of evidence: (1) tickets for travel out of the home country that show travel to a third country in situations where, if the time of travel between the third country and the United States is considered, entry into the United States should be calculated within the one-year filing period; (2) certified airline or ship manifests showing that a particular flight or ship route exists and that the vessel traveled that route on the dates that the applicant claims in testimony that she traveled; (3) tickets for travel in the United States shortly after crossing the border; (4) affidavits from workers at migrant shelters in northern Mexico who recognize the individual as having stayed at the shelter during a certain time period or who have checked a list of individuals who stayed during that time period and found the applicant's name; (5) affidavits from individuals who travelled to the United States with the applicant; (6) affidavits from individuals who housed the applicant before or shortly after crossing the border; (7) affidavits from individuals in the home country with knowledge of the timing of the applicant's departure or who received communications from the applicant about his travel to the United States and the dates for that travel; and (8) affidavits from family or friends in the area where the applicant arrived in the United States stating his arrival date. E-mail from Prof. Denise Gilman, University of Texas, Austin, to Jaya Ramji-Nogales (July 6, 2010) (on file with author).
24. 8 C.F.R. § 1208.9(b); *Matter of S-M-J-*, 21 I&N DEC. 722 (BIA 1997); Asylum Officer Basic Training Course, supra n. 19 at 21–22. ("While the burden of proof is on the applicant to show that there are changed circumstances that now materially affect his or her eligibility for asylum, many applicants affected by changed circumstances may not be able to articulate this. The unique nature of assessing an applicant's need of protection places the officer in a 'cooperative' role with the applicant. It is an asylum officer's affirmative duty 'to elicit all relevant and useful information bearing on the applicant's eligibility for asylum.'")
25. In cases in which the basis for an exception is that the applicant was in lawful status, the department's training materials state that "guidance offered by the Department of Justice

states that more than a six month delay would usually be considered unreasonable" citing language that appeared in the Federal Register in 2000, before the Department of Homeland Security was created. Asylum Officer Basic Training Course, supra n. 19, at 24. But that advice did not purport to apply to the reasonable time for filing after the occurrence of circumstances other than the termination of lawful status. Since Congress thought that it was reasonable for applications to be filed within a year, so long as the year remains the standard the "reasonable time" period should also be no less than a year. Even in cases in which an applicant waited more than six months to file after a lawful status expired, at least one court has held that the delay may be considered reasonable if he justifies it with "a cogent and well-documented reason." Wakkary v. Holder, 558 F. 3d 1049 (9th Cir. 2009).

26. One measure of this increased complexity is that the 1991 edition of Deborah Anker's authoritative work, *The Law of Asylum in the United States*, was 171 pages long, excluding tables. The 2012 edition is 659 pages long.
27. E-mail to Philip G. Schrag from Mary Margaret Stone, Chief of Operations, Asylum Division, Refugee, Asylum and International Operations Directorate, U.S. Citizenship and Immigration Services, Department of Homeland Security (September 24, 2012).
28. This change of procedure would be similar to the existing practice of assigning certain officers to represent applicants who are children.
29. An additional reason for requiring or at least preferring a law degree is that many law schools now have student loan forgiveness programs for graduates who enter into government service, but most of these programs only assist students who take jobs for which a law degree is required or at least preferred. Even stating a preference for law graduates would therefore enable DHS to attract a larger pool of applicants.
30. See, for example, Alice Clapman, "Hearing Difficult Voices: The Due Process Rights of Mentally Disabled Individuals in Removal Proceedings," 45 *New England L. Rev.* 373 (2011).
31. See, for example, Chris Guthrie, Jeffrey J. Rachlinski, and Andrew J. Wistrich, "Blinking on the Bench: How Judges Decide Cases," 93 *Cornell L. Rev.* 1, 31-32 (2007).
32. Shai Danziger, Jonathan Levav, and Liora Avnaim-Pesso, "Extraneous Factors in Judicial Decisions," 108(17) *Proc. of the Nat'l Acad. Sci. U.S.A.* 6889 (2011), available at http://www.ncbi.nlm.nih.gov/pmc/articles/PMC3084045/, citing Mark Muraven and Roy Baumeister, "Self-Regulation and Depletion of Limited Resources: Does Self-Control Resemble a Muscle?," 126 *Psychol. Bull.* 247 (2000).
33. Id. at 6892.
34. Id. at 6892.
35. We explain at page 97 of *Refugee Roulette*, supra n. 11, why the "cure" of quotas is worse than the disease of disparities.
36. Jeffrey J. Rachlinski, Sheri Lynn Johnson, Andrew J. Wistrich, and Chris Guthrie, "Does Unconscious Racial Bias Affect Trial Judges?," 84 *Notre Dame L. Rev.* 1195, 1231 (2009).
37. Representatives must file a G-28 form when they assist applicants. The February 28, 2013 version of this form indicates the type of representative who is filing it, facilitating coding of the type we suggest.
38. One recent empirical study, controlling for other variables, found that experienced public defenders were significantly more successful than those who had spent less time on the job. David S. Abrams and Albert H. Yoon, "The Luck of the Draw: Using Random Case Assignment to Investigate Attorney Ability," 74 *U. Chi. L. Rev.* 1145 (2007). It would be ideal if DHS and scholars could learn what characteristics of applicants' lawyers correlated with success, but that investigation would probably involve too much work for both the

agency and the lawyers who would be called upon to reveal information about themselves. It would require only some additional coding, however, for DHS to distinguish among members of the bar, law students, and other permitted representatives.

39. Applicants already disclose their educational levels on the asylum application form, but it is not coded in RAPS.
40. *See* the analysis of this issue at the end of chapter 5 and text of this chapter at supra n. 11.
41. The officer may also check a box labeled "none." E-mail to Philip G. Schrag from Mary Margaret Stone, Chief of Operations, Asylum Division, Refugee, Asylum and International Operations Directorate, US Citizenship and Immigration Services, Department of Homeland Security (September 24, 2012). If the claim is decided on more than one ground, the officer is directed to check more than one box.
42. The Canadian government codes asylum cases according to seventeen categories, although we would not recommend using the Canadian categories, as they are ill defined and substantially overlapping. See Sean Rehaag, "Troubling Patterns in Canadian Refugee Adjudication," 39 *Ottawa L. Rev.* 335, fn. 38 (2008) (listing categories used by the Canadian Immigration and Refugee Board's internal database).
43. At present, RAPS has a code for denials or referrals based on the bar for having been convicted of certain crimes. It also has a code for denials or referrals based on the applicant having persecuted others, having provided material support to terrorism, or being a danger to the public. But the code does not differentiate among those three different grounds.

INDEX

A companion website for this book at http://www.law.georgetown.edu/humanrightsinstitute/LivesInTheBalance includes the original data sets on which the studies in this book were based, a Methodological Appendix to the book, and other supplemental materials.

ABOUT THE AUTHORS

Andrew I. Schoenholtz directs Georgetown Law's Human Rights Institute, co-directs its Center for Applied Legal Studies as well as its Certificate in Refugee and Humanitarian Emergencies, teaches courses on refugee and immigration law and policy, and serves as the Deputy Director of the Institute for the Study of International Migration. He is the author of numerous publications on refugee and immigration issues. Before coming to Georgetown, he served as Deputy Director of the U.S. Commission on Immigration Reform.

Philip G. Schrag is the Delaney Family Professor of Public Interest Law at Georgetown University and the co-director, with Professor Schoenholtz, of Georgetown's Center for Applied Legal Studies, the clinic in which law students provide free representation to asylum applicants in immigration court proceedings. He is the author or co-author of fifteen books and dozens of articles on immigration, consumer protection, nuclear arms control, legal ethics, and other topics related to public policy.

Jaya Ramji-Nogales is Associate Professor of Law and the co-director of the Institute for International Law and Public Policy at Temple University's Beasley School of Law, where she teaches Refugee Law and Policy among other courses. Professor Ramji-Nogales has represented numerous asylum seekers in immigration proceedings and has authored several articles on the intersection of immigration law and international human rights law.

CPSIA information can be obtained at www.ICGtesting.com
Printed in the USA
LVOW11*1819250816

501855LV00008B/66/P